Body of Victim, Body of Warrior

SOUTH ASIA ACROSS THE DISCIPLINES

Edited by Dipesh Chakrabarty, Sheldon Pollock, and Sanjay Subrahmanyam

South Asia Across the Disciplines is a series devoted to publishing first books across a wide range of South Asian studies, including art, history, philology or textual studies, philosophy, religion, and interpretive social sciences. Contributors all share the goal of opening up new archives, especially in South Asian languages, and suggesting new methods and approaches, while demonstrating that South Asian scholarship can be at once deep in expertise and broad in appeal.

Funded by a grant from the Andrew W. Mellon Foundation and jointly published by the University of California Press, the University of Chicago Press, and Columbia University Press. Read more about the series at http://www.saacrossdisciplines.org.

Extreme Poetry: The South Asian Movement of Simultaneous Narration, by Yigal Bronner (Columbia University Press, 2010)

The Social Space of Language: Vernacular Culture in British Colonial Punjab, by Farina Mir (University of California Press, 2010)

Unifying Hinduism: The Philosophy of Vijnanabhiksu in Indian Intellectual History, by Andrew J. Nicholson (Columbia University Press, 2010)

Secularizing Islamists?: Jama'at-e-Islami and Jama 'at-ud-Da'wa in Urban Pakistan, by Humeira Iqtidar (University of Chicago Press, 2011)

Islam Translated: Literature, Conversion, and the Arabic Cosmopolis of South and Southeast Asia, by Ronit Ricci (University of Chicago Press, 2011)

Conjugations: Marriage and Form in New Bollywood Cinema, by Sangita Gopal (University of Chicago Press, 2011)

The Powerful Ephemeral: Everyday Healing in an Ambiguously Islamic Place, by Carla Bellamy (University of California Press, 2011)

Body of Victim, Body of Warrior: Refugee Families and the Making of Kashmiri Jihadists, by Cabeiri deBergh Robinson (University of California Press, 2013)

Body of Victim, Body of Warrior

REFUGEE FAMILIES AND THE MAKING OF
KASHMIRI JIHADISTS

Cabeiri deBergh Robinson

UNIVERSITY OF CALIFORNIA PRESS
BERKELEY LOS ANGELES LONDON

University of California Press, one of the most distinguished university presses in the United States, enriches lives around the world by advancing scholarship in the humanities, social sciences, and natural sciences. Its activities are supported by the UC Press Foundation and by philanthropic contributions from individuals and institutions. For more information, visit www.ucpress.edu.

University of California Press
Berkeley and Los Angeles, California

University of California Press, Ltd.
London, England

Cataloging-in-Publication Data is on file with the Library of Congress

ISBN 978-0-520-27420-4—ISBN 978-0-520-27421-1

Manufactured in the United States of America

22 21 20 19 18 17 16 15 14 13
10 9 8 7 6 5 4 3 2 1

In keeping with a commitment to support environmentally responsible and sustainable printing practices, UC Press has printed this book on Rolland Enviro100, a 100% post-consumer fiber paper that is FSC certified, deinked, processed chlorine-free, and manufactured with renewable biogas energy. It is acid-free and EcoLogo certified.

CONTENTS

LIST OF ILLUSTRATIONS

MAPS

FIGURES

LIST OF ABBREVIATIONS

AJK	Azad Jammu and Kashmir
AJKMC	All Jammu and Kashmir Muslim Conference
AJKNC	All Jammu and Kashmir National Conference
APHC	All Party Hurriyat Conference
BSF	(Indian) Border Security Force
IDP	Internally Displaced Person
ICRC	International Committee of the Red Cross
INGO	International Non-Governmental Organization
IRO	International Refugees Organization
ISI	(Pakistani) Inter-Services Intelligence
JKLF	Jammu and Kashmir Liberation Front
KRCRC	Kashmir Refugees Central Relief Committee
LoC	Line of Control
MAJ	Muhammad Ali Jinnah Papers (National Archives of Pakistan)
MFJ	Mohtarmah Fatima Jinnah Papers (National Archives)
MI	(Pakistani) Military Intelligence
MKA	Ministry of Kashmir Affairs
NAP	National Archives of Pakistan
NWFP	North West Frontier Provinces
PMLWC	Punjab Muslim League Women's Committee

QARF   Quaid-i-Azam Relief Fund
RAW   (Indian) Research Analysis Wing
UJC   United Jihad Council
UN   United Nations
UNAC   United Nations Appeal for Children
UNCIP   United Nations Commission on India and
        Pakistan
UNHCR   United Nations High Commissioner for
        Refugees
UNICEF United Nations International Children's
        Emergency Fund
WRC   Women's Relief Committee

NOTE ON NAMES, TRANSLITERATION,
AND PHOTOGRAPHS

In this book, I refer to the distinct governmental regions of the disputed territory of Jammu and Kashmir by the names by which they are identified in their own current constitutional documents. In Pakistan, the State of Azad Jammu and Kashmir is commonly referred to as "Azad Kashmir" (Free Kashmir) and in India it is known as "POK" (Pakistan Occupied Kashmir). I employ its full constitutional name except when I am presenting ethnographic materials, in which case I reproduce names like "Azad Kashmir" and "Occupied Kashmir" in order not to distort the speakers' intentions. For the sake of consistency and clarity, I refer to its government as the government of Azad Jammu and Kashmir. Likewise, I refer to the 1949 UN Ceasefire Line as the military "Line of Control," even though it wasn't officially renamed until the Simla Agreement of 1972.

Following anthropological convention, I use pseudonyms in my presentation of all ethnographic information. For unmarried youths and young men, I use only a single name. I use two names for older men to whom I owe the respect due to an elder, but in order to avoid the confusion that would result from using a fictive second name linked to descent-group identities, I use two male first names. Women generally have as a second name the first name of their father or of their husband; I use the second name "Bibi" for younger women and "Begum" for elder women. In my presentation of historical material, such as documents or memoirs, I use real names as recorded in the public or governmental record.

Transliteration of Urdu words follows the system standardized by John T. Platts in *A Dictionary of Urdū, Classical Hindī, and English* and reflects the standard spelling of the word as it is written. I do not use diacritical markings in any personal names, proper nouns, or adjectives generated from proper nouns (such as "Kashmiri" or "Pakistani") unless they are a part of an Urdu language phrase. In the case of political parties and militant organizations for which there are several alternative English transliterations in use, I employ a common one. The term *jihād* has entered into English-language usage in the past decade. As an English word, jihad is used to refer to Islamic religious warfare. As an Islamicate word, however, the term has a more variegated meaning; it can refer to a struggle in either spiritual or material realms. In this text, I retain the hard diacritic to mark the fact that it has also become a dialectical term, jihād, which refers simultaneously to its use within specific Muslim societies and to its integration into a global political vocabulary. I use the term as a foreign word *(jihād)* to mark its use (1) as an ethnographic distinction within translated ethnographic quotes to draw attention to the speaker's original use of the term; and (2) as a purely Islamic concept in religious texts. I deploy a grammatically unconventional plural in this text to make another ethnographic distinction; *muhājirīn* is the correct grammatical plural of *muhājir* (refugee) and *mujāhidīn* of *mujāhid* (warrior), but I use English plurals *(muhājirs and mujāhids)* to indicate a plurality of individuals as opposed to a collectivity. This is an important distinction in the greater Kashmir context, where people use a singular noun with a plural verb to mean groups of individuals; for example, *"yeh lōg mujāhid haiñ"* (those people are *mujāhids*). Thus, I use the word *mujāhids* when many individual militants are involved, but I use the word *mujāhidīn* when referring to a collective of militants acting or speaking as members of an organization.

I took all photographs used in this text. I have not used any photographs depicting people in close-up focus because of issues of confidentiality. For the same reason, names and identifying data have been removed from the document facsimiles reproduced here.

PREFACE:
THE KASHMIR DISPUTE AND THE CONFLICTS
WITHIN CONFLICT ETHNOGRAPHY

Since 1947, the peoples of Jammu and Kashmir have experienced three inter-state wars between India and Pakistan (1947–1949, 1965, and 1971), the unde-clared Kargil War of 1999, frequent border clashes, and an active antistate armed conflict in Indian-administered Jammu and Kashmir State that began in 1989 and is ongoing. Pakistan and India consider the greater Jammu and Kashmir region a disputed territory; both claim a historical and cultural right to political rule over its entirety, and both states claim that their sovereignty has been violated by the other's "occupation" of its territory. After bilateral nuclear tests in 1998, security and policy analysts began to discuss the Kashmir Dispute as more than a regional security problem; they began looking at the contested military Line of Control (LoC), where troops of the Indian and Pakistan armies engage in regular exchanges of heavy artillery and light arms fire, as a potential nuclear flashpoint. Invoking the specter of an outright war between India and Pakistan and the potential for increased regional instability in South and Central Asia, the international community once again turned its attention to Kashmir.

Kashmiris, however, have had their attention on the international community for decades. The phrase "Kashmir is now the most dangerous place on Earth" became a media trope during the Kargil War—and it has endured through the rise of the War on Terror, concerns about the nucle-arization of Middle Eastern states like Iraq and Iran, and border tensions between North and South Korea.[1] But those reporters, who stood gestur-ing toward the militarized border with trepidation, were standing in a place where people have lived for more than three generations caught between the gunsights of two opposing armies. People from the Indian Jammu and Kashmir State, Pakistan-administered Azad Jammu and Kashmir, and the diaspora of "overseas Kashmiris," particularly in London and New York, had worked with United Nations commissions since 1948. They also had been actively involved in documenting human rights abuses by state and paramilitary organizations since 1990. But while the appeal to human rights is relatively uncontroversial, knowing whose rights to champion over decades of oscillating hot and cold war is less so. Which victims should we protect? Against which perpetrators? As the international community became more involved in organizing humanitarian interventions around the world in the post–Cold War era, why the international community intervened to protect the victims of one conflict and not another became part of debates within Kashmiri communities.

In refugee resettlement villages across Azad Jammu and Kashmir (AJK), these debates became especially heated during the late spring of 1999, at the beginning of the Kargil War, when it was discovered that members of jihadist organizations, under the umbrella of the United Jihad Council and working with the Pakistan military, had occupied strategic posts on the Indian side of the LoC. Residents of AJK began preparing for an invasion by Indian troops by evacuating their families and supplying the camouflaged defense bunkers dug into the fields during previous wars and periods of border conflict. During the day, the sounds of gunshots reverberated off the mountains as villages retrained their defense committees. In the city of Muzaffarabad, the wail of ambulances announced the frequent arrival at the government hospital of casualties from the LoC. The atmosphere was tense, because many people believed a full-scale war was imminent. That belief produced both anxiety and hope: anxiety for the inevitable hardship and grief of warfare, and hope that a war would bring the international attention that would at last result in the resolution of the Kashmir Dispute.

Hajji Mohammad Rashid was an elder council member for a refugee village near the LoC whom I visited often during my fieldwork. He could not read, but he watched Pakistani, Indian, and international news programs on satellite TV and listened to the BBC and Voice of America–Urdu on the radio. In the spring of 1999, he was interested in what the American public thought about military interventions that were justified in terms of protecting civilians from widespread state and (un)civil violence, particularly the "humanitarian" military interventions in East Timor and Kosovo. He offered his own perspective as well; he was critical of an overreliance on direct intervention to resolve chronic conflict:

> Now the NATO has been dropping bombs on Kosovo. I have seen all these things on the BBC dish. So many people are suffering; it is by the grace of God that something is done. But your people are very modern and depend too much on machines. I think that this bombing would not be necessary now if you had remembered that a free market is not the same thing as a just society.

He shared some thoughts about what did make a just society before talking about the tensions in his own village that accompanied such debates. He was particularly concerned about the number of young men who were joining militant organizations to fight in what they called the "Kashmir Jihad":

> Some people say that we in this village should not call ourselves refugees since we are living in our very own Kashmiri homeland, but what this is, it is the practice of the Holy Prophet, peace be upon him, who said, that "he who steps even over the threshold to provide a moral life for his family, he is a refugee and therefore a defender of his people." I tell this thing to the young men when they are overtaken by emotion to join the *jihād* [armed struggle]. I tell them that *hijarat* [protective migration] is also a *sunnat-e-rasūl*—an honorable practice of the Prophet Mohammad, peace be upon him. I tell them, "Become educated, work hard, study Qur'an Sharif, honor your mother by marrying well, educate your children, especially your daughters." I tell them, "There are many ways to defend human rights and to fulfill your duty to humanity and to your nation."

Hajji Mohammad Rashid's attempts to convince young men not to join militant organizations point to three historical transformations in the regional political culture. The first is a change in the terms that people use to talk about their experiences of political violence and to express the value of resettlement and re-creating enduring social ties after periods of warfare and civil conflict. Among displaced Kashmiri Muslims in Pakistan and AJK, the historical response to political violence and to violence-related forced displacement has been the bodily practice of *hijarat* and the production of the *muhājir* (one who has done a hijarat, a refugee) as a social and political identity category within the postcolonial nation-state. The experience of political violence in the current conflict, however, is increasingly incorporated into social life through the concept of *jihād,* with the production of the *mujāhid* (one who fights in a jihād, a warrior) as a valued political subject.[2]

A second transformation reflects a concurrent shift in conceptions of sovereignty in Kashmiri political culture that has shifted the terrain of struggle from the territory of Islam to the bodies of Muslim people, a concern that people expressed by referring to the concept of human rights. Finally, there has been a corresponding evolution in how young men become mujāhids; the practice of jihād is increasingly regulated not by Islamic institutions, but by Muslim individuals and refugee families.

CONDUCTING AND PRESENTING ETHNOGRAPHIC
RESEARCH IN A TIME OF WAR

In this book, I investigate these transformations, focusing on the time period of 1947 (when the first refugees from Jammu and Kashmir were displaced into Pakistan) to 2001. I conducted ethnographic research in Kashmiri refugee communities between March 1999 and September 2001. I returned to Pakistan for field visits and archival research in 2003 and early 2005, and then, weeks after I returned to the United States in 2005, a massive earthquake quite literally changed the landscape of AJK. Several of the refugee camps where I had worked slid off the mountainside into the river, and all of their surviving residents were displaced into new camps. I returned to AJK a month after the earthquake and then again in 2006 and 2008. Earthquake relief and reconstruction effort changed the political and economic terrain of AJK as well as its landscape. Many militants refocused their struggle as a "humanitarian jihād," and the work of international humanitarian and development organizations that came to AJK for the first time opened up new spaces for civil engagement.[3]

September 2001 became a turning point in the scholarly as well as popular literature on jihadist movements and political Islam; it framed how we examine the "global" and "jihād" in ways that essentialize "Islamic" culture and misunderstand the relationship between Islam as a religious tradition and the social production of Muslims as political actors. By focusing on how Kashmiri Muslim refugees and militants negotiated Islamic and global values before they were widely assumed to be diametrically opposed, I hope to engage readers in this story of how people struggle, in very human and very modern, if discomfiting ways, with the problem of political violence so wrapped into the normality of everyday life as to be almost banal.

It has been my experience that, after presenting a scholarly paper or giving a public lecture, one of the questions will begin, "I appreciate your project to humanize Islamic militants, but. . . ." Such questions initially confounded me, and I've learned over the years that it helps if I am forthright about the process by which I came to do this research and eventually to the arguments that I present in this book. So first, I have never aimed to humanize Islamic militants. As I see it, the people who engage in violent politics by any name—militants, mujāhids, jihādīs—are always already human. They are members of communities and, like other people, the question of how they are socialized toward or away from violence (and whether that violence is seen as criminal or is sanctioned) is a core political and cultural question.

Second, I did not set out to study militants at all; I set out to work with refugees and other victims of the Kashmir conflict. I had worked in Indian Jammu and Kashmir State on a humanitarian mission from 1995 to 1996. During that time, I conducted hundreds of interviews with men who had been detained and interrogated during the anti-Indian insurgency. I decided to complete my training as an anthropologist rather than become a professional humanitarian worker because my observations in the detention centers convinced me that peacemaking in the Kashmir region would eventually have to grapple with the ways that experiences of violence have been incorporated into the political cultures of the regions that are a part of the Kashmir Dispute. I knew that I couldn't work in refugee camps in Pakistan without being willing to engage with militants, but a good field researcher has to be willing to be surprised. It surprised me to discover, for example, that youths from refugee resettlement villages had also become involved in jihadist organizations. I became increasingly uncomfortable with the assumed "deterrent effect of public exposure" in the anthropological literature of political violence.[4] I also discovered that public exposure— breaking the silences that obscure political violence—rather than charting a path toward peace actually underpins the social reproduction of political violence as a jihād in Kashmir.

Over several years of fieldwork, I began to understand that "victim" is an unstable political category. It is an easier moral category—and a much more comfortable place to locate compassion than "perpetrator"—but the long history of conflict in the Kashmir region has made many victims and many perpetrators, and many who are both victims and perpetrators. Peacemaking will have to deal not only with the pasts of all of them, but also with all of the parts of their pasts. Peacemaking will also have to engage the transformations of political culture, including the democratization of violence, that are the outcomes of decades of people grappling with normalized violence in the disputed borderlands.

Conduct and Confidentiality in the Ethnography of Armed Conflict

I am often asked how it was possible to conduct research among Islamic militants as a female scholar. In many ways, my gender has been an asset rather an impediment. Azad Jammu and Kashmir is a high-surveillance society and the frontier of an active conflict zone. No one can object to political vigilance in a security zone without bringing suspicion upon himself, but harassment of women is not socially acceptable in a context explicitly circumscribed as "Islamic." It was possible, therefore, for my interlocutors to critique political surveillance as a transgression of gender propriety and to include me in domestic spaces that are resistant to state oversight. It was in part because I could move in family networks that I was able to learn how Kashmiri refugees negotiate public and domestic spaces and how much the legitimacy of the practice of jihād depends on the family.

Many female anthropologists describe being treated as an "honorary man" in such situations, but I was never an honorary man. My presence as a female researcher was always explicitly discussed, balanced with the fact that I was going to be "a professor" and write "a book." Several influential elder men and religious leaders who generally do not meet with non-kin women publicly announced that they had decided to speak with me out of a shared "seeking-after-truth," even if the kinds of knowledge we sought were quite different. I do not, however, wish to imply that the gender of a researcher conveys a right to access. I found that the more my Kashmiri hosts negotiated me into the circumscribed domain of the family, the more a critique of my morality became a part of the state's political project of surveillance. Eventually, the security agencies' surveillance of my conduct as a researcher came to focus on "discovering" whether I was providing sexual favors to AJK government officials or local hosts in exchange for their assistance in my field research. That line of investigation illustrated that gender surveillance and political surveillance can each be transmogrified into the other. It also meant that my efforts to conduct myself in a way that was socially acceptable by my host communities' standards, rather than my gender per se, was what allowed me a continued place in their homes.

There were other ways that my identity allowed me to cultivate ethnographic access in a wide variety of contexts. I did not inherit the restrictions on sociality that come with having a presumed position in the social order, because I don't have a natal kinship network in Pakistan or Jammu and Kashmir. I found that people were eager to speak with me, because in me they saw access to a broader international public. So, being a non-Muslim Euro-American woman, on the one hand, helped me initiate relationships that granted ethnographic access to the diverse social worlds of Kashmiri refugees in Pakistan. On the other hand, anthropologists sometimes overestimate the extent to which our interlocutors replicate the markers through which we recognize ourselves. I have actually on several occasions during fieldwork been assumed to be a person of South Asian descent. For example, I had difficulty convincing residents of one refugee village that I was *angrez* (a white foreigner) because someone had seen me in the market and had determined from my bodily comportment that I was likely Muslim, perhaps from an overseas Kashmiri family. Another time, I was detained by the Rawalpindi police on suspicion of being an Afghan prostitute; the evidence against me was that I was "obviously" Afghan and driving an automobile without a male escort.

Unlike discussions of my gender, discussions about other aspects of my identity were rarely conducted in my presence, and I know less about how people resolved their anxieties about who I was. I was told on several occasions by members of militant organizations that they had used their networks to confirm that I had in fact visited members of their organization in Indian prisons when I was doing humanitarian work. Some of my interlocutors expressed a fear that I might not be a real scholar, but rather an intelligence agent for my government. The idea that the hand of the U.S. government might knock on the door of a village in the mountains of Kashmir might sound far-fetched to some readers, but for many Kashmiri refugees the presence of the state in their lives has been felt on their bodies. After 2002 particularly, the visible U.S. military presence in South Asia and the cooperation between the U.S. and Pakistani governments on practices of rendition has made the possibility that the U.S. government is now a part of the surveillance network in AJK a commonly accepted belief. These were mere hints that people were worried about how I would use their stories and, thus, also a testament to how much people were willing to risk to be in dialogue with a global public about who they are and who they hope to become.

To members of the various communities in which I worked, some of the stories recounted in this book are well known, and their tellers will be easily recognizable. I also assume that the places and groups with whom I worked are a part of any records that the state's intelligence services might have made of my research activities. The political situation, however, changes continuously, making it impossible to predict how people will be affected by the future use of their accounts. Markers like where people come from, where they resided when I met them, and where they are now may currently be transparent to some state authorities and obscure to others. Many of the refugees, and militants, whose stories I recount or reference explicitly, declared their intentions to return to their home properties in parts of Jammu and Kashmir administered by India. Several of my interlocutors now live in the United States, the United Kingdom, Australia, and Canada. Some organizations of which people were members when I met them are now on the terrorist watch lists of various countries. A number of former jihadists now work for nongovernmental organizations (NGOs) in postearthquake reconstruction efforts or as policy analysts overseas. For these reasons, I have changed all names and most of the specific places mentioned in this text, even though many people said they wanted their names and their stories to be explicitly linked in the publications that would result from my research.

Lies, Secrets, and Conflict Ethnography

In the practice of jihād as an armed struggle, the normative prescription is that it must be organized, conducted, and evaluated publicly; being a mujāhid is an honorable, if difficult, undertaking. On the other hand, people in AJK are well aware of the international equation of jihād and terrorism; the international disapprobation of religiously legitimated violence and the state of insecurity and paranoia about spies made its secretive practice at least potentially legitimate. Certain forms of knowledge production (such as surveys or interviews conducted independently of participant observation) are not good research methods in contexts where dissimulating about one's objectives, activities, or beliefs is necessary to one's survival or an integral part of the production of political society. Working in a conflict zone or high-surveillance society makes explicit that which is an inherent part of all ethnographic research—the recognition of both conscious and unconscious misrepresentation as an integral part of social and political life.[5] Ethnographic observations of and participation in social processes and relationships makes available to anthropological analysis the production of social and political power through conflict and even dissimulation.

Anthropologists recognize that, when conducting ethnographic research in conflict zones and high-surveillance societies, ethnographers have to make accommodations that include acknowledging limitations on where one can go, what questions can be asked, and what one can eventually write about given the dangers of research and the need to protect our interlocutors.[6] This recognition was fundamental to reformulating anthropological research on political violence, but it largely ignored the problem of "open secrets"— information that is widely known, and yet which people claim not to know. The importance of open secrets was a conceptual focus of older sociological writing on the conduct of politics and was recuperated in anthropology by Michael Taussig with the concept of "public secrecy," which took up the challenge of considering the work that "not knowing" does in processes of political violence.[7] What remains, however, is the problem of how one is taught what must be "not known," because the management of dangerous knowledge is embedded in social relationships.

Despite my years of living and working in Pakistan and Jammu and Kashmir before I began ethnographic research, and despite a rigorous human subjects review on maintaining the confidentiality and safety of my interlocutors, I had to be taught what constituted dangerous knowledge for them. Indeed, my attention was repeatedly drawn to the ways that people teach each other the things they need to not know in order to go about the work of living, and especially to how women passed and managed dangerous knowledge in domestic spaces. This recognition led to the arguments that I make in this book, and to the theoretical interventions that I outline in the introductory chapter. I thus suggest that conflict research needs to shed analytic light on the practices by which people reproduce dangerous knowledge as public secrets in order to better theorize the social production of all forms of modern political violence. For this reason, I have endeavored to make the moments in which secrets, lies, and uncertainties shaped my research a part of the ethnographic description and interpretive work of this book. By focusing on the social practices of managing dangerous knowledge as an analytic problem, rather than as a methodological one, I first recognized the centrality of the family as the site of social production of jihād among Kashmiri refugees in Azad Jammu and Kashmir.

ACKNOWLEDGMENTS

With a deep sense of gratitude and humility, I offer thanks to the many people who shared their memories, experiences, and insights with me. I am not able to acknowledge all of the numerous people in Azad Jammu and Kashmir and Pakistan without whose help and support this fieldwork would not have been possible. I am very grateful to the Kashmiri residents of Muzaffarabad, Hattian, Mirpur, Naya Kotarian, Rawalpindi, Muslim Colony, Islamabad, Murree, Mansera, and Abbottabad who extended hospitality and told me their stories. It was my great pleasure during my research to spend many hours with the families and extended families of my interlocutors, and I thank their spouses and children for their kindnesses, for conversations and sharing their opinions, and for some silliness.

I thank Khawaja Mohammad Awais, Junaid Mian, Abdul Mateen Khan, Rimmal Jamil, and Nadeem Mir for far, far more than I can say, but mostly for trust. I am especially thankful to Mohammad Awais and Rimmal Jamil for inviting me to be at home in their homes and for much good counsel. I thank Shakil-urRahaman for his contributions as a research assistant, and for many introductions. I thank the families of Abdul Hamid Malik, Mohammad Shafi, Abdul Waheed Khan, Zaffar Iqbal Mian, Altaf Hussain Qadri, Ibrahim Hydery, Abdul-urRahaman, and Hajji Qamar Ali Awan for their continuous hospitality. I thank Ghulam Muhammad Safi, Amanullah Khan, Shah Ghulam Qadir, Yasin Malik, Mohammad Qayyum Khan, Mushahid Hussain, and Tariq Masood for graciously sharing their time and their knowledge. Nadeem Akbar and Mazhar Awan exceeded their official duties and also shared bread on many occasions. I thank Zouhoor Wani and Raja Muzaffar for keeping me informed and for including me in their holiday celebrations.

For friendship, intellectual companionship, and much laughter in the company of women, I thank Homaira Usman, Shaista Aftab, and Asma Khan Lone. I am especially grateful to Homaira for the salt in the chai, to Shaista for the dream about the sandals, and to Asma for sharing her thoughts about women's voices. I also thank Humeira Awais for trusting my friendship with her husband and Fariha Rimmal for her example of graceful strength.

The research for this book was conducted over a number of years and was supported by a several grants and fellowships. Travel grants in 1998 and 2002 to Pakistan, India, and Geneva were awarded by the South Asia Program, the Peace Studies Program, and the Anthropology department at Cornell University. Research in Pakistan between 1999 and 2001 was supported by dissertation research grants from the Fulbright Foundation and the American Institute of Pakistan Studies. U.S. government restrictions on travel to Pakistan between 2002 and 2009 limited scholarly funding for follow-up research, and the Jackson School of International Studies and the South Asia Program at the University of Washington engaged in creative course scheduling that made it possible for me to make several field trips to Pakistan between 2004 and 2008. The Fulbright Foundation and the American Institute of Pakistan Studies offered administrative support, office space, and transportation to me during those field visits. I am particularly grateful to Grace Clark, who shared the hospitality of her Islamabad residence and who is always generous with her knowledge and introductions.

This research could not have been conducted without a great deal of institutional support in Pakistan. I thank the Government of Pakistan, particularly the Ministry of Education and the Ministry of Kashmir Affairs, for granting research and residency permissions. I offer deep thanks to the Government of Azad Jammu and Kashmir, particularly to the AJK Ministry of Refugees and Rehabilitation, for affording all possible support. I thank the Institute of Kashmir Studies at the University of AJK for extending affiliated status during my field research. I benefited greatly from the opportunity to meet with scholars at Quaid-e-Azam University and the University of the Punjab in Lahore. I enjoyed unparalleled support at the National Archives of Pakistan, and I thank the staff of the archives for their daily hospitality and their efforts on my behalf.

Friends, colleagues, and teachers around the world contributed to this book. I have had the unqualified privilege to study, work, and write in the company of outstanding people with whom distinguishing between intellectual engagement and personal support is nearly impossible. This book began as a Ph.D. dissertation in Anthropology, and I remain deeply indebted to the training of the scholars with whom I had the privilege to study at Cornell University. As members of my graduate committee, Kathryn March, David Lelyveld, and John Borneman offered years of scholarly support and have remained mentors. With profound respect, I also acknowledge Rima Brusci, Parvis Ghassem-Fachendi, Saadia Toor, and Allison Truitt, who commented on the original research proposal and remained engaged.

At the University of Washington, I have benefited from a generous and supportive community of scholars. Priti Ramamurthy, Kalyanakrishnan Sivaramakrishnan, and Anand Yang were unwavering in their enthusiasm for the completion of this book and in professional mentorship. I thank Purnima Dhavan, Sunila Kale, Christian Novetzke, and Arzoo Ozanloo for many conversations and insights. I thank my interdisciplinary colleagues in the Jackson School of International Studies for contributing to my understanding of the implications of my research beyond South Asian studies and also Marie Anchordoguy, David Bachman, Mary Callahan, Sara Curran, Resat Kasaba, and Joel Migdal for professional support. I also benefited from my interactions with students who came to my courses with eclectic backgrounds in political science, anthropology, Islamic studies, and international studies; they inspired me to think about how to explain my research to broad audiences. I was especially inspired by many conversations, about their work and mine, with my honors and senior thesis students: Marshall Kramer, Mohammad Bilal Nasir, Andrew Watkins, Lydia Wright, Kristen Zipperer.

Over the years, colleagues and friends in Pakistan studies contributed in myriad ways, especially Kamran Asdar Ali, Nosheen Ali, Hussain Haqqani, Rifaat Hussain, Matthew Nelson, Robert Nichols, Sayeed Shafqat, and Anita Weiss. Julie Flowerday and Mona Bhan shared many insights about doing ethnographic research in the Jammu and Kashmir region. I discussed the themes of this book in symposia and workshops at the Davis Center for Historical Studies at Princeton, Kroc Peace Institute at Notre Dame, Quaid-e-Azam University, the Stanford Humanities Center, the School of Historical, Philosophical, and Religious Studies at Arizona State University, the University of Michigan, and the Weatherhead Center for International Affairs at Harvard, and I benefited immensely from the thoughtful discussions.

In 2009–2010, I was a Fellow at the Stanford Humanities Center, where I completed most of the first draft of this book. I thank Aron Rodrique for the atmosphere he fostered as director, and I thank the other fellows for their engagement with this work and for making it such a wonderful year. I especially acknowledge Wendi Adamek, Nicholas Guyatt, Gwyneth Lewis, Gregory Mann, and David Marriott for their productive comments and questions on individual chapters. In addition, Arzoo Osanloo, Pamela Ballinger, Anna Holian, Christian Novetzke, Liisa Malkki and Joel Midgal commented on drafts of articles and chapters in ways that contributed to the final presentation of this book.

I am immensely indebted to those who read the manuscript in its entirety. Anand Yang offered thoughtful commentary and excellent advice. The anonymous reviewers of UCP and the SAAD series provided explicit suggestions and helped me streamline the presentation of the argument. I am particularly grateful for their comments on the final chapter, which improved it immensely. Suvir Kaul revealed himself as one of these reviewers; I am honored to be able thank him by name, because his marginal comments were invaluable. In addition, I thank the excellent readers of the penultimate draft of this book. My freelance editor, Julie vanPelt, contributed her word-craft. Amanda Snellinger read revised chapters at crucial intervals. Karen Robinson and Jasmine Brown offered detailed reflections on the interests of general readers, and Christopher Robinson practiced uncharacteristic restraint with his red pen, as promised. H. Paul Hammann provided constant feedback and made it possible to forge forward.

Reed Malcolm at the UCP was dedicated to this book, and I thank him for his enthusiasm. His comments in the early stages and his clear suggestions for revision have made it better. I also thank Stacy Eisenstark and the UCP editorial staff for their work in bringing the book to press and Bill Nelson for his cartographic renderings.

Much thanks to the family and friends who are now thoroughly acquainted with the terrors of academic writing. The voices and company of old friends Kristen Borges, Jennifer Lee, Teri Lanza, and Kathleen Loisel, and their assurance that there is a world before, during, and beyond the book, buoyed me many times. I thank Shoshanna Press for the stickers. My family offered immeasurable support through years of research and writing. My special remembrance to my great uncle John Strater, who gave the gift of an education without debt, a wondrous and liberating thing. I thank my brother, Kylian Robinson for his spirit and for dancing on the polo grounds in Hunza. I thank my parents, Karen and Christopher Robinson, for their visits to AJK and Pakistan, and for publicly bestowing on me the status of dutiful daughter, which was helpful, although not well deserved. H. Paul Hammann, my husband, has become my anchor and my sail; I thank him for his love, endurance, and for taking care while I tended to this book.

While many people commented on drafts of this book, I alone am responsible for any shortcoming or errors that remain. The interpretations and arguments offered here are also solely mine. I say this in recognition of the fact that some research participants do not agree with my conclusions; I offer them my special appreciation for the discussions and debates that we have had on these topics over the years.

Parts of Chapters 1 and 3 were previously published in the *Journal of Refugee Studies* (2012) as "Too Much Nationality: Kashmiri Refugees, the South Asian Refugee Regime, and a Refugee State, 1947–1974," 25(3): 344–365.

The Social Production of Jihād

IN THIS BOOK, I PRESENT an anthropological analysis of the social production of jihād among refugees who occupy a transnational space in the borderlands between Pakistan and India. For the first four decades after the Partition of colonial India, displaced Muslims from Jammu and Kashmir placed tremendous value on the Islamic practice of a kind of migration known as *hijarat* (protective migration). They defined themselves as *muhājirs* (refugees) and accorded spiritual value to the practice of reestablishing the Muslim family in exile. In the 1990s, a shift was discernible; more and more, Kashmiri refugees talked about the importance of becoming *mujāhids* (warriors) and participating in a *jihād* (armed struggle) as a way to defend their families and to make it possible to return to their homes. Through their incorporation in militant groups, Kashmiri Muslim refugees living in Pakistan and in the Pakistan-administered territory known as Azad Jammu and Kashmir (AJK) played a significant role in shaping the militant movement known as the "Kashmir Jihad." I use the tension between hijarat and jihād to tell the story of why "refuge-seeking" became a socially and politically devalued practice in the Kashmir region and how this devaluation made large numbers of refugee men available for militant mobilization. The tension between hijarat and jihād grounds this analysis in a set of debates in which Muslim Kashmiri refugees are deeply invested and which are both explicit in political discourses and implicit in social practices.

A long history of violent political conflict has shaped the lives of people who live in the disputed region of Jammu and Kashmir. During each period of interstate and intrastate armed conflict, people were forcibly dislocated across the military Line of Control (LoC) between India and Pakistan. In Pakistan and AJK, Muslim refugees from the Indian side of the LoC were given temporary property allotments and resettled in refugee resettlement villages and urban satellite colonies. Their resettlement was, and remains, legally temporary; international agreements provided for refugees to return to their home places and reclaim their properties when the territorial dispute between India and Pakistan will be resolved. In the interim, their documented legal status as "Kashmiri refugees" became the basis of the extension of political rights in Pakistan. That legal category includes both people who were themselves displaced and their descendants, and there are now over five million officially recognized Kashmiri refugees in AJK and Pakistan. These documented Kashmiri refugees now comprise a large percentage of the citizens of the provincial state of AJK.[1] Of these, none are recognized as conventional refugees by the United Nations or by international refugee organizations. While they successfully garner recognition as "Kashmiri" within Pakistan, they are increasingly categorized as "Pakistanis" in other contexts.

After the beginning of the civil armed conflict in the Indian valley of Kashmir in 1989, additional refugees entered AJK territory. They were settled in camps rather than offered resettlement provisions, and many of the men from these camps became active in militant organizations that fight in Indian Jammu and Kashmir State. The refugee camps became spaces both for providing relief and for organizing militant violence, and youths from resettlement villages and urban Kashmiri refugee communities began joining active militant organizations fighting on the Indian side of the LoC. They called this struggle the Kashmir Jihad (*jihād-e-kashmīr*). Young militants often endured the disapproval and discouragement of their elders, but they eventually garnered widespread public support. By the late 1990s, their participation had prompted the emergence of new jihadist groups that had little connection to established Kashmiri political parties and only loose ties to organized religious schools. The Kashmiri refugees who joined and supported these militant organizations had refashioned an insurgency as an Islamic jihād, but they also reframed popular understanding of what jihād is and how it should be practiced.

This book is organized in three parts, each of which integrates ethnographic with historical accounts to explore the relationship between these two social forms produced by displaced peoples' experiences with political violence: that of the muhājir (refugee) and that of the mujāhid (warrior). Part One, "Between Hijarat and Jihād in Azad Kashmir," examines the political and cultural paradigms through which Kashmiri Muslim refugees interpret and explain their personal and collective histories and express their aspirations for the future. Over their lives, displaced people sometimes claimed to be muhājirs and sometimes mujāhids. They did not always achieve the social recognition they sought, but their claims referenced symbolic meanings that connected refugees to other historical migrations and to periods of violent political struggle in other parts of the Muslim world. The designation "*Kashmiri*" also indicates people's awareness of their involvement in political contexts and historical processes that exceed the immediate context of daily life. Many people were displaced by historical accidents—by the unanticipated formation of new borders or by the border's propensity for wandering across terrain. But the production of Kashmiri refugees as political subjects was not an accident of history. Kashmiri refugees insisted on recognition as Jammu and Kashmir "hereditary state subjects" and on the institutionalization of their status as refugees, because they derive their rights claims in the postcolonial state from a polity that existed in the past (and that some still strive to re-form for the future): the former Princely State of Jammu and Kashmir. In this sense, national and transnational processes shaped Kashmiri refugees' experiences of incorporation into the postcolonial nation-state. "Being Kashmiri" and "being a refugee" now simultaneously secure rights claims and obscure intense social conflicts about how cultural affinities correspond to political identities.

The second part of the book, "The Historical Emergence of Kashmiri Refugees as Political Subjects," analyzes the formation and transformation of the Jammu and Kashmir state subject refugee (muhajir-e-riyasat-e-jammu-o-kashmir)—or simply Kashmiri refugee (muhajir-e-kashmir)—as a social and governmental category. In South Asia, a regional refugee regime developed to deal specifically with the displacements associated with the dismantling of the British Empire during the Partition. Kashmiri refugees had a distinctive place in that classificatory system. Refugee administrators, international observers, and the Pakistani public distinguished Jammu and Kashmir state subject refugees from Partition-era refugee-migrants. Jammu and Kashmir refugees and politicians also used the distinct category to make claims on legitimate governance over the former polity and to limit Pakistan's administrative penetration into AJK. The concept of being a refugee was thus imbued with political value, both by people's use of religious symbolism and by this specific historical formation. What it meant to be a Kashmiri refugee came into conflict with global cultural expectations, legal norms, and administrative practices that constitute the international refugee regime after 1989, when new groups of displaced people crossed into AJK. For Kashmiri refugees, the concept of hijarat no longer adequately explained the social or political experiences of violence-related forced displacement. Addressing the international community as a kind of humanitarian victim-refugee, required the de-politicization of the Kashmiri refugee subject. The terms *refūjī* (camp refugee), *panāh gazīn* (refuge-seekers), and *mutāsirīn* (affectees) became a focus of political and social debate and placed conflict-related forced displacement in a global political imaginary. At the same time, the terms mujāhid and *jihādī* (jihadist) became important as fighters emerged from refugee communities.

The final section, "Body of Victim, Body of Warrior," describes the contemporary social practice of jihād within Kashmiri refugee communities in AJK and Pakistan. The young refugee men who joined militant organizations fighting in Kashmir were not recruited through traditional Islamist political party networks or through fundamentalist ideological indoctrination in traditional religious institutions. Instead, they sought out militant organizations directly. Their primary sources of information about the conflict in Kashmir were networks of personal relationships (including residents of refugee camps and relatives living in Indian Kashmir) and public media (such as newspapers, satellite television, and the Internet). They describe the Kashmir Jihad as a defense of Kashmiri people from human rights abuses by the state rather than as a defense of Muslim territorial sovereignty (the fundamentalist paradigm) or a means of establishing Islamic legal rule within the modern state (the Islamist paradigm). Jihadist organizations accommodated this image of the mujāhid as the defender of victimized Kashmiri women, and this formulation of the Kashmir Jihad shifted the terrain of struggle from sovereign territory or the sovereign state to the sovereign body.

This story, thus, reveals a surprising convergence: Kashmiri Muslim refugees adopted the language of human rights and humanitarianism to rethink their position in relationship to wider regional, transnational, and global communities. In doing so, they forged a notion of "rights", as a hybrid of Islamic and global political ideas and practices, and reformulated the Kashmir Jihad as a project legitimized by the need to protect the bodies of Muslim people against torture and sexual violence. Kashmiri refugees emphasized their personal conscience and their understanding of the broader political context over doctrinal regulation. In this, they drew on modern experiences of the self to express ideas about how a Muslim person should respond to experiences of violent transgression of the physical and social body. While this formulation offered many different ways for people to participate in jihād and produced a significant amount of public support, it also loosened the institutional connections between political parties and militant organizations. Indeed, Kashmiri mujāhids and jihādīs cannot produce themselves through the ideological guidance and bodily disciplining of religious institutions, because this notion of rights was created as a relational concept within and by refugee families. Instead, for Kashmiri Muslim refugees who become Islamic militants, the family rather than the mosque or the religious school mediates entrance into jihadist organizations.

This ethnographic reality challenges many current understandings of what jihād is and how it is produced.

ON CONTEMPORARY JIHADS AND THE SPECTACLE OF JIHADIST VIOLENCE

Jihād is no longer a concept that is completely contained by the Islamic religious traditions. It has become an object of public culture on a global scale[2] and a concept that mobilizes political and military interventions in the name of multiple (and divergent) ethical goals.[3] At the end of the Cold War and through the first years of the so-called War on Terror, media and policy discourses produced a widespread understanding that it refers to Islamic religious warfare, or "holy war." Scholars of the Islamic traditions objected to this translation; they argued that the term rightly refers to a spiritual struggle for moral perfection rather than to practices of warring.[4] Despite these objections, the term jihād came into broad use not only as an indicator of religious warfare, but more specifically to denote terrorism legitimated by theocratic discourses. This created a demand for experts on "Islamic terrorism," many of whom were not trained in the history, culture, or languages of any particular Muslim society and approached jihād as a universal fundamentalist form of religiously mandated violence against nonbelievers.

In response, scholars with expertise in historical and contemporary Muslim societies turned their focus to jihād's relationship to the universalizing claims of "Islam" as a religious tradition, and three broad positions emerged. One emphasized trends of continuity within Muslim societies and historical attempts to maintain or regain religious purity, and linked contemporary violence to the origins of the Islamic religious traditions.[5] It has been critiqued for making violence central to the study of Islam and for presenting the culture of Muslim societies as unchanged by debates; as if, instead of being a "people without history," Muslims are a people with nothing but history for whom the work of culture-making is inherently already complete.[6] Another position emphasized the political and economic conditions, particularly those of inequality and domination, that shaped jihād practices in the modern era and made them analytically comparable with other (violent) anticolonial, anti-imperial, or liberatory resistance movements.[7] A third position has described the Islamic tradition as "hijacked"—the true spiritual meaning of jihād has been captured and corrupted by a very small number of Muslim people who do not represent the true religious tradition.[8] This perspective posits, on the one hand, a universal Islam (but one disassociated from violent politics) and, on the other, a historical misappropriation of that "real" universal Islam (by untrained, uneducated, or misguided Muslims who do not understand their own tradition). Critiques of these positions accuse adherents of being apologists for Islamic terrorism.

These studies have illuminated the actual diversity of jihāds, and they offer important challenges to counterterrorism policy analysts. Unfortunately, however, the dominant paradigm has been to analyze "jihād" as its own object. It is therefore not surprising that institutions (like religious schools or militant training camps), religious doctrines (such as Deobandi, Salafi, etc.), and political ideologies (like fundamentalism or Islamism) have been removed from their social contexts and posited as new sites of subject formation and regulation.[9] In addition, the methodologies employed to study jihād have had profound theoretical consequences.[10] Religious studies focus on the foundational texts and lineages of interpretive exegesis.[11] Historians, for their part, have taken up regional traditions and approach jihād as a paradigm that that Muslims have drawn upon in different ways at different times.[12] And social science studies of contemporary jihāds are predominantly based on statistical survey methods, structured interviewing, and analysis of testimony or statements of jihadists in detention.[13] Unfortunately, a focus on texts privileges doctrinal positions and the cultural productions of religious elites, and basing social analysis on preidentified jihadists presupposes understanding how someone becomes a fighter in a jihād. To actually ask people what jihād means to them, and to further observe how communities and individuals support or subvert processes by which people become mujāhids, requires a sustained ethnographic access that is extremely difficult to achieve and maintain.[14] But it is precisely such an approach that one must adopt in order to address the serious analytic challenges posed by the current approaches to the study of contemporary jihāds.

One such challenge is that emphasizing the essential spiritual meaning of the "greater jihād" does not explain how jihād as warfare or armed struggle (the "lesser jihād") can have a valued place in modern social life and why it cannot simply be de-fetishized by those Muslim scholars and intellectuals who argue the foundationally spiritual meanings of the concept. Another is that, as regards so-called Islamic violence, the role of culture in the process of sociopolitical transformation is contested and contingent; the eventual emergence of new social forms is neither epiphenomenal to cultural production nor culturally overdetermined. Islam in its many political forms provides several alternative models for how Muslims might act when confronted with oppression and violence—hijarat and jihād, for example, are both discussed in Islamic religious texts, both have the status of *sunnat* (models of behavior), and both address the issue of how to live with political violence. Therefore, why one model becomes more or less powerful at any given moment cannot be explained by a textual or historical hermeneutics that is internal to its object. Furthermore, there is no ritual process of subject formation that embodies Islamic ideology outside of specific historical and social contexts, and religious concepts, symbols, and interpretations are always connected with and inflected through worldly symbols and historical processes of meaning-making.[15] Thus, neither the social production of mujāhids nor muhājirs can be explained analyzing either textual explanations of Islam or historical precedent exclusively.

There is also the challenge of confronting the violence in/of jihād. Images of violence associated with jihād circulate on a global scale, yet the spectacle of that violence and the human experiences of suffering associated with it have no single, stable political meaning. Whether the suffering that first comes to mind was caused by the 9/11 attacks or by unmanned drones bombing a village suggests whether a person thinks of jihād as a practice that is offensive, even terroristic, or a legitimate use of violence to defend Muslim people from external aggression. Other spectacles of violence are even less stable; for instance, the marks of torture inscribed on the bodies of prisoners interrogated for their political activities or beliefs are read very differently across diverse publics. Even images of violence that are intended to reveal a simple truth about violent events instead reveal that the corporeal wound does not speak for itself. The most eloquent expression of this that I have encountered is from Susan Sontag's *Regarding the Pain of Others*. She wrote that photographers think about their material "as unmasking the conflict, but those same antiwar photographs may be read as showing pathos, or admirable heroism, in an unavoidable struggle that can be concluded only by victory or defeat."[16] Divergent interpretive publics come to very different conclusions about what the corporeal wound is evidence of, and they come to very different conclusions about how they should respond to what they see and what they "know". In this sense, the interpretive processes by which Muslim publics evaluate violence carried out in the name of Islam are quite similar to the social practices of evaluation and rationalization that are a part of the process of legitimating modern political violence in general.

The Kashmir Jihad and the Pakistani State

Here, I would like to clarify what my argument is *not*. It is well documented that the Pakistani state funds various militant groups as part of a long-term proxy-war strategy vis-à-vis India and that international Islamic organizations have links with some of the militant groups active in the Kashmir region.[17] I do not deny that they exert influence. The people who participate in the Kashmir Jihad, however, are very well aware of the different uses that various states will make of them, and they have their own uses for state and non-state sponsors as well. The common analytic perspectives that explain changes in the social mobilization of violence on the ground by analyzing the intentions and stratagems of Pakistan or any other government are insufficient. I am also not focused on political elites or their explanations of the political goals of their movements; many of the young men involved in militant organizations, both those allied with political parties and those purely organized to conduct jihād, are members of multiple political associations, some of which have contradictory ideological underpinnings or political goals. Overt statements about political affiliations might or might not represent aspirations or commitments for Kashmiri refugees in the current context; and in many cases, people have many different political affiliations that they deploy as needed in different local, regional, national, and transnational contexts. This reality presents a problem to anyone seeking to correlate party or organizational membership, or even participation, with a specific political or religious position. Furthermore, they often join associations explicitly for the infrastructural support that they offer, rather than as an endorsement of a position. Rather than being the end point of separating young men from the family, the life histories of Kashmiri refugees who have become jihādīs suggest that the family, as a model and moral structure and as an aspiration, penetrates even into the militant training camp. Conflict analysis in the Kashmir region has remained firmly on states and political elites,[18] but in order to understand how decades of armed conflict have changed the regional political culture, it is necessary to take serious measure of the new social formations that have emerged from people's long struggles with and against violence.

It is also not my argument that Muslim refugees in AJK are the only victims of political violence in the Kashmir region, or that they haven't perpetrated great violence upon others.[19] It is a terrible truth that there are many victims in this long conflict and that basing political claims on the defense of victims has heretofore contributed to greater victimization rather than to the emergence of sustainable systems of accountability or to a durable peace. Understanding the emergence of jihād on the ground requires engaging an important social reality: violence is actually a very small, if highly visible, part of the practices of jihād—most of which are not violent most of the time. These practices raise ethical debates, produce new cultural aesthetics, and shape the desires and aspirations of the social imagination.

Regarding the Modernity of Politicized Islam and Personhood in Muslim Societies

My argument that contemporary jihāds, like other modern violent political movements, unfold over time through discussion, debate, and conflict over legitimate practices and limitations, brings into question the role of Islam as a religious tradition in the process of sociopolitical transformation. It also engages two theoretical debates in the interdisciplinary study of political movements—including violent ones—that employ an Islamic moral language. One of these debates is about whether Islam as a religious tradition is inherently already political or whether it requires some kind of social work to make it politically accessible. The other, a corollary in some ways, is about how to explain the paradox of overtly politicized uses of Islam—that both fundamentalist ideology (which argues that individuals should model their behavior on the past as a site of authentication and authority) and Islamist ideology (which argues that the state apparatus should enforce traditional Islamic legal systems to reform Muslim society) depend, in their appeal and practice, on modern political forms and subjects. I contend that it is important to make analytic distinctions between "Islamic fundamentalism," "Islamism," and "political Islam."

Islamic fundamentalism and Islamism are distinctly modern movements, even though they rhetorically claim a return to an uncorrupted and universal past.[20] As modern ideological forms, however, fundamentalist and Islamist trajectories have important distinctions.[21] For this reason, while there are legitimate objections to the use of the word *fundamentalism* in application to Islam, it is a valuable marker of the debate among Muslim intellectuals in which Islamist ideologies diverged from their reformist and revivalist influences. Fundamentalist thinkers (whose arguments first cohered and became prominent in the 1920s and 1930s) argued that individuals should model their behavior on the past as a site of authentication and authority. They were interested in establishing a proper Islamic sociopolitical order, and they argued that it would be achieved through organized movements to reform individual Muslims and society more broadly. In this, the intellectual task was the excavation and reaffirmation of foundational principles and the organized effort to reshape society by those principles.[22]

Islamist thinkers (whose arguments diverged from the fundamentalist position in the 1940s and became prominent in the 1960s), on the contrary, were explicitly interested in articulating a political ideology based on this foundational Islam. Islamist ideologues argued that Islam constituted a total system for the governance of public and political life as well as for individual piety and social organization. Indeed, the term *Islamist* emerged from these thinkers' explicit effort to distinguish themselves from other Muslims in general, and from fundamentalist thinkers specifically; an Islamist is someone committed to what Abu A'la Maududi, ideologue of the South Asian Islamist party the Jamaat-e-Islami, termed in Urdu the *"nizām-e-islāmī"* (the total system/order of Islam).[23] Eventually, Islamist thinkers argued for the total institution of Islamic governance and the institutionalization of Islamic law. Yet, "because Islamic symbols are filled with different patterns of meaning... there exists no clear consensus on how to determine the substance of the posited concept of order,"[24] and Islamist positions vary on what form Islamic governance should take and on the specific character of the law. Significantly, Islamists' arguments were not based on classical notions of caliphate and territorial sovereignty but were instead interested in the modern bureaucratic state and the use of political parties to organize formal institutional politics.[25] Islamist political parties are typically made up of closely affiliated associations; the political party itself, which may be concerned with administration or diplomatic efforts; a wing concerned primarily with charitable activities and the provision of social welfare; and a militant wing, which may or may not be active.[26]

One of many vexing questions in the study of Islamic fundamentalism and Islamism is how to measure their success. The posited "total system" of

Islam rejects a foundational distinction between social order and political order and, on one hand, Islamism failed as a global political ideology if its focus was to capture and transform the modern state. Islamist parties have rarely been successful electorally. When they have had electoral success, they have been suppressed by authoritarian regimes often supported by external powers. Where they have had electoral or revolutionary success, the paradox of Muslims, including Islamist leaders, having different conceptions of the Islam on which the order of society and state should be based becomes an object of immediate dispute. But the social work and political organizing actually carried out on the ground by fundamentalist and Islamist social activists extended the cultivation of disciplined, self-reflective Muslim personhood and demonstrated that people could be the agents of their own political possibilities.[28] As Islamist activists and parties reinterpreted Islamic precepts for application in state legal practices and institutions, they had to make arguments that were convincing and compelling to people in the emergent political public sphere. In this process, overtly nonpolitical reform and revivalist movements contributed to the formation of modern political subjects, through their focus on the self-reflective moral reform of individual Muslims and the inculcation of conscious bodily practices of piety.[27] Religiously inflected moral terminologies were integrated into discursive arguments about the rationality and value of political practices, but in ways that confounded doctrinal regulation and actually produced hybrid political forms.[29]

The concept of "political Islam" should be understood and applied as an analytic concept distinct from but related to both Islamic fundamentalism and Islamism. Political Islam properly marks epistemological and ontological orientations—rather than ideological ones—that have become legible though the central role that cultural processes and cultural conflicts play in modern political forms of rule. Questions of authoritative interpretation remain contested issues in Muslim societies, but in practice, neither traditionally trained scholars nor political ideologues, control the actual social debates and cultural process of evaluation by which people evaluate the "good" use of power or the legitimacy of political practices, including the use of violence to achieve political ends. Instead, the forms of knowing and being in the world that correspond to the politicization of Islamic cultural forms in late modern societies are connected to Muslim political subjects' awareness of and engagement in local, national, and global social, political, and economic processes.

One of the theoretical strengths of anthropology has long been its ability to explain how systems of cultural categorization operate to frame the conditions of politics. This book explains the coherence and contradictions within and between systems of categorization that shape who qualifies as a Kashmiri refugee. What appear to be merely taxonomic struggles actually reveal social and political struggles over, and anxieties about, who is Kashmiri, Pakistani, or Indian; who qualifies as a refugee as distinct from a citizen; and whose violent pasts are worthy of solidarity and care (such as refugees or victims of human rights abuses) as opposed to those whose pasts are not (such as militants and terrorists).

Some have argued that the young men who joined militant groups in the 1990s came to think of themselves as Kashmiri refugees as a result of an effort by Pakistan to recruit them to a proxy war in Indian-administered Jammu and Kashmir.[30] This perspective is underwritten by two misleading assumptions about political violence in Jammu and Kashmir. The first is a tautological but pervasive culturalist argument that has held that Kashmiri society is fundamentally nonviolent and religiously syncretic and that it therefore follows that a political struggle based on violence or legitimated in a religious discourse must by definition be "unKashmiri" and carried out by people who are not Kashmiri and come from outside of Kashmir.[31] However, the category "Kashmiri" also emerged as a distinct rights-bearing political subject through the cultural, social, and political work of Jammu and Kashmir politicians and political activists who struggled to maintain the Princely State's categories of legal identification. Through their efforts, the Hereditary State Subject provisions remain wrapped into the political and social fabric of the divided regions of the former state; they undergird struggles for political belonging in ways often obscured by the claims of the postcolonial states of India and Pakistan for legitimacy and domination in the region.

The second misleading assumption is that there is a single real (universal and unchanging) refugee subject against which disjunctures or contradictions can be held up as a sign of inauthenticity. In fact, categorical incommensurability is a familiar problem in accounting for displaced people in many parts of the world.[32] One of its causes is a failure to recognize the different symbolic systems that order the management of refugees. Another is a failure to examine how and why these systems change over time. The refugee regime concept illuminates the different processes through which people displaced by political violence in Jammu and Kashmir became refugees at different historical moments and the varying social, institutional, and cultural meaning accorded to it. It renders visible the changes in meaning that derive from refugees' place in the regional, transnational, and international cultural and political order. The category "Kashmiri refugee" has a historical continuity, and its relational meanings to other political forms have changed over time. Indeed, that refugee camps could become spaces for organizing militant violence as well as for offering relief to refugees, while disturbing to many observers, was a comparatively well-known phenomenon by the 1990s. In fact, the issue of the humanitarian dilemma (that long-term support for displaced peoples perpetuates conflicts by supporting women and children and freeing men for militant labor) was by then a topic of debate among humanitarian practitioners.[33] Taking serious inventory of the relationship between the category of the Kashmiri refugee and the classificatory system of the South Asian refugee regime, thus also renders visible the process of problem of regime change.

Refugee Regimes and Refugees in South Asia

Examining violence-related forced mass displacement in postcolonial South Asia within the rubric of refugee studies has long been a problem for the field. This is due in no small part to the emergence of a new "conventional" definition of a modern refugee during the Partition of colonial India. The final version of the 1951 Convention Relating to the Status of Refugees defined a refugee as an individual who has crossed a national boundary and has a well-founded fear of persecution in the country of origin for reason of race, religion, nationality, or political opinion.[34] Although it took several years to set this definition, in part because states' representatives had serious disagreements about the principles of recognition that should be applied, the standards of categorization and management that developed became normative on a global scale, and this system is now commonly referred to as "the international refugee regime."

The idea that refugees are people deprived of their nationality had the effect of excluding displaced people who could be argued to have multiple claims on nationality—particularly people displaced by decolonization processes. It became a generally accepted argument that Partition-era displacement was a mass migration in which Partition's displaced did not lose the protection of their states and that therefore Partition "migrants" were not subject to United Nations (UN) refugee agreements.[35] But as the historian Mark Mazower has argued about that formative period in the creation of the UN, "the origins of legal regimes lie in a set of cultural, political, and ideological struggles."[36] These legal regimes did not merely reflect an obvious distinction or institutionalize a preexisting agreement—it shaped them. In the words of B.S. Chimni, a legal scholar and former advisor to the United National High Commissioner for Refugees, "the problem of defining a refugee is a debate about the epistemological principles which inform its elaboration."[37] This epistemological ordering of displacement—the process of identifying a person as a refugee, or defining a group as a refugee population—is an inherently political project that orders international relations by categorizing migration and assigning different values to dislocation experiences.[38]

In the social sciences, political scientist Aristide Zolberg and anthropologist Liisa Malkki refocused the study of the international refugee regime; they approached it as a set of transnational expectations, provisions, and representations that constitute a symbolic system for ordering the material practices of refugee administration, including legal adjudication, security provision, and relief distribution.[39] This regime analysis approach shifted the scholarly study of refugees away from purely legalistic consideration of juridical status to a focus on the symbolic as well as material practices that organize power relations through the care and administration of dislocated people. It also made it possible to examine other systems that developed to deal with modern mass dislocation and to coordinate refugee practices across nation-states.

One such system was the South Asian refugee regime, which developed to deal with the ten million to twelve million people who crossed the newly international borders of India and Pakistan between 1946 and 1951 as part of the Partition of the colonial provinces of Punjab and Bengal into East Punjab (India) and West Punjab (Pakistan) and East Bengal (Pakistan) and West Bengal (India).[40] Partition is still too often approached as a historical event that produced an immediate and clear rupture between Pakistan and India. It is better understood as a long process of creating a new categorical and classificatory system that established political and cultural (rather than simply territorial) separations between the new nation-states.[41] The identification, management, and rehabilitation of displaced people were a central part of this process, and India and Pakistan developed bilateral laws and practices that produced the "refugee" as a governmental and social category in postcolonial South Asia. The South Asian refugee regime was based on a political notion of what it means to be a person displaced in the world and has generated political power for the state. The identity category "Kashmiri refugee" developed within this regional refugee regime.

Human Rights, Humanitarianism, and Depoliticization

The international refugee regime has changed over time, and it adopted and adapted symbolic and material practices from several world contexts.[42] In the post–Cold War era, the refugee became a subject whose main reference is not the nation-state but the human rights of the individual.[43] In the 1990s, Kashmiri refugees engaged in documenting their status as a certain kind of humanitarian subject—the human rights victim—for the international community, effectively claiming inclusion in what Jonathan Benthall has called the humanitarian narrative.[44] The international refugee regime's use of human rights and humanitarian discourses and practices emphasized the "victim" status of refugees in ways that challenged the historical construction of refugee subjectivity in the Kashmir region. Those claims were first made in the iconic "humanitarian" space of the refugee camp, but they became a part of wider rethinking of the relationship between being Kashmiri and having rights that depoliticized Kashmiri refugee identity. One effect was a new gendered distinction between female and male refugees that led to the depoliticization of refugee women and the militarization of refugee men in the 1990s.

The depoliticization of Kashmiri refugee women may have been facilitated by globally reinforced images of victimization, in which violence "is strongly sexualized, and the distinction between perpetrators and victims of violence is often represented as a gendered difference."[45] Still, it was striking given that practices of sexual violation of women in other armed conflicts in the same decade were explicitly theorized as a form of political violence characteristic of modern politico-territorial disputes.[46] Feminist scholars have objected to the uncritical acceptance of the trope of women as victims as "a positioning [that treats] women as 'objects' [and that] denies their agency and voices."[47] Unfortunately, critical responses have often taken the form of efforts to recuperate women's agency by finding counterexamples of women's militant activism or subversions of hegemonic domination.[48] Instead, I offer a perspective on the constitution of Kashmiri refugee women as victims that reveals the social value produced by people who can be recognized as victims by global political communities.

The shift away from the South Asian refugee regime toward the international refugee regime required a tremendous amount of social work, and it illustrates that depoliticization is an active process that produces its own political effects. The depoliticization of women in modern Muslim contexts cannot be explained by reference to globalization or renewed enforcement of a posited universal Islamic gender symbolism.[49] And gendered depoliticization in postcolonial South Asia is not a product of the ideological reformulation of the domestic sphere by nationalist elites, making women a repository for a privileged sphere of "culture" or "tradition" that serves as a site for political claims based on cultural identity.[50] Instead, we must look to the difficult social work required to produce certain kinds of experiences as "political" and other kinds of experiences as "cultural" or to fix the unruly boundaries between "the public" and "the domestic."[51]

The transformation of Kashmiri refugee subjectivity thus brings to the forefront the question of what it means to live a "politically qualified life"— by which I mean not only the kinds of values that shape formal recognition of political belonging (like nationality or citizenship) but also the ways in which some experiences of the world are coded as "political." Social processes and cultural categorization shape how people struggle to occupy, in Hannah Arendt's still-cogent words, "a place in the world which makes opinions significant and actions effective."[52]

ON THE AZAD STATE OF JAMMU AND KASHMIR

Azad Jammu and Kashmir (AJK) is a part of the former Princely State of Jammu and Kashmir. In Pakistan, it is commonly referred to as Azad Kashmir (Free Kashmir), although in India it is known as POK (Pakistan Occupied Kashmir). It has a semiautonomous regional government and has been administered internationally by Pakistan since 1949, but it is not constitutionally a part of Pakistan and its people are not represented in the Pakistan National Assembly. Under the 1949 UN agreements on Jammu and Kashmir, Pakistan was recognized as temporarily in charge of AJK's international status. Successive governments of AJK have struggled to maintain their control as "local authorities," in the UN treaty terminology, over AJK's internal administrative structures and governance practices. Formally, AJK operates as a limited parliamentary democracy, as established in the Azad Jammu and Kashmir Interim Constitution Act, adopted in 1974. The territory of AJK

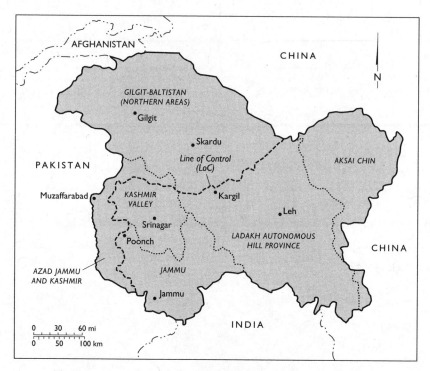

MAP 1. The Former Princely State of Jammu and Kashmir (2012).

comprises about five thousand square miles of the former State of Jammu and Kashmir, one of the largest Indian Princely States during British colonial rule in South Asia (see map 1). The borders with Pakistan's Provinces of Punjab and Khyber Phaktunwa (formerly known as the NWFP, North West Frontier Provinces) determine its territorial boundaries to the west and south. The military Line of Control (LoC) between India and Pakistan demarcates the eastern border. At the time I was doing field research, AJK was comprised of six administrative districts, all of which bordered the LoC (see map 2).[53] To the north, another part of the former princely state known as the Northern Areas, until it was renamed Gilgit-Baltistan in 2010, has a separate governmental and administrative structure.[54] It is governed directly through the Ministry of Kashmir Affairs and Gilgit-Baltistan in Islamabad.[55]

AJK's political status within Pakistan is complex and widely misunderstood, because its internal governance is marked by a long history of tension between the formal structural limits on Pakistan's power and the informal influence and coercion wielded by Pakistani bureaucrats and military

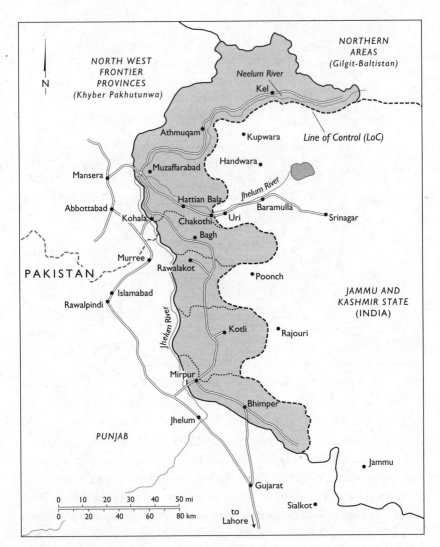

MAP 2. The Azad State of Jammu and Kashmir (2001).

personnel. Study of AJK politics has been dominated by a kind of proxy government theory, which explains political developments in AJK by analyzing the interests and influence of Pakistan.[56] This perspective keeps the focus firmly on the international politics of the Kashmir Dispute and denies the political agency of Kashmiri peoples in producing the conditions of their own political lives. It also overemphasizes formal institutional politics and underestimates the role that Kashmiri politicians, administrators, and political society played in shaping political practices and institutions as they developed in the postcolonial period. As a result, a consensus opinion in the scholarly literature is that the institutionalization of refugee representation in the AJK government was a deliberate strategy through which Pakistan guaranteed itself representation in AJK internal politics.[57]

On the contrary, displaced Jammu and Kashmir hereditary state subjects (the "refugees" who are guaranteed representation) have a long history of actively demanding recognition from and a role in the AJK government. In fact, the "Kashmiri refugee" as a political identity emerged in part through efforts by AJK political elites to define an exclusive domain of state power. By restricting all forms of state patronage—including government employment, property ownership, and registration in government schools—to recognized Jammu and Kashmir state subjects (including refugees), they were able to limit Pakistan's control over the administrative machinery of the AJK government. That government provides most of the public services available in AJK, and it employs only legally recognized Jammu and Kashmir state-subjects and bases civil service appointments on its own exam system.[58] Since the 1980s, small industry and private businesses, like construction firms, hydroelectric development projects, and private English-medium schools[59] have been a growing sector of the regional economy. Private employment opportunities also grew exponentially after the earthquake of 2005 with internationally funded rehabilitation and reconstruction. Historical restrictions on property ownership and employment created opportunities for AJK residents and documented state refugees to provide contract labor for international agencies and establish new local businesses, because Pakistani-owned firms did not have a foothold in the state. The political party or coalition in charge in the capital of Muzaffarabad supervises a vast structure of service provision, administration, and governance and therefore controls an important regional patronage system.

Under the Interim Constitution, the executive branch of the AJK government is comprised of a Prime Minister, elected by a Legislative Assembly, and a Council of Ministers. The Assembly and the Ministry of Kashmir Affairs jointly elect a President, and the AJK Supreme Court and the High Court of Azad Kashmir exercise judicial oversight. The current Legislative Assembly is made up of forty-nine seats. Of these, forty-one seats are directly elected: twelve are elected by refugees living in Pakistan, and twenty-nine are elected by AJK residents. The elected members of the Assembly make appointments to eight reserved seats, of which one is for "overseas Jammu and Kashmir

State Subjects."[60] The AJK government is responsible for all internal law and order and internal security. It maintains its own police, whose elite investigative unit is the AJK Special Branch. AJK does not have its own professional army; the Pakistan Army provides border defense. A special regiment of the Pakistan Army called the "Mujahid Regiment" was established in the late 1980s. It recruits only Jammu and Kashmir state-subjects and is deployed only on the front line of the LoC. The AJK government has also developed an active civil defense program, which trains village-level militia to defend against external (Indian) invasion.

Pakistan has always been sensitive about its international reputation on matters pertaining the UN resolutions on Jammu and Kashmir. For that reason, outright annexation was not a political option. Instead, Pakistan's administrative penetration into the AJK state government was accomplished by making political alliances with AJK political leaders.[61] The government of Pakistan legally exerts authority in AJK internal politics through the Azad Jammu and Kashmir Council, through supervision of the state administrative services, and through control over the state budget.[62] In addition, candidates for elected office are required to support Jammu and Kashmir's accession to Pakistan, and all government employees are required to sign an oath to that effect. For this reason, the nationalist, pro-independence political parties cannot forward candidates for election in AJK, and anyone in government service cannot be a registered member of a pro-independence party. This constraint has effectively kept independence parties (both pan-Kashmir and AJK-based) out of political office, although they have a presence in nongovernmental political contexts. It has also led to a widespread practice of multiple party affiliation, some that are documented for the purpose of employment and others that people espouse clandestinely.

The Pakistan Army exercises coercive power but has to limit its interventions to those that can be hidden from international public scrutiny or that it can legitimate in the name of defending against external aggression. Pakistan treats the entirety of AJK as an area of security risk, because the former Princely State of Jammu and Kashmir has been at the center of regional instability since 1947, and because it is claimed by India. Pakistan exerts the most direct administrative influence within the official Military Security Zone, which covers a 16-km band along the LoC and encompasses areas within range of Indian Army artillery. Within the zone, the Military Intelligence (MI) of the Pakistan Army, the Inter-Services Intelligence (ISI), which recruits both from the Pakistan Army and the Pakistan Civil Services, along with the Federal Investigation Authority (FIA) oversee the activities of the local population, and the military carries out identity checks at regular check posts. These practices remind the people who live there that AJK is an insecure state under constant impending threat of external armed aggression, and it allows Pakistan to suppress dissent in the name of security.

Politicians, administrators, and civilians in AJK express deep suspicions about the indirect influence that representatives of the government of Pakistan play in their political lives. The rise of international access to AJK after the earthquake of 2005 facilitated vocal public critique.[63] Despite Pakistan's influence, however, the reality is that the state of Azad Jammu and Kashmir plays a key role in organizing the experiences of daily life and in shaping the national historical consciousness of people who derive aspects of their political identity from its regulatory regime. For residents of AJK and for Kashmiri refugees resident in Pakistan alike, living a political life means negotiating AJK's semiautonomous institutional structure, political parties, and civil associations, as well as the Pakistani state's surveillance and oversight.

ON THE RESEARCH, SITES, AND METHODS

I conducted the fieldwork upon which this book is based between 1998 and 2008. That fieldwork included twenty-two months of ethnographic research with Kashmiri refugees in Azad Jammu and Kashmir and in Pakistan and four months of archival research at the National Archives of Pakistan. I maintain connections with overseas Kashmiris based in the United States and in England, and over the years I have met with Kashmiri political party leaders on extended political or personal visits in New York, London, and Geneva. My primary methods were participant observation, life-history interviews, and archival research. I also conducted numerous structured interviews on topical issues with government officials and administrators, politicians, and religious leaders. Published scholarship on AJK is limited, and a number of relevant sources are available only in Urdu. I use the available materials— including histories, pamphlets, and memoirs—to contextualize my analysis of the historical development of Kashmiri refugees as a political category, and I draw on government documents from the National Archives of Pakistan, which holds the original records related to Kashmir refugee relief in Pakistan from 1947 to 1965. I also examined jihadist publications, including magazines and taped lectures and songs *(tarānas)*. The conclusions that I present in this book emerged from a sustained analysis of various kinds of information considered in light of others.

I designed my research around the different categories of refugees rather than the places where I could encounter them. I thus met with men and women, displaced during each of the wars and from various parts of the Jammu and Kashmir region living in both AJK and Pakistan. This design accommodated the theoretical issues involved with working with Kashmiri refugees as well as the pragmatic concern that my access to any particular place could change unexpectedly. I was always aware that any number of factors could affect my ability to work with a particular community in a particular place, including the escalation of tensions between Pakistan and India or a decision by the Ministry of Kashmir Affairs that local conditions were dangerous for foreigners. On many occasions I adjusted the timing of meetings with people or visits to certain places in order to allow people to evaluate my project and reputation among other communities. In the first year of my research, I avoided developing close ties with political parties and formal associations to keep my research separate from their political projects, although I did visit a number of nongovernmental organization (NGO) projects on request. Once I felt that my research was well established and that I was not seen as affiliated with any particular group or party, I began meeting with political representatives. Over the years, my fieldwork within AJK has been made feasible by some of these connections.

When I was resident in AJK, I was based in Muzaffarabad city. I made day trips to refugee camps and spent extended periods of time in refugee resettlement villages in the district. When I was resident in Pakistan, I was based in Rawalpindi or Islamabad, and I met with settled refugees living in urban allotments, unsettled refugees living in three different labor camps, and camp refugees who were living and working in Pakistan illegally. I also met with people displaced from villages near the LoC who had come to Pakistan seeking temporary wage labor. I made many short trips to Muzaffarabad and Mirpur for important social and political events, and I moved around a great deal, often following networks of kinship alliances. People from refugee communities in AJK added me to their broader networks of visiting, which were connected to wage-labor migration and kinship obligations between AJK and Pakistan. I, in turn, also traveled these networks to meet with Kashmiri refugee families in cities in the northern Punjab and Khyber Pakhtunwa (NWFP), such as Murree, Abbottabad, and Mansera. One spring, I accompanied a family group of migratory goat headers *(bakerwals)* on the seasonal migration from a village near Rawalpindi to the high grazing grounds of Skardu, meeting other Kashmiri *bakerwals* along the route. I turned back as they embarked on the last leg of the journey, a dangerous stretch that passed within firing range of the LoC.

As a female researcher, it was more appropriate and easier to travel in public spaces and to work with unrelated men when a male companion accompanied me. I therefore worked with a research assistant who came with me on most of my field visits from June 1999 through December 2000. For reasons of protocol, he almost never accompanied me on official meetings with government officials or politicians. For reasons of his security, I never had him accompany me on visits to places like refugee camps or to meet people that I knew were likely to be under high surveillance. My assistant had extended kin relations in several refugee resettlement villages in Muzaffarabad District, and he identified two families who had been displaced from resettlement villages on the LoC who were living in labor camps in Rawalpindi and Islamabad; those families gave me my first entrance into communities of unsettled Kashmiri refugees living in Pakistan. I have not worked with a research assistant since 2001. I have sometimes been the guest of government officials in AJK and, at other times, members of local families who have assumed collective responsibility for me have escorted me to and from meetings.

I was almost always allowed to record life-history interviews. Many of my interlocutors insisted that they wanted their life histories to be preserved in their own words, and one of my research assistant's primary jobs was to transcribe Urdu- and Pahari-language interviews. I also took cameras into refugee resettlement villages and made short films of rituals and ritualized events. I never took photographs in refugee camps, which are already profusely, if selectively, photographed. In retrospect, I rather wish I had photographed those things that underscore the "getting-on-with-life-ness" of living ten years in a refugee camp. At the time, however, I found that *not* having a camera in the camps facilitated my research: foreigners often came to the camps to take pictures as documents of human rights abuses or to "expose" the presence of militants in the camps, so without a camera it was easier to abandon that official script and access the daily life of the camps.

Over time, I found that some of my interlocutors took up the life-history part of my project in ways I had not expected. Several people who were present during my interviews with other people made their own recordings of their experiences of displacement or resettlement and gave me the tapes. On two occasions, I received recordings from young men who I have no record or recollection of having met, but who sent their stories to me. Others took pictures or made videos of events or people who live in places where I was not allowed to go (such as the Security Zone) and asked me to view them. The viewings were always social occasions, with others who for various reasons could not go to these places also watching, explaining, commenting, and asking questions. Like viewings of videos received from across the LoC, these were often heterogeneous social events, with men and women from several generations participating. On one occasion, I received the taped life-history interview of a member of a jihadist organization who did not feel comfortable meeting me. Someone who had been present during my conversations with several other young refugee men conducted the interview, entirely on his own initiative. He said later that he knew the man's story well and felt that I needed to know "the whole dirty truth" about the Kashmir Jihad.

Indeed, many people gave me materials that they thought I should consider in my research. For example, people sometimes brought me jihād manuals or other publications such as recordings of lectures and militant songs, things they had bought at fairs or from militant organizations. Once, I received a pamphlet in the mail from a town near Peshawar. The pamphlet explained the "necessity of organizing *jihād* to combat injustice and protect the innocent" from the abuses of unchecked power; the accompanying anonymous letter, painstakingly penned in English, explained that the sender hoped I would give serious attention to the continuity between spiritual and political jihād and attempt to understand why "*jihād* is not a terrorist practice." Not infrequently, the same thing was given to me from radically different stated motives; one person brought me a collection of jihadist magazines so that I could better understand why jihād is a legitimate form of "resistance against a terrorist state [India]," and another brought me one of the same magazines so that I could see how it "exploits the uneducated [and has become] a terrorist business [which is] ruining Pakistani society." Many people risked social or state disapproval to show me the truth as they understood it.

The ethnographic quotations in this book come from my transcripts of recorded interviews and from my own original field notes. To maintain the confidentiality of my interlocutors, I have identified people by a combination of fictive name and a general time frame for the interview. I don't use specific identifying information except when the significance of the information cannot be conveyed without knowing that information. In the process of analyzing the life histories and narratives that refugees constructed for me, I tracked the different markers in the narratives that would make the speakers recognizable. I did this originally in order to obscure such markers, but in the process of doing so, I came to a much clearer perception of how Kashmiri refugees as historical subjects are implicated in multiple sites of power, both informal and institutional. Twice, I have attributed a quotation or a piece of a life story to a new speaker when in fact the narrator had already appeared in the text under another name. I did this because the information conveyed was so specific that to use the same name twice would have effectively revealed the actual identity of the person. However, none of the stories represent compilations of multiple accounts. I have selected narratives and accounts that are good examples of the personal experiences, sentiments, and concerns expressed by many people over the years. The selection of stories represents my own final understanding of the development and transformation of refugee political life in AJK and Pakistan.

ORGANIZATION OF THE BOOK

Chapter 1 discusses the history and historicity of Kashmiri political subject formation in order to explain the apparent paradox of the Kashmiri refugee collective identification—that the very existence of the Kashmiri refugee as a politicolegal and sociocultural identity both underwrites and challenges the structural foundations of the postcolonial nation-state in South Asia. In the colonial-era Princely State of Jammu and Kashmir, the first political movements produced a highly territorialized definition of political belonging in the greater Kashmir region. The historical patterns of dislocation in the region between 1947 and 2001 then created a dispersed population of people who became categorized as "refugees from the State of Jammu and Kashmir" living in Pakistan and Pakistan-administered Kashmir. The identity category Kashmiri refugee emerged as a subject position, within a domain of rights claims, as the sovereign ground of the disputed state of Jammu and Kashmir. For this reason, the state's territorial borders provide neither the empirical nor analytical language needed to express the relationship between being Kashmiri and political activism.

Chapter 2 delves into competing ideas about what it means to be a refugee in the Kashmir region, aided by life-history narratives of men and women, young and elderly, who have been forcibly displaced because of interstate wars or intrastate insurgency. In their lifetimes, displaced people can move between being muhājirs (refugees) and mujāhids (Islamic warriors). The chapter examines the Islamicate concepts of protective migration (hijarat) and struggle (jihād) to show how Muslim societies have used them to integrate suffering, social responsibility, and political activism in both historical and religio-moral terms. Community discussions of what it means to do hijarat or to participate in jihād show that both practices are continually debated and evaluated; even within communities and families, individuals often come to very different conclusions about the value of each practice.

Chapter 3 examines the national contexts in which Kashmiri refugees emerged as rights-bearing political subjects in the postcolonial period. After 1947, the dominant modes of interpreting what it means to "be a refugee" established Kashmiri refugees as active political subjects with rights claims over political institutions in Pakistan and in India, as well as in the province of Azad Jammu and Kashmir. Within the South Asian refugee regime, Kashmiri refugees in AJK used their status of "difference" from Partition refugees and the "temporary" nature of their resettlement to enforce limits on the coercive power of the Pakistani state. The practices established in this period firmly ensconced a high cultural, social, and political value for hijarat as a model for political engagement.

Chapter 4 discusses the transformation of Kashmiri refugee political subjectivity as displaced Kashmiris renegotiated their multiple relationships with social and political sites of power to include the international community. This precipitated a fracturing of the previous sociopolitical consensus about the relationship between refugees and broader AJK society. For Kashmiri refugees in the 1990s, addressing the international community as "refugees" required the depoliticization of the Kashmiri refugee subject. This process of depoliticization was contested and remains incomplete, but it produced a new gendered distinction between female and male refugees. As it became progressively more difficult for men to claim the political and religious recognition of hijarat as a valued political practice, jihād acquired an enhanced social value as a model for political engagement.

Chapter 5 examines how "human rights" became a part of jihād discourses and practices in transnational Kashmiri communities. The Kashmir Jihad that emerged in Pakistan during the 1990s employed an Islamicate vocabulary but was not primarily defined by Islamic doctrine or Islamist ideology, and the process of drawing young men into militant organizations was not regulated by ideological education or bodily disciplining. Instead, as human rights discourses and practices localized in AJK, refugees drew on concepts of justice, rights and obligations to formulate a concept of jihād as a project legitimized by the need to protect the bodies of Muslim people against human rights violations. This articulation challenged both liberal humanist understandings of human rights and Islamist ideologues' regulation of jihād. The personal narratives of young Kashmiri refugee men who were active members of militant organizations reveal that jihadist organizations (as opposed to political-party-based militant groups) proliferated in the mid-1990s because they accommodated Kashmiri refugees' ideas how a Muslim person should respond to the experiences of violent transgression of the physical and social body.

Chapter 6 argues that for Kashmiri Muslim refugees, the family rather than the mosque or the religious school mediates entrance into Islamic militant organizations. Kashmiri mujāhids depend on the family for the social recognition of "discernment" (which one gains through sacrificing for others) and for the evaluation of "good intention" (which one gains through moral training in familiar and public domains); together, discernment and good intention established the armed struggle as an extension of an internal moral transformation linked to an awareness of mujāhids' obligations to society. Yet, their close association with those who inspire strong personal attachments of love and physical desire, especially children and wives, produced a tension around issues of sexuality and sexual purity. The mujāhid in life and the "martyr" in death alike are enmeshed in social relationships and are subject to ongoing social evaluation about the meaning and value of their actions, including their use of violence.

The Conclusion describes the significance of the emergence of a social distinction between a mujāhid and a jihādī. The book ends with a brief Postscript. It describes the continuing negotiations over the meaning and significance of jihād in Azad Jammu and Kashmir's political culture by discussing how the earthquake of 2005 led to the emergence of a practice that Kashmiri jihādīs call "humanitarian jihād," which in turn is transforming how people there think about security, welfare, and their struggles for sovereignty.

PART ONE

Between Hijarat and Jihād in Azad Kashmir

ONE

Between War and Refuge in Jammu and Kashmir

DISPLACEMENT, BORDERS, AND THE BOUNDARIES OF POLITICAL BELONGING

THE PRINCELY STATE OF JAMMU AND KASHMIR was formed by treaty agreement between the British Colonial Government of India and the Sikh governor of Jammu in 1846. The state was ruled by the Dogra Maharajas until 1947, when internal political and armed resistance and war between the new postcolonial nation-states of India and Pakistan ended monarchical rule. The Indian Princely States were not subject to the partition of the British territories in 1947; the accession of each principality was negotiated between the monarch of the State and the leaders of both the Indian National Congress and the Pakistan Muslim League—the political parties that ran the first postcolonial governments of India and Pakistan during the period of constitution formation. When the British Government of India transferred power to the independent postcolonial states of India and Pakistan on August 14, 1947, the monarch of the Princely State of Jammu and Kashmir had acceded to neither India nor Pakistan. Within months of independence, India and Pakistan had troops on the ground in the Princely State's Kashmir Province. This first war between India and Pakistan was ambiguously resolved with a United Nations–negotiated ceasefire in 1949. The state was functionally divided, and nearly a quarter of its people were displaced within the territories of the former Princely State or into India and Pakistan.

This politico-geographical division was supposed to be temporary, until a United Nations–recommended referendum could be carried out. There was, at first, no question of changing the terms of legal political belonging to the Princely State of Jammu and Kashmir. The people of the Indian Princely States were "state subjects," not British colonial subjects; unless an Indian monarch had acceded to one or the other of the Dominions before the Partition, the ruler's displaced subjects were not counted as refugees who would have to be rehabilitated. Both people who were displaced by political violence in the Princely State of Jammu and Kashmir between 1947 and 1949 and relief administrators in Pakistan and India made an important distinction between those (Kashmiri) refugees who were to return to their homes and those (Partition) refugees who would be resettled as permanent immigrants; "hereditary state subjects" of the Princely State of Jammu and Kashmir were supposed to return to their homes, lands, and properties. By the time the matter of princely state subjects was negotiated in the Karachi Agreement of March 1949, the (former) Princely State of Jammu and Kashmir was a "disputed territory" and the subject of a UN resolution. Its refugees were a specifically named part of the dispute-resolution process. Practices of identifying, regulating, and documenting Kashmiri refugees developed historically in the context of regional and international concern for (and dispute over) a Jammu-and-Kashmir that is both a former and a not-yet or a never-to-be political entity. The Hereditary State Subject provisions were adopted by the provincial successor states of both Jammu and Kashmir State (in India) and Azad Jammu and Kashmir (administered by Pakistan) as the basis of their legal frameworks for recognizing citizen-subjects of the disputed former Princely State of Jammu and Kashmir.

The 1949 UN Ceasefire Line—now called the LoC (military Line of Control)—simultaneously symbolizes and obscures the historical experiences of people who live in the divided regions of the former Princely State. On post-1949 maps of India and Pakistan, the LoC is a dotted line, representing its contested status. On the ground, it has been a permeable boundary without exact demarcation that has nonetheless shaped people's apprehension of the political landscape. It forged a frontier through landscapes that people had previously experienced as contiguous, and these displaced people encountered the line not as a specific place but as a profound shift in the ways they experienced political power. Paradoxically, the LoC has had a more concrete presence when its physical location has been less certain—during periods of warfare. Thus, the line has had a cyclical as well as historical temporality; it has become more borderlike over time, but it has shifted in each war and has been serially revisited as a site of possible territorial settlement between India and Pakistan. This speculation has made it possible to envision the LoC gone or redrawn, even while it has become more entrenched. It has become an object of ideological struggle in daily life, even as the act of transgressing it has been criminalized by the state. The LoC becomes a real social object at the moment when people encounter new regimes of power, but it does not exclusively regulate the conception of either relatedness or political belonging. Instead, the social dynamics within bisected regions of the (former) Princely State of Jammu and Kashmir reveal the importance of cross-border alliances—including those that are interrupted—to the ongoing cultural construction of social relatedness. In this sense, the greater Kashmir region was, and remains, a borderland in which forms of social regulation contest rather than buttress the regulatory processes of the state.[1]

The Kashmir Dispute is often called the "unfinished business of Partition." Explanations of the dispute paradigmatically begin by recounting the origins of the territorial dispute between India and Pakistan.[2] The story I tell here is different, and it has a different history. The continuing conflict in the Kashmir region is fundamentally *not* a territorial dispute between states. It is a struggle by the ruled to establish limits on the sovereign power of their rulers. Social groups, political parties, and the regional successor states of the monarchical State of Jammu and Kashmir employ the symbolic territoriality inherent in categories of political identity to make claims on absent and lost geographic territories through the territory of the political body. In the context of unresolved political status, the Kashmir borderlands extend not only across the disputed LoC or into the "occupied" territories but also through the indeterminate sovereignty of the bodies of the borderlands' subjects.

The background to this story is about the conflicts and contestations for political recognition that were happening at the time of decolonization, when Kashmiri peoples' struggles for political rights were with the monarch of Jammu and Kashmir, not with the British colonial power or with the post-colonial nation-states of India and Pakistan.

THE PRINCELY STATE OF JAMMU AND KASHMIR
AT THE END OF EMPIRE

The Partition of British India was a long process of creating political and cultural (rather than simply territorial) separations.[3] In this process, the postcolonial states were formed not only by dividing colonial holdings but also by dissolving the borders of hundreds of tributary polities and integrating the semi-autonomous Indian Princely States and their peoples.[4] The postcolonial historiography of India and Pakistan has highlighted the forms of modern collective politics that were prominent in British India, but the decolonization and partition process was also shaped by political forms that emerged in the Princely States and that disappeared after their integration.[5] In the Princely State of Jammu and Kashmir, an articulation of subject peoples as rights-bearing subjects developed during the period when sovereignty was vested with the monarchical court. This idea of the distinct identity and rights of the people-of-the-state *(awām-e-riyāsat)* or people-of-Kashmir *(awām-e-kashmīr)* still underlies and competes with other postcolonial articulations of political and cultural belonging.

The Indian Princely States were governed by hereditary monarchs under relationships of suzerainty and paramountcy with the British colonial government of India. How autonomous these states really were is the subject of significant debate in the historiography of South Asia.[6] One of the challenges in the historiography of the Indian States, specifically in evaluating their relative sovereignty, has been their vast differences in size and historical state formation. There were numerous small states that commanded little autonomy (on the scale of Jammu and Kashmir's smaller *jagīrs* and much smaller than its internal *wazārats*).[7] There were also much larger Indian States, like Jammu and Kashmir, with composite political structures, heterogeneous regional cultures, and transregional networks of relationships to other Princely States that exercised aspects of sovereign control over their subjects.[8] The monarchs of these more autonomous states had to establish new forms of legitimate authority over their subjects as they centralized their power during the colonial period.[9]

The Treaty of Amritsar, signed in 1846, demarcated the territorial borders of a new Princely State of Jammu and Kashmir—the *riyāsat-e-jammū-o-kashmīr*. Unlike established Indian States with hereditary thrones, Jammu and Kashmir had not had a political center of historical state expansion, and sovereignty within the state was dispersed. Like other Indian Princes, the Maharajas' political universe included limitations on their influence in matters outside their territorial boundaries, but they enjoyed considerable security at the treaty boundaries of the state. While the Maharajas of Jammu and Kashmir struggled with British attempts to influence the internal politics of the court, the real challenge of kingship in the Princely State was to centralize power and establish new relationships between the ruler and his subjects and between the state and its political community, which eliminated the intermediate forms of layered sovereignty within the treaty state.[10]

The first political movements in the Princely State of Jammu and Kashmir developed out of demands for protections against arbitrary rule and guarantees of patronage and employment for its subjects . Out of those movements, the "hereditary state subject" emerged as the primary category of political identity for the State's peoples, and the legal provisions for state subject recognition were codified and elaborated by the Maharaja's government between 1912 and 1932.[11] Protections from arbitrary rule were linked with establishing and recognizing land-holding rights, both usufruct and proprietary, which created a distinction between the monarchy's sovereignty over territory and its sovereignty over its subjects. The first articulation of this distinction emerged during the period of agrarian land reforms, and the category *mulkī* (the people of the land) emerged as a legal–administrative category in the Kashmiri Nationals' Law of 1912. The Hereditary State Subject Order of 1927 (amended 1932) clearly distinguished between state subjects who had rights to government office and land use and ownership versus those (non-state subjects) who did not have such rights. The concept of the *awām-e-kashmīr* or *awām-e-riyāsat* became a political category through which it was possible to articulate new limits on princely sovereignty, and Jammu and Kashmir state subjects demanded further political recognition in the form of representation and franchise.

At the historical juncture of liberation struggles against monarchical rule and the dissolution of colonial India, the relationship between land rights and protection from arbitrary rule informed both elite and popular political mobilization in the Princely State of Jammu and Kashmir. Between 1947 and 1949, the "Azad Kashmir Government" based in the town of Pulandri, in the Poonch Jagir, maintained the state subject as its definition of Kashmiri political identity, as did the "Emergency Interim Government of Jammu and Kashmir State" based in the city of Srinagar, the summer capital of the Princely State. After 1950, both India and Pakistan began to integrate the regions of the former Princely State that were under their control. The Princely State's own competing successor regimes—the Government of Azad Kashmir (in Pakistan-administered territory) and the Government of Jammu and Kashmir State (in Indian-administered territory)—struggled to maintain regional autonomy from the administrator states of India and Pakistan; they did this in part by maintaining the historical distinction between the subject-citizens of the former monarchical state and citizens of the new nation-states of Pakistan and India.

The Awām-e-Riyāsat: Making the State, Making Its Subjects

In 1846, the new Princely State of Jammu and Kashmir had been a unified polity only in name, and only at its borders. The Treaty of Amritsar, which set the state's territorial borders, was part of the negotiated settlement that ended a war between the British and Sikh rulers of the Punjab and brought the Punjab under colonial control. Within the new state were numerous hereditary estates and chieftainships that had been awarded by the Sikh court at Lahore and by the Mughal, Afghan, and Tibetan monarchs who had once had feudatory arrangement with rulers within the treaty borders.[12] With the borders of the new state secure, but internal control uncertain, the Dogra Maharajas of Jammu and Kashmir focused on consolidating political and administrative authority.[13]

The eventual internal organization of the Princely State reflected localized sociopolitical alliances as well as the monarchs' uneven consolidation of political power within the borders established by the Treaty of Amritsar—a process by no means complete in 1947. Jammu Province, Kashmir Province, and the Frontier Ilaquas (Frontier Areas) made up the state's three large administrative units. The administrative hierarchy was most consolidated in Jammu and Kashmir Provinces; each was divided into districts that were in turn distinguished by taxation units called *tehsils*. Chenani Jagir and Poonch Jagir were incorporated into Jammu Province only in the 1930s. The Frontier Ilaquas consisted of the Ladakh Wazarat, the Gilgit Agency, the vassal states of Hunza and Nagar, and the tribal region of Chilas (which was never successfully surveyed by the monarchical state). These areas had a semi-autonomous feudatory status within the Princely State, which had limited administrative control.[14]

To establish their power, the Princely State's first Maharajas (Gulab Singh and Ranbir Singh) began consolidating the dispersed *jāgīrdārī* system of land tenancy and revenue administration, in which the revenue of a territorial estate (*jāgīr*) and the responsibility of governing it accrued to an appointed official (*jāgīrdār*) who owed allegiance to the monarch.[15] Establishing a consolidated administrative hierarchy involved bringing the semi-independent hereditary *jāgīrs*—such as Chenani Jagir and Poonch Jagir—into a subordinate relationship with the Maharaja's court and enforcing the state's claim that all land was government property *(khālsah)*.[16] The Maharajas also extended the system of containment and exit permits *(rehdārī)* that had been used by the Sikh governors of the Kashmir Valley to the whole of the Princely State, in an effort to prevent people who were subject to taxation in the form of compulsory corvee labor *(bēgār)* from leaving the state or migrating out of their taxation divisions.[17]

Identifying *awām-e-riyāsat* (people of the state) as a category of political belonging, administration, and governance first developed in the 1880s, during the agrarian land reforms of the *jāgīrdārī* system.[18] During that period, famine and excessive *bēgār* led to large-scale migrations to the Punjab.[19] The colonial administration of Punjab wanted a stable rural agricultural population; the British India Office considered migrations a security issue because the Princely State of Jammu and Kashmir had become a frontier between the British colonial empire and Russian imperial projects in Central Asia.[20] The land-settlement assessments in the state began in 1887, carried out by an officer of the British colonial government. British colonial permanent settlement practices were associated with the introduction of capitalist revenue systems and gradually transformed occupancy rights into proprietary rights. However, in the Princely States, these settlements transferred usufruct rights but not proprietary rights, which remained instead with the monarch, albeit in attenuated form.[21] In Jammu and Kashmir, land reforms focused on imposing limitations on *bēgār* by establishing taxation assessments in cash or as a share of agricultural product and by granting occupancy and usufruct rights to cultivators. The Jammu and Kashmir Land Settlement Act identified people—*kashmīr mulkī*—who had usufruct claims on land and who had rights to state patronage in the form of government employment. The legislation also articulated a category of people who did not have such rights—the *gairmulkī* (people not of the land).[22]

After the permanent settlements in Kashmir Province and Jammu Province (1887–1905), successive Maharajas faced pressure to recruit only state subjects for employment in state administration. Populist demands to reserve "Kashmir for Kashmiris" erupted, and the state's first political parties organized protests.[23] The Kashmir for Kashmiris demand required a clear definition of who a Kashmiri was, and Maharaja Pratap Singh first established a bureaucratic definition of Jammu and Kashmir nationality in 1912. That definition was based entirely on the conferment and recognition of land occupancy and proprietary rights, and it limited state patronage to those who possessed an *ijāzatnāmah* (document of permission [to hold land]) issued by the Maharaja's Darbar, or the state administrative bureaucracy. The Maharaja had full discretion to confer state-owned community land; therefore, he was empowered to confer or to withhold subject status.[24] This popular demand for an articulation of state identity was at first primarily about patronage, but it became increasingly connected to rights claims through the franchise and antitaxation movements of the 1920s.

The 1912 nationals definition excluded nomads and migratory people such as the Gujars and Bakerwal herders, whose grazing lands were generally held as *khālsah* (government property).[25] It also excluded residents of Jammu and Kashmir's internal feudatory dependencies (e.g., Poonch Jagir, Chenani Jagir, and the frontier chieftainships). In mass protest movements in the 1920s and 1930s, members of excluded groups demanded the benefits of recognition as state nationals. In 1927, Maharaja Pratap Singh instituted the Hereditary State Subject Order of 1984 (1927 C.E.),[26] which defined hereditary state subjects as "all persons born and residing in the State before the commencement of the reign of His Highness the late Maharaja Gulab Singh Sahib Bahadur (1846 C.E.) and also persons who settled therein before the commencement of Samvat 1942 (1888 C.E.)."[27] The 1927 state subject definition established that subjects of the monarchy had durable rights. By limiting the Maharaja's ability to confer land rights and by restricting employment in government institutions to established state subjects, it also created a legal mechanism though which they could make claims on the Princely State. At the same time, state subjects also became the site of new forms of control, regulation, and political contestation. Whereas the regulatory acts of the nineteenth century had focused on the border, during the 1920s to 1940s, the Maharaja used the legal category "state subject" to exert claims over his subject nationals when they were in foreign territories. The category also facilitated the development of legal mechanisms to exclude foreigners and seditious (i.e., antimonarchist) ideas from the Princely State.[28]

Demands on the Maharaja's government for patronage and legal recognition of proprietary rights continued into 1931, culminating in riots at religious sites in the Kashmir Valley, Mirpur district, and the city of Jammu.[29] The subsequent Glancy Commission Report reflected British colonial anxieties about communal politics in British India. However, the commissioners' recommendations reflected the emphasis within the state on legal and rights-based definitions of political belonging; the report recommended that government jobs be reserved for state subjects, that full proprietary rights be allocated to land occupants, that the state pay for all forms of labor services as a resolution to remaining *bēgār* taxation, and that state subjects participate in state government.

Between 1932 and 1936, Maharaja Hari Singh redefined the state subject and accepted the Jammu and Kashmir Constitution Act of 1996 (1934 C.E.),[30] which established the state's first Legislative Assembly—the Praja Sabha. An amended Hereditary State Subject Order (1932) was drafted concurrently with the Constitution Act of 1934; it established three classes of state subjects and a hierarchy of rights firmly based on claims to immovable property and agricultural land, bureaucratic labor, and limitations on taxation.[31] Although these rights were not directly linked to political representation, the Praja Sabha representatives (who were appointed by the Maharaja) used the recognition and distribution of land rights as a means of conferring political rights. The Praja Sabha passed a number of regulations that prevented the commodification of property and transferred some of the power of conferring political status from the Maharaja to the Legislative Assembly. Similarly, the Maharaja's council used the connection between land rights and state subject status to extend its own administrative control in the many internal feudatories it did not fully control. Poonch Jagir, for example, was not represented in the first Praja Sabha because in 1934 it was still an independent *jāgīr* with its own hereditary Rajas. In 1939, the council brought the Poonch Jagir into the Princely State's direct administrative structure—and more pointedly shifted the right of taxation to the Maharaja—by conferring land rights, and thus state-subject status and Praja Sabha representation, to residents of the Poonch Jagir.[32]

In the late 1930s, political parties and subaltern movements began to argue for direct franchise rights for state subjects. The Praja Sabha allowed for only minimal direct popular participation and had only advisory power. Its formation, however, legalized political parties in the Princely State, and a number of regional and transregional parties developed after 1932. Political party development in Jammu and Kashmir was not a simple extension of anticolonial and nationalist movements in British India. Parties developed from networks of educational reading groups and religious associations that had been legally permitted formal associations before 1932. During the agitations of 1931, members of these groups, including the prominent leaders Ghulam Abbass, Sheikh Mohammad Abdullah, and Prem Nath Bazaz, met in the Maharaja's prisons. They went on to found a number of parties, including the Praja Parishad, the Dogra Party, and the Kashmir Kisan Mazdoor Party, as well as the All Jammu and Kashmir Muslim Conference (AJKMC), which later split, forming a new AJKMC and the All Jammu and Kashmir National Conference (AJKNC).[33] After 1941, the AJKMC was generally referred to as "the Muslim Conference" and the AJKNC as "the National Conference."

Party leaders were influenced by global anticolonial, nationalist, and socialist thinking, but political parties in Jammu and Kashmir took up the issues that were of particular concern to the subjects of the Princely State.[34] The Quit Kashmir protests, centered in the Kashmir Valley, and the armed Azad Kashmir insurrection, which began in Poonch, indicate how strongly the connection between land and rights influenced Kashmiri political identity and grounded political movements in the Princely State of Jammu and Kashmir by the 1940s.

Azad Kashmir and the Quit Kashmir Movement

A working committee of the National Conference first articulated the concept of popular sovereignty as a right of Jammu and Kashmir state subjects in its *Naya Kashmir* (New Kashmir) Manifesto, which the party adopted in 1944.[35] The manifesto blended socialist land reform with sovereign rule by the people of the state, defined as "the people of the Jammu, Kashmir, Ladakh and the frontier regions, including Poonch and Chenani Ilaquas."[36] This notion of self-rule was extended in the call for *āzād kashmīr* (Liberted/Free Kashmir) at a meeting sponsored by the Kashmir Kisan Mazdoor Party in May 1946. Representatives of various state political parties from Kashmir Province, Jammu Province, and the former Poonch Jagir attended the meeting, including members of the National Conference, the Muslim Conference, the Dogra Party, and the Praja Parishad. The meetings concluded with a demand for the liberation of the Princely State of Jammu and Kashmir and the creation of a free state in which the "people of the state" would be sovereign.[37]

Sheikh Abdullah, a politician educated at the modernist Aligarh University and well versed in European social and political theory, also demanded self-rule under the slogan "Quit Kashmir." The Quit Kashmir Declaration of 1946 held that the "people of the state" henceforth abrogated the Treaty of Amritsar between the British and the Sikh princes, in which the people of the state has been ceded as well as the land itself.[38] In a telegram to the Cabinet Mission officials responsible for partitioning British India, which was printed in the Srinagar newspaper *Khidmat,* Sheikh Abdullah announced the Quit Kashmir Movement as the last stage of Kashmiri peoples' struggle for self-rule.[39] This movement was led by Sheikh Abdullah and the AJKNC party, but it depended on multiple party affiliations and interregional networks. The movement's popular appeals invoked a sovereignty based in the region's previous land-rights movements and protests.

The AJKMC and other regional political parties did not initially endorse the Quit Kashmir statement, and the National Conference provided the public leadership of the movement. However, the involvement of the state's various parties became clear as prominent party leaders were arrested by the Maharaja's government in 1946 and 1947. By the end of 1946, supporters of the National Conference and of the Muslim Conference were engaged in a violent struggle for control of the Quit Kashmir movement. This so-called Sher-Bakra conflict resulted in the exodus of the National Conference's political opponents from the Princely State, either as direct exiles from Srinagar or as political exiles from the Maharaja's detention centers.[40] When the Maharaja, beset by internal revolt and external invasion, signed the Instrument of Accession to India in November 1947, the National Conference was the clearly dominant political party in Srinagar.

The Quit Kashmir movement began with a clearly articulated political ideology and organized, party-led protests. The armed Azad Kashmir movement coalesced around a tax protest in the Poonch Jagir, where the Maharaja's government had been attempting to regularize and increase land-revenue assessments since 1940, when it had been integrated into the Princely State. In June 1947, the Kashmir State Dogra Army began to disarm Muslim peasants and redistribute the weapons to Hindu and Sikh landlords. Men from Poonch brought women and children to towns on the border of the Princely State and the NWFP, notably to the army cantonment towns of Murree and Abbottabad, and returned to Poonch with weapons that they smuggled across the Jhelum River into the Princely State.[41] By late August, the tax protests had shifted to a full revolt against the Maharaja's authority; armed fighting began between Kashmir State Dogra Army troops and protesters in Poonch who concurrently made demands for Azad Kashmir and *ilhāq-e-pakistān* (accession to Pakistan).[42]

Political leaders in Poonch declared in August 1947 that they had overthrown the Maharaja's government, and in October, they announced the establishment of what they called the Provisional Revolutionary Government of Azad Kashmir: "Maharaja Hari Singh's title to rule has come to an end from August 15, 1947 and he has no constitutional or moral right to rule over the people of Kashmir against their will. He is consequently deposed with effect from October 4, 1947. All the Ministers and officials of the State will henceforth be duty-bound to carry out the orders of the Provisional Revolutionary Government. Anyone disobeying this duly constituted Government of the People of Kashmir or in any way abetting the Maharaja in his usurpation of the rule of Kashmir will be guilty of an act of high treason and will be dealt with accordingly."[43] The Revolutionary Government described itself as a war council. It formed an army it called the "Azad Forces," with three zones of military command—one in Kashmir Province, one in Jammu Province, and one in the former Poonch Jagir.

Several weeks later, prominent AJKMC leaders reconstituted the Provisional Revolutionary Government as the "Azad Kashmir Government," run by the Central Committee of the Muslim Conference. This committee included leaders from the Kashmir and Jammu Provinces of the Princely State—such as Sardar Mohammad Ibrahim Khan (a Praja Sabha representative from Poonch), Ghulam Abbass (who had been recently released from Jammu Jail), and Yusaf Shah (the Mirwaiz of Kashmir, who was in exile from Srinagar). On the matter of political rights, the Azad Kashmir Government addressed India and Pakistan, not the Maharaja, whom it considered already deposed: "The Azad Government hopes that both Dominions [India and Pakistan] will sympathize with the people of Jammu and Kashmir in their efforts to exercise their birthright of political freedom. . . . The question of accession of Jammu and Kashmir to either dominion can only be decided by the free vote of the people in the form of referendum. . . ."[44] As Sardar Mohammad Ibrahim Khan, the president of the first Azad Kashmir Government, announced in November 1947: "Our Government is [a] Government of the people and has behind it a majority of the elected representatives in the Kashmir Assembly. Today the major portion of the State Territory is in our hands and we alone are the real government of Kashmir. . . . On the other hand, the despotic Maharaja has brought foreign aid [and] armies of occupation are pouring in from the Indian Union."[45]

In late October 1947, loosely organized *lashkars* (militias) of Pathans from the Northwest Frontier Provinces (NWFP) of Pakistan entered the Princely State of Jammu and Kashmir at Muzaffarabad, the frontier administrative outpost of the Kashmir Province, and advanced along the Jhelum River road toward the capital of Srinagar.[46] Maharaja Hari Singh quickly signed an Instrument of Accession that conferred defense, foreign affairs, and communications to the Government of India. The accession agreement reserved all residual powers for the Princely State government, and the Maharaja ceded internal administration to the National Conference party.[47] In Srinagar, Sheikh Abdullah declared the National Conference to be the state's "Emergency Interim Government,"[48] and he mobilized civil defense committees.[49] Indian Army forces joined the Kashmir State Dogra Army in fighting on the Jhelum road at Baramullah and in the Poonch region of Jammu. The government of Pakistan did not accept the Maharaja's accession and sent in its own army troops to prevent the capture of Jammu and Kashmir by India. Thus, by mid-November 1947, the armies of the newly independent nation-states of India and Pakistan were fighting their first war in Jammu and

Kashmir, and two different internal governments claimed to be the government of the entirety of the former Princely State and its state subjects.

Local Authorities and Successor States

During the war of 1947–1949, both the "Emergency Interim Government" based in Srinagar and the "Azad Kashmir Government" based in Palundri, claimed to function in place of the Praja Sabha (the state's legislative assembly). International representatives and relief workers recognized both of these governments as "local authorities." They negotiated with both administrations on pragmatic issues, such as entry into specific territories, and on humanitarian issues, such as refugee relief, protection of minorities, and prisoner exchanges.[50] The United Nations Commission on India and Pakistan (UNCIP) tacitly acknowledged both the Interim Government and the Azad Kashmir Government in Security Council resolutions on Kashmir. The resolutions distinguished the Azad Kashmir Government from the Government of Pakistan and the Interim Government from the Government of India, instructing the UN to work with local authorities in reestablishing law and order and arranging for a popular referendum to determine the political future of Jammu and Kashmir.[51]

Neither government recognized the authority of the other, however. The National Conference and Sheikh Abdullah (who represented Jammu and Kashmir at the UN in Geneva), claimed to be the local authority for the whole of the former Princely State.[52] The Muslim Conference identified the Azad Kashmir Government as the government of both "territories of the State of Jammu and Kashmir which have been liberated by the people of that state" and of "the people of the state of Jammu and Kashmir" as a whole.[53] As soon as the 1949 ceasefire between India and Pakistan was established, this recognition of local authorities became a central problem for UN mediators, who were trying to carry out the Security Council resolutions by arranging a popular referendum on the future political status of the state. The Government of India and the National Conference's Interim Government refused to recognize the Muslim Conference's Azad Kashmir Government, suggesting instead that all officials in AJK territory be replaced with Kashmir State officials appointed by Sheikh Abdullah. They also insisted not only on the withdrawal of Pakistan Army troops but also on the complete disbanding of the Azad Forces and Azad Government Police Services, to be replaced by Kashmir State Troops. The British Commonwealth appointed mediators in 1950 and in 1951, both of whose proposals eventually failed, at least in part, over the question of recognizing the actual authority of the Azad Kashmir Government.[54] During these negotiations, refugees from Jammu and Kashmir were recognized as a nascent political constituency when the Government of India agreed to keeping civil armed forces in Azad Kashmir territories, provided that the troops consisted of "residents of the territories who were not followers of the Azad Government," preferably refugees from the Kashmir Valley.[55]

The National Conference's Interim Government and the Muslim Conference's Azad Kashmir Government each operated under the legal provisions and practices established by the Maharaja's court.[56] Each government attempted to establish its legitimacy by claiming to represent displaced people who were dispersed across spaces not under the governments' actual territorial control. By 1951, the definition of a "refugee of Jammu and Kashmir" had been firmly established through principles laid out in bilateral Inter-Dominion agreements between India and Pakistan and in the actual administrative practices of allocating temporary land and properties to people displaced from and unable to return to their homes and lands. A Kashmiri refugee was defined as a state subject of the Princely State of Jammu and Kashmir who was displaced from his or her home or who could not return as a result the war of 1947–1948.

Jammu and Kashmir State maintained a distinct "permanent resident" status that conferred separate state rights and privileges even after the Delhi Agreement (1952) gave Indian citizenship to Jammu and Kashmir state subjects.[57] This separate status was important for many reasons, not least because it recognized the continuing and uninterrupted status of displaced state subjects resident in Azad Kashmir territory and in Pakistan. In his address to the Constituent Assembly of Jammu and Kashmir on August 11, 1952, Sheikh Abdullah instructed the representatives to recognize the rights of "State Subject Evacuees [who were] living as refugees in [Pakistan and Azad Kashmir]."[58] The constitution that the assembly drafted based Jammu and Kashmir state "permanent resident" status on the 1932 Hereditary State Subject definition[59]; the rights reserved for permanent residents of Jammu and Kashmir were the same as those granted state subjects under the Maharaja's government. These included the exclusive right to acquire and hold property in the state, to stand for election or be employed by the government, and to receive any form of patronage, such as scholarships.[60] Adopted in 1956, the Constitution of Jammu and Kashmir State defined the state as "all the territories which on the 15th day of August, 1947, were under the sovereignty or suzerainty of the Ruler of the State."[61] This included the territories actually controlled by the Azad Kashmir Government and by Pakistan, for which twenty-five seats in the new Legislative Assembly were reserved and held vacant for representatives from the "Pakistan-Occupied territories."[62]

Unlike Jammu and Kashmir State in India, Azad Jammu and Kashmir did not adopt a formal constitution until 1970; instead, a series of provisional orders defined the state's administrative structure until the Azad Jammu and Kashmir Interim Constitution Act was ratified in 1974. In the 1960s, political leaders in AJK debated the transition to a democratic legislative system.[63] The Muslim Conference particularly resisted the transition to an electoral system on the grounds that "the institution of democracy would damage the freedom movement and that the area [AJK] would become a settled territory and not a base camp for the liberation of the State."[64] Also unlike Jammu and Kashmir State in India, AJK is not represented in the federal Pakistan Legislative Assembly, and it maintains constitutional autonomy from Pakistan as an internationally disputed territory.

Successive administrations of the Azad Kashmir Government, like those of Jammu and Kashmir State (India), extended citizenship recognition to all hereditary state subjects. The Rules of Business of the Azad Kashmir Government of 1950 reserved state employment and property ownership for state subjects and recognized all displaced state subjects as Kashmiri refugees. Once franchise rights were made a part of an electoral process, all hereditary state subjects were guaranteed electoral representation, AJK political parties demanded that the 1932 Hereditary State Subject law be integrated into the constitutional definition of state citizenship when the first Interim Constitution Act was drafted in 1970.[65] The Azad Jammu and Kashmir Interim Constitution Act of 1974 structured the state as a parliamentary democracy, with an elected Legislative Assembly. The franchise was extended to "any state subject who left the Indian-occupied part of Jammu and Kashmir due to the "War of Liberation" and who was living in Azad Kashmir territory or in Pakistan[66] and to state subjects who left their homes after 1947 due to the "Indian occupation of the State."[67] Under the Act, displaced state subjects (*muhājarīn-e-riyāsat-e-jammū-o-kashmīr*) living in Pakistan elect representatives to twelve seats in the Assembly. These seats are not linked to residential electoral areas but rather are allocated according to constituencies based on the last district of residence in the former Princely

State. Six of the seats are allocated for refugees displaced from the Kashmir Province and six for refugees displaced from the Jammu Province.

The reservation of refugee seats carries an important representational force with lasting political effects. The equal division of AJK assembly seats does not proportionally represent the refugee electorate, since the overwhelming majority of refugees living in Pakistan were displaced from Jammu Province and most refugees from Kashmir Province are resettled in AJK territory. Instead, it represents the state's territorial claims through the property claims of refugees in Pakistan. Their participation in AJK elections serves as a ritual that demonstrates the continuous and distinct identity of people from the former Princely State of Jammu and Kashmir, and their registration by district of origin maintains the AJK government's claims over territories that it does not administer.

LOCATING DISPLACEMENT: THE LINE OF CONTROL AND ITS REFUGEES

When the war between India and Pakistan ended with a UN-negotiated ceasefire on January 1, 1949, the former Princely State of Jammu and Kashmir had two successor political regimes, each of which claimed the legitimate right to rule over the whole state. The so-called UN Ceasefire Line divided the former Princely State's Kashmir Province, Jammu Province, and the Frontier Areas into regions controlled by India and those controlled by Pakistan. It re-oriented historical regional routes of trade and travel such as the Jhelum River Road, which had connected Muzaffarabad city to Srinagar, to the silk route and the Central Asian cities of Kabul and Kashkar, to Leh and the Tibetan Plateau, and to the Punjabi cities of Lahore and Amritsar. It also restructured the former Princely State's internal relationships among administrative districts, social networks, and political authority (see maps 3 and 4).[68] The decades after the 1949 division of the Princely State saw the Ceasefire Line become a frontier of political as well as military control. The Ceasefire Line moved with the front of military control during the 1965 and 1971 wars, and it was renamed the Line of Control (LoC) in the Simla Agreement of 1972 that ended the 1971 war. No plebiscite as envisioned by the original UN agreements was conducted in the former Princely State. In the absence of an internationally recognized political status for the territories under Indian and Pakistani control, the LoC became the de facto border

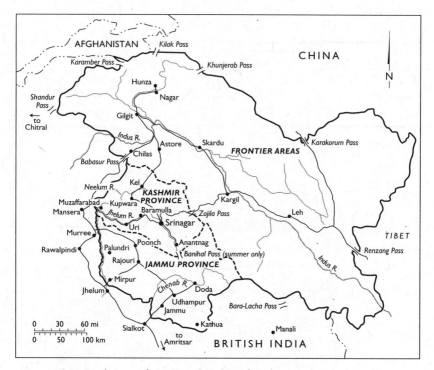

MAP 3. The Princely State of Jammu and Kashmir (1946).

between the semi-autonomous provincial states of Jammu and Kashmir State and the Ladakh Autonomous Hill Province (administered by India) and Azad Jammu and Kashmir and the Northern Areas (administered by Pakistan).

Both the movement of people and the movement of borders created a population of refugees from the State of Jammu and Kashmir living in Pakistan and Pakistan-administered Kashmir. In 1947 and 1948 there were only military front lines that shifted, sometimes drastically. Some people found themselves on the same side of the line as their lands and properties; others found themselves not temporarily displaced but "refugees" only miles from their former homes. Many who became refugees did not know that there was an Azad Kashmir distinct from the Jammu and Kashmir where they had always lived; many had never heard of Pakistan, or if they had, did not know what or where it was. In 1949, seven hundred fifty thousand people were displaced, nearly twenty percent of the four million state subjects enumerated in the census of 1941.[69] More were displaced in the wars that

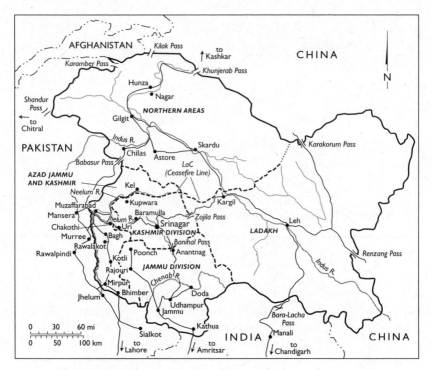

MAP 4. The Divided Territories of Jammu and Kashmir (after 1950).

followed the dissolution of the former Princely State. During the wars of 1965 and 1971, and during the armed conflict in the Indian Jammu and Kashmir State (1989–present), refugees crossed territories marked by the LoC. Some displaced people only came to know that they had migrated in retrospect, when the creation of a new border made returning to their homes impossible. For others, migration was planned and intentional. These latter refugees were acutely aware of the presence and location of borders and the competing claims of local, regional, and national centers of authority and power.

Revolt, Massacre, Incursion, and War (1947–1949)

In the Poonch district of Jammu Province, the first displacements were closely linked to the Azad Kashmir movement and the armed revolt against the Maharaja's rule that began in August 1947 as an antimonarchical tax rebellion. The insurgency had a communal element, and between 1947 and 1948, members of minority religious communities were expelled from their homes and killed in areas held by both the Azad Kashmir Forces and by the Kashmir State Dogra Army.[70] After the Pakistani and Indian Armies became directly involved in the fighting, the front lines of engagement shifted dramatically in the lower mountains of the Jammu Province, often displacing the residents of entire villages. Minorities in each of the controlled territories were also collected at refugee transit camps, similar to those organized in the Punjab, and sent to territories held by the opposing armies.[71]

In other parts of Jammu Province, Muslim state subjects were forcibly displaced by the Kashmir State's Dogra Army in a program of expulsion and murder carried out for three weeks in October–November 1947. In mid-October 1947, Kashmir State Dogra Army troops began forcibly expelling Muslim villagers from Jammu Province.[72] The refugees were sent on foot toward West Punjab, where most were accommodated in refugee camps in the districts of Sialkot, Jhelum, Gujarat, and Rawalpindi that had been originally established to accommodate the large numbers of refugees arriving from East Punjab. The Pakistan Central Ministry of Refugees undertook the first census of refugees in Pakistan in March 1948. The census enumerated two hundred fifty thousand refugees from the Princely State of Jammu and Kashmir in government-run camps in West Punjab.[73] Registration records from the Sialkot, Jhelum and Rawalpindi refugee ration depots confirm that these first arrivals came from the Jammu district.

The Muslims of Jammu City were instructed to congregate at the state grounds known as the Police Lines. There and at the city's Rosin Factory, they joined people who had been displaced by fighting between insurgents and Kashmir State Dogra Army troops in Poonch. State soldiers secured the areas and the inmates were visited by state officials, who informed them that they were being deported to Pakistan. By the end of October, representatives of the Muslim Conference were sending repeated urgent telegrams to officials of the Pakistan government informing them that water and food supplies were being withheld from the approximately five thousand people collected in Jammu City, warning of impending violence and requesting intervention.[74] The "Jammu massacre" began on November 5. Kashmir State Dogra Army soldiers began an organized evacuation of the Muslims, but instead of taking them to Sialkot, the trucks drove into the forested hills of Rajouri District, where the evacuees were executed. The first news of these killings began circulating in Pakistan as individual survivors found their way to populated areas and were brought to established refugee camps in Punjab or to military hospitals and aid stations. Pakistani hospital and refugee camp personnel reported that of the five thousand people deported from the Jammu Police Lines Ground and Rosin Factory deportation centers, two hundred survivors arrived in Pakistan.[75]

The patterns of violence and displacement in the Kashmir Province were profoundly different; mass displacement was caused by the incursion of Pathan *lashkars* (militias) along the Muzaffarabad–Srinagar road in October 1947, their subsequent retreat through the mountains, and the advance and retreat of the Indian and Pakistani armies during the war of 1947–1949. The *lashkars* entered the Princely State from Abbotabad, arriving at the settlement of Domel (now a part of the Muzaffarabad Municipal Corporation), at the confluence of the Jhelum and Neelum Rivers, and proceeded along the Jhelum River road toward Srinagar. As an unregimented and unsupplied military force, they supported their incursion by appropriating supplies from the local population. People fled from settlements directly on the Jhelum River Road, because the *lashkars'* push toward Srinagar was relatively focused; villages on the other side of the river were mostly unaffected. The Pathans's incursion into the Princely State stopped in Baramullah and Uri, where the *lashkars* looted the local population. Many people abandoned their villages for safer areas in the mountains around Baramullah. When Kashmir State Dogra Army Troops, first backed and then joined by the Indian Army, began pushing the *lashkars* out of the Princely State in November, the Pathans retreated, pushing through the mountain passes of upper Baramullah and Muzaffarabad districts as well as by the road route, confiscating wealth and women as they passed. They were followed by Indian Army troops advancing along the main road and by Pakistani and Indian military operations and aerial bombings in the mountains. People living along the paths of the advancing and retreating *lashkars* and then of the military operations vacated their homes and villages, temporarily depopulating areas that encompassed what became the Ceasefire Line in 1949.

In territory held by the Azad Kashmir Government, displaced people took refuge at shrines, were accommodated by local residents, or established squatter camps that grew in size, prompting local leaders to organize relief depots to supply the ad hoc camps. As the ground and air war intensified through 1948, ground fighting and aerial bombing forced approximately one hundred thousand people into refugee camps near the towns of Mansera and Abbottabad, just over the Princely State's border in NWFP. In June 1949, six months after the UN Ceasefire Order that ended the first war between India and Pakistan, the International Committee of the Red Cross (ICRC) conducted a transregional survey of Jammu and Kashmir refugees. Its final report put the Kashmiri refugee population in India and in Indian-held Jammu and Kashmir State at 180,000 and in Pakistan at 535,000, of whom 155,000 were in Azad Kashmir territory.[76] In 1951, based on the ICRC survey, the AJK government estimated the total refugee population in AJK at two hundred thousand out of a total population of seven hundred thousand.[77]

Displaced people moved between AJK and Pakistan and across the Ceasefire Line/LoC without border restriction between 1949 and 1953. Many moved in search of livelihood opportunities; others attempted to return to their home villages. Refugees who had spent most of the war in informal camps in Muzaffarabad district presumed that they could return to their home villages when the armies stopped fighting. But the road route turned out to be impenetrable, due to an Indian and Pakistani army presence, and those with young children did not try to make it back by using mountain routes and passes. Others successfully made their way to their home villages but found staying there untenable, often because of harassment by Indian Army troops or by neighbors who saw them as Pakistani sympathizers. They then returned to AJK, sometimes with family members previously left behind or from whom they had become separated. Refugees found it particularly difficult to establish themselves in the rural areas of Poonch district, and many who had initially taken refuge in those areas shifted to the refugee camps in northern Punjab, which already accommodated large numbers of refugees from the Jammu Province. Some refugees—especially those in NWFP refugee camps in Mansera and Abbottabad—moved back into AJK territories, and others who were not successful in establishing themselves in local communities in AJK moved into Pakistan.

Refugee movement slowed after 1954, when the government of AJK began making provisional allotments of evacuee property to Kashmiri refugees. In Pakistan, Kashmiri refugees remained in refugee camps into the early 1950s. Kashmiri political party leaders began advocating for provisional resettlement of refugees within Pakistan in 1951, and the official "temporary resettlement" of Kashmiri refugees began in 1954. Refugees who had been accommodated in West Punjab and NWFP refugee camps were settled in the cities of Sialkot, Gujarat, Rawalpindi, Abbottabad, and Mansera. In AJK, where relief administration had not been institutionalized, refugees had begun occupying rural and urban properties and cultivating the lands formally held by Sikh and

Hindu landholders. The government of AJK began formally allocating properties after 1954 by surveying and legalizing these de facto holdings.

Border Evacuation and Political Persecution (1965–1971)

The wars of 1965 and 1971 brought 50,000 new refugees into Azad Jammu and Kashmir.[78] The greatest number of people displaced during the wars of 1965 and 1971 were from areas where the front lines of warfare altered the boundaries of military control, such as the former Jammu Province districts of Poonch, Rajouri, and Mirpur. Border villages on the Indian side of the LoC were under considerable pressure to evacuate as the Indian Army created an ever-widening security line, emptying areas of people who might become casualties of warfare or whose loyalties were considered questionable. On the Pakistan side, civilians were largely pressured *not* to evacuate, as their presence was considered an additional impediment to an Indian ground advance. In the Jammu Division of (Indian) Jammu and Kashmir State, many people who left their villages chose to evacuate east and south within the Indian-administered territories. Most of the people who crossed the LoC knew they would not be able to return to their homes after the fighting ended. They came to AJK in family groups and chose to settle in areas where they had kinship connections.

In the high mountain regions of Muzaffarabad, Kupwara, and Baramullah districts, the LoC did not shift a great deal. In these areas, many people who crossed into AJK were young men, unaccompanied by family. Many were young male residents of border villages where they were under heavy pressure from security personnel, who suspected them of facilitating an invasion from Pakistan. Others came from towns farther from the LoC, especially from the strongly pro-Pakistan neighborhoods of Srinagar. Many of these refugees spoke the Kashmiri language, had close ties with pro-Pakistan political parties, and were advocates of Kashmir's accession to Pakistan. Identified as pro-Pakistan activists, they left their homes to escape persecution. Such refugees were not resettled through government programs; most entered into negotiated alliances with local residents, such as through marriage. These marriages were arranged by families through cross-border kinship connections or by the leaders of political parties who, in addition to mediating such marriage alliances, secured government jobs for the refugees.

The changing contours of the preexisting LoC made for some displacement predicaments. For example, in 1965, residents of several villages in

AJK's Poonch district found their villages on the Indian side at the end of the war. When they left their homes and crossed the front lines into Pakistan-held territory, they found that they were not eligible for rehabilitation as refugees because they had been previously acknowledged as residents of AJK. Although these people no longer had access to their properties, the AJK government considered their villages "occupied by" India but not "in" Indian-administered Jammu and Kashmir State.

Insurgency and Counterinsurgency (1989–2001)

In January 1990, refugees from Jammu and Kashmir State began crossing the LoC once again. This time, the context was a militant insurgency in the valley of Kashmir. The government of AJK provided relief supplies to 35,000 registered refugees between 1990 and 2004, of whom 17,000 constituted a permanent camp-resident population.[79] Unlike refugees from the previous periods of intrastate conflict, the AJK government did not grant them rehabilitation allotments or recognize their right to own land. The people who came to AJK after 1990 lived in temporary tent camps until October 2005, when a severe earthquake forced relocation of all established refugee camps.

The first refugees during this period entered AJK's Muzaffarabad district from the Kupwara and Baramullah districts of Jammu and Kashmir State's Kashmir Division. Indian military and security force activity in border regions kept residents under constant pressure from the military forces, who suspected local people of aiding militants, and from insurgents, who suspected local residents of collaborating with the Indian military. Indian military and security forces used interrogation, torture, and harassment against those suspected of activities or sympathies that supported pro-Independence or pro-Pakistan insurgents.[80] In situations in which a suspected militant could not be located, his male relatives were likely to be detained for interrogation. His female relatives were often subjected to severe public mistreatment. Thus, most refugees who crossed the LoC into AJK came in family groups, and the residents of several border villages migrated to AJK together.

In addition, there have been periods of intense military engagement at the LoC in the form of heavy artillery fire and border skirmishes. These were pronounced after the bilateral nuclear test of 1998; the Jammu districts of Jammu and Kashmir State saw an increase in fighting and a corresponding increase in the numbers of people who crossed into the AJK districts of Kotli,

Bagh, and Rawalakot. During the (undeclared) Kargil War of 1999, large numbers of people were displaced from AJK and the Northern Areas into Pakistan. Many people from border villages were repeatedly displaced, and others have not been able to return to their villages since the summer of 1998. The Government of AJK provided canvas tents, but they did not register these people as refugees or make relief provisions. The AJK government estimates that more than three hundred seventy thousand residents have been displaced within AJK and Pakistan due to LoC firing since 1990. However, as the AJK Minister for Refugees and Rehabilitation explained to me during our first meeting in 1999, this number is compiled from the records of military checkpoints within the Security Zone, and it likely reflects people who evacuated from their homes on multiple occasions.

The Line of Control and Its Disputed Territory

For much of its history, the LoC had neither the absolute place nor the solid materiality that its representation on maps of Jammu and Kashmir suggests. The Indian military began planning a boundary fence known as the Indian Kashmir Barrier in the mid-1990s, but for decades there was no boundary line marking the place in a stream or on a hillside that ceased to be (Pakistan-administered) Azad Jammu and Kashmir and became (Indian-administered) Jammu and Kashmir State.[81] Indian and Pakistani Army posts faced each other across mountain ridges, marking the LoC's contours, but in many places its specific location was in doubt. Occasionally people wandered across the LoC by mistake, something they had perhaps done many times, until the day they encountered an army patrol and discovered that they were carrying the wrong identity cards. Sometimes such people said they were collecting fruit from a tree that had been in the family for years, claiming that it was the army patrol that had wandered across the line.

As a social boundary, the LoC was permeable, often fluid, and sometimes irrelevant. Many people traversed the line in the first decades after its establishment. Most of these crossings had nothing, overtly, to do with politics. Villages near the LoC had close links with villages and communities on the other side. Families and social groups were divided across the India- and Pakistan-administered regions, and people continued to reaffirm their kinship ties. Residents of villages on the line crossed it to attend important ritual events like weddings and funerals. The reinforcement of kinship ties through marriage and the continued participation in exchanges of ritual labor were particularly important for refugees as an expression of their social commitment to the idea of return. Refugees who thought of themselves as temporarily resettled sought to reinforce their social networks in the villages from which they had been displaced.

It became progressively more difficult and dangerous to make such crossings after 1971, when both India and Pakistan began treating the LoC like a border. Parts of the LoC were mined, and people caught crossing it were subject to arrest, investigation, and imprisonment. In other places, people experienced the LoC as an absence, a place across which contact with family members ceased. For divided families, the LoC marks where social interaction has become circumscribed and restricted and where interaction with "the other" places a person at risk.

Ideologically, the LoC marks a clear boundary. India has always regarded the events of October 1947 as a military invasion of Jammu and Kashmir orchestrated by Pakistan; it claims that the monarch of Jammu and Kashmir legally joined India in 1947, that the territory currently administered by Pakistan is therefore illegitimately and illegally occupied, and that the entirety of the former Princely State of Jammu and Kashmir—including Pakistan Occupied Kashmir (POK)—is an integral part of India. Indian officials regularly accuse the government of Pakistan of attempting to internationalize the Kashmir issue, but in Pakistan the Kashmir Dispute has historically been viewed as an inherently international problem.[82] Pakistan had no Instrument of Accession for Jammu and Kashmir, disputed or otherwise, but it claimed that the Maharaja's accession to India was illegitimate and illegal and that interim constitution formation and elections did not invalidate the UN resolution calling for a general referendum. In Pakistan, people call AJK Azad Kashmir (Free Kashmir) and refer to Jammu and Kashmir State in India as *muqbūza kashmīr* (Occupied Kashmir) or Indian Held Kashmir.

The process of legitimizing India's claim in domestic political discourse involved linking the dispute to the central concerns of Indian national political culture, and Jammu and Kashmir came to represent the secular claims of Indian democracy. As Jawaharlal Nehru, India's first prime minister, argued several years after the Partition, "the Kashmir dispute [is] symbolic for us as it has far-reaching consequences in India. Kashmir is symbolic as it illustrates that we are a secular state."[83] This symbolic relationship's asserted importance to the stability and security of the Indian Union is now fully validated in policy analysis and academic studies of the Kashmir Dispute.[84] In this formulation, the Kashmir Dispute is not just a conflict between India and Pakistan; it is a struggle to secure a modern secular state in South Asia.

In Pakistan, political thinking on the Kashmir Dispute focused on state security issues, on the illegitimacy of the electoral process and constitution formation in Indian-administered Kashmir, and on the imperative of international intervention to enforce the UN resolutions until the 1970s.[85] After 1972, the two-nation theory underwent crisis with the secession of East Pakistan (Bangladesh) in 1971, and Islamist parties acquired influence in Pakistan's national politics.[86] New slogans such as "Kashmir is the jugular vein of Pakistan" *(kashmīr shāhrag-e-pakistān hai)* and "Kashmir will become Pakistan" *(kashmīr pakistān banegā)* emphasized the purported common (Islamic) cultural identity of Kashmiris and Pakistanis and the "natural" relationship between Jammu and Kashmir and Pakistan. In this formulation, the Kashmir Dispute "concerns the life and the destiny of a people who have been historically and culturally an integral part of the nation that achieved sovereignty through the establishment of Pakistan."[87] In short, the Kashmir Dispute was reconceived as nothing less than a struggle for the very existence of Pakistan as a viable nation-state.

India and Pakistan now consider border crossers of all kinds national security risks. Residents of border villages and nomadic herders, who have a reputation as potential crossing guides, are subject to surveillance and suspicion by all sides in the conflict. In tracing family life histories, it was evident to me that marriages connecting families across the LoC continue, but people are now taciturn in discussing the movement of marriage parties. To talk about clandestine LoC crossings now is to admit to an activity that is associated with either terrorism or spying. For many people living in the Kashmir borderlands, cross-LoC alliances represented a continuation of old patterns of social, economic, and political alliances. Over time, it became more difficult to maintain these connections and more important to forge and solidify social bonds that connected people to networks in the broader postcolonial national contexts. Therefore, it was primarily refugee families who were committed to continuing these trans-LoC alliances, especially if they maintained a hope of return to their predisplacement homes.

The Kashmir Problem and the Line of Control

India and Pakistan consider the Kashmir Dispute a territorial dispute but Kashmiri refugees living in Pakistan and Azad Jammu and Kashmir refer instead to the *masʾalah-e-kashmīr* (Kashmir Problem) to talk about the border in Jammu and Kashmir and its impact on their lives. The *masʾalah-e-kashmīr* is not a territorial dispute between states but a problem of the incomplete realization of the rights of the people *(haqūq-e-awām)*.

When Kashmiri politicians, public intellectuals, or refugees use the term *mas'alah-e-kashmīr,* they place the Kashmir conflict in the context of a freedom movement *(taharīk-e-āzādī)* that began as a struggle to force the Maharaja to recognize the sovereignty of the people and that has become a struggle for the same recognition against the postcolonial state and in the international system of states.[88] None of the UN resolutions envisioned the option of a third independent state in South Asia, but in the 1970s, Jammu and Kashmir nationalist thinkers introduced the possibility of an independent (unified) state to the popular understanding of the options that the promised referendum would present. They argued that the plebiscite *(rāye-shumārī)* called for in the 1949 UN resolutions referred to the right of self-determination *(haqq-e-khudirādīyat),* which they linked to the Universal Declaration of Human Rights (1948) and the International Covenant on Civil and Political Rights (1966).[89] Contemporary discourse on the politics of the *mas'alah-e-kashmīr* has established a firm link between the promised future of *haqq-e-khudirādīyat,* the historical *haqūq-e-awām,* and the continuing integrity of the dispersed *awām-e-riyāsat,* or *awām-e-kashmīr* (people of the state of Jammu and Kashmir).

Arshad Sohail was working as a Central Committee member of the Organization for the Rehabilitation (Settlement) of Unsettled Refugees of Jammu and Kashmir when I met him in an unofficial refugee settlement colony in Rawalpindi in 2001. It was a chance meeting, and he greeted me warmly, recalling that we had met in passing at a social gathering in Murree, a hill station in the northern Punjab. I didn't remember meeting him, as I had spent most of the day with the women guests, but I did remember that the gathering had been to remember the death of a family member of the hosts—a young man who had been a member of the militant wing of the Jammu and Kashmir Liberation Front (JKLF). Arshad Sohail said that he had been a district organizer for the JKLF's political wing and told me about his own history as a refugee displaced from Baramullah in 1971.

His recollection caught my attention because I knew that the family I was visiting were registered members of the AJKMC (although likely with Kashmiri nationalist sympathies because they had a picture of Maqbool Bhat—an iconic nationalist martyr—hanging on the wall of their shack). I also knew that the Organization for the Rehabilitation (Settlement) of Unsettled Refugees drew its membership primarily from Jammu and Kashmir refugees living in Pakistan, where the AJKMC had a large base of support. Refugees from Jammu and Kashmir are often members of multiple political parties, because these multiple alliances express different political ideologies, aspirations for the future, and investments in networks of patronage in the places where they live and work. They might be members of one political party that was effective in "getting it done" in their daily lives and another that connected them to the places from which they had been displaced, and to where they hoped to return. It is important to pay attention to this multiplicity of affiliations, because often the organizations to which Jammu and Kashmir refugees belong espouse contradictory political ideologies. It is impossible to deduce people's political proclivities or to predict their behavior from their political affiliations. However, I was interested to know how Arshad Sohail had become a Central Committee member for an organization that not only served members of a different political party than his own but also primarily served people who had been displaced from the Jammu region.[90]

He explained that his standing in the Kashmiri refugee community derived in part from his role in organizing refugee participation in a 1992 protest march from Muzaffarabad toward Srinagar, which was intended to meet marchers from Srinagar at Chakothi/Uri and thus "break" the LoC. The refugees he organized were all registered with the Organization for the Rehabilitation (Settlement) of Unsettled Refugees living in Rawalpindi, and they were also members and supporters of a variety of different political parties in AJK and Pakistan. In fact, he said, although the 1992 march had been a JKLF initiative, the first organized attempt to break the Ceasefire Line had been in 1958 by activists of the Azad Jammu and Kashmir Liberation League. During the years of Muslim Conference party rule in Azad Jammu and Kashmir, successive party leaders and AJK presidents had led public marches to break the LoC.[91] Kashmiri refugees living in Pakistan always participated in these marches, Arshad Sohail said, because the LoC needed to be revealed as an irrelevant boundary and made visibly permeable to Jammu and Kashmir state subjects:

> We are all Kashmiri. When this *mas'alah-e-kashmīr* is resolved then one day we will return to our homes, but even now this LoC– it does not apply to us. The LoC was an agreement between India and Pakistan, but the UN never said to *awām-e-kashmīr,* "this is your LoC." The *haqq-e-khudirādīyat* is a political right that we were promised, but some conditions were not met and we are still waiting—and by the grace of God if the UN does not give it to us then we will grasp it ourselves.

Being Kashmiri, according to Arshad Sohail, cannot be interpreted within a worldview that privileges the territorial division of Jammu and Kashmir between India and Pakistan. He continued:

> That LoC? Well, that is a thing which Pakistan must know and India must know, but I do not know any LoC. I am a *muhājir* in Pakistan, but if I accept this LoC between my home and my family and my own self, then I will be a refugee in the whole world and I will have no home.

BEING KASHMIRI, THE BORDERLAND OF THE BODY, AND THE TERRITORY OF THE STATE

The existence of the *muhājir-e-jammū-o-kashmīr* (Kashmiri refugee) as a politico-legal and sociocultural identity both underwrites and challenges the foundational narratives that legitimate the postcolonial nation-states of Pakistan and India. It challenges citizenship categories and destabilizes a major material line of separation and identity—the border. For this reason, the border does not provide the language that can illuminate the relationships between ways of "being Kashmiri" and the "Kashmir" to which they correspond.

Despite the guarded maintenance of the predivision Jammu and Kashmiri hereditary state-subject status as the basis for recognizing Kashmiri state subjects on both sides of the LoC, arguments about the proper use of the term erupt regularly in daily life. Three cases illustrate the constant work required to maintain the category Kashmiri as a political identity. In each of these cases, political organizers, appointed delegates, and elected representatives disputed the limits of inclusion in the community of Kashmiris and deployed the designation Kashmir in very different ways when they were speaking in formal political contexts versus when they used the word in casual interpersonal speech. Each, in speech not circumscribed as political, used the word to describe a sense of cultural difference and the speaker's affective attachment to that difference.

Farida Begum criticized a political rival for implying that anyone within the borders of the state (as they had been in 1947) could possibly be a refugee. Her objection to the use of the term muhājir highlighted the utility of the term Kashmiri to reject a political distinction between hereditary residents *(qaumī bāshindah)* and resettled refugees (muhājirs) that might delimit a differential evaluation of rights based on the current divisions of territory. Yet, in private discussions with me, Farida Begum was very interested in drawing distinctions between "this and that Kashmiri" in the domain of culture and language. Likewise, as an official diplomatic representative, Arif Obaid maintained a similar although apparently inverse distinction to the one made by Farida Begum—that the same relationship to territory that makes people "refugees" also secures their identity as "Kashmiri." In personal conversation, however, Arif Obaid expressed his interest in refugees from the cultural center of the Indian Kashmir Valley; while he had a political obligation to the "mountain people" as a representative of a transnational Kashmiri political party, he clearly did not feel an affinity with them. In Islamabad, the residents of one squatters' colony so effectively mobilized their claims to be "Kashmiri refugees" against the government of Pakistan that their colony, located within view of the parliament, was one of the last *kacchī ābādīs* remaining in the capital of Islamabad after residents of other such settlements had been forcibly relocated to the outskirts of the city. Their representative to the AJK Legislative Assembly, however, denied their requests for patronage, because the government of AJK, concerned primarily with tracing the contours of displacement across the LoC, was uninterested or unwilling to take up issues particular to the condition of people displaced from the other Pakistan-administered areas into Pakistan.

In AJK and Pakistan, not all people who self-identify as Kashmiri garner recognition from others in all domains; informal, casual slippages often belie formal political speech, revealing rifts of cultural attachment and social ambivalence. In speaking to and about each other, Kashmiris sometimes become vexed by the multiple possible references of the designation, and these disagreements reveal the ambiguous and contingent quality of the term.

"Not Refugees in Their Own Homeland"

The municipality of Murree has historically been an important crossroads between the NWFP (now Khyber Pakhtunkhwa), the Punjab, and the Jammu and Kashmir territories. The town has had a resident community of Kashmiri refugees since 1947. In 1946, it was a hill station retreat for the colonial administrators of British India and a military outpost for the British Colonial Army. Organizers of the tax rebellion in the Poonch region in 1946–1947 smuggled weapons into the Princely State of Jammu and Kashmir from Murree and brought their families to the town in order to protect them from the Maharaja's army. In 1948, refugees arrived in Murree from the other areas in Jammu District that were most profoundly affected by frontline fighting between India and Pakistan. In the same period, prominent political supporters of the Muslim Conference from the Kashmir Valley came to Murree after being forced out of Srinagar during the violent political party contests between National Conference supporters and the AJKMC. This community of political elites from the Kashmir Valley made Murree a hospitable resettlement community for other exiles who supported the pro-Pakistan movements during the Indo-Pak wars of 1965 and 1971 and had to leave Indian Kashmir because of later political retaliation. Murree is now a center for the constituency of one of the six KV (Kashmir Valley) seats and for one of the six JC (Jammu City) seats that are reserved for *muhājir-e-kashmīr* (Kashmiri refugees) in the Legislative Assembly of AJK.

Farida Begum was my hostess for several days while I stayed in the town, meeting with Kashmiri refugees. Her husband had been a Member of the AJK Legislative Assembly on several occasions, elected to one of the town's refugee seats. She herself had been a close partner in his campaigns, advocating his candidacy in women's circles and household networks. My hostess had lived in Srinagar until she was a young woman when her family arranged her marriage to the son of a friend who was living as a refugee in Pakistan. Her own closest connections were to other Kashmiri-speaking refugees from Srinagar who traced family connections through several generations and several villages and urban neighborhoods on both sides of the LoC. Farida Begum was eager to talk about the importance for muhājirs (refugees) from the Kashmir Valley to maintain their language and traditions; she said that it was more difficult for them than for refugees from Poonch or Jammu, where the regional languages were closer to the Hinko and Punjabi their neighbors spoke in town and to the Urdu their children spoke at school. She and her husband spoke only the Kashmiri language (Koshûr) to their children, and she hoped to give her daughter in marriage to a Srinagar family so that her family's connection to Srinagar would remain strong until they could all return to their proper homes.

One day, we were invited to the home of the former president of the other major political party that represented the town's refugee community. We were graciously received, and we waited a short time in the formal guest receiving room, where there were many photographs of the political leader. He had served several terms as the Prime Minister of AJK, and the photographs showed him shaking hands with several of the Prime Ministers and Military Administrators of Pakistan, including Nawaz Sharif, who was then in office. Our hostess, the politician's sister, received us with tea and refreshments and discussed the specific history of her family's contribution to founding AJK and establishing a place for Kashmiri refugees in its territory and within its government.

As she spoke, Farida Begum became increasingly agitated. At last she interrupted our hostess: "We are all Kashmiri, there is no difference that you can name to draw a distinction between this Kashmiri and that Kashmiri. Is it not so?" Our hostess agreed by inclining her head slightly to the side, but it seemed like a polite acquiescence to me, the kind a hostess might extend to a guest. Apparently Farida Begum was not satisfied, because she interjected again:

> Then what is this that you are speaking of *muhājirīn* [refugees] in Poonch? Yes, it is fine, you may call me this, a *muhājir,* and you may even call yourself a *muhājir,* since you are now in Pakistan and not in Poonch. But how can you call a *muhājir* those people who are living in their own country? They have not crossed any border that you should call them *muhājir.* It is all our one Jammu and Kashmir, and they are not refugees in their own homeland!

The lady of the house agreed, but in a way that suggested that she was loathe to contradict, and she resumed answering my questions and talking about her family's history. But she found it difficult to tell her story without using the words that upset my companion.

Soon Farida Begum turned to me and suggested that we ask to be excused. We began the long walk back to the center of town, and I noticed how very angry she was. Her lips pursed slightly and she walked quickly. She had pulled her veil briskly about her face and the broad cloth draped her shoulders and torso, but I could see the rigid set of her shoulders, and on the busy streets and narrow alleys, men pulled slightly aside to let her pass. I struggled to keep pace with her as we wound our way through the steep back alleys of the Pakistani hill town. When we arrived at her house, I tried to beg her pardon for asking her to accompany me to the home of a political rival. She dismissed my concern:

> I campaign for my husband, she campaigns for her brother, that's just politics. Didn't you notice how well she received us for tea? After all, we are all Kashmiri. But she should not call them *muhājirs* when they are in their very own homeland!

"Just Mountain People"

On a hot summer afternoon, I arrived at the Islamabad offices of the All Parties Hurriyat (Freedom) Conference (APHC), where the five members of the executive committee greeted me. The chairman represented the party that held the chair on the executive committee APHC in Srinagar, and he introduced each of the other delegates, each appointed by their respective political parties. He and his colleagues were used to meeting with diplomats and government officials, representatives of nongovernmental organizations, journalists, and scholars, and he presented the APHC's official position on the Kashmir Problem succinctly: the current struggle in the valley of Kashmir is an indigenous liberation struggle of the people of Jammu and Kashmir, who are fighting for their right to exercise their right of self-determination, a basic human right according to the UN charter and, moreover, a specific right that was promised to the people of Jammu and Kashmir in 1949 by the United Nations. I listened to his presentation and then asked him to explain the APHC's policy on refugee return.

He explained that the APHC, while cognizant of the refugee issue, did not have a specific unified position on the refugee question. He gave two reasons for this. First, he said, the right of refugees to return to their homes and reclaim their properties was a principle of state law. Second, Kashmiri refugees would not be able to return to their homes until the end of armed fighting and abuses of civilians on the Indian side of the LoC. At that point, the issue would be moot, because refugees and all the people of Jammu and Kashmir would participate in the UN-mandated plebiscite and express their preferences for the future status of Jammu and Kashmir—accession to Pakistan, accession to India, or an independent state. The chairman said that he was himself personally worried about the provisions for future refugee return, but he emphasized, "Kashmiri refugees are Kashmiri people"; the parties represented in the APHC had many refugee members and organizers, as the group's only requirement for participation was that members be Jammu and Kashmir state subjects.

It was a long meeting, and after the official presentation the APHC members spoke openly about their own circumstances as exiles from the valley of Kashmir. While they each traveled extensively around the world, either on APHC or party work, none of them could return to their homes on the Indian side of the LoC because their prominent political work and human rights advocacy had made them targets of the Indian security forces. As we talked, it became clear that each of them had been appointed to their positions because they had already been in danger in the Valley for their political activities.

At the end of the afternoon, Arif Obaid, one of the APHC representatives, offered to drop me at my residence on his way home, and we had a chance to speak more as we traveled. He asked me to tell him more about the refugees in the camps in Muzaffarabad. I began to list names of the towns and villages outside the towns of Kupwara, Handwara, and Uri that I had heard mentioned most often in the camps when I asked people where they had lived before coming to AJK. He sighed and said disappointedly,

> Oh, I thought you said that they were *kashmīrī* refugees, but they are just *pahārī lōg* [mountain people].

"Not of Concern to the Government of Azad Jammu and Kashmir"

During the monsoon season of 2001, a flash flood washed through the city of Rawalpindi. In some neighborhoods, buildings were flooded to the third story, and less sturdy homes, livestock, and people were swept away with the rushing waters. In the lowest-lying neighborhoods, families lost all of their possessions and counted themselves lucky not to have lost loved ones. The AJK Legislative elections had just announced returns, and Sabur Qadir had won election to a refugee seat from the Rawalpindi constituency expected to receive a Ministry assignment in the formation of the new government in Muzaffarabad. In the days after the flood, he was busy visiting Kashmiri refugees in neighborhoods around Rawalpindi, where he informed himself of their condition and compiled a list of families who suffered losses. He also promised to advocate for relief funds from the AJK government on his next trip to Muzaffarabad.

I accompanied him for several days on his rounds. Hanging on the remains of several houses we visited were the tattered election campaign posters of his rival, but Sabur Qadir was recognized and welcomed at each house. At each, he spoke with the head of the house, and his secretary made an entry in an account book. Privately, he expressed concern that he would not be successful, or at least not very successful, in securing relief for the flood victims. The damage was extensive; entire neighborhoods had become structurally unsound. In many cases what people needed were new homes. The biggest problem, in his view, was that the Kashmiri residents of Rawalpindi were widely distributed across different parts of the city, and there was thus little that the government of AJK could do to provide relief to Kashmiris as a group. Sabur Qadir said that he also found it personally very difficult to visit Kashmiri refugee families in their urban neighborhoods and to walk past their neighbors, who were just as profoundly affected. He found it extremely difficult that, while he might do little more than write the name, address, and an estimate of losses suffered by the Kashmiri residents, for the others he could not even do that much.

One day I did not accompany him and went instead to the *kacchī ābādī* (squatter settlement) on the outskirts of Islamabad, where I had spent a great deal of time during earlier fieldwork. One of several *kacchī ābādīs* in Islamabad and Rawalpindi, the colony had begun as a labor camp during the building of the capital of Islamabad in the 1960s. Over the years, the laborers living there had built mud and stone shacks, but the state power and water agencies refused to provide services to illegal habitations; the laborers hijacked electricity from main lines but had no water or sewer connections, although they lived within view of the Pakistan parliament and the official hostels for legislators that many of them had helped build. The Pakistan government had tried on several occasions to forcibly dislodge the inhabitants and destroy the slum. Unlike other *kacchī ābādīs* around the capital, however, 80 percent of the residents of this labor colony were Kashmiri.[92] They had successfully prevented the Islamabad Central Development Authority from bulldozing their homes, and they attributed their success to having threatened to publicize the government's "lack of concern for Kashmiri refugees." The oldest residents, who claimed to have lived there since the capital was being built, were from Gujar or Bakerwal families who had had their winter camps in the Poonch and Rajouri regions and were displaced by the wars of 1965 and 1971. Over the years the colony had grown; it attracted people from AJK because the other Kashmiris living there helped them find work, build a shack, and bring their families. The labor colony expanded and became more densely populated in the 1990s, when LoC firing brought more people from border villages in search of wage work to supplement their disrupted agricultural production. After 1996, Shina-speaking refugees from Kargil (on the Indian side of the LoC) and Baltistan (on the Pakistan side) moved there, and such a significant number of people had moved to the colony from the Northern Areas during the Kargil War in 1999 that the Imam of the Shi'ia mosque had become the colony's recognized spokesperson.

I had asked about the colony immediately after the flash floods and had been told that it had not been affected, so I was surprised when I arrived to discover that, while the colony had not suffered flooding, the heavy downpours had collapsed many roofs and had washed out the mud-constructed huts. Many of the colony's residents had lost their possessions and many were staying with neighbors or were sleeping in the mosque. They asked me to bring Sabur Qadir back to the colony, because they were a part of the refugee constituency that had elected Sabur Qadir, and he had campaigned there. They wanted to record their names and losses in his account of Kashmiris affected by the flood. I conveyed the request, but he was uninterested in visiting the colony again:

> Those people are not of concern to the government of Azad Kashmir. There are in the whole colony only a few Kashmiri refugees, the rest are from Baltistan.

TWO

Protective Migration and Armed Struggle

POLITICAL VIOLENCE AND THE LIMITS
OF VICTIMIZATION IN ISLAM

AS A YOUNG MAN, Nasir Waseem was displaced from his village in Rajouri District during the 1965 Indo-Pak war. He had been allotted property in a Kashmiri refugee settlement in Punjab, but he had not been able to make a living from that land; instead, he supported his family by doing wage labor for a construction firm. He was living in a labor colony *(kacchī ābādī)* near Islamabad when he spoke with me on a sunny winter day. We were sitting cross-legged on a woven rope bed called a *chārpāī* and sipping sweet milky tea. The *chārpāī* had been pulled out of the living and sleeping room of his two-room shack and set in the center of his small compound, made somewhat private by the mud walls that separated his domestic space from the neighboring shacks and the colony's pounded dirt alleys and drainage canals. Nasir Waseem said that he accepted his life as a muhājir. He told me that he regretted not being able to return to his natal village, but the difficulty of resettlement in Pakistan had enabled him to achieve a spiritual consciousness he might not otherwise have achieved:

> To do *hijarat,* to cultivate the land, to make it habitable and productive, and to render it populated, that is a great act of devotion to God and accrues blessings.

His words were incongruous with the squatter slum where we sat, where almost nothing grew, where during the monsoon the open sewers overflowed, and where during the summer the corrugated tin roofs made the interior of the houses hotter than the courtyards in direct sun. He further explained to me what it meant to render the land habitable and populated: he meant creating a place where it is possible to live a respectable life as a good Muslim, and he saw no shame in being poor, as long as he earned an honest livelihood.

For him, doing hijarat meant undertaking the duty of living an honorable life, a duty that included taking care of people who were dependent on him.

Not all residents of the *kacchī ābādī* considered earning a living for their families a sufficient way of responding to the history of displacement that had led, at least in part, to their present material conditions. Shafiq had grown up in a resettled refugee village and had been displaced by the nearly constant artillery fire on the Line of Control (LoC) during and after the Kargil War of 1999. Shafiq was a member of a muhājir family, but he did not put as much value on the practice of hijarat. After careful consideration, he had decided to join the armed struggle in Kashmir:

> It is good to go to school and to take a profession, but no one asks who defends the rights of oppressed Kashmiris. It is a *farz* [duty] as a Muslim that you should protect the rights of the oppressed. So it is also my *farz* as a Muslim to go for this *jihād,* and I joined a militant organization and began my training.

He had grown up a muhājir, but he said, "I am a *mujāhid* in my heart."

His parents disagreed. Indeed, his father had recently retrieved him—very much against his will—from a militant training camp by convincing the camp commander that Shafiq could not legitimately participate in jihād. On several occasions, Shafiq expressed that he remained at odds with his parents, and I noticed that someone accompanied him to and from work and to do errands at the market. His father had apparently recruited a significant amount of community support to prevent his son from going back to Azad Jammu and Kashmir to join another of the militant groups based there.

Hijarat and jihād provide moral frameworks through which Muslim refugees interpret the relationships between personal and collective suffering, social responsibility, and political action. By applying the concepts, Kashmiri refugees relate their personal experiences to those of other Muslims living in other places and times. People employ the terms in evaluating the conditions under which they are obliged to endure political violence or permitted to perpetrate violent struggle in the name of political and social ideals, such as the sovereignty of the polity or the duty to the protect the community. Yet, neither hijarat nor jihād presents a simple mytho-historical model for how to respond to and live with political violence. The meaning of hijarat and jihād are embedded in present-oriented domains of power, both local and global, and practices of becoming a muhājir or a mujāhid do not index an exclusively Islamic symbolic order of cultural, social, or political belonging. As social and political practices, they are continually evaluated and debated.

Even within families, individuals come to very different conclusions about what it means to be a Muslim refugee or to be a defender of Muslim peoples, and people's assessments of how to balance religions obligations with social responsibilities change over time.

ISLAMICATE WORDS, MUSLIM SOCIETIES, AND FUNDAMENTALIST MYTHO-HISTORIES

As Islam became a global religious tradition through conversion, conquest, and migration, important Arabic key words were adopted into many languages and thereafter developed their own regional etymologies. Some, such as the words *hijarat* and *jihād,* now reference multiple historical events, theological debates, and philosophical concerns in societies in which Islamic traditions are a source of cultural meaning and value. These terms thus carry multiple meanings; in some social usages, these multiple meanings are condensed; at other times, they are dispersed. In this sense, they have become dense Islamicate concepts through which Muslims can organize, express, and debate their experiences with violence in the contemporary world.

I draw here on a distinction, suggested by religious historian Marshall Hodgson, between the use of the word *Islamic* to mean "pertaining to Islam in the proper religious sense" and *Islamicate* to refer to "the social and cultural complex historically associated with Islam and Muslims."[1] This is a useful distinction, because it creates an analytic space in which it is possible to examine how the religion of Islam contributed to the symbolic systems of Muslim societies. But it has some problems. One is that the distinction rests on the possibility of disambiguating essential religious meanings—the Islamic—from historically mediated social and cultural meanings—the Islamicate. However, religious authorities argue about the authentic meaning of religious terms and concepts; debate occurs across sectarian divides regarding the authority of interpretation, between the four orthodox Sunni schools of jurisprudence,[2] and within the Sufi philosophical lineages. Different kinds of so-called proper Islam developed in each of these traditions, and some scholars have suggested there are actually multiple "Islams."[3] Still, Islam—or these multiple Islams—makes universal claims on its confessional community, and efforts to reform members of that community, whose Islamic sensibilities seem too cultural, are a recurring theme in Muslim societies.[4] Hodgson did not mean that Islamicate concepts were distorted derivatives of authentic Islamic ones, but the distinction can replicate and therefore evade core debates within and between Islamic traditions and Muslim societies, unless those debates are explicitly acknowledged.

The symbolic systems of historical Muslim societies have also influenced how Muslims understand and experience Islam as a global religious tradition. Hodgson did not consider the question of how those systems shaped or determined Islam, in the "proper religious sense," but field researchers have often noted an emphasis on orthopraxy over orthodoxy in Muslim societies.[5] As Dale Eickelman has cogently argued, "[the] practice and significance of Islamic faith in any given historical setting cannot readily be predicted from first principles of dogma or belief."[6] In fact, with the emergence of modern politico-religious institutions and political parties (jamā'ats), scholars trained in the traditional Islamic sciences ('ulemah) have struggled to retain their positions as arbitrators of proper Islamic religious practice in contemporary Muslim societies.[7]

Several influential recent studies of violence-related forced displacement distinguish Muslim refugee communities from other global refugee populations by asserting a fundamental link between hijarat and jihād. Indeed, "refugee-warrior" has been increasingly adopted as an English translation of the word muhājir. This translation wrongly asserts an inevitable developmental relationship in which the practice of jihād follows inherently from the performance of hijarat. Some Muslim refugees involved in militant organizations do explain their practices by referencing the Qur'anic verses on jihād,[8] but to assume that becoming a muhājir requires a displaced person to also become a refugee-warrior infers that Muslim refugees are inherently militant and that "from a personal point of view, [hijarat] renders the refugee almost a fighter, and from a collective point of view, it binds the group to the very sources of Islam."[9] The adoption of this specific ethnographic explanation as social analysis unfortunately reproduces a mytho-historical conception of the Islamic past—one that replicates a fundamentalist worldview. As such, it has no analytic distance from which to engage the paradoxical social production of that worldview.

The social production of muhājirs and mujāhids cannot be reduced to an analysis of either textual or historical Islam, because neither hijarat nor jihād reference monovalent historical events or uncontested scriptural imperatives. There is no single uncontested doctrine on either hijarat or jihād among formally trained Islamic scholars and even less agreement among the Muslim intellectual elites of the nineteenth and twentieth centuries. Furthermore, the relationship between them is mediated by diverse positions on territorial sovereignty and religious duty. As dense Islamicate concepts, they serve as conceptual frames for theorizing the regulation and limitation of violence and articulate the conditions of Muslim people's responsibility to act to achieve collective social and political goals.

"Hijarat" and "Jihād" as Dense Islamicate Concepts

The Islamicate concepts of hijarat and jihād condense multiple historical, political, and spiritual references. They both have the status of *sunnat* (habits or behaviors that serve as models of conduct), and Islamic scholars of the classical period (seventh to eleventh centuries, C.E.) forged doctrinal connections between the terms in textual exegesis, philosophical studies, and juridical literature on the topics of territorial sovereignty *(dār)* and religious duty *(farz)*. In response to the emergence of world-historical political systems and modern states, modernist and reformist Islamic scholars in the eighteenth, nineteenth, and early twentieth centuries transformed the accepted classical doctrines.

There are a number of Islamic terms that describe religiously endorsed and valued forms of migration and travel.[10] As a kind of migration, *hijarat* conveys a sense of "flight"—of movement necessitated by conditions of political isolation, threat, and persecution that lead a Muslim group to seek a secure community life elsewhere.[11] Several historical hijarats are mentioned in the Qur'an. The first was the migration of Abraham to Syria, a journey that marked his transition to prophethood. As a proper noun, Hijarat refers to the migration by the prophet Mohammad, his disciples, and his followers from Mecca to Medina in 622 C.E., following a period of religious persecution. It marks the beginning of the Islamic calendar, because this Hijarat led to the formation of the first Muslim political community (the *ummah*), which was comprised of the Meccan *muhājirūn* and their supporters in Medina (the *ansār,* or hosts). In addition, many hijarats occurred after the lifetime of the prophet Mohammad; while not a part of Islamic sacred history, they are important in the histories of specific Muslim communities. In the esoteric traditions, hijarat references a spiritual journey, like a believer's interior journey into the heart or a migration of the self to the divine. In many Qur'anic verses, use of the term indicates a transformation of the political relationship between family and tribe as well as a change of geographical location.

The term *jihād* also has multiple meanings.[12] In diverse Muslim societies, jihād is widely understood as a striving for moral perfection or spiritual salvation. For this reason, the *'ulemah* reject translating the term as "holy war." There are also several other terms used to discuss the relationship between violence and politico-religious practices—these include internal dissent *(fitna)*, fighting *(qitāl)*, and war *(mukātala)*.[13] Classical Islamic scholars attributed most of the Qur'anic references to jihād to the historical period in which the *muhājirūn*, supported by their Medinan hosts, organized a prolonged armed struggle against the Meccan tribes. Their success after eight years of war enabled the *muhājirūn* to return to the Meccan homeland. The historical association of jihād with the Hijarat to Medina developed in the Islamic classical period through scholarly exegesis and a genre of analysis *(naskh)* that correlated Qur'anic verses with events in the prophet Mohammad's life, as known through the Hadith literature, and in Qur'anic references; "verses employing the derivative *hajāru* (they migrated) are often paired with *jahādu* (they waged war), thus implying a close association of hijarat with jihād."[14] It is this interpretive association that established jihād, in its sense of armed struggle, as a practice of religious warfare foundational to the survival of the Muslim community.

The founders of the classical Islamic traditions were very concerned with securing a stable polity for Muslim people and with practices of migration and warring, but in the formation of doctrines on the practice of hijarat and jihād, there was a tremendous diversity among different Islamic scholarly lineages. The different schools of Islamic interpretation, philosophy, and jurisprudence place different weights on the Qur'anic *suras* (verses) and the Hadith literature (collected sayings and explications attributed to the prophet Mohammad) and *sunnat* (habits or behaviors of the prophets *[sunnatul-rasūl]*, which serve as models for personal conduct) as the foundation of Islamic jurisprudence *(firqh)*. These elements are given meaning and applied to contemporary questions by members of the *'ulemah*, each versed in their own authoritative lineages of scholarly exegesis and precedents based on subsidiary sources of law such independent reasoning *(ijtihād)* and consensus *(ijma')*. In practice, "there are times when the *sunnat* seems to take precedence over the Qur'an in the formation of consensus and the exercise of independent reasoning."[15]

There were several points of broad consensus. With few exceptions, the classical Islamic scholarship on political sovereignty focused on the control of *dār* (sovereign territory) and the people living there. Early Hadith scholars established a distinction between the *dārul-islām* (the land of peace/faith) and *dārul-harb* (the land of war/dissent). A classical consensus emerged that hijarat was a political practice necessary for the establishment of *dārul-islām* and was no longer obligatory after *dārul-islām* was secured.[16] Normative justifications of warring assumed the unity of religious authority and political leadership in Islamic polities,[17] and the early scholars were especially concerned with limitations on the practice of jihād (as an offensive or defensive form of armed struggle) and with questions about who had the authority to declare and conduct jihād. There was a diversity of opinion about the conditions under which jihād could be practiced to establish or extend *dārul-islām*, but there was consensus that Muslims had a duty to wage jihād in order to defend *dārul-islām*. In general, the classical scholars emphasized the importance of formal declarations of jihād, usually by a recognized political leader vested with religious authority.[18] Classical Islamic scholarship also established that both hijarat and jihād had the status of *farz,* a divinely instituted obligation that an individual owes to the Muslim community. Islamic scholarly analysis of *farz* distinguished between *farzul-'ayn* (individual duty) and *farzul-kafāya* (collective duty), and the majority of Hadith scholars agreed that both hijarat and jihād were collective duties.

The Limits of Violence

Hijarat and jihād became concepts that expressed limits on the conditions under which people were required or permitted to live under the threat of violence or to use violence to political ends. In the case of jihād, the orthodox schools of Islamic law developed such elaborate systems of regulation that contemporary humanist and social science scholars compare orthodox doctrines of jihād, as a form of warfare, with Euro-Christian just war theory.[19]

Classical doctrines established that neither jihād nor hijarat could be undertaken individually (unlike for example, prayer, which is *farzul-'ayn*). *Farzul-kafāya* is a collective endeavor undertaken in different ways by different individual members of the community; the spiritual benefits of doing so were considered to accrue to all members of the community. Each of the Islamic schools laid out detailed guidelines for how individuals were to participate in collective duties. Some of these conditions restricted only sons or men who are the sole sources of support for their families from participating in combat.[20] Others described categories of people whose contribution to jihād were to take the form of providing material support or maintaining the ongoing social life of the community. The exception was that jihād was *farzul-'ayn* in the case of an external invasion of Muslim lands.

The expansion of European colonial empires that were ideologically secular and that, in theory, protected community religious practices from direct intervention by the colonial state challenged these foundational points of consensus. During the colonial period, Islamic reformists and modernists developed new politico-territorial categories such as *dārul-sulk* (domain of truce) and *dārul-aman* (domain of peace), which expressed the space of sovereignty as a political sphere where living as a Muslim was possible.[21] These new categories accommodated notions of political communities that corresponded to the concepts of "nation" *(millat)* and "state" *(dawla).* These developments were both the result and the cause of contentious debates between Islamic scholars and the new schools they founded (such as the Darul-Uloom, based in Deoband, India, and generally known as the Deobandis). One issue of debate was the status of territory as *dārul-islām* or *dārul-harb* under colonial rule. Another issue was what obligations the Muslim community (the *'ummah)* had to reestablish Muslim rule in the territories where they lived. The Sunni schools (especially the Hanifi and Maliki) examined these issues during the British colonial occupations of India and Nigeria and occasioned the reformulations of hijarat and jihād doctrines.[22] Although classical scholarship emphasized the use of jihād to extend and consolidate the politico-territorial domain, reformist and modernist formulations of jihād held that its practice outside of *dārul-islām* was possible only to counter direct oppression. These formulations also solidified the doctrinal link between jihād and hijarat. Reformist and modernist scholars argued that hijarat was a collective duty not only because it ensured the safety of the community but also because it allowed for the organization of movements to liberate Muslim lands. They also argued that hijarat was necessary only when preceded by a declaration of jihād or when religious persecution or restriction on religious freedom prevented Muslims from practicing their religion.[23]

Arguments about the declaration and regulation of hijarat and jihād continued and distinguished divergent modernist, fundamentalist, and Islamist positions in the nineteenth and twentieth centuries.[24] By the early twentieth century, much Islamic scholarship on sovereignty had reconceived *dār* as a domain within which political authority is exercised rather than a literal territory. This shift accommodated the nonunity of the Muslim world, the proliferation of different Islamic states, and the religious tolerance of secular democracies. It acknowledged that "in the era of nation-states . . . where rights to worship are protected by covenants of citizenship, the question of the mutual definition of *hijarat* and *dārul-islām* and *dārul-harb* [had become] less relevant."[25] Then, in the mid-twentieth century, the first Islamist ideologues emphasized the idea of "defensive" jihād and effectively recuperated jihād as an individual duty *(farzul-'ayn)* for the purpose of political reformation and consolidation.[26]

The most profound shifts in Islamicate formulations of jihād came at the intersection between popular movements and formal Islamic scholarship. None of the classical traditions emphasized the role of either individual or collective conscience in the declaration, practice, or evaluation of jihād.[27] The Islamic revivalist and reform movements of eighteenth and nineteenth centuries were especially concerned with the influence of regional culture on religious rituals and devotional practices, and they sought to reform devotional practices that permitted intermediaries between the individual and god. The new institutions that developed during these movements emphasized personal efforts of individual Muslims to conform with Islamic tradition in order to shape a just social and political order.[28] They focused on the bodily disciplining of (their interpretation of correct) ritual practice[29] and on creating self-conscious, pious Muslim subjects.[30] In South Asia and in other regions where modern Islamic reform movements shaped the discourse and practice of anticolonial movements,[31] late-colonial and postcolonial jihād movements were marked by a concern that the individual mujāhid develop a self-awareness of his own practice. It was no longer sufficient that he conduct himself properly according to the Islamic law on warring and not warring (in any particular doctrinal manifestation), but also that he had the spiritual capacity to evaluate his conduct as a religious practice. This trend is now evident in the late twentieth century and early twenty-first century Salafi fundamentalist movements, to which Middle Eastern ideological and sociological origins are usually attributed.[32]

Embodied Ideology and Fundamentalist Mytho-Histories

Scholars and political analysts have treated jihād—particularly when its practitioners claim that their jihād is defensive—as essentially different from non-Islamic responses to oppression or occupation. As the religious studies scholar Bruce Lawrence has argued, jihād "embodies ideology, translates thought into action, [and] mobilizes the committed for a cause perceived as both just and necessary."[33] In other words, this theory of "embodied ideology" suggests that jihād disciplines the political consciousness and integrates the personal body with the religious collective without mediating social processes. It is implicit in a great deal of contemporary social science writing on militant politics in Muslim societies and has impeded the understanding of contemporary jihāds and the social production of actual mujāhidīn. It does, however, offer an important insight into how violence connects jihād, and hijarat, as *sunnat* to modern politics.

The problem it presents is twofold. First, the deceptive simplicity of the word *ideology* reveals little about any specific jihād, because there is so much diversity between the Islamic scholarly traditions, and because Islamist political parties also articulated political doctrines of jihād in the twentieth century, which were at odds which those of the established *'ulemah*. It also replicates a mytho-historical construction of the past,[34] through which Islamic fundamentalists and Islamist ideologues sought to legitimate their reinterpretation of the relationship between jihād practices and the modern state. Their predecessors—the reformist and revivalist movements of the eighteenth and nineteenth centuries—had sought to purge Muslim societies of "impurities" and "historical accretions," which are a part of the historical process but to which they attributed Islam's global political decline in the era of European colonial expansion. By questioning the lineages of orthodox scholarly interpretation and exegesis through which scriptural authority had been made meaningful for Muslim societies, the reformists paradoxically revived the concept of *ijtihād* (independent reasoning) as something referred to in the originary past but done only in the present.[35] Although *ijtihād* as a principle of scholarly practice and legal application had developed as a specific response to the recognition that the Qur'an and the Hadith do not in and of themselves tell Muslims how to live, but rather had to be interpreted and adapted in the present, it was revived as a way of revisiting the past without engaging history. At the same time, the reformist cultivation of self-reflective piety indicates that reasoning, interpretation, and meaning making are no longer the sole prerogative of trained scholars or even lay intellectuals; pious Muslims have to be convinced of the authenticity of their own practices. Thus, by drawing on this dehistoricized vision of authentic Islam,[36] fundamentalists and Islamists present a paradox; the analysis of their ideology (be the source textual or ethnographic) has to engage the process by which the image of an authentic tradition was reinvented for contemporary Muslims.

The concept of *sunnat* is key to understanding the insights of the embodied ideology theory in Islamicate political cultures. The observance of *sunnat* connects mundane with ritual practice, the individual with the religious collective, and both the individual and the collective to a temporal and spatial community that far exceeds the here and now of any personal experience. In contemporary anthropological terms, *sunnat* incorporates aspects of what the sociologist Marcel Mauss called "techniques of the body"[37] as well as the disciplinary mechanisms of political power that work by making such techniques and physical habits simultaneously self-conscious and available to external regulation, as described by the historian Michel Foucault.[38] In the global political culture of late modernity, the body itself has become "a political institution" and a "bearer of seminal political messages."[39] Thus, the explicitly self-conscious internalization of religious authority through the bodily practices, habits, and behaviors experienced as *sunnat* suggests a union of "Islam" and "the political" at the site of the body.[40] This is a union that cultural modernity otherwise eschews through the ideological separation of religion and politics.

Still, this does not explain why embodied ideology might reenter the political sphere as jihād specifically, since there is nothing more inherently bodily about jihād than about any of the other *sunnats*. Unlike many of the *sunnats,* however, jihād and hijarat both deal with the interpretation, regulation, and production of violence and were reinterpreted as tools of political accommodation and liberation across multiple Muslim societies as they developed modern political cultures. The question of why individual or community responses to oppression or political violence would assume either the discourse and practice of hijarat or of jihād remains unresolved. This indeterminacy makes the process of embodying Islamicate values and ideals a social problem, rather than a strictly religious one.

MOUNTAIN JOURNEYS AND THE UNEVEN TERRAIN BETWEEN MIGRATION AND STRUGGLE

The following are stories of how five people became muhājirs or mujāhids at different points in their lives. Of the three muhājirs whose stories I invoke here, Mahmood al-Khabar and Shireen Begum were senior residents of a refugee resettlement village. The third, Mohammad Ibrahim, was living in a labor colony. All three had come to AJK several decades earlier, and were reflecting back on how they had rebuilt their lives, and so their stories had a sense of completeness. The stories of the two mujāhids, Shafiq and Zahid, are incomplete, because the process of becoming a mujāhid was incomplete; in fact, each young man was at odds with his family about whether he was or could become a mujāhid. I selected these stories not because they are unique, but because they are in many ways ordinary, invoking paradigmatic themes that recur in the lives of many of the refugees I encountered.

Mahmood al-Khabar and Shireen Begum used the term hijarat to describe their experiences of becoming displaced. They did not, however, emphasize the doctrinal connections between hijarat and the protection of the Muslim community in the abstract. Rather, they focused on the protection, reconstruction, or defense of the family and its domestic life as a social site from which a just Muslim society is created. The hijarat they described was not an ordered, intentional migration, and their stories did not valorize their migration experiences. For men as well as women, the question of a muhājir's conscious intent at the time of his or her migration was subjugated to an overwhelming concern for his or her participation in the social work of reestablishing family life, a moral community, and a secure political space in the place of resettlement. In this sense, the domestic sphere was not relegated to the "private" or juxtaposed with the "public," outside world.

This emphasis was even more pronounced in the stories of people who came to AJK as refugees in 1965 or 1971 and had to negotiate with resettled muhājirs for recognition and inclusion. Territorial places have a very different status in Mohammad Ibrahim's story than in the narratives of Mahmood al-Khabar and other refugees of 1947, for whom place names were always specific, such as Hattian, Muzaffarabad, or Rawalpindi. In Mahmood Al-Khabar's and Shireen Begum's stories, for example, India and Pakistan and Azad Kashmir aren't places; they are ideas represented by institutions of power, such as the army or ration depots. In Mohammad Ibrahim's story, on the other hand, Azad Kashmir is a general place where, he imagined, one could live in freedom from the constraints of an occupying army. Going there for him was an explicit decision, not an accident of geography as it had been for so many people displaced before the borderlines were drawn. Yet Mohammad Ibrahim never referred to the concepts of dārul-harb or dārul-islām when he recounted leaving his home. Instead, like Shireen Begum, he spoke about creating a social place for himself through domestic and ritual labor. For him, as for other muhājirs, labor exchange and service to others reestablished and reproduced social bonds and opened a route to positions of authority and influence. Their concept of hijarat encompassed gendered social roles and acknowledged both men and women as political actors because of their place in domestic relations.

In contrast, the refugee youths I spoke with had difficulty claiming hijarat as a political activity that accorded them recognition as both refugees and men. Even those who intentionally crossed the border to escape political violence found it somehow not enough to pursue an education, support a wife, and raise children. It was instead by returning (or proclaiming the intention to return) to their home places as defenders of those left behind that they achieved recognition as good Muslims. This shift toward thinking about the protection of the family as an act of warfare as opposed to an act of migration is now very pronounced among the youth in refugee communities.

It is worth recalling here the words of Hajji Mohammad Rashid, an elder member of the village council of another refugee resettlement village, who told the young men of his village that "*hijarat* is a *sunnat-e-rasūl,* an honorable practice of the Prophet Mohammad (PBUH), [who said] 'He who steps even over the threshold to provide a moral life for his family, he is a *muhājir* and a defender of his people.'" Hajji Mohammad Rashid was *hafīz-e-qur'an,* which meant that he had memorized the Qur'an in its entirety and could recite it in full. He had completed the Hajj pilgrimage to Mecca, and he led Friday prayers at the village mosque; his opinions on religious matters commanded significant respect. However, they were no longer convinced by his counsel, he said. He still advised them that it was honorable and respectable to live the life of a muhājir. He still told them to "become educated, work hard, study Qur'an Sharif, honor your mother by marrying well, educate your children, especially your daughters." He told them that these were also ways to "defend human rights and to fulfill your obligations." However, he said sadly, every year more muhājir youths joined militant organizations and crossed the LoC in the name of jihād.

Many of them claimed to have joined the Kashmir Jihad because, in Shafiq's words, it is a "*farz* as a Muslim to protect the rights of the oppressed." Shafiq spoke always in very personal, even intimate terms, about the violation of houses, families, and bodies. He neither invoked scriptural references nor referred to religious leaders who had declared the armed movement in Kashmir as a jihād. Instead, he concluded that the struggle was a jihād, and one in which he had a duty to participate, based on his own knowledge of the conditions of violence under which people in border villages lived in the 1990s. For him, the threat that necessitated jihād was not the violation of the sovereign territory *(dār)* of Islam but the violation of the rights *(haqq)* of Kashmiri people and the bodies of Kashmiri women.

The final young man's story is about the indeterminacy of becoming a muhājir or a mujāhid. It was common for refugees to have been both muhājirs and mujāhids at different points over their lives. For most of the older refugees I met, their own conflicts about the better way to serve and protect had been resolved years before, and when they told me about those conflicts it was from the position of knowing the resolution. For Zahid, whether and how he would establish himself as a valued man in his community, as a muhājir or as a mujāhid, was not yet clear. Zahid told me two different versions of his life story. In one, he told me about becoming and living the life of a mujāhid; in the other, about becoming and living the life of a muhājir. Parts of at least one of Zahid's stories are untrue. The story I tell here is the story of his lie; it is the story of the indeterminacy of how to become a man as either a muhājir or as a mujāhid in the context of the ongoing-armed conflict.

The Uneven Terrain between Hijarat and War

Mahmood al-Khabar, was a founding resident and a respected elder on the village council of a refugee resettlement village in Muzaffarabad district. Some of the families in the resettlement village had abandoned their homes in what is now Indian-administered Kashmir in response to the brutality of the Pathan militiamen who invaded the Kashmir Province in October 1947. Others had stayed as the Pathans passed through only to flee later when the Princely State's Dogra Army, backed by Indian troops and modern warfare technologies, began pushing the Pathans and their supposed sympathizers out of the Baramullah and Uri districts. Still others had fled into the mountains during the aerial bombings of the subsequent Indo-Pak war (1947–1949). When the fighting stopped, they found themselves behind Pakistani army lines. Their villages—and in some cases their near and extended families—were on the other side of a new not-quite-international boundary. They had become refugees only a few miles from what had always been their homes.

The first time I met Mahmood al-Khabar was for a formal interview at his request; he wanted to interview me to evaluate whether or not I should be allowed to come and go within the village and to meet residents of the community. The decision was not his alone, but his word carried a lot of weight. It was important to him to know why I wanted to talk to refugees. It was also important to him to know that I would be a good guest and not behave in ways that would bring undue scrutiny to the village. When he was satisfied with the nature of my research and my integrity, he offered to tell me his own story.

Mahmood al-Khabar was a boy when he and his parents were displaced. He began by remembering his life in his natal village and then explained how he and his parents had left in 1947:

> By the time the Pathans arrived in Uri, there had already been a lot of trouble and many people had left their homes, but we didn't know that until later when we met people camping here. We just knew that the Pathans were there and the market was closed and shuttered. One of the residents of our village was from a Pathan family and he spoke to them in Pashto and for this reason we were spared and gave only some food as a gift. But then people started coming from Baramullah and the villages nearby with stories about the cruelties of the Pathans. No man or woman was prepared for the calamity that had befallen them. Women had leapt up from cooking and left, and didn't know where their children were. Men had left the field and didn't know where their wives were. There was confusion every way. My parents helped some people, and we didn't know what to think was happening, but we weren't worried because this person in our village knew their language. Then the word came that the Indian army was coming and everyone thought things would be alright again. But when the army came to our village, they were searching the houses and threatening the men, saying, "you have helped the invaders." People were leaving by the road and into the hills. My parents took me and we were with a small group of people from our village. On the way, we passed children sitting crying and lost—that is what is was like, women alone without their husbands or brothers, mothers grabbed up one child and left the other—people had to leave before everyone had been gathered up and found. People ran in different directions and only afterwards they tried to find each other.

His description of the chaos of departure was similar to the remembrances of many people who had been displaced in 1947. Indeed, a common trope of these narratives was some shameful act that had been a part of leaving. In the stories of men, it was often that they had left without even looking for mothers or sisters or wives. In the stories of women, it was that a child had been left behind or unburied in the mountains. Things were also unspoken or only hinted at in these stories. Both men and women recounted seeing someone put a child down on the side of the trail and turn to walk away. They admitted passing by without taking up the child, but only one woman said that she herself had abandoned a baby; she had been alone with three young children and could only carry two of them. These stories were cloaked in shame not just for the individual's actions past but also for the complete breakdown of basic rules of kinship and sociality.

Mahmood al-Khabar's account of his family's departure emphasized that leaving home had been unexpected and unintentional. As he continued, he told me about how the refugee village had been settled without express intent:

> We stopped when we arrived at [the town of] Hattian. A lot of people were camped there. We stopped because we wanted to go back as soon as it was safe. Then the airplanes came and dropped bombs and more people came and passed us and went on to Muzaffarabad, but we stayed because we wanted to go back [to our village]. . . . When the bombing stopped, some people tried to go back, but it was not possible. We started staying on some open land and the women and young children stayed together in the houses [that had been abandoned by previous Sikh landowners]. . . . Finally, we made a village where each woman felt safe in her own house at night. The people on that land planted some corn and some boys went to Rawalpindi for work.

He talked about planting crops and going to the city to earn cash to supplement what the refugees could produce. This, he said, was how he "became a *muhājir.*"

His goal had been to return to his family's home village when the war ended. Although return had not been possible, he still held out hope. The idea of return in his story was specific; it would be a return to the village, the house, the fields that he remembered from his childhood and that he would have inherited from his father:

> I still remember that house where I lived as a child, and I have always told my children that we will return as soon as it is safe for us, which means when Kashmir is free from occupation. It is my right to return to that land and to give those walnut trees planted by my forefathers to my children.

In this matter, too, his thinking was similar to many of the residents of these resettled refugee villages; he talked about his claims to that original land as enduring and unchanged by the labors of time. I asked him whether he thought that his house had been empty all these years, the walnut trees untended, and whether the new residents didn't have some claim on that land. He shrugged and asked me whether I thought that the village where we sat had been built on unsowed land. "When Kashmir is liberated," he said, "the owners of the house will come back, and we too will have to leave this temporary home."

Shireen Begum, was a refugee resident of the same village and distantly related to Mahmood al-Khabar by marriage. She did not share his standing in the village council, but she also was one of the village founders and kin to many of its residents and thus one of the holders of its stories. I met Shireen Begum on many occasions, but it was only when she was visiting as a guest in the Rawalpindi home of her married daughter that she had time to converse with me at length.

Like Mahmood al-Khabar, she often spoke of her natal village to her children and grandchildren, sometimes nostalgically. But when the topic turned to how she had arranged marriages or the suitability of a match for one of her daughters or granddaughters, the discussion required detailed consideration of where the proposed groom's family lived and how the bride's visitations and routes of travel would be affected by returning to the groom's home village when the Kashmir conflict ended. If the boy was from a muhājir family, the deliberations involved considering who would return and what the share of inheritance would be for the sons and daughters in both the resettlement and natal villages. When she had arranged the marriages of her sons and grandsons, she had negotiated similar concerns expressed by the proposed bride's family.

When men spoke about settling the refugee villages, they often used a shorthand similar to Mahmood al-Khabar's statement about the end of his life in a refugee camp: "Finally, we made a village where each woman felt safe in her own house at night. The people on that land planted some corn and some boys went to Rawalpindi for work." I found that women remembered more detail about the work of making a village, and this figured prominently in Shireen Begum's account of her first years in Azad Kashmir:

> I cannot say that there was any time we decided not to go back. For the first months we were waiting and discussing daily. I was an [unmarried] girl then and I was not asked my opinion. But I remember the other women were not in favor of going back until there was some announcement that it was safe while some of the men were in favor of going back as soon as the bombing stopped. We cooked together with rations from the depot at the camp, but sometimes there was nothing available. The people in town helped with this and that and took a lot of people into their own homes, but when the rations came we were supposed to use those rations. . . . When we could not go back right away we went to stay in the houses of the landowners who had left. We used only what we needed in that house because we knew they would be coming back to reclaim it, but sometimes we found some pinch of salt or stores of butter, and then some person would begin crying, remembering the preserves

she had put up and wondering if they would be there when we were able to go back. . . . The women all stayed in the house at night, but sometimes there was news that the Indian army was coming or the owners of the house, and then the cry would go up "the Sikhs are coming" and people collected their children and preparations were made to leave again. I do not remember that a decision was ever made not to go back, we all tell our children even now in old age that "Kashmir is heaven and that is where I will return when I die." But after one winter some women began to plant a garden and then all around that communal household, there were small plots.

In many women's experiences, living in a refugee camp and the first squatter settlements were experiences of relative autonomy and independence. In their natal or affinal homes, they were members of extended families, but the conditions of displacement had divided and dispersed families and households. Some older women discretely indicated that as young women they had enjoyed establishing their own domestic spaces, separate from the oversight of in-laws. Still, the overwhelming emotion that women recalled was the isolation, loneliness, and insecurity of being separated from people who had enduring social obligations to them. The communal cooking fires and kitchens in refugee camps and squatter settlements that later grew into resettlement villages were sites of arguments and competition for rations and space. But they were also where women forged enduring relationships with other women who were not relatives.

Women nurtured these relationships by continuing exchanges of mundane and ritual labor. Paradoxically, refugee men's searches for the wage labor that would make them good marriage prospects often took them far away from their resettlement communities and their families:

> The women did the work of keeping the children close to their parents and cooking the food for people to eat and then of making plots for each family. Women stay in the village and keep the house. Men, you never know, they go for labor or some government job in the city, and they come back for planting and harvest; they come back because the women have kept the house and children together in the village. They come back because the women have a *farz* to visit with others, and to share their work, and to keep the ties of relationship strong. Women, we are the ones here to celebrate the happinesses and mourn the tragedies of our family and neighbors.

Shireen Begum's emphasis on the importance of celebrating and mourning was a common feature of muhājir women's accounts of the process of establishing and maintaining resettlement communities, either villages or urban neighborhoods *(mohallah)*. As she explained, women used their networks of women-friends *(saheliyoñ)* to arrange marriages for their children, making family *(ristadār)* of friends.

Mohammad Ibrahim was a refugee from a village close to the LoC near Handwara town in Kupwara district. He had migrated to AJK as an unmarried youth several months before the war of 1965. When I met Mohammad Ibrahim, he was living in the same *kacchī ābādī* outside Islamabad where Nasir Waseem and Shafiq lived. He comported himself as a pious man but said that he had not particularly been so in his youth. Religious community became important to him first as a place where he could establish new social relationships with other people:

> When I first came to Azad Kashmir, I had nothing and nowhere to go. A family took me in and I used to do labor for wages during the planting and harvest season. But when you are standing on the labor market, one day you are bought by one person, and the next day by another. I started going to the mosque and there did service for the mosque committee, cleaning and organizing. When there was some wedding or funeral, I went to that household and contributed labor by carrying wood or cooking the food. After a few years, someone [from the mosque committee] noticed that I was a young man and was not married. He began looking for a girl for me, and he knew a family who was from a village near mine, who had come here [to AJK] in 1947. They accepted me to marry their daughter and put some of their land in her name as her dowry and the people whose happiness and sadness, weddings and funerals, I had celebrated, well, they came and built a small house on that land. That land was not enough to support my family, so I came to work in the city and I found some labor job with other refugees who work here, but we harvest the corn every year, and during Ramadan and on 'Eid, we offer food to our neighbors and guests.

In Mohammad Ibrahim's account, the income from wage labor supported him as a young man and his family after marriage, but it did not help him re-create a valued social identity. He established himself within Azad Kashmir's networks of social exchange by doing volunteer work for the mosque and that eventually led to an arranged marriage. Maintaining those exchanges, through the collective and reciprocal work of harvesting crops and serving food on ritual occasions, was the work through which he became a good Muslim man.

His desire to migrate, as he told it as an older man, was something of a folly of youth. It was an emotional decision, inspired by humiliation and insults to his honor, in part, but also based in a desire for greater opportunities:

> The Indian army was building bunkers in the hills. They would come to our village and take the men and boys out of the fields and from the market.

There was nowhere to escape from them, because there was a big army camp near our village and always there was work to do and always they were coming to the village to make us do this work or that work. When they took us into the hills, we had to work on the roads and bunkers closest to the Line of Control. The Pakistani soldiers shot at us sometimes, and the Indian army soldiers stayed back, and made us carry the loads in the open. Some boys who refused to do their work were beaten and killed. Some boys were arrested and questioned if they were Pakistan supporters. We had no choice but to do their work. I was a young man then and very emotional. I would discuss with my friends about how we were making it possible for the army to kill Kashmiris and also Pakistani soldiers. One day one boy would stand up and say, "I will refuse to do their bidding" and the rest would hold him back and say, "no no, think of your mother and how she would weep if you were beaten," or "think of your young brother who is still in school, if you refuse they will take double labor from that child." So in this way we all proclaimed the heat in our hearts, but kept each other cool when the guns were pointed at us.... One day though, I was working with some older boys. They already had a plan to do *hijarat* and one of the boys knew a man who knew all the crossing routes over the mountain and how to slide past the Indian and Pakistani army posts. Another boy had family in a village across the river. He said, "I am going to Azad Kashmir to start a new life. I am not going to do this business for the Indian army any longer." One evening, after finishing our labor job, instead of walking down towards the village, we went towards Azad Kashmir.

At the end of his story, Mohammad Ibrahim relinquished the opportunity of claiming religious value in his intention *(niyat)* to migrate. He suggested that his migration did not have an inherent religious value because it had prevented him from fulfilling another important obligation—taking care of his mothers and sisters. Instead, he suggested that, by being a good father, he had been given the opportunity to subjugate his own desires in deference to those who depended on him:

> I am an old man now. I have been blessed with these beautiful daughters because God is kind and forgiving, I have faith that he will bless them with many sons. I did not have sons, but I was given the opportunity to earn blessings by caring for daughters. But they never met their grandmother, and I never saw my mother or my sisters again.

He claimed in retrospect that he had made a hijarat of what had actually been an abandonment of his family as a young man. He had accomplished this by fulfilling his role as a father and providing for his daughters—one of whom, he told me with pride, was completing her metric degree[41] and the other of whom was already well married to a government employee with a secure salary.

His final words were tinged with the regret of a man looking back on his life and concluding that he had made the best of his path but that perhaps his choice of paths had not been the wisest or most considered of decisions:

> You asked me what I intended when I left? Well, I can only say that I was young and I wanted to be a man. I thought that I would go back when the armies were gone, having made something of myself.

The Uneven Terrain between Refuge and Jihād

It was not a sanguine period of Shafiq's life when I met him, and he was grieving and angry. His elder brother had been killed in their village near the LoC by artillery fire several months earlier. His family had left the village, and he was living in a *kacchī ābādī* (labor colony). Our meeting had been arranged by other Kashmiri refugees in the colony who had suggested that I meet him because he could tell me what it was like to live in a village within the sights of Indian guns.

When I arrived for the interview, it was clear that Shafiq did not want to talk to me, which was a problem for both of us. It was a problem for him for practical reasons: his community had decided he was going to talk to me. The *mullah* of the *ābādī's* mosque was present, in addition to Shafiq's cousins and one of his uncles, who repeatedly ordered him to "tell her your story." These elders had legitimate authority to make decisions on his behalf; he was unmarried and therefore a "boy," although he was twenty-two and worked to help support his family. His reluctance was a problem for me both ethically and practically. The concept of "consent" in ethnographic fieldwork is foundational, and "informed consent" is a legal requirement of research institutions. Yet, even though researchers are required to establish the consent of individuals, in many societies consent is negotiated collectively. While I had the impression that Shafiq would not have met me if he could have avoided it, I knew that if I did not conduct the interview, I would be insulting the *mullah* and Shafiq's uncle by not recognizing their authority in the community and the household.

I decided that my best course of action was to be an inept interviewer; I would create a situation where Shafiq would not need to answer any questions he did not want to answer, and I would let the interview fizzle, drink my tea, and publicly thank Shafiq's uncle for inviting me into his home. At the prodding of his audience, Shafiq made a few perfunctory statements about the cruelty of the Indian Army snipers who shoot at the cattle in the fields because "Kashmiri cows must not be holy like Indian cows." After a while, he stopped looking at his uncle and asked me, "Do you want to hear about the bombed-out houses and the firing-line martyrs, or are you willing to hear about the unspeakable things?" I told him that I was willing to hear whatever he wanted to say. He instructed me to get out my tape recorder.

As he spoke, it was clear that he was addressing two audiences. One audience consisted of me and of the readers of the book I would write. The other was the audience before him. Shafiq and his parents were in a dispute over his membership in a militant organization *(tanzīm);* his father had removed him from a *tanzīm's* training camp after convincing the leader that Shafiq was not a legitimate candidate for "walking in the path of a *mujāhid*." The interview gave him a forum to present his case, uninterrupted, to people who might be able to influence his father. He was ostensibly talking to me, but he was also arguing his case to the *mullah,* to his uncles, and to his cousins and rebuking them for preventing him from fulfilling what he saw as his duty.

Shafiq's father had been displaced during the 1965 Indo-Pak war. His mother came to Azad Kashmir from a village in Indian Kashmir's Handwara district to marry his father in 1973. As a child, he had heard stories of his parents' natal villages and of the relatives on the other side of the LoC. His father had spoken of how they would return there when his village was no longer "occupied." Shafiq recalled that he first learned about the armed conflict in Indian Jammu and Kashmir from refugees who stayed in their village after crossing into Azad Kashmir. His mother, he said, had emphasized that the refugees were neither guests nor supplicants—they had the right to demand shelter and food as they passed through:

> We always fed them and at first we kept some [refugee] people in our home, but later the [Pakistan] army came and took them to the camp in Hattian. My mother said to us that one accrues blessings for feeding a guest or sheltering a traveler who asks for refuge *[panah],* but she said, "You receive no blessings for offering food to these *muhājirīn* [refugees]. It is your *farz* [duty] to feed them and it is their *haqq* [right] to eat this corn."

Shafiq had been born in AJK and had never been to either of his parents' natal villages, but he spoke about the people who lived there in intimate terms.

As youths, he and his brothers had listened to refugees tell the villagers why they had left their homes and recount tales of violent persecution by (Indian) state military and paramilitary forces:

> Once I became aware of these [practices of torture and rape by security forces in Indian Kashmir], it was not possible for me to sit at home with my mother and my sister. My older brother became a *mujāhid* first. *Muhājirīn* [refugees] and *mujāhidīn* [warriors] passed though our village often [in 1990 and 1991] and they told us about what happened to them and why they left their homes.

He never spoke of the occupation of Muslim sovereign territory *(dār)*. Instead, he talked about the violation of "the rights of Kashmiris." At other times he referenced specific kinds of violence—sexual torture of men or the rape of women or the destruction of houses or schools:

> My mother always asked [the refugees who passed through the village] for news of her family, but we did not get specific news. Still, we never forgot those stories that they told us, about how the Indian soldiers came to their houses and that the women were unsafe. About what they did to any person if they were looking for some *mujāhid*—it didn't matter if they find his son or his brother or his cousin, even his old father. They would take that person and torture him too. They told us all those things and more that I can't say to you [a woman] although you say you study Kashmir so you should already know [about rape and sexual torture].

Shafiq never said that he had doubted their stories, but he referred to his brother's return to the village after going to Indian Kashmir as a turning point, after which he knew that all the accounts had been true:

> The first time [my brother] came back to our village [after completing his first mission in Kashmir], he told me that all those accounts [of torture and rape] that we had heard were true. And he said that he could not tell our mother about the village where her family still lives because so many houses have been burned and so many people had died that she should not know these things.

By 1994, when his brother returned from his first "mission," international organizations had documented widespread human rights violations in Indian Kashmir, and Pakistani state television carried nightly news coverage of the conflict in Occupied Kashmir. For Shafiq, however, the indisputable source of information was his own brother's testimony.

Shafiq recalled that when his brother had joined a militant organization he had made two arguments. The first was an intimate argument: the women in Occupied Kashmir were like sisters, and he had a duty to care for them and protect them just as for his own sister. The second was an argument of principle: he had a duty to defend the "rights" of Kashmiris.

> My brother joined a *tanzīm* [militant organization] in 1993. My parents did not want him to join, but he was able to convince them because he said, "I am unmarried and you have two more sons who are home with you and who will support you. My sister is not yet ready for marriage and, as God is willing, we are already able to give her rightful dowry. There is no debt which I have not paid and no one can complain that I am unfaithful. It is my *farz* to protect my sisters and defend the rights *[haqūq]* of Kashmiris." My parents relented.

In Shafiq's recollection, his brother's arguments had prevailed, and his parents had consented to his joining a *tanzīm* and becoming a mujāhid. In Shafiq's own argument with his parents, he was making a similar, but unsuccessful, case about his *farz*.

In this argument, there was little appeal to doctrinal positions on jihād or reference to religious authorities. As he recalled, the leaders of militant organizations had a presence only after his brother had already joined a militant group:

> After taking training, [my brother] left to cross the LoC, and later the *tanzīm* leaders came to our village and congratulated my parents. My mother was crying, but everyone said to her, "Don't cry, he is walking the path of the *mujāhid* now, and if God is willing, he will return to you when Kashmir has been liberated from occupation and when it is safe for all of us to return to our rightful homes." The second time he went [on a mission], he did not come back. Only some representatives came [on behalf of the *tanzīm*] and some of his brothers [other *mujāhidīn*] to say that he has been martyred. My mother began to weep but they told her not to weep. But after they left, both my mother and father wept. After they left, the women of our village came and sat with my mother and when she was tired and could not raise her voice, some other women began to wail. My father did not have a body to bury, but the other men came and did the funeral prayer with him.

Shafiq lingered on his parents' mourning for his brother. It's an important point, one that appears in many accounts of how families receive the news of a loved one's becoming a *shahīd* (martyr). Jihadist ideologues teach that it is a matter of celebration when a mujāhid becomes a *shahīd* and that the traditional funeral prayers, in which the living appeal to God for forgiveness and entrance into heaven on behalf of the dead, are unnecessary because, for those who walk the path of the mujāhid, a special prayer is made before they go to "the battlefield." Shafiq's account of his mother's grief and his father's recitation of the funeral prayers illustrated that these teachings had not shaped the affective life of his family.

Shafiq referred repeatedly to the suffering of the victims of oppression and concluded that, like his brother, he had a personal obligation to protect and defend his "sisters." Both he and his parents agreed that he had a duty to serve his family. But they had very different ideas about how that duty should be fulfilled:

> It is a *farz* as a Muslim that you should protect the rights *[haqūq]* of the oppressed. So it is also my *farz* as a Muslim to go for this *jihād,* and I joined a *tanzīm* and began my training. But it is not allowed for me to walk on the path of the *mujāhid,* [because] my other brother was killed [in 1998] in LoC firing, my sister is married and lives in the house of her mother-in-law, and we cannot live in our village any more [because of heavy artillery firing]. So now it is my *farz* to support my parents and so I am working here doing [wage] labor. My father went to the training camp and said to the *amir* [the in-charge of the training camp], "This son is my only descendant. It is forbidden for him to fight *jihād.* He will marry and have children, may God will it."

His father's argument was not based on whether the conflict in Kashmir did or did not have the status of a jihād. Instead, his father argued that Shafiq had a greater duty to fulfill—not just to ensure that his parents would be supported in their old age, but to have children himself and ensure the continuation of the family. In making this argument, Shafiq's father was drawing on the understanding that jihād, as a *farzul-kafāya* offers individuals alternative ways of fulfilling their religious obligations. Shafiq, on the other hand, said that the *jihād-e-kashmīr* was a duty on him as an individual.

A River Crossing: Muhājir or Mujāhid?

I met Zahid on a hot afternoon in August. I had spent some time in the village where his wife lived, and I had met with other villagers and their relatives who resided in the cities of the northern Punjab. Several people told me of a young man I should talk to, to learn about the situation in Occupied Kashmir from a recent migrant. I was particularly interested in meeting Zahid because he was a relative newcomer in a muhājir resettlement village that was primarily inhabited by families displaced in 1947 and 1948 and because he lived in the refugee resettlement village rather than in one of the district's refugee camps.

Like many men from refugee villages who earned a living in one of Pakistan's cities, he "lived" in the village but for most of the year did not reside there. For most of the year, he worked in Karachi, where he shared rooms with other laborers. During our first meeting, Zahid and I sat cross-legged with our hosts on a carpet in the middle of the community room of the family home where I often stayed. Before he arrived, the women told me that Zahid was newly married and that his wife was expecting their first child. His wife was related by marriage to my hostess's niece, so he qualified as kin. After bringing tea and fruits, the women of the family settled around us, staying to listen to Zahid and to observe the interview. Zahid sat quietly while my host formally introduced him, telling me that he was called Sher Khan (tiger chief) because he had proven himself at an early age to be both brave and strong.[42] In 1991 he had left his home village alone—a boy of only 14 years—and crossed the mined forest and the swift Jhelum river, eluding Indian patrols to reach the village of Chakothi in Azad Kashmir. The observers in the room asked him to tell me about why he had left his village.

Zahid began telling his own his story, however, by announcing that he was a mujāhid, not a muhājir. He fixed his eyes firmly on mine and asked if I was interested in speaking with him, since I had come to interview a refugee instead. I told him that I was, and he nodded and instructed me to keep my tape recorder on. Then he leaned back against a bolster and began to speak.

Zahid told me that he had decided to leave his home village when he was preparing for his metric-level graduation exams. The armed struggle against the Indian state had begun in the valley of Kashmir a few months before. The Indian BSF (Border Security Force) and the RR (Rashitrya Rifles) were building bunkers in the hills and commandeering the labor of the men and children of his village. Those who refused were either beaten into compliance or arrested on suspicion of supporting the armed struggle. Therefore, refusal was not an option. Zahid described his growing awareness that neutrality in the independence movement would not be an option for him. The day he took his last exams he did not go home. He waited until dark and then headed into the forest, using the route he knew through the mined hills; he swam the river and walked into the AJK town of Chakothi in search of his maternal uncle.

After several days at his uncle's home, his relatives took him to the local police station to report his presence. The police detained him for several days while the security services tried to determine whether he was an Indian spy. His uncle secured his release by emphasizing that he was a mere child and by assuming full responsibility for him. He brought Zahid to a nearby refugee camp where he was registered as a refugee, but he lived with his uncle for two years and went to the refugee camp only to collect his allowance.

Zahid told me that he moved to the refugee camp when he was 16. There, he joined a *jihādī tanzīm* (jihad organization) and began doing administrative work for it. He soon became a recruitment officer and began to travel to cities in Pakistan that have large Kashmiri populations—Rawalpindi, Lahore, and Karachi—providing information about the persecution of Kashmiri Muslims, recounting human rights abuses and the rape of Muslim women on the Indian side of the LoC, and enlisting recruits.

In 1997, his uncle arranged a marriage for him to the daughter of a relative. The girl's parents refused to give their daughter in marriage until they had secured assurances from his uncle that Zahid would not take active duty as a mujāhid fighting in the Kashmir Valley; they did not want their young daughter to become a widow, even the widow of a martyr. In the rest of his story, Zahid expressed dedication to the liberation of Kashmir, his struggle to fulfill his responsibilities as a mujāhid, and his sadness and frustration at a situation that he presented as a moral paradox: his simultaneous duty to return to the valley of Kashmir as a fully adult man and to fight to protect his mother and sisters from victimization at the hands of the Indian army and his inability as a mujāhid to transgress the code of moral rectitude that required that he honor the promise his uncle had made on his behalf when he married.

It was quite late when Zahid finished telling his story. We decided to continue talking several days later so that I could ask him some questions. That evening one of the young men of the family took me aside and shared a confidence he asked me to keep secret so that Zahid, who had been a guest in his home, would not be embarrassed: Zahid had lied. This confidant said that while he could not say for sure that Zahid had never registered his name in the membership books of a *jihādī tanzīm,* he knew for certain that he had not done the work he had claimed. He claimed that Zahid had gone to Lahore to become an apprentice electrician and that he now worked as a master electrician for a construction firm. Moreover, he had often expressed his desire to marry and raise a family to his friends.

I found myself faced with methodological, theoretical, and ethical dilemmas. I had conducted an interview whose epistemological status was doubtful: Was the narrative a life history or a personal fantasy? I had had no reason to doubt Zahid's story during the interview. The story itself had been descriptive, and the details about his service with the militant organization complemented what I already knew about how such organizations operated. More important was the social and public context of the interview.

The people I knew in this refugee village had wanted me to meet Zahid; they had set up the meeting and introduced us. Everyone in the room—his friends and marital kin—would have known that he was lying. Yet they had listened, nodding approval and making small sounds of sympathy. I considered the possibility that he had not lied. Perhaps my host had become uncomfortable with how openly Zahid had talked about the *tanzīm* of which he claimed to be a member and that was indisputably active in the district. Something had made my host anxious enough that he was willing to transgress the rules of hospitality to accuse his guest of lying. I decided that I had to discount the interview; I would not be able to pursue the veracity of the story without revealing what my host had told me—something that would in turn reveal his breach of hospitality or his own lie. But for the same reason, I decided not to cancel my follow-up interview with Zahid.

Much to my surprise, at the second interview Zahid confessed his lie. I was the hostess at my residence in Muzaffarabad, and I had set out tea and biscuits. Zahid began recounting his life history in the same way that he had at our first meeting. He told me about crossing the LoC and the two years at his uncle's home. Then he stopped and said that he did not know which story he should tell me. For a while he looked unspeaking at my open notebook, at the tape recorder, and at the cup of tea in his hand. Then, he said that since I had received him as a guest, he was obligated to tell me the simple truth.

He said that he had moved from his uncle's house to the refugee camp because he couldn't bear to look across the river at his natal village. At times he could see his mother from a distance, and he felt a tremendous urge to return to her, but he could not go back without putting his family in tremendous danger. He had wanted to become an engineer, so he stayed in the refugee camp only a short time before he left for Lahore to pursue an education. However, his Indian diploma was not acceptable for admission to Pakistani colleges, and he became an apprentice electrician. When he began earning enough money to support a family, his uncle selected a girl for him. The girl's family had ensured that she would stay in the village and that the couple's children would have property by giving her dowry of agricultural land. Zahid said that he had made it clear that when Kashmir achieved liberation, he would return to his mother's home and bring her daughter-in-law with him; his wife's family had agreed because they too intended to return to their ancestral homes after the liberation. For now, he said, he worked as an electrician in Karachi and earned a good wage that supplemented the income from his wife's land.

Every ethnographic field researcher occasionally misses an opportunity to pursue an important issue. This was one of my missed opportunities. I did not ask Zahid why he had lied, and I never attempted to confirm either of his stories. The simplest reason for this is the least satisfactory: I did not trust my interlocutor. I had already decided that I would not use Zahid's life history or any of the information from his interviews. However, I recorded other, more complex concerns and speculations in my field notes.

I was puzzled by the paradox of the two stories, the "lie" and the "confession"; by his second account, he had lied when he told me his life story in public, before an audience that would have known he was lying, and then later told the truth in private, to an audience that could only acknowledge that lie once he had confessed. His lie would not have convinced kin and neighbors in a small village that he was a mujāhid, and he had not lied because he wanted me to believe that he was a mujāhid. I was also not sure that his second story was more "truthful" than his first had been. Perhaps my hosts in the refugee village had wanted me to meet a mujāhid; several of the elders, including Hajji Mohammad Rashid, had talked about their concern for the path the young men were taking. Had they set up the interview because they didn't know whether I would be willing to meet one of the militant youths to whom they had referred? Going over my recordings of the interview, I am still surprised by the details Zahid gave about the militant organization of which he claimed to be a member. Some of those details I now know were not common knowledge.

At the time, I was also worried. Zahid's story, in both its versions, hinted at the suspicion directed at Kashmiri refugees in the geopolitical context of the dispute in the Kashmir region, especially since the beginning of the armed insurgency in Indian Jammu and Kashmir. And Kashmiri mujāhids are caught between the demands of multiple moral and political prescriptions, between an imperative to be perfectly open and public about their activities and pressure to operate secretly. Zahid's reasons for changing his story might have had to do with a concern for truths deeper than "the simple truth." In his home village, Zahid had found that any refusal to aid the Indian army troops made him an object of suspicion, a possible militant sympathizer. On the Pakistan side of the LoC, he had to prove himself not an Indian spy. He could not return to his natal village without being suspected of being a member of a militant organization, and he could not leave AJK without joining one. He might have been encouraged to reconsider his assessment of what was secret information for an audience that included a foreign researcher. If he had misassessed the boundaries of divulging information and dissimulation, then who had reimposed these boundaries? The possible answer to that question had very different implications for Zahid and for the people who had arranged our meeting. There were several obvious possibilities: members of the armed militant organization for which he worked; members of state security agencies; and members of the refugee community who had, according to Zahid's first telling, pressured him to abandon his aspirations of participating in the armed struggle for the liberation of his homeland. If Zahid had changed his account under some kind of external pressure, I felt that I needed to act as if I believed his second account.

In the end, I find Zahid's story—not his life history, but the story of his lie—striking because it reproduces the tension of a community struggling to alternately preserve and transform the dominant values of its political culture. It reveals the tremendous difficulty that young refugee men experience in claiming hijarat to understand and explain their relationship with political violence—a claim that makes them both refugees and valued political subjects. Older muhājir men tell stories of reestablishing domestic life after accidental displacement, but young men who actively decide to cross the border from a domain of insecurity and political violence find that their desire to pursue education, adopt a profession, find a wife, and raise children does not receive the social approbation that it did in the past. It is primarily in returning to their home places as armed defenders, or professing an intention to return, that they achieve recognition as moral political subjects. For a young man living among resettled refugees to recount that he could have been a great warrior, but was impeded by restrictions his own kin had tricked him into accepting, emphasizes that such debates occur not just in refugee camps but are moving into settled communities—communities that are themselves becoming sites of support and recruiting grounds for jihadist organizations.

PART TWO

The Historical Emergence of Kashmiri Refugees as Political Subjects

THREE

Forging Political Identities, 1947–1988

THE SOUTH ASIAN REFUGEE REGIME AND REFUGEE
RESETTLEMENT VILLAGES

IN THE YEARS IMMEDIATELY FOLLOWING WORLD WAR II, forced displacement was a global phenomenon. In addition to the people displaced across Europe, there were tens of millions of displaced people in East Asia and millions more in the Middle East and North Africa. In South Asia, approximately 10 million people were accommodated in refugee camps during the Partition of colonial India. Yet in 1951, Nehemiah Robinson, the Israeli delegate to the Geneva Conference of Plenipotentiaries, which drafted the final version of the Convention Relating to the Status of Refugees, observed, "For the purposes of the Convention, there were practically no refugees in the world other than those coming from Europe."[1] The contemporaneous conclusion that Partition's forcibly displaced people were not refugees because they suffered no loss of nationality[2] tautologically reproduced a deliberate but contested exclusion from the regime of refugee recognition that was just coming into being. The provisions for refugee recognition established in the 1951 Refugee Convention did not reflect a natural differentiation between displaced people; rather, the legal provisions that determined who received recognition as a refugee at the end of WWII and the beginning of the era of global decolonization reveal the political and cultural struggles involved in the creation of the "international community" and the United Nations. In the international body's formative years, it was unclear what the international community would actually be, how the agencies of the United Nations (UN) would work and whom they would serve.[3] And questions of what, how, and for whom were key points of debate in defining the people—refugees— who would be objects of special care for the international community.

The representatives from various countries who drafted the Refugee Convention aspired to a definition of "refugee" that would be beyond the

politics of states, but the official minutes of the drafting committee meetings show that many of the representatives who participated in writing the
definition thought that it did not represent the universal ideals enshrined
in the UN charter. Some delegates argued that the Convention should not
apply to Greek, Arab, Kashmiri, or Indian refugees and that China's refugees
need not be considered since China had not sent a delegate to the drafting
conventions.[4] Both India and Pakistan objected to focusing on European
displacement as the foundation of a new regime of international care for
refugees. Their delegates participated in the early meetings of the UN committee charged with drafting the Refugee Convention and establishing the
UN High Commission for Refugees (UNHCR). They argued repeatedly for
a definition of refugee that would recognize the millions of displaced people
in South Asia.[5] They also protested contributing funds to refugee relief projects in Europe when the new international community was unwilling to
contribute to the cost of administering aid to the millions of refugees in
camps in the subcontinent; the Government of India's unsuccessful bid for
refugee aid from European governments was a part of its decision to stop
contributing to the International Refugees Organization (IRO) in 1947.[6]

Ultimately, neither India nor Pakistan participated in the July 1951
Conference of Plenipotentiaries, which drafted the final definition for
the Refugee Convention, and neither India nor Pakistan ever ratified the
Refugee Convention (which went into effect in 1954) or the 1967 Protocol
Relating to the Status of Refugees.[7] By 1951, they had developed bilateral
treaties and parallel legal instruments that regularized relief administration
and resettlement programs in South Asia. These laws and practices were in
turn shaped by transnational representations that shaped the emergence of
refugee as a distinct governmental and social category in postcolonial South
Asia. In this South Asian refugee regime, Partition's refugees were defined in
part by the political violence of state formation and in part by their disrupted
(and later reestablished) proprietary relationship with immovable property
in each of the new states.

Displaced people from the Princely State of Jammu and Kashmir had
a distinctive place in this symbolic system and, indeed, in the new classification system of postcolonial nationhood. Between 1947 and 1948, the
"Kashmiri refugee" emerged as a distinct political subject within the South
Asian refugee regime through public charitable activity and administrative
and bureaucratic practices. After 1949, international treaties, bilateral legal
provisions, and provincial legislation excluded *muhājir-e-jammū-o-kashmīr*

(Jammu and Kashmir refugees) from both India's and Pakistan's national refugee resettlement projects. The presumption in the first international agreements was that these refugees would not become nationalized citizens of the Pakistani and Indian nation-states; rather they would reclaim their properties and homes in the former Princely State and participate in the mandated plebiscite as Kashmiri citizen-subjects. This referendum was neither carried out nor abdicated, however, and over time Kashmiri refugees demanded temporary land allotments while maintaining that they would return to their hereditary holdings when it was safe to do so. These places are defined by claims on properties, lands, and houses that are recognized in the legal and political systems of the current administrator states. When the semi-autonomous successor states constitutionally framed their political constituencies, the state's citizen-subject reflected the prior status of hereditary state subject, as guaranteed by the recognition and confirmation of the Jammu and Kashmir refugee.

HUMANITARIAN INTERNATIONALISM AND THE REFUGEE REGIMES IN THE POST-WAR ERA

In contemporary social and political analysis, humanitarianism and refugee relief have become inextricably connected domains of practice and theory. That link has been so successfully forged that the concept of the international refugee regime is almost interchangeable with that of the international humanitarian regime.[8] However, this was not always so. Humanitarian law (which seeks to regulate the practice of warfare) and refugee law constitute two separate international legal domains; each are distinct from "humanitarianism," as a cosmopolitan ideal of care for strangers to whom one does not owe direct social or political obligations.[9] Yet, diverse postwar humanitarian relief projects contributed to creating recognized refugee populations, because humanitarianism not only "functioned as an alternative welfare state for stateless people; it also fashioned modern political asylum practices by sorting 'true' from 'false' refugees."[10] Humanitarian workers took part in the cultural, political, and ideological struggles that produced the legal mechanisms, institutional practices, and categorical systems developed to administer aid to dislocated people. In part, they did the cultural work of regularizing and naturalizing symbolic systems—by, for example, distinguishing the suffering of refugees from that of other poor and displaced people impacted by the vicissitudes of war economies. In selectively recognizing suffering and responding to particular kinds of need, relief projects helped distinguish population categories and thus also to shape political practice and refugee law.[11]

Although it has become a commonplace observation that the international community did not become involved in the refugee crisis in South Asia during the Partition because Partition-era displaced peoples were not deprived of their nationality (and were therefore not refugees), there are several problems with accepting this assertion. The first is empirical: international humanitarian organizations and voluntary societies from around the world were, in fact, both indirectly and directly involved in the vast project of aid distribution and administration in South Asia. The political leaders and state civil servants who framed the administrative practices and legal provisions for refugee administration understood the expectations, concerns, and practices of the international humanitarian community and audience. Indeed, appealing to the "market of international compassion"[12] was a strategy of the newly minted Pakistan Ministry of the Interior, as evidenced by an October 1947 internal memo that recommended, "Photographs showing destitution and misery of the refugees may be sent to Indian [sic] representatives abroad. Such photographs should be circulated by them and displayed. This would be an excellent method of arousing sympathy and obtaining help."[13]

The strategy was sufficiently successful that establishing a Pakistan Red Cross Society quickly became a priority for the government of Pakistan, because international charities accepted the Red Cross as a neutral intermediary for philanthropic funds and because Red Cross societies around the world were sending material and human resources.[14] In addition, a worldwide campaign of the United Nations International Children's Emergency Fund (UNICEF) reached into Pakistan and India in 1948. Its practices of fund-raising habituated those national publics to new philanthropic forms of caring that were not defined in terms of religious charity. It also schooled the governmental elites who coordinated the campaign to the expectations of international donors. Finally, the International Committee of the Red Cross (ICRC) sent delegates to India and Pakistan in 1947.[15] Their work with Kashmiri refugees influenced the UN indirectly because when their mission ended at the conclusion of the first India–Pakistan war, their practices of identifying Kashmiri refugees were inscribed into the first UN resolutions on the Kashmir Dispute.

The second problem is more theoretical: there was nothing obvious or natural about how to resolve the ambiguities of having too much nationality or too little. Being potentially both Indian and Pakistani put people at risk just as surely as being stateless.[16] The new UN's refusal to deal with the Partition's refugees was just that: a refusal. Moreover, it was the result of a process of exclusion that the Indian and Pakistani state representatives had actively protested. The South Asian refugee regime, thus, formed in dialogue with, and in deliberate opposition to, the refugee regime that was developing at the same time in Europe.

PARTITION AND THE SOUTH ASIAN REFUGEE REGIME

In the study of the Partition and postcolonial South Asia, historians and social scientists have focused on decentralizing national histories and on discovering the meanings of the dislocations of Partition through the recovery of silenced voices and the excavation of memory.[17] Instead, a close examination of the legal and administrative management of displacement and resettlement reveals the underlying the epistemological principles that organized competing and even contradictory images and definitions of what it meant to become a refugee.

The legal provisions of the South Asian refugee regime have their origins in the Inter-Dominion Conference negotiations, which resulted in the Inter-Dominion Agreements (1948–1951). Through the agreements, India and Pakistan developed interconnected and reciprocal national and provincial legal frameworks, administrative practices, and institutional forms for dealing with Partition's refugees. Partition refugees and evacuees were defined, in part, by their relationship to the boundaries of the new states of India and Pakistan and to the political violence of state formation and, in part, by their proprietary relationship to immovable property in each of the new states. These definitions were intertwined in the bureaucratic documents of refugee administrators, and were sorted out later in the bilateral agreements.

The political elites who ran the various governmental department and ministries charged with the care of refugees attributed Partition's violence and dislocation to religious conflict and subsequent communal violence, but they also approached the care of those refugees as a core political issue. Officials working for India's Rehabilitation Department argued that the Indian government had a moral obligation "to succor and rehabilitate the victims of communal passion."[18] Pakistan's Minister of Finance expressed a similar ideal in 1948 when he invoked the notion of sacrifice in an appeal for a greater budget for refuges relief: "Whether we can escape disaster depends on the speed and the completeness with which refugees can be rehabilitated.... This can only be done if those whose domicile falls within the boundary of Pakistan are ready to make large-hearted sacrifices and undertake grievous burdens to re-establish their unhappy brethren, and to fulfill a duty which is enjoined by the sacred precepts of Islam and in which their own existence is inextricably bound."[19]

In September 1947, when Mohammad Ali Jinnah, Pakistan's first Governor General, established a public charity to fund refugee relief, his first public appeal connected the care of refugees to the building of the new state of Pakistan: "[This] appeal to the Muslims to divert a portion of their earnings in a common pool and live a life of austerity and self denial is reminiscent of the situation when our Prophet and a handful of Muhajerins [refugees] migrated from Mecca to Madina where the Ansars [hosts] exhibited unparalleled hospitality to the Muhajerins by offering half their wealth and property. . . . By helping the Muslims of India, remember, we are strengthening the foundations of Pakistan."[20] That fund specifically defined its mission as aiding Muslim refugees in Pakistan,[21] but the projects it funded were not focused on securing religious subjectivity for nation-building nor, for that matter, on redressing victimization through compensating losses or suffering.

Instead, the primary concern of relief and rehabilitation projects in both India and Pakistan was to reestablish class relations in order "[to secure] for refugees an orderly entrance into the economic life of [India]"[22] and "[remove] dislocation in the social and economic life of Pakistan."[23] At the Inter-Dominion Conferences between 1948 and 1951, the basic provisions for refugee administration were negotiated bilaterally so that there was a single legal frame for the resettlement of people displaced between India and Pakistan. While there were many points of difference concerning refugee and evacuee law and policy, Indian and Pakistani representatives evidenced a central concern for the problems of land and property ownership as well as a shared assumption that the formalized exchange of evacuee property would be a cornerstone of rehabilitation.[24] The eventual Agreements were first enacted as ordinances or ministerial-level policy directives in both India and Pakistan, and the negotiated provisions were later passed as acts of law by federal and provincial legislatures.

Like other refugee regimes, the South Asian regime regularized systems of exclusion as well as inclusion. Legal provisions excluded large numbers of refugees who crossed the new Bengal border after 1949, the agreed-upon end point of Partition in the Inter-Dominion Agreements.[25] And with the focus firmly on the opposition between India and Pakistan, the South Asian refugee regime had no provisions that recognized people displaced within India or the homeless within Pakistan. There was also no land reform or new property distribution associated with refugee rehabilitation[26]; refugees who had owned neither land nor property and who had no rights in the "enjoyment" of land or property received no allotments. Urban property was distinguished from rural property, commercial from residential, and agricultural from nonagricultural. Land was allotted to refugees who would not cultivate it themselves but who would (re)establish tenancy rents, and those who had been tenant cultivators were allocated the right of tenant occupancy. Exchanges of evacuee property provided allotments based on the value of property that a refugee family could claim to have "enjoyed" before the Partition.

The South Asian refugee regime was based on a political notion of what it meant to be a displaced person. Refugees' own understanding of their displacement experiences was not linked solely or even primarily to their identities as Muslims or as victims of communal violence. New associations formed in refugee relief and transit camps; these groups influenced regional political parties in at least two ways: through direct efforts to influence party agendas and through their members becoming party workers themselves, bringing along their experiences as they rose in party ranks to participate in government practice and policy formation.[27] Refugee political subjects in turn became new social groups that transformed the politics of the subcontinent in the postcolonial period.[28]

Evacuee Property and the Deprivation of the Refugee

The Inter-Dominion Agreements, along with governmental directives and provincial legal instruments, defined refugees only in part by their movement across physical boundaries in the wake of the political violence that accompanied state formation. Partition refugees were also defined based on their proprietary relationship to property in each of the new states: specifically, refugee as a legal category meant someone who had been deprived of their ability to access and make use of their immovable property in the dominion from which they had been displaced. Such property was known as "evacuee property," and a vast bureaucracy developed to evaluate its value, collect rents, and regulate exchanges through state institutions. India and Pakistan conferred to refugees the use of and tenancy rights to evacuee property through two connected departments known as the Board of [Refugee] Rehabilitation and the Office of the Custodian of Evacuee Property. These agencies were established at the provincial level and were charged with rehabilitating refugees by assessing the kind of property a refugee had claim to before Partition and by restoring to "him" [sic] an equivalent form and value of evacuee property in the new dominion of residence.[29]

In Pakistan, a series of reports from the Pakistan-West Punjab Joint Refugees and Rehabilitation Council recommended refugee and evacuee management policies that shifted Pakistan's focus from questions of communal violence and the provision of temporary relief to the distribution of property rights and the process of resettlement.[30] As reflected in the Secretary of the West Punjab Board of Economic Enquiry's 1947 census of refugee camps,[31] these reports disambiguated the mass category of displaced people who were to receive relief aid into differentiated social classes who would contribute to the economic, social, and political stability of the new state. One report stated, "Clearly, we want to devise some method whereby the man who was a peasant proprietor in the East Punjab should be set up as a peasant proprietor in the West Punjab."[32] In these internal reports, the problem as identified by refugee administrators was not only the sheer numbers of displaced people in need of rehabilitation; it was the type of property required to rehabilitate people in their proper social roles. Thus, administrators argued that while the "sudden absorption of [21 lakhs (2,100,000) more people than we lose] in a population of [17,200,000] would in itself be a sufficiently difficult problem, [the] problem with which we are faced is far worse."[33] They pointed to the refugee census and concluded that "the excess in the case of agriculturalists is [1,310,000] in the case of non-agriculturalists, [808,000]."[34]

In these documents, refugee administrators referred to the religious identity of refugees in reference to landowner occupations and to the issue of control over land revenue. One report for example argued, "It would be undesirable to have in Pakistan large Hindu or Sikh zamindars [feudal landlord] or Jagirs." Yet, the report recognized that property ownership in the new state could not be limited to residents, because "to confine ownership of real property to persons domiciled in Pakistan raises very wide and difficult questions indeed," and would put foreign investment at risk in Pakistan.[35] Ultimately, the administrators concluded, "Practical consideration would seem to indicate that when the transfer of population is complete and accounts are settled, ownership must pass from the evacuee [to the resettled refugee]."[36]

The first bilateral provisions for legal recognition of refugees were established in January 1948 in the first Inter-Dominion Agreement on property management, which established the Evacuee Property Management Boards. In the first agreements, India and Pakistan defined a refugee as any person who was ordinarily resident in the territories that came to comprise the dominions of India/Pakistan and who went to the other dominion because of either the Partition or the civil unrest and communal violence that preceded it. At first, the central governments framed provisions for recognizing returned evacuees and restoring their property to them (upon payment of fees for management of said property in their absence). In 1949, representatives of India and Pakistan decided to permanently transfer property rights to refugees. The parallel national legal instruments—the Indian Administration of Evacuee Property Act of 1950 and the Pakistan Administration of Evacuee Property Ordinance of 1949—shifted the definition of refugee slightly: a refugee was not just someone displaced across the borders of the new states, but someone "deprived of the enjoyment of immovable property in [Pakistan/India] or other proscribed territories;" someone "(1) who left the territories which came to comprise India/Pakistan any day after the first of March, 1947 on account of the setting up of the Dominions of India and Pakistan or an account of the accompanying civil disturbances; (2) who acquires any right or interest in any evacuee property in Pakistan/India or territory occupied by Pakistan/India; or (3) who is resident in the territories occupied by Pakistan/India and is therefore unable to manage his property in India/Pakistan."[37]

Once India and Pakistan began redistributing evacuee property, the definitions of evacuee and refugee acquired an explicitly corporate aspect and implicated not individuals as property holders but families as the social unit of rehabilitation. The respective Department of Rehabilitation in India or Pakistan allotted evacuee properties to refugee families in exchange for the lands, residences, and businesses they had lost in the other dominion.[38] The focus had thus shifted from administering property to evaluating property types and value and regulating exchanges through state institutions.

Partition refugees formed advocacy associations in all parts of former colonial India and in many of the former Princely State; their activities illustrate a broad social acceptance of this definition of refugee status. A few, such as the Muhajir Council of the Pakistan Muslim League, were associated with political parties, but most formed in transit camps or resettlement sites independently of political parties (e.g., the All Pakistan Mohajir Board and the Mohajir Claims-Holder Association—the word mohajir in these names is an alternative transliteration of the word muhājir). Some, such as the Pakistan Kutchi Mohajir Agriculturalist Jamait (Pakistan Party of Refugee Agriculturists from Kutch), advocated for particular classes of refugees that would correspond to the categorization of "agricultural land," "urban property," and "commercial property." There was neither court oversight nor external review of the Custodians of Evacuee Property in the assessment of allotments, and these associations intervened to advocate on behalf of refugees with the office of the custodian in specific matters of property assessment and allotment. These groups intervened when refugees could not document their holdings and were unable to claim the extent or type of allocation to which they were entitled; letters of appeal written by these organizations only rarely requested reconsideration of a case when the basis of the request was that the claimant should be compensated for personal suffering by a property award that would better the conditions of his family's life. After the first All Pakistan Muhajir Convention in January 1953, when one hundred forty-one refugee associations from West and East Pakistan met in Lahore, representatives from the convention began to advise the central government on formulas for assessing property value. In their role as advisors to the central government, they sought to establish and solidify their political identities by reestablishing the political, economic, and social forms generated by usury and proprietary claims.

Funding Refugee Relief in Pakistan

The Inter-Dominion Agreements constructed a common rationalized legal system for managing refugees and evacuees from what was already being worked out in administrative practice on the ground. District administrators, local police, the military, and political party volunteers organized locally to deal with the millions of displaced people moving through and across India and Pakistan. Party volunteers shaped government practice through their involvement in relief services and administration. In Pakistan, the quasi-governmental organization and administration of refugee relief funds, the mobilization of social participation in refugee aid fund-raising, and the development of new civic and political associations to support relief, rehabilitation, and resettlement projects brought social groups into the project of making the postcolonial state.[39]

Mohammad Ali Jinnah, Pakistan's first Governor General, established the Quaid-i-Azam Relief Fund (QARF) to fund refugee relief carried out though the government bureaucracy, especially via the Ministry for Interior, Refugees, and Rehabilitation. Federal, provincial, and district-level committees were comprised of appointed government officials and functioned as collection and distribution organizations. The Central Committee, which included Mohammad Ali Jinnah (as the Governor General), the Finance Minister, and the Minister for Refugees and Rehabilitation, oversaw provincial committees headed by the Provincial Governors. These, in turn, oversaw district committees. The Central Committee coordinated national and international fund-raising campaigns and allocated resources to government agencies and projects. The Provincial and District Committees were charged with collection activities and consolidating donations for deposit in the federal account. The clear federal, provincial, and district-level organization of the QARF committees created a national administrative structure for fund-raising. This structure blurred the boundaries between voluntary and governmental work and spread practical knowledge about the process of fund-raising outside of bureaucratic and political party networks.

The QARF was a national fund that supported relief projects in East and West Pakistan,[40] but the campaign for funds and practices of fund-raising were shaped by international influences in two ways. First, contributions came from all over the world, many from Muslim communities or from the South Asians living in other parts of the British colonies. The Central Committee launched its first fund-raising campaign in September 1947. Jinnah began the effort by radio broadcast, and the campaign printed speeches and appeals in Pakistan's major national English, Urdu, and Sindhi newspapers. In his appeal, Jinnah called on the nation to "stint no sacrifice" and said that "the people themselves, and private charity . . . can accomplish much which the Government organizations and aid alone cannot do."[41] The Central Committee also appealed to foreign governments and the rulers of the Princely States for large contributions.[42] People sent monetary donations for the QARF from all over Pakistan. It was common for previously existing labor committees or mosque associations to mobilize their networks and organizational capacity to collect monies, and in South Africa, Burma, Qatar, Bahrain, Iran, and the East Africa Protectorate (later Kenya and Uganda), new organizations also formed to raise funds for the QARF, using names such as the "Pakistan Central Relief Committee." Many of these organizations later became significant donors to other causes in Pakistan, particularly to the Kashmir Fund.

The social practices of fund-raising were also shaped by the institutional expectations of the international organizations that were involved in fund-raising in Pakistan at the same time. Mohammad Ali Jinnah's sister, Fatimah Jinnah, managed several of the most important nongovernmental funds, and functioned as a liaison between the QARF Central Committee and the international humanitarian organizations that were operating in Pakistan during the Partition.[43] As President of the Pakistan National Committee of the United Nations Appeal for Children (UNAC), which was a one-year global fund drive for UNICEF, Fatima Jinnah negotiated the terms of Pakistan's participation directly with the office of the UN Secretary General, with the result that the Pakistan National Committee received ninety-five percent of the funds it raised for relief projects in Pakistan. She also ensured that UNAC's publicity materials, fund-raising practices, and principles of distribution satisfied the appeal's mission as a "world-wide appeal for non-governmental voluntary contributions to meet emergency relief needs . . . without discrimination because of race, creed, nationality status or political belief."[44] The Pakistan National Committee received frequent reminders of UNICEF's requirements for the allocation of funds and the connection between the "humanitarian endeavor" of the appeal and the right of national committees to use the name of the United Nations. Fatima Jinnah reassured UNAC officials by directing proceeds from the appeal through the Pakistan Red Cross.[45] She was also the president of that organization, and as such, she oversaw the transfer to the Pakistan Red Cross of the two large refugee camps and field hospitals (Lahore and Rawalpindi) that had been established by the British Red Cross Commission, and she attended meetings with the ICRC and Indian Red Cross in Switzerland regarding cooperation in Jammu and Kashmir.[46]

The QARF was a national charitable fund, but it operated in a domain in which global humanitarian imperatives were shaping the practices of giving, and the strategies and practices used to solicit contributions for one set of appeals were used for other purposes as well. Local committees that first formed in response to the QARF appeal later organized donations to the Pakistan Red Cross and for UNAC. People sent letters to the fund administrators, along with their contributions. The letters show that people were thinking of their work as both charity and as a contribution to the process of rebuilding Pakistan and that charity work came to be seen as an appropriate union between domestic and public work. Many of the letters specifically mention schoolgirls and young college women organizing social events, such as plays or poetry readings, as fund-raisers. Other letters talk about women's groups or labor committees that donated pooled resources. Donors demanded receipts, and many of the letters included long lists of contributors and requested that the receipts list each individually.

After the UNAC drive, which encouraged people to donate the equivalent of a day's income, letters and receipts show that very small individual donations were also sent directly to the QARF and later to the various funds dedicated to Kashmiri refugees. Donors were starting to think of themselves having a direct and personal impact on the new political community. The formation and incorporation of a new Pakistani public into the state relief project, and the formation of voluntary associations around that project, joined political elites, the state bureaucracy, and the public in a shared charitable effort of relief-fund collection and distribution. Formal and informal associations that developed out of these fund-raising drives in turn helped strengthen and secure the Pakistani state through focusing on the collective care for refugees who would be rehabilitated as citizens. In this process, moments of uncertainty were politically productive, and public and social expectations shaped administrative and governmental practices.

THE SOCIAL DIFFERENCE OF KASHMIRI REFUGEES, 1947–1950

During the first war in Jammu and Kashmir (1947–1949), the general assumption had been that Kashmiri refugees would return to their homes. Jammu and Kashmir state subjects were not considered Partition refugees, its monarch's state subjects were not counted as refugees who would have to be rehabilitated, and their rights to immovable property were not included in the accounting of evacuee property available for resettlement. India and Pakistan agreed to retroactively include the state subjects of all former Princely States that joined either India or Pakistan after August 1947 (in the Karachi Agreement of 1949), but by that time, the UN-negotiated ceasefire had set out guidelines for the permanent resolution of the Kashmir dispute and for the preservation of Jammu and Kashmir state subjects' political rights in their places of origin. Even before the Inter-Dominion Agreements or the UN resolution on the status of the territorial state, resettlement administrators and relief workers distinguished refugees from Jammu and Kashmir from Partition and other state-subject refugees and excluded them from the governmental planning for refugee rehabilitation in Pakistan.

Recognition of Kashmiri refugees was at first the result of a process of exclusion and default: they were known in Pakistan and India because they were excluded from the national relief and resettlement projects; they were known in the Princely State because there were hundreds of thousands visibly displaced on the frontiers of the war zone. During the war, how to pay for relief for refugees from Jammu and Kashmir became a serious issue for central and provincial governments and refugee administrators. The institution of separate relief funds for Kashmiri refugees in 1948, and the practice of their collection and distribution, demonstrates that there was a broad social and political consensus that Kashmiri refugees were not to be absorbed into the citizen-making process but held in abeyance as a sign of the incomplete resolution of the Kashmir dispute between India and Pakistan.

Recognizing Kashmiri Refugees in Pakistan: The Ministry of Refugees and the Kashmir Funds

For Pakistan, two related issues were at stake in identifying Jammu and Kashmir state-subject refugees. The first was the need to differentiate between those who would be resettled in Pakistan and those who would not. The second was how to pay for the short-term relief of hundreds of thousands of refugees who were not accounted for in the relief budgets of provincial governments. In Pakistan, civil servants first excluded refugees from Jammu and Kashmir from the projected numbers of "state refugees" who would have to be accommodated in West Pakistan resettlement programs in the administrative census of refugees undertaken in March 1948 by the Pakistan Central Ministry of Refugees.[47] By July, the Pakistan Army was feeding and providing medical care to Kashmiri refugees in refugee camps near the Jammu border run by the West Punjab government, which claimed it had no budget for Kashmir refugee relief.[48] Then in September, the Pakistan Refugees Commissioner issued policy directives that excluded "refugees from Jammu and Kashmir who have not to be rehabilitated [sic] in West Punjab" from the bureaucratic accounting of resettlement needs.[49]

In principle, relief administrators relied on the political category of the hereditary state subject in assessing a person's status as a refugee from Jammu and Kashmir. The most direct way of documenting identity as a state subject of Jammu and Kashmir was through the possession of a Hereditary Jammu and Kashmir State Subject certificate issued by the Maharaja's court (figure 1). However, few of the subjects of the Princely State possessed

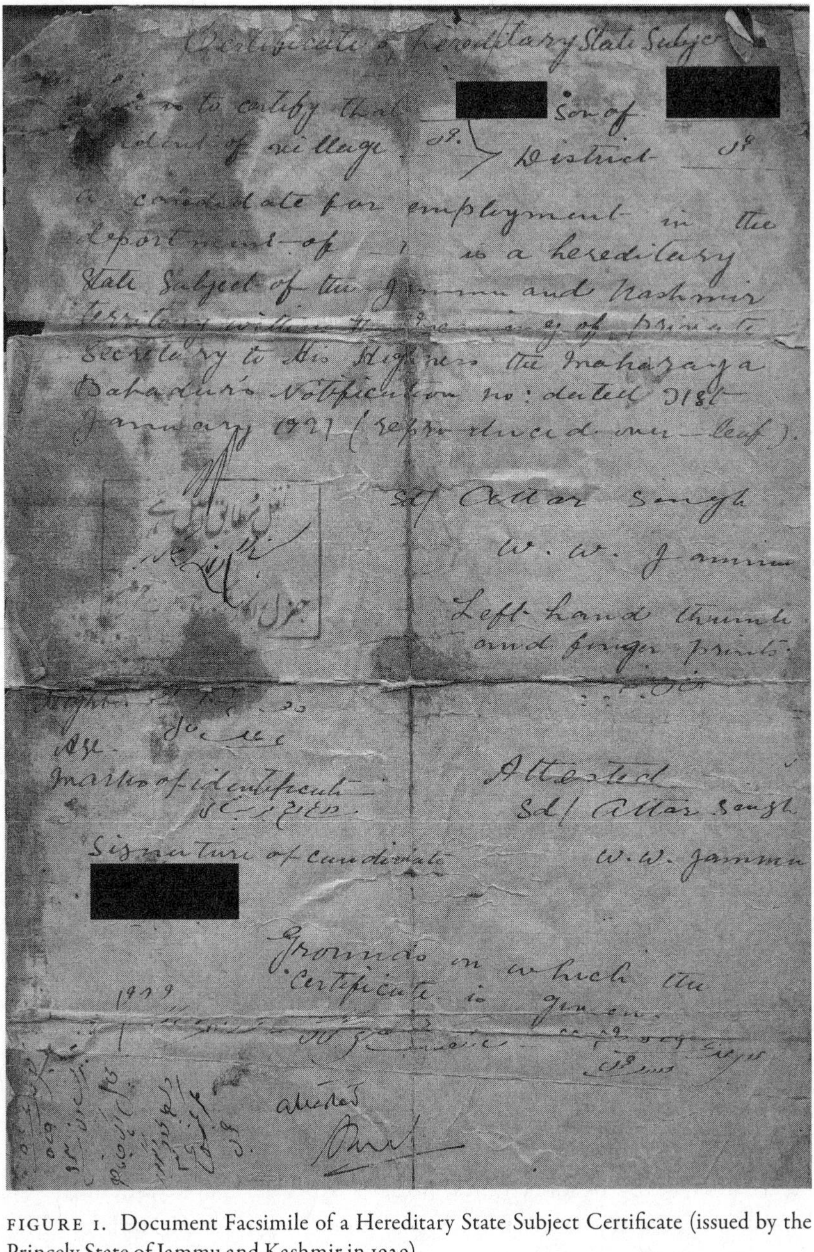

FIGURE 1. Document Facsimile of a Hereditary State Subject Certificate (issued by the Princely State of Jammu and Kashmir in 1929).

material evidence of their status in 1947. Only those employed in the state administration and members of the enfranchised classes had need of official documentation; in primarily agrarian or trading communities, almost no one possessed such a certificate. In any case, people who left their homes during periods of armed conflict rarely had such documents in their possession.

At first, refugee relief administrators identified refugees of Jammu and Kashmir primarily by establishing their places of residence as within the territory of the State of Jammu and Kashmir. These administrators then issued refugee ration cards that identified the place from which a refugee had been displaced. The ration cards were issued to heads of household and, along with place of origin, also listed all members of the refugee family on the card. The regularization, documentation, and legalization of the category of the "refugee of Jammu and Kashmir" came later, when most people who had been displaced were not, in fact, able to return to their homes.

There were no governmental budgetary provisions for the support of Kashmiri refugees in Pakistan's relief camps, and most of the resources that supported them were raised though national and international fund-raising projects. Initially, there was no formal account dedicated to Kashmir in the QARF, but the treasurer accepted monies sent to QARF that the donors designated for Kashmiri refugees. In April 1948, Fatima Jinnah established an independent Kashmir Fund to provide financial support to projects and agencies specifically offering relief to Kashmiri refugees.[50] Voluntary groups that had first formed during the previous QARF and UNAC fund drives organized collections for the Kashmir Fund. Some people donated one day's income—the charitable model that had been established in the UNAC fund drive. Others wrote to say they were donating the proceeds from cultural events such as plays or poetry readings. Formal associations mobilized relief-fund collection committees that consolidated funds before sending them to the overall fund collectors, and women's groups pooled resources or contributed goods, such as collections of household items and clothing.

Popular conceptions of the Kashmiri refugees as different from other Partition-era refugees shaped these initiatives, because public philanthropic funds were foundational to the project of supporting Kashmiri refugees. The donors' demands about how their contributions should be used led to the establishment of four different Kashmir Funds in the relief-charity domain in Pakistan between 1947 and 1949. The first two were the Kashmir (Refugees) Fund account within the QARF and the Miss Fatima Jinnah Kashmir Fund. A third general fund was the Kashmir (Refugees Relief) Fund, which was the only one that was controlled by an organization based in Azad Jammu and Kashmir (AJK), known as the Kashmir Refugees Central Relief Committee (KRCRC). A final fund, known informally as the Kashmir Mujahideen/ Bombers Fund and formally as the Women's Relief Committee's Kashmir (Mujahideen) Fund, was established because other funds received donations not only for Jammu and Kashmir refugees but also for fighters on the Kashmir Front, and there was no previously existing account through which contributions could be routed to the paramilitaries in AJK.

Fatima Jinnah created the Women's Relief Committee's Kashmir (Mujahideen) Fund to separate projects that satisfied international requirements from those that satisfied public and social demands. This relief fund for Kashmir front-line mujāhidīn did not, strictly speaking, have the administrative status of a fund with a designated bank account. Instead, it was actually a new charitable action undertaken by the Women's Relief Committee (WRC), a previously existing subcommittee of the Punjab Muslim League Women's Committee (PMLWC) with its own bank accounts.[51] Fatima Jinnah was one of the central organizers of the WRC, and she became Chairperson of the Women's Relief Committee's Kashmir (Mujahideen) Fund. She kept its books, and she used its accounts to collect the donations labeled for Kashmir mujāhidīn that donors were already sending to the Fatima Jinnah Kashmir Fund, the QARF, and the Red Cross.

The WRC consulted with the Defense Ministry and the All Jammu and Kashmir Muslim Conference (AJKMC) provisional government and received lists of goods and supplies needed by "the Kashmir mujahideen and the Kashmir refugees."[52] The WRC's record book and correspondence shows that the Committee considered sending aid to fighters on the Kashmir front as one of its primary projects.[53] This emphasis was also a part of the WRC's publicity for its activities and fund-raising. Fatima Jinnah announced her participation with the WRC and her dedicated efforts to fund-raising for Kashmir refugee relief in September 1948[54]; her first direct fund-raising effort began two weeks later, with a request for charitable contributions for the Kashmir war effort: "On this I'd-uz-Zuha [sic], please reserve the skins [of sacrificial animals] for the defenders of Kashmir. Arrangements have been made by the Karachi Women's Relief Committee for house-to-house collection by the Pakistan Boy Scouts, who will give receipts for skins received."[55] In response, donated animal hides and monies resulting from their sale arrived from across Pakistan and from overseas. The WRC sent its first shipment of 5,000 parcels to AJK in November 1948. An article in the newspaper *Dawn* described committee members packing parcels for Kashmiri "mujahideen." On the facing page was Fatima Jinnah's next appeal: "Mujahideen of Kashmir Require Blankets: Miss Jinnah's Appeal."[56]

Donations in response to her appeal came from East and West Pakistan and also from overseas groups that had contributed to the previous QARF, UNAC, or Red Cross campaigns. The people who mobilized their social networks to organize collections did not differentiate between raising funds for displaced people engaged in active conflict and collecting donations for displaced Kashmiris in general. Clothing donations often designated women's and children's clothing for "Kashmiri refugees" and men's clothing for "the Kashmir fighters." Many of the letters that accompanied contributions show that, in public perception, there was no clear distinction between "Kashmiri mujahids" and "Kashmiri refugees."

Recognizing Kashmiri Refugees' Place in the Kashmir Dispute: The United Nations Committee on India and Pakistan

During the war of 1947–1949, India's, Pakistan's, Jammu and Kashmir's political elites assumed that displaced people from the princely state would not be resettled in India or Pakistan. This was also the understanding of Indian and Pakistani government officials as well as of the Kashmiri political party leaders who functioned as local authorities in Azad Kashmir (the territories held militarily by Pakistan) and in Jammu and Kashmir State (the territories held militarily by India).[57] This view informed the perspective of ICRC delegates, British Dominion advisors, and representatives of the United Nations Commission on India and Pakistan (UNCIP), and it shaped the first United Nations Security Council resolutions on Kashmir.

The UNCIP representatives (including Joseph Korbel) worked closely with the governments of India and Pakistan and had frequent meetings with political party leaders in Azad Kashmir (specifically, the Muslim Conference) and in Jammu and Kashmir State (specifically, the National Conference).[58] They also met with the ICRC delegates who were working with Indian, Pakistani, and local authorities and who had conducted the transregional survey of Kashmiri refugees that produced the displacement estimates that the UNICP used in its own reports.[59] UNCIP recommendations specified that Kashmiri refugees (defined as forcibly displaced Jammu and Kashmir state subjects) "who have left [the State] on account of disturbances are invited, and are free, to return to their homes and to exercise their rights as such citizens"[60]; refugee repatriation was one of the listed responsibilities of the appointed Plebiscite Administrator.[61]

Recognizing Kashmiri Refugees in AJK: The Kashmir Refugees' Central Relief Committee and the Azad Kashmir Government

During the war from 1947 to 1949, there were few formal refugee camps in AJK.[62] The largest camp was on the outskirts of Muzaffarabad near the shrine of Sahi Saheli Sarkar and was run by the Pakistan Military. Most displaced people were clustered temporarily at various places along their routes of travel away from the fighting. Many arrived at shrines and tombs, traditional sites of refuge and respite, and stayed there; others camped in groups at the edges of towns; still others moved into the houses of local residents or into houses and surrounding lands vacated by others who had, in turn, fled the area. The AJKMC and the Pakistan Military ran ration depots that provided basic supplies to displaced people as well as to local residents whose lives were disrupted by the war.

In April 1948, the AJKMC leadership informed the government of Pakistan that they had formed the Kashmir Refugees Central Relief Committee (KRCRC).[63] The KRCRC requested direct allocation of funds from the Quaid-i-Azam Relief Fund for the purpose of providing aid to the Kashmiri refugees who were excluded from the refugee provisions (administrative, legal, and budgetary) of the government of Pakistan. The committee pointed out that in West Punjab and the North West Frontier Provinces (NWFP) there was no provision in the budget for Kashmiri refugees, although refugees from Jammu and Kashmir needed general services such as hospitals and dispensaries as well as accommodation and rations in refugee camps. Their request emphasized the connection between the interim relief for Kashmiri refugees in Pakistan and the future political relations between the anticipated free State of Jammu and Kashmir and Pakistan: "The Abdullah Government has launched a subtle drive to lure [the refugees] them back into the State [of Jammu and Kashmir, India] by holding out promise of a sweet and smooth rehabilitation. . . . It is, therefore, imperative to give them immediate and adequate relief and also make provision for their interim rehabilitation till, by the Grace of God, they are able to march back onto their homes triumphantly with the banner of Pakistan in their hands."[64]

Jinnah responded in a personal letter to Ghulam Abbass, the chairperson of the AJKMC. He informed him that the QARF Central Committee had allocated five lakhs (500,000 rupees) and authorized the KRCRC to conduct relief work anywhere in Pakistan but "only among the refugees from Jammu and Kashmir."[65] The KRCRC set up district relief committees composed of AJKMC party members, many of whom were themselves refugees. These party workers oversaw relief projects and services provided to Kashmiri refugees by District Commissioners in Pakistan and were paid by the AJK government through the fund run by the KRCRC. The KRCRC also cooperated with the Pakistan Army, which was deeply involved in providing basic medical services to the nearly two hundred thousand refugees in AJK territory.[66]

The first serious dispute between the government of Pakistan and the AJK government was over the formation of the Kashmir portfolio and specifically over control of funds for Kashmir refugee relief. In 1949, the Ministry of Kashmir Affairs was established to serve as a link between the government of Pakistan and the AJKMC in its role as the Azad Kashmir Government. The formation of the Ministry was a point of contention between the Government of Pakistan and the leaders of the new Azad Kashmir Government, which resisted Pakistan's direct involvement in state administration. One of the first assignments of the new Minister for Kashmir Affairs, as the Chairman of the Ministry's Subcommittee on Kashmir Relief, was the consolidation and administration of all relief funds. Leaders of the AJKMC, strongly objected to the changes: "[The KRCRC] has been the one connecting link between the Muslim Conference and the Kashmir refugees on the one hand and the Government on the other. . . . I am afraid the liquidation of this committee and the consequent centralization of powers with the [Pakistan] Government will not at all be expedient at this stage, especially if the plebiscite is to take place in time to come."[67]

For a while, the KRCRC operated parallel to the Subcommittee on Kashmir Relief. Then, the QARF Central Committee decided that all future allocations of aid for the KRCRC would be routed through the Ministry. All of the KRCRC members refused to work with the new subcommittee until, in June 1950, the AJKMC was given executive and administrative representation on the Subcommittee on Kashmir Relief.[69] During AJKMC party rule in the 1950s, all refugee relief funds were directed through the AJKMC offices. Party members acted as direct advocates and distributors of refugee relief items to Kashmiri refugees in Pakistan and in the territory of AJK.

POLITICAL RECOGNITION OF THE KASHMIRI
REFUGEE AFTER 1950

By late 1949, it was clear that people displaced from the Princely State would not or could not simply go home. The provisions for recognition of the Kashmiri refugee and the continuing importance of the category of state subject after 1950 resulted from the efforts of Jammu and Kashmir politicians to define and maintain an exclusive domain of state power through the rights and patronage claims of its subjects. Like the provisions for refugee identification, administration, and resettlement developed by India and Pakistan, those enacted by Azad Jammu and Kashmir (Pakistan) and Jammu and Kashmir State (India) were largely reciprocal, based on the legal code of the Princely State of Jammu and Kashmir and on explicit extension of Partition-era East and West Punjab refugee laws and administrative practices.[70] Each of the Jammu and Kashmir governments made claims to the legitimate rule of the entirety of the former Princely State, and each framed its refugee policies and legal definition in terms of the entirety of the State and the totality of its peoples.

The refugee provisions of the two Jammu and Kashmir governments bore significant resemblance to the provisions of the South Asian refugee regime as it was developing between India and Pakistan, but there were a number of crucial differences. The greatest continuity was that the legal definition of refugee developed in relation to evacuee property—property of which a displaced person had been deprived by the formation of new territorial states. Unlike Indo-Pak definitions, they made no reference to identity categories such as occupation or community. For Jammu and Kashmir state-subject refugees, having been "deprived" of property was actually having been deprived of the proprietary or usury rights as the basis of political recognition. The first definitions of the Kashmiri refugee thus revolved around both the displaced person's status as a hereditary state subject (of Jammu and Kashmir) and his or her inability to enact the rights claims that accrued to that expression of political belonging.[71] Unlike Pakistani or Indian courts, which after Partition considered the deliberate adoption or renunciation of citizenship irrevocable, the highest courts of AJK and Jammu and Kashmir State repeatedly upheld the premise that the provision of Pakistani or Indian citizenship to state subjects did not negate their state-subject claims or their claims on property in any part of the former Princely State.

Once a need for resettlement was articulated, provisions for the allotment of evacuee property to Jammu and Kashmir state-subject refugees were not assigned in exchange for specific properties but on the basis of people's categorical identity as a Kashmiri refugee *(muhājir-e-riyāsat-e-jammū-o-kashmīr)*. Each of the successor governments maintained the unity of the state through the continuity of its provisions for recognizing the political rights of the state subject. The allotments were also not permanent; each of the Princely State's successor governments eventually made the allotment of evacuee property *ārzī* (temporary), just as the "occupation" of territory was to be entirely provisional and temporary until a plebiscite or referendum could be held. Establishing and maintaining political rights, rather than requiring that the allottee relinquish a property claim on the other side of the border, actually depended on the allottee maintaining his claim.[72]

In Pakistan, identity documentation began as an extension of the distinctions that provincial camp administrators and rehabilitation made between Partition refugees and Jammu and Kashmir refugees. Identity documentation was, in other words, the product of previous practices of exclusion. In AJK, resettlement allotments depended on a process of positive or inclusionary identity documentation. The history of these practices produced a system in Pakistan and AJK in which some people have legal refugee status because they could prove their identity as hereditary state subjects of Jammu and Kashmir and others have legal state-subject status because they were identified as having been displaced from the Princely State.

Legal Definitions and Political Recognition in AJK and Pakistan

The regularization of the nominally temporary resettlement of large numbers of Jammu and Kashmir state-subject refugees in Pakistan in the late 1950s led to a dual definition of Kashmiri refugee in AJK law. The Azad Jammu and Kashmir Refugees Rehabilitation Finance Board Act of 1960 gave the legal status of refugee to state subjects who were displaced within the territory of the (former) Princely State "who, though resident in Azad Kashmir territory, [had] been deprived of the enjoyment of immovable property in the Indian occupied part of [the State]."[73] The Azad Jammu and Kashmir Refugees Registration and Representation Act of 1960 also recognized as a refugee "any state subject who (1) left the Indian-occupied part of Jammu and Kashmir due to the 'War of Liberation' [against the Maharaja, 1947–1949] and took refuge in Pakistan or (2) who could not return from the territory of Pakistan as a result of the war or (3) who could not return to their home any other country."[74] These provisions distinguished how refugees would be represented in the AJK government; refugees "domiciled"' within areas under the territorial control of the government of Azad Kashmir (defined at the time as the districts of Mirpur, Poonch and Muzaffarabad) participated in AJK elections as part of residential electorates, and there were reserved seats for refugees living in Pakistan.

The clause "due to the War of Liberation" was later amended to include those who left due to the 1964 war, and AJK politicians later amended the wording again in the Azad Jammu and Kashmir Electoral Rolls Ordinance of 1970 and the Administration of Evacuee Property (Amendment) Ordinance of 1971 by extending Kashmiri refugee status to include any state subjects who left their homes after 1947 in the "Indian Occupied portions of the State."[75] That change recognized the reality of the slow but constant movement of people caused by political conflict in Jammu and Kashmir as well as armed conflict between India and Pakistan. It also accommodated the refugees of the 1971 Indo-Pak war and reflected a growing political belief in AJK that the resolution of the Kashmir dispute (and the promised referendum) was not immanent.

Two principles underwrote the definition of a Kashmir refugee in all of the legal provisions drafted and enacted by AJK political leaders. The first was the underlying connection between the Princely State's standards for state-subject recognition as the articulation of political belonging for the totality of the state's peoples. The second was the temporary nature of displacement and resettlement and thus of all property allotments made to Kashmir refugees settled in both Pakistan and in AJK itself; these remain subject to cancellation "at, during, or before the holding of plebiscite as envisaged by UNICP Resolutions" (see figure 2). Because *muhājir-e-jammū-o-kashmīr* were legally just temporarily resettled until a final agreement on the postcolonial status of the former Princely State of Jammu and Kashmir, their rights and protections depended on the maintenance of property rights and land claims and ultimately on the inheritance of Kashmiri refugee status. Therefore, the process of securing a refugee allotment became a central means of securing recognition as a Kashmiri refugee and ultimately as a state subject.

In Pakistan, displaced people from Jammu and Kashmiri have a long history of actively demanding recognition from and a role in the Azad Jammu and Kashmir government. Refugees were the first to pursue widespread documentation of their status as state subjects. A refugee's identity as a state subject established access to relief services and later to all the administrative

OFFICE OF THE CUSTODIAN OF EVACUEE PROPERTY
AZAD JAMMU AND KASHMIR

PROPRIETARY RIGHTS TRANSFER ORDER

ORDER NO. ▓▓▓ ....   Serial No. ....
         Whereas allottee Mr/Mrs. ▓▓▓▓▓▓
S/O, D/O,W/O. ▓▓▓▓▓▓▓▓ ...caste. ▓▓▓▓ ....Tehsil. ▓▓▓▓
District.. Muzaffarabad ..... previously resident of village/city.. Naribal ....
Tehsil . Sopur ... . District . Baramula ....(Indian Occupied Jammu
and Kashmir), Now resident of village/city.. ▓▓▓▓ .... Tehsil.. Hattian
District... Muzaffarabad ....Azad Jammu and Kashmir/Pakistan has claimed
Proprietary rights of Evacuee Property mentioned in schedule below ; cost of which
has been assessed as Rs. 3000.00

         And whereas, the Rehabilitation Commissioner has issued a certificate
of Entitlement under Section 18-A (3) of the Administration of Evacuee Property
(Amendment) Ordinance 1980 in favour of the said allottee/old tenant ;

         NOW, therefore, in exercise of the powers vested in the Custodian
under Section 18-A (2) and under other Acts, proprietary rights in the said Evacuee
Property are hereby granted to the said allottee/old tenant subject to the terms and
conditions mentioned herein and those laid in the said Ordinance, the allottee/old
tenant/his successor/transferee shall hold the same rights in the Property as were held
by the Non-Muslim owner/occupancy tenant at the time of migration from Azad
Jammu & Kashmir;

         In case, the evacuee/owner/occupancy tenant/his successor/his/her
transferee returns in AZAD JAMMU AND KASHMIR at, during or before the
holding of plebiscite as envisaged by UNCIP Resolutions, and such a person
puts in a claim, the allottee/old tenant/his successor/transferee shall surrender the
property to such a person on issuance of a declaration and determination of
cost and dues etc: by the Custodian and payment thereof by such a person ;

         The allottee being refugee is granted proprietary rights free of cost
subject to the provisions of Section 18-A—(2) (b) under Pakistan Administration of
Evacuee Property (Amendment Ordinance No LIX of 1986.

                    SCHEDULE OF PROPERTY
Land measuring Fourteen Kanals..... Seven ... Marlas, Survey No/Nos. ▓▓▓ .....
....
....
....
House/Shops consisting of ....Rooms situated in village/city ▓▓▓ ....
Tehsil.. Hattian ....District.. Muzaffarabad Azad Jammn & Kashmir, left
by.... ▓▓▓▓▓▓
....non muslim evacuee
Dated 26-12-1989.   EVACUEE PROPERTY A.J.K.
                                         CUSTODIAN

FIGURE 2. Document facsimile of a Proprietary Rights Transfer Order (issued by the Azad Jammu and Kashmir Custodian of Evacuee Property in 1989).

processes that require legal documentation, including employment and school registration. At first, the fact of land occupancy and residence in AJK territory sufficiently established a de facto identity as a state subject. As AJK developed formal representational systems and expanded its government administration, identity documentation also became increasingly important for the *qaumī bāshindah*—hereditary residents who had not been displaced from their lands in 1947 or in the subsequent wars between India and Pakistan.

Documenting Identity, 1950–1959: The Azad Kashmir Rules
of Business, the Ministry of Kashmir Affairs, and
Temporary Resettlement

Until 1960, the Azad Kashmir Government was essentially a single-party government controlled by the AJKMC that had functioned as AJK's local authority during the war from 1947 to 1949.[76] From 1950 to 1960, three policy documents known as the Rules of Business of the Azad Kashmir Government vested executive and legislative control in the party and in the Ministry of Kashmir Affairs. The Rules of Business of the Azad Kashmir Government, 1950, provided the first official framework for organizing power and governmental authority between AJK and Pakistan. It instituted a party system of government, whose political constituency were the state subjects of Jammu and Kashmir, and identified the AJKMC as the "Supreme Head" of the Azad Kashmir Government and thus the local authority with which Pakistan would work. Under the 1950 Rules, the President of the Muslim Conference was the head of state, with full authority to appoint a Council of Ministers and court justices and to approve all pieces of legislation. The Rules of Business were rewritten in 1953 and 1958; changes allowed the Ministry of Kashmir Affairs (MKA) greater executive control over AJK.[77]

As stipulated in each iteration of the Rules of Business, only Jammu and Kashmir state subjects were permitted to be employed by the state, and the Azad Kashmir Government and the MKA were jointly responsible for displaced state subjects living in Pakistan.[78] The maintenance of these provisions were a matter of repeated conflict between the AJKMC and the government of Pakistan, which tried on several occasions to dissolve the structures for refugee representation and to eliminate the provisions that restricted Pakistanis from serving in the state's administrative services. The correlation between Kashmiri identity and a struggle to define the differences between AJK and Pakistan became an explicit part of distinguishing the domains of state authority after a series of agitations in Poonch, in which the government of Pakistan called in the Punjab police forces. Reports of the Punjab Constabulary's extremely violent repression of the Poonch agitations led AJK leaders to demand the recall of all "non-Kashmiri" officers from AJK and the formation of a legislative assembly to be democratically elected by all Kashmiri state subjects.[79]

The first demands for Kashmiri refugee resettlement came from members of the KRCRC, who were among the leadership of the AJKMC, many of whom were themselves displaced. They argued that the Government of Pakistan should extend resettlement provisions to the people displaced from Jammu and Kashmir: "These people domiciled in West Punjab [who] suffered heavily in the Jammu genocide. . . . [They] have to lead a life of forced exile till the battle for Kashmir is won. . . . [T]hey have been in Pakistan for over a year and in spite of repeated representation the Government has not thought it advisable to grant them the status of refugees. The Government was justified in their attitude in the past as it was the impression all round that the Kashmir refugees would have to return very soon to the State. But unfortunately the political situation has now changed and the Kashmir issue is likely to hang fire for some time. This being the case it is very necessary that arrangements should be made for the temporary rehabilitation of Kashmiri refugees in Pakistan."[80]

Besides advocating for the provision of relief supplies to Kashmiri refugees, the committee founders also recommended the interim rehabilitation of the refugees. This rehabilitation, they argued, should be "purely temporary and subject to cancellation as soon as [refugees'] return to their homeland is made possible. . . . Their problems are identical with those of the refugees, though in a different way. They need immediate relief in the shape of food, clothes, and in some cases, houses. . . . In any battle of arms or vote in Kashmir, these people are our only assets, and the sooner they can be relieved of their distress the better from every point of view."[81]

Between 1950 and 1953, the AJKMC advocated publicly for Kashmir refugee resettlement provisions, against the policy programs of the Pakistani rehabilitation authorities and West Punjab rehabilitation administrators. These demands for resettlement continued into the mid-1950s, when Ghulam Abbass cautioned the Prime Minister of Pakistan not to accept the boundaries of the Ceasefire Line/Line of Control (LoC) as the basis for regional plebiscite or regional elections and warned that Kashmiri refugees expected to return to their homes in the part of the state under Indian administration.[82]

Temporary Allotments and Kashmiri Refugee Resettlement after 1954

Temporary resettlement provisions were enacted in Pakistan and AJK in 1954, but the explicit legal provision for refugee return was first established by the National Conference government during the process of constitutional formation in Jammu and Kashmir State and the debate over

(Jammu and Kashmir) provincial and (Indian) national citizenship.[83] The process of temporary resettlement followed different processes in Pakistan and in AJK until the 1960s, when the formation of electoral constituencies led to the regularization of the processes by which Jammu and Kashmir refugees were able to document their legal identities.

In Pakistan, the official transfer of allotment rights to Kashmiri refugees began in 1957. The MKA acquired land for new developments (satellite colonies) and issued temporary allotment documents on the basis of the ration-card records; the head of household on the ration card became the primary allottee for each family unit.[84] Jammu and Kashmir nationals were moved to what became Kashmir Refugee Camps or were accommodated in (evacuee) abandoned institutional buildings in the urban areas of the northern Punjab, such as Rawalpindi and Sialkot. These temporary allotments were not issued to Jammu and Kashmir state-subject refugees in exchange for specific properties but rather on the basis of their categorical identity as Kashmiri refugees. The allotments were temporary and subject to cancellation, and maintaining a claim on them depended upon the refugee's successfully maintaining a claim to political belonging on the other side of the Kashmir boundary (unlike Partition refugees who had to relinquish their claims in exchange for property allotment).

The AJKMC remained one of the principle advocates for temporary refugee resettlement, and party workers submitted evacuee property applications for refugees and intervened to regularize ad hoc holdings. However, Kashmiri refugees also began organizing through other parties and associations and participated in the All Pakistan Muhajir Convention in January 1957, a meeting of over a hundred refugee associations from West and East Pakistan. In the convention chairman's public statement, the associations "assured the Kashmiri refugees that the Convention would ... help solving their problem and would continue to stress its demands for an early resettlement of Kashmiri refugees."[85]

A fundamental difference between the creation of rural villages and urban satellite colonies for Kashmiri refugees in Pakistan compared to the process of resettlement in AJK was that in AJK the process of allotment essentially legalized de facto land and property use.[86] To formally allot a property or legalize de facto holdings, the AJK Rehabilitation Commission registered the address of a refugee family in the "occupied territory" on the Indian side of the LoC and the date that the family had entered AJK. Some displaced people were able to produce land-revenue documents sent (or brought) to them by family members on the other side of the LoC, which established their proprietary, usury, or tenancy rights in land or immovable property. Many displaced people had no way of producing such documentation, and thus in the first period of settlement, people's connection to specific properties, and their state-subject status, was established by testimony. AJKMC government officials used party alliances and networks to find party members who (being refugees themselves) had known a refugee's family in their home place and would give sworn testimony with regard to their identity as a state subject. In some cases, the local land revenue record-keeper *(patwārī)* of a district revenue sub-division *(tehsil)* was himself displaced and was able to testify for members of all the families for whom he had kept records over the years. In some rural areas, the process of recognizing and regularizing land use as legal allotment continued well into the 1980s.

The allotment of urban evacuee property in AJK was contentious, and there was a great deal of secondary displacement in cases in which people who could not prove their state-subject status were expelled and the properties they had occupied were allotted to other refugees. This legal and administrative process of regularizing land use and expelling non–state subjects was linked to the development of electoral constituencies and provisions for refugee citizenship.[87] Once a refugee had secured an allotment, the record of said allotment established the identity of all the members of the family, and their descendants, as state-subject refugees for the purposes of the AJK state.

Another difference was that, in AJK, the resettlement process broke up historical large landholdings and created new rural spaces that were enclaves within which resettled refugees were able to enact a limited amount of political and social autonomy by excluding Pakistani state representatives from direct oversight of their affairs. For example, off of the main road between Muzaffarabad and Srinagar there is a refugee resettlement village that residents access using a footbridge that spans the steep banks of the Jhelum River, which separates the village from the road and small town on the other side. At the top of the path leading down to the bridge is a small sign stating concisely, "No Photography, No Peddlers, No Police." The location of the village's only market stall at the top of the path enforces this dictum; the comings and goings of all—residents, guests, and strangers alike—are easily monitored. Villagers have been known to "arrest" officials trying to cross the bridge by detaining them for hours in the small grocery store. The resettled refugees have established their own village council for resolving disputes, and if disputes arise that they cannot mediate or forcefully resolve, they deport the offenders to the town on the other side, with its police station and magistrate. Children go across the river to attend the government secondary school, and the primary school is privately run and staffed by teachers who reside in the village. The refugee resettlement village is a space that keeps others out—the stranger, the spy, and the merchant, but most particularly agents of the state.

Documenting Identity, 1960–1988: Basic Democracies, the Interim Constitution, and the Kashmiri Refugee Electorate

Refugees from Jammu and Kashmir were guaranteed electoral representation in the Azad Kashmir government from the first time franchise rights were accorded to state subjects. In 1960, the Basic Democracies Act created an electorate for the first time by establishing a government consisting of a President and an Azad Kashmir Council within the Ministry of Kashmir Affairs, to be elected indirectly by "local bodies" that were themselves directly elected by Jammu and Kashmir state subjects. Of the twenty-four Azad Kashmir Council members, twelve were elected by Jammu and Kashmir refugees living in Pakistan and the others by people living in areas under the territorial control of the Azad Kashmir government. The Council's legislation had to be ratified by the Chief Advisor, who was an MKA appointee,[88] but the ministry did not have unfettered control over the practice of politics. Refugee seats were eliminated in 1964 at the MKA's behest. However, Jammu and Kashmir refugees living in Pakistan protested and demanded representation in the AJK government.[89] Political leaders criticized the Government of Pakistan for eliminating refugees from the electoral process, protesting that, "since 1930, the people of the state have been fighting for political rights, [denying refugees voting rights] has cut down on the rights of Jammu and Kashmir nationals and it would be very sad if the government of Pakistan took away that right from the people of the Azad Jammu and Kashmir territory."[90] Refugee seats were reinstated in the council in 1968.

AJK formed a Legislative Assembly and instituted a party-based electoral system in 1971 under the Azad Jammu and Kashmir Government Act of 1970, which recognized all state subjects of Jammu and Kashmir as potential electors.[91] The refugee seats were divided by the Provincial Division of property rights holding, with six seats for people deprived of land and property in Jammu Division and six for people who were deprived of land and property in the Kashmir Division. The number of directly elected seats for AJK districts grew over time. In 1970, the provision was for a total of twenty-five seats (twelve AJK districts, twelve refugees, and one reserved seat for women). The current Legislative Assembly is made up of forty-nine seats, of which twenty-nine are for AJK by district of residence and eight reserved seats are appointed by the elected members of the Legislative Assembly.

In a very real sense, AJK is imagined to be something more than a territorial state. The twelve seats elected by Jammu and Kashmir refugees living in Pakistan have remained stable, as have the division of six seats for Kashmir Valley refugees and six for Jammu refugees. These seats represent an important symbolic claim for the State of Azad Jammu and Kashmir, which claims legitimate political succession over both the liberated territories and all the people of the former Princely State of Jammu and Kashmir as a whole. AJK makes these claims in part by including state subject refugees in its elections. All refugees temporarily resettled in the territories of AJK participate in elections according to their residential electoral district; all refugees temporarily resettled in Pakistan participate in elections according to constituencies based on the last district of residence in the (former) Princely State. Refugee participation symbolically and materially demonstrates and reinforces the continuity of the political identity of state subjects, and their registration by district of origin within Jammu and Kashmir maintains the AJK government's claims over territories that it does not administer.

Two forms of documentation regularized the legal recognition of Jammu and Kashmir hereditary state subjects in Pakistan—the Azad Kashmir Certificate of Domicile (āzād kashmīr domisīl sirtifiket), issued by the AJK Government, and the Jammu and Kashmir State Resident Certificate (jammū-o-kashmīr riyāsatī bāshindah sirtifiket), issued by the Kashmir Council in Islamabad (figure 3). The Resident Certificate is the formal equivalent of the Hereditary State Subject Certificate once issued by the Princely State of Jammu and Kashmir. Based on this document, a Jammu and Kashmir state subject can acquire the other documents of political identity required by the Pakistani State for various legal and administrative purposes, including a Pakistani identity card and a passport, each stamped "National of Jammu and Kashmir." For Jammu and Kashmir refugees, the process of establishing the legal identity of a state subject was secured through the documentation of their status as a Kashmiri refugee; the regularized temporary allotment allowed them to secure the State Resident Certificate, which in turn could be used to get a Certificate of Domicile from the AJK government. This made the holder eligible for any seats reserved for Kashmiris in Pakistani educational and government institutions.[92]

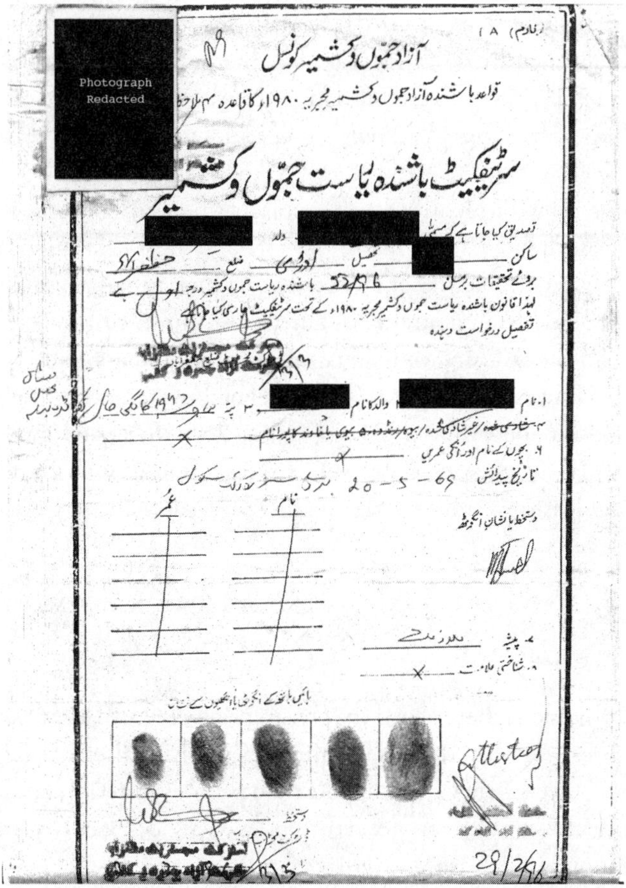

FIGURE 3 Document facsimile of a Jammu and Kashmir State Resident Certificate (issued by the Azad Jammu and Kashmir Council in 1996).

For those heredity residents *(qaumī bāshindah)* who had not been displaced, acquiring a Resident Certificate for the first time involved first acquiring an Azad Kashmir Certificate of Domicile by establishing the fact of residency and proprietary rights to property now in AJK territory. The first person in a family to document his status generally did so by providing landholding or land-use records from the *tehsil* division land records office, showing land-tax payments, permanent settlement records, and testimonials from already documented neighbors. Establishing such a history for the first time required a great deal of administrative labor and usually was not possible for women, who were rarely legally recognized heads of household before refugee resettlement in AJK in the 1950s. Once a documented land-holder established his legal identity, his direct descendants could use his Certificate of Domicile to establish his or her own legal identity as a Jammu and Kashmir state subject without again petitioning based on a claim to land rights.

Documenting the identity of state subjects who were not refugees became important in the 1970s and 1980s. As AJK became increasingly integrated into the larger national life of Pakistan, it became necessary to distinguish not only refugees from nonrefugees but also Kashmiri citizen-subjects from Pakistanis. As possessing individual identity documents for employment, school enrollment, state services, and travel became important in both AJK and in Pakistan, hereditary residents and settled refugees used their legally recognized land rights to secure public recognition of political identity as Jammu and Kashmir subject-citizens and thus legal rights in Pakistan.

TEMPORARY RESETTLEMENT AND KASHMIRI REFUGEE FAMILIES

The legal provisions that created the presumption of return arose out of a specific historical context. There is nothing inherently unalterable about them. Over time, however, they framed more than people's material conditions and their political identities: refugee return became a social fact that influenced the formation of the Kashmiri refugee family.

For example, the idea that her settlement in AJK was a temporary arrangement was a basic presumption of Shireen Begum's life. It factored into many important decisions that refugees made, such as arranging marriages:

> Women always have to consider many things when considering to give or accept a marriage proposal: where does that family live now and do they have some claim on land? Where does that family come from [in Indian Kashmir] and it is close to the place where we will return to?

These considerations changed over time and lead to repeated debates between family members about the temporality of refuge and the spatiality of refugee resettlement:

> Now, the men sometimes say that when Kashmir is liberated and we are all in our own homeland, we will be able to visit from Srinagar to Muzaffarabad as easy as from Muzaffarabad to Rawalpindi, but we [women] always preferred

to arrange marriages with people from villages near our own village. Later, after land was allotted to *muhājarīn,* whenever possible we kept some land in the girl's name when she married.

Such debates have made the possibility of imminent return a part of what it means to be a Kashmiri, temporarily resettled in Pakistan, for each new generation of Kashmiri refugees.

Questions of return have also shifted the normative practices, if not the ideals, of how kinship is ordered in refugee families. When asked about kinship, many people articulate the paradigm of patrilineal and patrilocal joint family (with a general preference for cross-cousin marriage), but refugee family histories reveal instead that egalitarian social alliances forged through labor and ritual exchanges and women's premarital kin groups have become more important than patrilineal descent groups in structuring refugee families. In each first generation of dislocation, kinship alliances were re-created by first forging networks of social obligations and exchanges, rather than by making claims on descent groups. This work of forging networks is evident in families' histories through the relative importance of male and female peer groups over descent lineages, as represented by the *dost* (male friend) or *sahēlī* (female friend) over the *bhaī* (brother) or *bahen* (sister) as a prime social bond in arranging marriages for single men or for the daughters of displaced people. The importance of female-centered networks is evident in the emergence of some matrilocal residence patterns in muhājir communities, as a result of the practice of putting land titles in women's names at marriage (either as dowry from the woman's family or as the *haqq maher* paid by the groom's family as a part of the Islamic marriage contract). As landholders, refugee women have shown a preference for, and ability to arrange, cross-cousin and parallel-cousin marriage in their own patrilines in the second generation of settlement.

Kashmiri muhājirs developed kinship practices that inscribed the experience of being a refugee daily life in ways unrelated to the formal, institutional politics of refugee identity. Genealogy among Kashmiri refugees now expresses the institutionalization of reciprocal social exchanges as kinship. It has also tied the affective life of the refugee family to the politics of the Kashmir dispute.

"The UN Has Made a Refugee of Me!"

I had been to the home of Bashir Ahmed and his wife Munirah Begum on several occasions when I wandered into the middle of a family debate that had begun as a question of the suitability of a marriage proposal for their daughter. That Bashir Ahmed did not like his current residence was something I had known since I had first met him. His greatest dissatisfaction was that he did not own land and that he lived in a rented house. For years he had earned his living as a tailor, a skill he had acquired as a boy after arriving in Pakistan from his village outside of Uri. Then he had moved his family from the hill town where they had lived for many years to a village close to the city where his son was employed in a shop. He would have liked to stop working and enjoy his grandchildren, but his son did not earn enough on his own to support his parents and his wife without a supplemental income.

They moved on several occasions over the years during which I visited them regularly, but on this occasion they were living in a rented section of a house in a village between Islamabad and Rawalpindi. Each time I went there, I found it disconcerting to leave the transit van on the main thoroughfare—with its six wide, freshly paved lanes, regulated traffic lights, and large luxury automobiles speeding by—to step just a few paces over the curb and find myself sharing a rough dirt road with women carrying bundles of fodder on their heads, motorbikes carrying entire families on the handlebars, water buffalo pulling carts, and an occasional goat, pursued by the errant child on whose watch it had gotten off its lead. At certain times of day, I shared that passage with girls in school uniforms and with youths wearing jeans and tight shirts, hair slicked back in a style decidedly reminiscent of the popular Hindi film style. The house, a newer style made of concrete, with its steel support bars exposed on the roof to leave room for expansion on a second story, had a tank on the roof for storing water when the pump was actually running; this village was subject to the scheduled and unscheduled loss of power (called "load-shedding") to which many homes in the nearby cities were no longer subject.

When I arrived, Bashir Ahmed's wife was urging him to reconsider his refusal of a marriage proposal for their youngest daughter. The conversation began again after I arrived, since my presence was an opportunity to present the case again to Bashir Ahmed by telling me the story of the argument that they were having. That afternoon, the mother and sisters of the proposed son-in-law had arrived, bearing sweets, at their house for the second time and had asked Munirah Begum to reconsider her own refusal of the week before. They reminded her of a time when their families had lived close to each other in the town of Abbottabad, of how they had exchanged visits on the 'Eid holidays and of how their fathers had been the kinds of neighbors that one would call a *dost* (friend); in giving her daughter to them for their son, that old *dostī* (friendship) would become kinship and tie the two families together in the future. Munirah Begum expressed some reservations: the family had a successful business and had become wealthy enough to purchase property in Pakistan. Would they really go back to a rural life in their home place (a village in Baramullah district, which was actually the home place of the proposed groom's grandfather) when Kashmir was liberated? Yet, she said that she was becoming more and more convinced that her husband should reconsider the match. She had no objections to the boy himself, and she liked his family. Moreover, they owned a house and a small shop in Abbottabad, and being the owner of one's own home and shop provided security and respect—no small thing. Her husband, however, did not think it a suitable proposal:

> I should not accept this proposal because it is not a good thing that a daughter should be settled so far from her parents. When Kashmir will be reunited and we go back to our own house, then it will be a long journey and she will only come when her husband accompanies her on the trip. We will not be able to see her often, and will not know the joys and sorrows of her heart. And God have mercy and forbid that the day ever arise that she ever needs us, how would we know?

After a while, Munirah Begum's brother came to see her. She told him about the proposal and asked his advice. Munirah Begum seemed to feel that she had support in the form of her brother's presence, and she began to argue her case vehemently:

> It's just like a man to speak as if only you know to be concerned for your daughter. Am I not her very own mother? Am I not thinking of my daughter's happiness when we talk of giving her to such a family, whose very father, may he rest in peace, was the *dost* of my own beloved father?

Her voice rose as she motioned towards the young woman moving about in the courtyard:

> Will they not treat her like their own child, like I treat the child of my very own sister [my daughter-in-law]? You should be thinking of the family.... And are we not all Kashmiri? Is it just you that will go back to your own house? Are we not all waiting for the day that it is safe to go back and to live in the houses that belong to us and to see the fruit that the trees bear after all these years? Do you think that it is only you that eats rice from the market instead of from his own fields?

If Bashir Ahmed even looked at his wife, it was with a quick glance that I could not see from where I was sitting. His hands moved deliberately under the sewing machine needle, and he spoke in the same soft voice. One might almost think that he was speaking to himself, except that we could hear him easily despite the drone of the fan spinning overhead:

> No, dear wife, it is not like for our family in Azad Kashmir where we are all waiting to return to our own homes and living as *muhājirs* in our own homeland. How do we know that they will return to their house in Kashmir? They now have a big house and a shop in the town, and there is no guarantee except for this desire in one's own heart to live in one's own house and to know that this is my rightful property and inheritance.

He raised his eyes and motioned to me with his chin, keeping his hands on his work:

> I told her this story of how we came to be in living in Abbottabad and of how my father did not stop on the road but came directly to that town and did work. I told her that in those days Qayyum Sahab [Mohammad Qayyum Khan] was making uniforms for the *mujāhidīn* and that as a small child, I sewed the badge of the Azad Forces on the sleeves of their uniforms and that I was given a watch in recognition of my service. We always knew that we would not stay in Abbottabad and later when Pakistan made allotments for Kashmiri *muhājirīn,* we knew that we would not stay in Pakistan. I said to my father, "I am going to return to my home as soon as we are allowed to return," and later when we could not return I learned to be a tailor and I said to my father, "Father, do not accept property because we will not stay here and we will not give up our very own property," and I told him to take a house on rent. I have tried to buy a house here for my family, but I am not able to do it. It is the condition of a *muhājir* that I am separate from my very own property, but I did not accept any other to replace it, and when the conditions are right, my children will see that home that they did not know they were longing for.

I had indeed heard this story on several occasions, but there was some part of the story that I suspected I had never heard, the details of which I could only guess—some dishonor, perhaps some implication of impropriety; something still embarrassing and uncomfortable enough that the story skirted its edges. In my focus on understanding the details of life stories, my repeated questions had occasionally resulted in someone speaking aloud some fact about the past that was nearly unknown to the current generation—for example, several older women admitted in front of their surprised grandchildren that they had been married more than once. For men, wives left behind or lost were a part of their stories; second wives and first wives' children caused, not embarrassment, but a lament for the home left behind, especially if the second match was not well made. For women, however, those first marriages ended by the losses of war—by death or by abandonment—often at first appeared in the parts of their stories that didn't make sense.

In Bashir Ahmed's story, I had never fully understood how it was that he had not gotten a refugee allotment. It was several years before anyone let me see what part of the story had been withheld. About three years after the argument about the marriage proposal, I met with residents of the resettlement village where Munirah Begum's parents had lived and where her brother now holds the family allotment. We were talking about how it had come to be that some of the villagers no longer owned their land but instead leased it from other refugees. People told me that just after the 1971 war a number of the villagers had become convinced that the Kashmir dispute was going to be settled and that they would be able to go home to their natal villages in Indian Kashmir. People had debated whether it would be best to wait until the UN announced a resolution or whether they should leave immediately. Some people, one elderly woman said darkly, had been foolish and greedy. They had sold their allotments—sure that they would be cancelled in any case—thinking that they would take the cash proceeds back home and also reclaim their hereditary holdings. She said, "Those people, did they forget? Land is our honor, land is our right! Who sells their honor? Who sells their rights?"

On the day that the marriage of her daughter was proposed for the second time, Munirah Begum might have presented her case more slowly if her brother had not stopped by. She might have invited cousins and friends to tea and to meals during which the intricacies of the offer could be examined within hearing of her husband, in an attempt to convince him that it was an excellent match for their child. Instead, in the presence of her brother, she shifted from telling me a story about an argument she was having with her husband to repeating the argument and bringing her brother into it.

After listening for a while, Munirah Begum's elder brother took a long sip of tea and leaned back against a pillow, stretching a bit, and without looking at anyone in particular, spoke into the room:

As Allah is willing, all of our children will return to their homes very soon. Truly this situation cannot continue for long and then when there is a solution to this problem we will all return to our own houses. We know, brother, that you will return and so your daughter-in-law will not come to her natal home like a guest but her daughter will be a frequent light-giver to the house of her parents.

Then, he paused and looked directly at his sister's husband:

> But you should also be thinking about your young daughter. The boy is educated and his family has property. Your daughter will never be subject to the winds of uncertainty and she will always live with honor in her own house, even now while we are all still waiting to go home after so many years. We will give her a generous dowry, but we will stipulate that in the marriage contract that her *haqq maher* should be paid by a portion of property in her own name.

The implications that he had not properly provided for his family's security, by not preserving land in his name for them, touched Bashir Ahmed in a way that his wife's complaints had not. He was among relatives—all Kashmiri refugees—and should therefore not have had difficulty in securing social recognition of his status as a muhājir. Yet, as someone who had not successfully secured or maintained a claim on property for his family, he was not able to exert his parental decision about this daughter's marriage. The engagement took place several months later, but that day Bashir Ahmed already knew that he had lost the argument. He threw down his work and jumped up. He looked from his wife, who sat with downcast eyes, to his wife's elder brother, who looked at him in silence. In the courtyard all sounds of tea-making had stopped. For a moment all I heard was the drone of the fan and a child crying in a house nearby.

Suddenly, his eyes filling with tears, Bashir Ahmed turned, pointed his finger at me, and shouted: "The UN has made a refugee of me! Do you understand what I mean? The United Nations made a *refūjī* of me and then forgot me!"

FOUR

Transforming Political Identities, 1989–2001

REFUGEE CAMPS IN AZAD JAMMU AND KASHMIR
AND THE INTERNATIONAL REFUGEE REGIME

IN 1990, hundreds and then thousands of refugees began arriving in Azad Jammu and Kashmir from the Indian side of the Line of Control (LoC). AJK government representatives for the first time requested assistance from the United Nations High Commissioner for Refugees (UNHCR) in protecting refugees and administering relief. The AJK government's request amounted to an appeal that the UN recognize displaced people in AJK as prima facie refugees. The UNHCR, however, declined to become involved on the basis that Kashmiri displaced people were "internally displaced" within the former Princely State of Jammu and Kashmir and therefore outside of the UNHCR mandate, because the LoC is not an internationally recognized border. Despite this refusal, the AJK government reorganized its administrative system of rehabilitation and resettlement to forge a space of recognition within the international refugee regime; the government made displaced people visible as victims of human rights abuses and therefore as "humanitarian refugees" as opposed to as emigrants. The emergence of this new social category—the humanitarian *refūjī*—inserted conflict-related forced displacement into a global political imaginary, transformed the relationship between Kashmiri refugees and the state, and had a tremendous impact on AJK and Pakistani society and political culture.

For the AJK government, making displaced Kashmiri people recognizable as humanitarian refugees required reorganizing its system of rehabilitation and resettlement. In Pakistan, international humanitarian organizations had been involved with relief and development projects for Afghan refugees in the 1980s. That experience familiarized politicians, civil servants, and the wider public with some of the global cultural expectations and administrative practices that constituted the international refugee regime. State subjects who came to AJK after 1990 were neither recognized as (already) citizens of AJK nor registered as electors for the selection of representatives to the refugee seats in the AJK legislature, unlike people displaced by previous periods of interstate conflict. The AJK government did not issue identity cards to these newly displaced people, nor did the government provide rehabilitation allotments. Instead, the government established tent camps outside of the Military Security Zone and registered refugees for rations and living stipends. Refugees from the conflict in Indian Jammu and Kashmir remained in what were referred to as "tented refugee camps" for well over a decade; they lived in camps first established in 1990 and 1991 until 2005, when an earthquake created a new disaster displacement geography that resulted in the movement of most of the established refugee camps.

The refugee camps were the spaces where displaced people documented their experiences of political violence and presented them as evidence of as human rights abuses to the international community. The camps also became the focal point of debates between different groups of Kashmiri refugees as they renegotiated their multiple relationships with social and political sites of power to include the international community. Different terms described and ordered displaced Kashmiri peoples' relationships with each other, with established communities in AJK, with the state, and with the international community. Some of these terms, like *panāh gazīn* (refuge-seekers) and IDPs (internally displaced persons), gained little social currency in AJK. Their continued use, although limited, revealed the ongoing struggle to make displacement in AJK visible to an international audience. Others, like the Urdu word *mutāsirīn* (affectees) and the word refūjīs—which was adopted from English into the Urdu language to refer specifically to camp refugees—marked the contested emergence of new social experiences and political identities.

One AJK government official, who traveled frequently to Geneva, New York, and London to meet with representatives of foreign governments, to attend international symposia on the Kashmir issue, and to attend the UNHCR and UN General Assembly meetings, suggested to me that it was strange that the UN treated the LoC as a nonborder in the matter of violent displacement but did not enforce Kashmiri people's right to cross it. On our first meeting in his office, Mumtaz Rafi said to me:

> Kashmiri people crossing the LoC are not "refugees" but "internally displaced" because the LoC is not a border and there is no division of Kashmir for Kashmiri people. And honestly, even though we say *refūjī* here [in Azad Kashmir], we should really say "IDP" because it is good for the UN people to remember that Kashmir is one county.

Like many other politicians and activists, Mumtaz Rafi saw advantages to designating people displaced within the former Princely State as internally displaced persons (IDPs), because he thought that it reminded the international community that Jammu and Kashmir is a disputed territory. Yet, I observed that when we were in his home or when he was speaking in Urdu to members of his constituency, he always used the term refūjī to refer to the residents of refugee camps.

That there are political, social, and cultural differences between a refugee and a refūjī is not immediately obvious when representatives address the international community in English at international forums or in political speeches or media discourses. In AJK, people use the word refūjīs to distinguish camp refugees from muhājirīn as categories of displaced people. This was evident in even mundane disputes that I observed many times while doing my fieldwork when one party thought another was misusing either of the words and requested clarification. For example, one person would say, "*Hum muhājir haiñ* [We are *muhājirs*]," and another would respond, "*Matlab, āp lōg refūjī haiñ, nah*? [Don't you mean, you are *refūjīs*?]" The distinction between muhājirs and refūjīs is socially important in Azad Jammu and Kashmir; it is not a simple indication of a difference in awareness of the international vocabulary of displacement.

The new Kashmiri refūjīs are not conventional legal subjects. Instead, they embody the illegitimate use of violence by the state and represent a human rights crisis set within a historical political dispute. Mumtaz Rafi referred to one important point of difference when he endeavored to explain to me why he used the word refūjīs when he spoke in Urdu, even though he had told me that it important for politicians to say "IDPs" to refer to camp refugees in AJK:

We call them *refūjīs* because of the persecution in occupied [Indian] Kashmir, because the men have been tortured and, well—you know the things that happen to women, may God have mercy, I don't have to say it.

Like humanitarian refugees in the contemporary symbolic order of the international refugee regime, refūjīs are known in part for the human rights abuses levied against them. The Kashmiri refūjī is furthermore both a victim of Indian state violence and (perhaps therefore) not a threat to the Pakistani state. As the Muzaffarabad District Refugee Commissioner explained to me during a formal interview in 1999:

First we must satisfy ourselves that this person has migrated because of torture and humiliation and that he is not a RAW [Indian intelligence] agent, so the police or army must first catch and interrogate any person who comes here. When we are sure that this person is a real *refūjī,* then that person is handed over to the civil authorities at district headquarters.

The word refūjīs also illuminates a conflict between camp refugees and muhājirīn as categories of displaced people: to what degree can refūjīs claim recognition as fully active political subjects versus primarily being seen as victims of political processes and events with no historical agency? This conflict, as it unfolded after 1989, fractured the previous sociopolitical consensus about the relationship between refugees and broader AJK society, and it transformed what it meant to be a Kashmiri refugee. Furthermore, the attempt to depoliticize violence-related forced displacement—and to reincorporate displaced people into a global symbolic order in turn produced a split that was markedly gendered. Refūjī women became visible as victims of human rights abuses and therefore as preeminent representatives of the humanitarian crisis produced by armed conflict. Organized militant groups *(tanzīms)* provided political recognition and offered refūjī men a place within wider social networks as mujāhidīn, actual or potential. Over time, this split led to an increased social value being put on jihād as a mode of political engagement.

THE INTERNATIONAL REFUGEE REGIME IN THE LATE COLD WAR ERA: FROM CONVENTIONAL TO HUMANITARIAN REFUGEES

The international refugee regime is international not because it is a symbolic system for ordering material practices across nation-states but because its material practices and systems of categorization and distinction have become, over time, normative on a global scale. During the Cold War era, the UN expanded the scope of refugee recognition to deal with "refugee-like situations" (in which the displaced people in question were not juridical subjects in a strict reading of the refugee conventions). The emergence of the "humanitarian refugee" as a subject of aid and intervention was an important factor in the globalization of the international refugee regime.[1] Refugee relief projects became dependent on human rights projects to identify their object, the humanitarian refugee.

By the 1980s, a "new humanitarian" approach to refugee-like situations consisted of two discernible strands.[2] The first, as Alex de Waal has argued, was a response to African famines and a critique of the relations of power and dependency that linked state development aid to geopolitical considerations; in the 1970s, groups like Oxfam and Save the Children worked with governments and launched large-scale relief projects in Africa, seeking to address the structural causes of starvation and food insecurity.[3] UN relief projects also began to operate on a development paradigm, and the UNHCR became a central coordinator of relief-development projects.[4] The second strand of the humanitarian approach, as Thomas Weiss has argued, formed in situations of conflict and political turmoil that displaced large numbers of people within state borders or without individual claims to direct persecution.[5] The emergence of the IDP as a category was one way of classifying who was eligible for this kind of humanitarian response.[6] Another was the emergence of a "rights-based humanitarianism" and the practice of offering temporary protection to people who could be shown to be victims of human rights violations.[7]

International relief provision now relies on identifying refugees through their victimization and situating humanitarian work within the framework of universal human rights.[8] The categorical association between the human rights victim and the humanitarian refugee made its way into institutional policy concerning humanitarian crises, a process driven in no small part by international nongovernmental organizations (INGOs). INGOs advocated a rights-based approach to humanitarian action that privileged solidarity with the victims of human rights abuses.[9] The domestic and international influence of the human rights movement also made states more willing to cooperate with the UNHCR.[10] States developed domestic legislation that incorporated human rights evaluations into their foreign policy agendas and led to regional legal norms that expanded refugee recognition or altered the kinds of responses that were seen as fulfilling international legal obligations.[11] Thus, Bill Frelick, director of the International Rescue Committee, counseled the U.S. Senate Judiciary Committee (Subcommittee on Immigration) in February 2002 that "governments ought to take a searching look at the degree to which they honor not only [the Refugee Convention's] minimalist requirements as a legal instrument, but also its fundamental underlying meaning as providing a regime of international responsibility on behalf of a particularly compelling class of people whose human rights have been violated."[12]

Whether relief aid and interventions should be embedded in a human rights framework is now one of the core practical, philosophical, and ethical questions of humanitarianism.[13] Providers of humanitarian relief have argued that it remains, by definition, apolitical; changes in the structural relations of war and armed conflict, not of the humanitarian project, have mandated broader recognition of the refugee in the late–Cold War and immediate post–Cold War period.[14] International humanitarian law traditionally assumed that wars were carried out between states, and that dictated the application of refugee law. But armed conflicts within the borders of sovereign states, or involving militant or so-called warlord groups that fulfilled some of the traditional functions of the state—a situation Mary Kaldor has called "the new wars"[15]—necessitated changes in the how refugee law was applied. By the end of the Cold War, the UN Security Council repeatedly "linked situations of internal disorder and resulting population displacement to threats to international peace and security,"[16] bringing mass displacement issues, both interstate and intrastate, within the UN mandate.[17]

As refugees became classified as victims, both by their suffering and by their nonresponsibility for that suffering, refugees had to be not only located and identified but actively produced. This meant that in order to recognize refugees as apolitical, people had to be depoliticized in the process of becoming refugees. Depoliticization depends on many different cultural and social processes, but several are paradigmatic. One is in the field of representation and draws on discursive forms that originate outside of the refugee's own subject position. In the international refugee regime, the visual prominence and global translatability of women and children as "embodiments of refugeeness," reflect institutional and international expectations of the helplessness of refugee experience.[18] They also draw on transcultural representations of women as inherently less political than men—an attitude that expresses itself in the refugee domain through the fact that boy children become, over time, a problem for the humanitarian project in a way that girl children do not. Another cultural process of depoliticization inheres in the ways that the humanitarian narrative, what Jonathan Benthall calls a "moral fairy story,"[19] frames the search for victims; the helplessness of the refugee is important because it drives donor aid by making the donor, empowered by the aid agency, the one who can rescue the victim.[20]

The refugee camp has been treated as the privileged social site where such persons are transformed into the depoliticized humans we know as refugees. From one perspective, the refugee camp functions as a technology of power to constitute refugees as a social-scientific population.[21] As a political space, it epitomizes the political modernity of the nation-state as a political form, which, as Hannah Arendt noted, privileges natural life over organized political associations and action.[22] Liisa Malkki, slightly differently, approached refugee camps as spaces that depoliticize refugees by excluding the refugee from the national order of cultural citizenship.[23] Refugees are not stripped of all forms of recognition, but their cultural claims on belonging are rendered politically impotent. The refugee camp has become the ideological locus of "humanitarian space," which is "separate from the political"[24] and "detached from the political stakes of conflict[s]" that produce refugee displacements.[25] The (collective) political innocence of refugees must be revealed, and if it cannot be discovered then it must be produced and enforced.

Refugee Camps and the Politics of Refugee Humanitarianism in Pakistan

International organizations became involved in the care and management of refugee populations in South Asia for the first time in 1971, during East Pakistan's secessionist war with West Pakistan (Bangladesh's "War of Liberation").[26] At the time, the UNHCR's effort in India was the single largest operation ever run by the UN, and it led to a quick expansion of the UN operating budget. The UNHCR also consolidated the development paradigm, begun in the 1960s, of working with governments to provide emergency assistance in a variety of humanitarian relief projects. UNHCR expansion occurred through working in refugee-like situations, although such situations did not fit within the agency's mandate under the Refugee Convention and 1967 Protocols.[27]

Working in refugee-like situations undoubtedly had a tremendous impact on the UNHCR, but it also had a profound effect in South Asia, where the material and symbolic practices of refugee recognition began to change. A distinctive feature of global refugee management as it developed in South Asia was that the responsibilities of identifying, documenting, and protecting refugees were separate from providing refuge relief. This pattern of split responsibilities developed in refugee camps set up for people displaced from

East Pakistan; the UNHCR functioned as a coordinating agency for relief funds and development aid in the refugee camps (provided by groups such as UNICEF, the World Food Program, and the World Health Organization), while documentation and daily administration was carried out by Indian state officials.[28] Although India is still not a signatory to international refugee conventions, successive Indian governments adopted this model by administrative order for dealing with later groups of refugees (Sri Lankan Tamil refugees in the 1980s, for example). Indian bureaucrats and legal activists have invoked such practices as signs of India's conformity to the requirements of international law, of India's humanitarian morality, and, more generally, of the rational modernity of the Indian state.[29]

In Pakistan, Afghan refugees began arriving in large numbers after the Soviet invasion of 1979, and a formal structure for the administration of Afghan refugee relief developed through joint accommodations among the government of Pakistan, foreign governments, and international humanitarian organizations. Policy commentators and academics pointed to Afghan refugees' accommodation in Pakistan as an example of the success of a long-term humanitarian relief project. Through the 1980s and early 1990s, they praised the willingness of the Pakistani state to treat displaced people from Afghanistan like refugees even in the absence of international treaty obligations.

The government of Pakistan undertook responsibility for identifying Afghan refugees, who were supposed to return to Afghanistan, and who had to be supported in Pakistan without compromising their home-country citizenship status. The UNHCR and international governments required that Afghan refugees move out of urban areas and into contained refugee camps, where the UNHCR and INGOs could distinguish between Afghan refugees and Pakistani nationals and direct and concentrate relief money.[30] The government of Pakistan remained responsible for the political oversight of Afghan refugees, and their accounting of Afghan refugees was used to direct the relief activities of humanitarian organizations.[31] By the late 1980s, the UNHCR was only one of more than a hundred INGOs administering aid to Afghan refugees in Pakistan. INGOs coordinated with hundreds of local counterparts, which often meant that the UNHCR and other INGOs functioned to raise money internationally while local NGOs carried out the actual distribution of relief.[32]

Pakistani state and civil institutions became a buffer between the international humanitarian community and the political and militant activism of

Afghan refugees. The Pakistani civil administration relied in part on organized political parties to identify people as they left Afghanistan or to confirm their identities by using religious and kinship networks among refugees already resident in Pakistan. Refugees registered as members of political parties, which in turn helped them secure a refugee ration book. Pakistan's camp administration relied on the ration books to identify family groups as Afghan refugees, and Western aid organizations relied heavily on party membership cards to identify individual refugees.[33] Militant organizations kept a jihād book of registered and sponsored military absences so that male refugees who left the camps to fight in Afghanistan could continue to collect relief for their families in the camps. In this close nexus of military funding and relief aid, international funding was also sent through political parties and their allied militant organizations fighting the Soviets in Afghanistan, and the numbers of mujāhidīn that a party could claim was used to determine proportional distribution of aid and military supplies.[34]

Early commentators attributed the success of Pakistan's Afghan refugee program to social affinities that supposedly produced a common political culture; they pointed to the influence of Islamicate norms of hospitality and charity[35] and to the historical connections between Pushtun communities in Afghanistan and Pakistan.[36] However, the so-called success of the Afghan refugee program in Pakistan was framed by the Soviet invasion of Afghanistan and resulting geopolitical interests, which encouraged the development of a large irregular army based in Pakistan for the purpose of fighting communism in Afghanistan.[37] Afghan militants of multiple political, religious, and social lineages were collapsed under the rubric of the "Afghan mujahidin" and widely accepted by the noncommunist allied states as "freedom fighters."[38] When the geopolitics of the Cold War changed in the 1990s, the "freedom fighters" supported by Western aid agencies throughout the anticommunist struggle in Afghanistan became "warlords,"[39] and Afghan refugees in Pakistan were increasingly criminalized for precisely the activities that had defined their supposed success in the 1980s. After the U.S.-allied military action in Afghanistan began in October 2001, the Government of Pakistan refused to register new refugees, citing its inability to distinguish refugees from mujāhids.[40] The refugee camps in Pakistan, which were undoubtedly sites for militant recruitment, had gone from being safe havens for "freedom fighters" during the war against Soviet troops, to havens for "criminals" during the Afghan civil war, and to "terrorist" recruitment grounds during the American and European intervention in Afghanistan.[41]

The militarization of Afghan refugee communities in Pakistan was not culturally predetermined.[42] It was the aim of state policy and the outcome of how refugees interpreted their interactions with the international community, represented in the refugee camps by aid workers. Nonetheless, it presented serious problems for humanitarian INGOs and aid workers who were committed to the ideology of apolitical humanitarianism. The paradox of humanitarian relief work is that relief institutions and funding are allied with military funding and indirect intervention, although the ideal of relief work in conflict zones is to alleviate suffering. Even when militant mobilization is not a policy goal, the international community can support a large civilian population in displacement for years. Over time, refugee populations constitute a recruitment pool for militant organizations and they legitimate militants who claim the status of protectors of the community.[43] In the Afghan refugee camps in Pakistan, INGOs came to focus development activities on women with the tacit assumption that women were not involved in militant politics, particularly religious militant politics.[44] Afghan women, it was said, "found themselves caught up in the political machinations of their leaders, the leaders of Pakistan, and donors with strong Islamic fundamentalist convictions."[45] This focus on refugee women as ideal, if not actual, apolitical subjects revealed little about Afghan refugee political culture. It did reveal a need at the heart of refugee humanitarianism: the need for a depoliticized subject.

REFUGEE CAMPS IN THE AZAD KASHMIR SOCIAL WORLD

That the AJK government understood the expectations of the international community, as represented by aid workers, foreign diplomats, and journalists, was demonstrated by the new forms of refugee administration that developed in AJK after 1989. The legal foundations for recognizing the *muhājir-e-jammū-o-kashmīr* (Jammu and Kashmir state-subject refugee) did not change, but administrative practices and government policies created sharp distinctions between muhājirs (as domiciled refugees) and refūjīs (who reside in relief camps) and between refūjīs and *mutāsirīn* (people internally displaced within AJK). Unlike refugees who had arrived in AJK before 1989, the camp refugees had no access to refugee resettlement provisions and did not participate in AJK electoral politics. Rather than serving as transit sites from which people formed settled communities through property allotments, wage labor, or marriage relations, the camps became sites of semipermanent residence. During the 1990s, refugee camps in AJK became an important place to disseminate information about conditions on the Indian side of the LoC to foreign visitors, and the camps were also where people displaced by Indian state violence encountered the "international community."

Since 1990, the AJK Department of Refugees and Rehabilitation has registered 35,000 refugees and has administered relief aid to a consistent camp-resident population of approximately 20,000 refugees. In the early 1990s, antistate and paramilitary violence on the Indian side of the LoC was centered in the Kashmir Valley districts of Indian Jammu and Kashmir State, and the first people displaced by the insurgent and counterinsurgent violence arrived in AJK's Muzaffarabad District. The first tented refugee camps—Kel Camp and Hattian Camp—were established in that district in 1990. Refugees were transferred into camps farther from the LoC; in the mountainous terrain of Muzaffarabad District, this effectively meant the expansion of the camps close to the city of Muzaffarabad—easy to supply and staff, and easy to visit. In the mid-1990s, refugees began to cross the LoC from the Indian Jammu districts of Poonch and Rajouri, and smaller refugee camps were established in other districts.

By 1996, there were 14 refugee camps in Azad Jammu and Kashmir. Eleven were in Muzaffarabad District and accommodated the majority of refugees who had been displaced by the armed conflict in the Kashmir Valley. Kamsur and Manikpian Camps were officially divided into administrative sections—Kamsur I and II and Manikpian I, II, and III; representatives of the AJK Department of Relief and Rehabilitation considered them separate camps, but most refugees referred to the camps by the place name only, without section number (map 5). The camps closer to the LoC became seasonally occupied by *mutāsirīn;* Hattian and Kel camps were used almost exclusively for displaced AJK residents after 1998.

Resettled refugee villages were spatially ordered and located to exclude strangers, outsiders, and the agents of the state. Refugee camps, on the other hand, were open and permeable spaces that faced the main roads connecting the Needlum Valley with Muzaffarabad city, Muzaffarabad and Chakothi at the LoC, and Muzaffarabad with Islamabad at Kohalla. In addition to a primary school, a medical dispensary building, and a mosque, each camp also had a meeting platform where official government visitors, diplomats, journalists, and representatives of aid and human rights organizations held meetings or conducted interviews with the camp residents. As the nominally

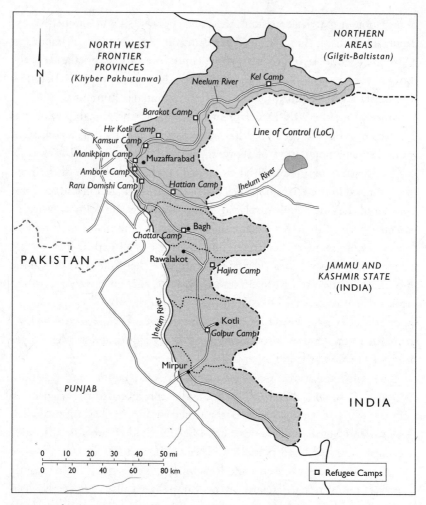

Map 5. Refugee Camps in Azad Jammu and Kashmir (1990–2005).

temporary camps became more permanent, this spatial orientation was maintained. Until 1997, most camps actually were communities of tent shelters. The Department of Refugees and Rehabilitation issued canvas tents every two years, and refugees constructed stone and mud foundations and low walls over which they pitched the tents. In 1998, a Saudi Arabian charity donated tin roof sheeting to the department, which began distributing it to refugees in lieu of new tents. Refugees in well-organized camps such as Kamsur Camp had soon transformed many of their tent encampments into roofed huts with mud walls built on the original tent foundations. By 2000, almost all of the refugee camps in Muzaffarabad were communities of small huts with tin roofs, clustered and stretched out along the main roads of the district.

Refūjīs, settled muhājirs, and other residents of Azad Kashmir addressed themselves to the international community of people and institutions concerned with protecting those who through various circumstances were not adequately protected by their states.[46] The work of documenting violence-related forced displacement was carried out in the refugee camps, and it was there that Kashmiri refugees learned that it was their status as victims of a particular category of political violence—the human rights abuse—that garnered international attention.

Over the years of the intrastate conflict in Indian Kashmir, as the cycles of interstate tension and border conflicts waxed and waned, refūjīs told their stories to numerous journalists, diplomats, and human rights researchers. They were asked to focus on selected events that helped investigators document patterns of human rights abuses. Photo documentation of these testimonials shows women mourning, disheveled and lost-looking children standing before torn canvas tents on mud foundations, and young men without arms or legs, or with scarred backs and thighs. But in my role as anthropologist, I saw another side of life in the camps. When the human-rights-abuse script was exhausted, refūjīs were quite excited to discuss the daily business of running the camp, the principles of selecting members of the Camp Welfare Committees, arranging marriages for the young people, and the difficulty of supporting a family on the stipend afforded by the AJK government. They also took very different kinds of photographs. For example, one proud uncle took pictures of his niece's fifth birthday party, which he intended to send to relatives across the LoC; the honored child, wearing a frilly pink frock and a "Happy Birthday" crown on her head, sat on her father's lap in front of a shack with a satellite dish on its tin roof.

Refugee camps are not, in the end, self-contained and isolated spaces that function exclusively as technologies of power for the state or for the international community. Instead, refugee camps develop as social worlds of their own. The people living there develop internal structures and hierarchies of relationship and difference.[47] They develop mediated and unmediated connections with the people and places around them that are not of the camp and yet provide it broader context or space in the world.[48] Finally, people in the camps become integrated into, and aware of, the wider national and international context of recognition and refusal in which refugees and refugee camps are located.[49]

"Having Done Hijarat, Now We Are Just Living Like Refūjīs"

In 1989, the LoC, while not a border in international law, was widely recognized as a boundary that defined the contours of state political power. This meant that in the 1990s, most of the people who crossed it knew they were going to Pakistan-administered Kashmir, unlike in earlier periods of war-related migration when people sometimes found themselves in AJK without explicitly planning to go there. I met many people living in refugee camps who told me that they had made an explicit decision to migrate as a public political protest against Indian state excesses in their communities.

Altaf Lateef was a resident of Kamsur I, the first of three subdivisions of the overall camp known as Kamsur Camp, who told me that he had "done *hijarat*" to AJK. He, his wife, and their five children had left their home in Handwara Tehsil along with many other residents of the village and its headman in 1991. They had spent a few weeks camped near the town of Neelum, where dispersed members of the village had reconvened and other villagers left behind had caught up with them:

> [Our village] is near the LoC and the Indian security forces were coming into our village and doing searches and taking the boys for interrogations and the girls were unsafe even in their own houses. The army would come and demand the men go with them to the hills to build bunkers and carry supplies, and then our boys were in the line of fire from Pakistan Army positions. Other times the *mujāhidīn* crossed in our village and demanded food, and then the army would come and say that we were supporting terrorists. We were discussing in the village that perhaps we should do *hijarat* in protest of these violations. The headman was in favor that we should migrate to Azad Kashmir and declare this a *hijarat* in protest of the violations in our village. But some people were not in favor and so it was still under discussion. Then the army came and there was a big crackdown, and the army set fire to some shops in the market and burned houses. Everyone was running helter-skelter and the word went out that people are leaving the village. Some people had time to take some of their possessions—jewelry and clothing and some cooking pots—but other people were not ready and left the village with only what they had in their hands when they heard the news. We arrived on the other side of the [Neelum] river in small groups, but when we arrived we saw more and more of our village. Everyone collected their family members and reported to the headman that we have done the *hijarat* which we had planned.

A decade after migrating to AJK, Altaf Lateef still lived in a camp. He was the head of household for his family—his wife, three daughters, and one teenaged son who studied at a private English-medium school in Muzaffarabad. His two older sons had married and established new households for their wives and children. His sons, he told me, worked in the gravel mines north of the camps on the Neelum Valley road, "when they were in Azad Kashmir." He regretted that they had to do that work—one was a qualified engineer and the other a certified schoolteacher—but, he said, they could not get government (public sector) employment in AJK or Pakistan. Over the years, he said, his sons had spent time "fighting for the liberation of occupied Kashmir," but the AJK government stipend was not enough to meet the needs of their families, and so now they mostly lived in the camp and took wage-labor jobs. Altaf Lateef said that the Camp Welfare Committee had successfully found jobs for most of the young men who wanted to work, but the wages were "unfair" because employers knew that refūjīs had limited opportunities, and that kept their wages low. Altaf Lateef had served on the Camp Welfare Committee himself several times, but said he was no longer willing to serve because the camp women bothered his wife with complaints about goats eating their kitchen gardens or skirmishes between children—all problems he said were impossible to solve until some "real land" was allocated to them.

Altaf Lateef claimed that he had done hijarat, but he did not call himself a muhājir. His experiences living in the camp required other words to express the experience of being a refugee:

> We agreed to move to the Kamsur location near Muzaffarabad City because we had no intention to return to [our home village] until conditions became safe for living. All in all, almost half of the village became a *muhājir* that day. But having done *hijarat*, we are just living like *refūjīs*.

Identifying Refūjīs

AJK established procedures for identifying and documenting refūjī status between 1989 and 1992, the years during which larger-scale migrations occurred. When people crossed into AJK, they were usually met by Pakistan Army patrols or by the intelligence and security services. Military and security agencies transported large groups traveling together directly to a civil police station. When they found individuals traveling alone or in small groups, or when they located border crossers staying in the homes of AJK residents, the intercepting agencies held them for investigation until satisfied that they were "real refugees." Determining who was a real refugee could last hours or days, and the process revealed how state security evaluations overlapped with cultural categories.

Village communities or extended families who crossed into AJK together often avoided investigation, or at least only the leaders of the group were questioned by authorities. The determining intelligence agency often needed only for a refugee group to be connected to a border village where the Indian Army or Border Security Forces had carried out a raid; or it was sufficient for one member of the group to declare that they had "done *hijarat*." Several intelligence agents who worked in the Security Zone in the early 1990s told me that if a big "action" occurred on the Indian side of the LoC, the military expected an influx of refugees. If one family in the newly arrived group could establish a kinship relationship with an AJK resident, intelligence agents took that as sufficient confirmation that the entire group was made up of real refugees. This was rarely difficult, as the history of clandestine border crossings and trans-LoC marriages in the region meant that residents of border villages had extensive ties with villages in AJK and with previously resettled refugees.

In the case of small family groups or individuals traveling alone, however, security agents investigated more extensively. In these cases, investigation involved evaluating the motives for crossing the border. Women refūjīs recalled telling "the police" about what had happened to them or to their family members during crackdowns by Indian security forces. Young men traveling alone were held for investigation for longer periods of time. In cases in which their bodies bore visible scars of torture and a relative could be located in one of the refugee camps, they were released to the civil authorities.

In other cases, however, a young man would claim that he was not a "muhājir" but a "mujāhid" who had come to join a *tanzīm*—a militant organization fighting in Indian Jammu and Kashmir. If the *tanzīm* agreed that the youth was a member, he was released to its *amīr* (leader). The *amīr* was then charged with responsibility for the youth's conduct in AJK. Young men who crossed the border alone, who could not identify kin in AJK, and who did not have visible scars of torture, spent weeks or months in detention. During my field research, I met only a few men who claimed to have crossed the border alone when they were not members of militant groups. In each case, they were unable to prove that they were real refugees and were only released once they joined a *tanzīm*. The migrants who first joined a *tanzīm* in this way were vague on the details of how their "release" to the *amīr* had been carried out. Of those who elaborated, several claimed that the *amīr* had come to see them with an intelligence agent during their investigation by state security authorities. Others said they had been brought to a militant camp or office where they were interviewed by the *amīr* and then released to his supervision.

Once the security and intelligence services were satisfied that a border crosser was a real refugee, that person was transferred to the care and responsibility of the civil authorities—usually the local police. If the group of border crossers was large, and the investigation had been conducted in the place where the group had temporarily camped, the refugees' first substantial contact with the civil authorities was often through the Department of Refugees and Rehabilitation, which registered them, assigned them to a refugee camp, and oversaw their transport to the official camp. That process often took several weeks. However, refūjīs who had migrated together and lived for at least the first year in the same camp rarely remembered being in the care of "the police." Instead, they talked about their hosts *(mezbān)* in the local community who shared food and let them camp in the fields. Individuals or small groups who had been held by the military for investigation were brought to a civilian police station, where they were housed until the Department of Refugees and Rehabilitation sent a representative to bring them to a camp. Those who spent time in the police stations recalled them as places where they were sheltered and offered hospitality by the police and members of the community. In AJK, detained persons are usually fed by their families because police stations do not have facilities for cooking; refugees recalled that the police officers offered them tea and food from the market and that local residents brought food for them.

Administering Refugee Camps

The AJK Department of Relief and Rehabilitation oversaw overall administration of the refugee camps. Education for primary students, electricity use, and medical care in the camps were provided directly by the department, and Camp Welfare Officers had direct oversight over the daily running of the camp and were charged with arranging for public services. The officers provided each head of household with a ration card that recorded the names of his dependent family members. The card entitled the family to a monthly stipend, and births and deaths were recorded on the ration card and in the department's records. The head of household collected the ration stipend in person in the camp he was assigned to and where he officially resided, but he or members of his household might spend most of their time living elsewhere. As of 2001, refūjīs received a living stipend of 2,000 rupees per person and 2,900 rupees paid to the head of household on a monthly basis, and secondary-school children received an additional educational stipend of 100 rupees per month. The ration card issued by the AJK Department of Refugees and Rehabilitation did not convey legal rights or allow for travel, employment, or political representation, but it came to function as an identification document. Refūjīs used the card when they left the camp, and the local authorities accepted it as a legitimate form of documentation.

Refūjīs resident in camps in the Muzaffarabad district also organized their own Camp Welfare Committees. In each camp, the committee served as an authoritative body that mediated internal disputes and advocated for camp residents with the Department of Refugees and Rehabilitation. The first such committee was organized by residents of Kamsur I around the time it was first established. Kamsur Camp was completely destroyed by an earthquake in 2005, but it had been a well-organized and fairly prosperous camp since its founding in 1991. Its prosperity was due in no small part to the formation of its Camp Welfare Committee and its successful model of internal self-advocacy. The committee helped refūjī men find work outside the camp in the gravel mines in the mountains or in domestic service in the city of Muzaffarabad. It established that refūjī women who had been teachers in the government schools in their home villages would staff the camp's primary schools. Over the years, the Kamsur Camp Welfare Committee successfully prevented the Department of Refugees and Rehabilitation from transferring people into or out of the original part of the camp without its approval; so as camps were consolidated and expanded, Kamsur II and III came to house refugees from Handwara and Kupwara tehsils almost exclusively.

There was no formal connection between camp welfare committees in different camps, but they shared a common structure. Each committee was comprised of senior members of the major kinship lineages or of the villages of origin represented in the camp; each of these groups selected its own representatives. In Kamsur I, where the majority of residents had migrated en masse from a single village in Indian Kashmir, the Camp Welfare Committee resembled a village council *(jirga),* with the same headman who had led the villagers in their migration. In Ambore, Barakot, Hir Kotli, and Raru Domishi Camps, the headman-ship of the committee was established by election or rotation. Representatives needed to command some authority within the lineages represented in the camp in order to mediate the camp's internal concerns. However, in order to advocate for camp residents with the

Department of Refugees and Rehabilitation and to represent the camp to delegates from political institutions and charitable organizations, the camp headman also had to be fluent and literate in Urdu and proficient in English. The Camp Welfare Committee, therefore, usually included the more educated camp refugees, even if they were younger than more senior members of a lineage or of their own families.

In the camps that were most visited by foreign and Pakistani dignitaries—Kamsur, Ambore, and Raru Domishi Camps—the chairman of the Camp Welfare Committee was selected as much for his ability to represent refugees diplomatically as for his ability to mediate disputes within the camp or to work with the AJK Department of Refugees and Rehabilitation. The chairman of one camp, for example, spoke English and German in addition to Kashmiri, Pahari, and Urdu. That proficiency, he told me, allowed him to speak directly with foreign representatives if he chose to do so.

Documenting Victimization

Representatives of diplomatic missions, international humanitarian and human rights organizations, embassy officials, and journalists visited the camps as part of their fact-finding missions. For reasons of protocol and security, such visits were formally organized affairs, and they began with an official orientation meeting, during which an official of the Department of Refugees and Rehabilitation provided the delegation with a copy of the department's annual report, The Details of Refugees Coming from Indian Occupied Kashmir. The report gave an overview of refugee arrivals by month, relief provisions supplied by the government, and information about refugee-camp populations. It also included a list of "atrocities committed in the Kashmir Valley by Indian forces since 1990, with numbers of people killed, women raped, men rendered impotent by sexual torture, houses burned, value of property destroyed, and number of corpses retrieved from the Jhelum River and buried in Azad Kashmir." Then, representatives were escorted to one of the refugee camps, where the Chairman of the Camp Welfare Committee met the guests.

The visits in the camps had two parts: first a tour and then interviews with individual refūjīs. Tours were led by members of the Camp Welfare Committee and a Camp Welfare Officer, and visitors were invited to look inside the huts or tents to view the conditions of the camp. For the interviews, the visitors were invited to a meeting platform or a central square, where the Camp Welfare Committee chairman called upon selected individuals to explain what had happened to them in Indian Kashmir and why they had come to AJK Photographs taken on these official visits, particularly of women or orphaned children and of men with visible bodily traces of physical harm, such as amputations or severe scarring, were incorporated into the reports written about the conflict in Jammu and Kashmir. Although journalists did not welcome government escort, refugees in the camps told me that they only spoke with journalists when a "handler" was present. A member of the Camp Welfare Committee would inform the Department of Refugees and Rehabilitation that they were giving interviews and would invite an officer to observe. Thus, journalists' interactions in the camps had a similar ritualistic structure and content to official diplomatic visits.

"You Can Take My Picture"

I met Naseema Bibi for the first time in Manikpian camp. It was not one of the camps that foreign representatives usually toured, and I had the impression that Naseema Bibi had not known that she would be asked to tell her story. At the same time, it seemed she had been selected to meet me because she had told her story many times. She had lived for five years in Ambore Camp and had moved to the Manikpian Camp after Ambore's Camp Welfare Committee had arranged her marriage to a refūjī man living there. She told me that she had been introduced to many foreigners over the years. Hers was a strange testimony, because she claimed to remember nothing of her life before the Ambore camp:

> I don't know how I got here [Azad Kashmir]. I don't remember. I was a child. They say they pulled me from the [Jhelum] river. Who knows? If someone brought me here I don't remember. I was unconscious. When I was a child, they brought me many times to meet some *angrez* (foreigners) to tell my story and have my picture taken, but I had no story to tell. I remember nothing, but everyone in the camps said "this is a Kashmiri orphan who lost her parents by the cruelty of the Indian Army."

The other women encouraged her to say more, but she repeated, "I remember nothing, I had no story to tell, all I know is that I am a Kashmiri orphan." She offered, "You can take my picture," and seemed confused that I did not have a camera with me.

She insisted that she couldn't tell me anything that would be of interest to me about the refugee camp, but she was willing to say a little about her experience of moving from her foster home in Ambore camp to her marital home in Manikpian camp. She knew nothing about how the marriage had been arranged. Before she married her husband, she only knew that he was older than she, that he was a mujāhid who had fought for many years for the liberation of Kashmir, and that she would move to live with him in the Manikpian Camp. She said that she was afraid to go to the *bazār* (market) even with her husband, because she feared she would be unable to bargain for good prices and would thereby mishandle the household monies. In her marital household, she was responsible for exchanging work with other women, but she felt that she "didn't know how to do anything."

These were the things, after five years of living in a refugee camp that concerned her: "I had no one but now he married me. He teaches me the things I need to do. His sister shows me how to cook. He [does wage labor] to earn extra money and he takes care of me. I have no complaint." Her husband's elder sister sat with us. She was a widow and her brother was the head of household of record for her and her two children. She told me that the committee had considered the marriage to Naseema Bibi mutually beneficial: an orphaned young girl would have a husband to take care of her, and a mujāhid who had lost many members of his family would have a new family.

Months later, I met Naseema Bibi again in Rawalpindi, where she and her husband Abdul Majid were living in a *kacchī ābādī* (labor colony). One day, drinking tea when there were no men present and when her sister-in-law, to whom she showed great deference, was not with us, she said:

> I don't know my own story. But now I know all his stories. He has many scars on his body. The first time I saw those scars I was scared. When I was less shy, one day I asked his sister. She told me all those details about how he got those injuries. She told me about how he was tortured. A lot of the men have scars like that, on their backs, on their legs, burn marks, beating marks. Some [have] a lump in a bone where it was broken. The women, when their husbands are away, talk about these wounds.

Naseema Bibi's sister-in-law told me that in 1991, shortly after coming to Azad Kashmir for the first time, Abdul Majid had told his story to the *angrez* (white foreigners) and had allowed them to photograph the scars on his back. Abdul Majid and I had many long conversations in his hut in the labor colony and sometimes in his taxi when he drove me to my residence. He talked to me about his life in Kashmir before the armed freedom struggle began, about becoming a mujāhid, about his hopes for his new daughter, and about working illegally as a taxi driver in Islamabad. I took a number of pictures of him with his wife, one of which he laminated and hung on the wall. But he never told me about being tortured or about baring his back to have his picture taken.

"Why Do You Say Mutāsirīn? We Are All Muhājirīn in Our Own Homeland"

Residents of villages in AJK territory who were displaced by border sniper fire and heavy shelling by the Indian and Pakistani armies did not qualify for the relief support that was offered to people who migrated across the LoC in the 1990s. Department of Refugees and Rehabilitation administrators developed a new Urdu term for firing-line-affected people: *mutāsirīn*. This terms evaded the distinctions inherent in the international legal terminology of "refugee" and "IDP" and became a common term in everyday speech in AJK, in the Urdu-language press, and in governmental reports and administrative documents. The forced displacement of *mutāsirīn* presented the AJK government with challenges different from those that presented themselves with people who crossed the LoC. *Mutāsirīn* were documented residents of AJK with domicile certificates—whether they were either hereditary residents *(qaumī bāshindah)* or resettled muhājars—and therefore also with Pakistani identity cards. They had strong connections to other AJK residents and communities, and they were already integrated into the Pakistani state's networks of social and political surveillance. Therefore, the local authorities were not under pressure from Pakistani security agencies to confirm that these people were "really" refugees.

Still, the scale of displacement was profound, as was the impact that displacement had on people's livelihoods. The official AJK government count of people displaced within AJK and from AJK into Pakistan from villages on the LoC was nearly 372,000 in 2001. However, because the government does not register *mutāsirīn* in camps, this number actually reflects the human traffic through military and police check posts and thus includes people who have left and returned to their homes on multiple occasions. Patterns of displacement from the villages near the LoC are also cyclical and seasonal, because the intensity of LoC firing correlates to the level of interstate political tension and tends to increase in the late spring and summer and decrease in the winter months.

There were no budgetary provisions for the support of *mutāsirīn* as opposed to *refūjīs* and therefore no rations or living stipends for them. Instead, the Department of Refugees and Rehabilitation administered one-time compensation for losses suffered as a result of LoC firing incidents. Individuals received payment for injuries or the loss of body parts, and the head-of-household was compensated for collective or family losses, like the destruction of houses and the death of adult household members and male children.

For *mutāsirīn,* refugee camps were at first temporary residences—places families moved when it became impossible to live in their home village by staying in the houses during the day and working the fields at night (and thus escaping sniper fire). *Mutāsirīn* moved into existing refugee camp infra-structure and used the camp facilities, like electricity and bathing areas, and national and foreign charities provided some material aid. After the mid-1990s, Kel Camp and Hattian Camp predominantly housed *mutāsirīn.* Men returned occasionally to their villages to look over their properties, and families moved back to their villages when periods of intense shelling dropped off. After the bilateral nuclear tests of 1998 and the Kargil War of 1999, nearly constant LoC firing forced residents of villages located close to the LoC to entirely vacate their homes and agricultural lands. Between 1998 and 2003, entire families moved seasonally between border villages and the tent camps. Over the years, more and more sought semipermanent, stable lodgings. There were no camps for Kashmiri *refūjīs* or *mutāsirīn* in Pakistan, but *mutāsirīn* families often vacated the tent camps and migrated to cities in Pakistan in order to secure wage labor that could support the family in the absence of agricultural income and to arrange for their children's schooling.

Many *mutāsirīn* rejected the AJK governmental vocabulary that desig-nated them as "affectees" and equated their own situation of displacement with that of the muhājirs. Omar Saleem, for example, who was displaced from his village near the LoC by artillery fire, was living in the former refu-gee camp at Hattian in the summer of 2000. He had organized a men's work group composed of a preexisting labor-exchange group from his own home village, and he had arranged for the work group to earn wages harvesting fodder grasses for Faisal Naseer, who ran a profitable shop in Hattian and could afford to hire help during the harvest. After Faisal Naseer referred to

Omar Saleem as an "affectee," Omar Saleem explained that the word *mutāsir* was not appropriate for his condition:

> We also had to leave our homes seeking safety for our families. First in 1947, then '65, then '71, and now we've been here [in the camp] for four years. Like all of these people here [in the village], we too are from [a village] in Indian Kashmir. We are *muhājirīn* so why do you say *mutāsirīn*? We have spent six months a year here for the past seven years and we can't go back to our own lands. We are all *muhājirīn* in our own homeland *(watan)*.

Other men from the camp were listening to the conversation and nodded in agreement, but Faisal Naseer disagreed. "He was affected (*mutāsir huē*) by LoC firing," he said. "That means they are all *mutāsirīn* not *muhājirīn*." Omar Saleem stopped sipping his tea and turned toward me in a way that suggested his disagreement, but he did not directly contradict his patron.

CATEGORICAL CONFUSIONS: REFUGEES AND MILITANTS IN AZAD JAMMU AND KASHMIR

Each of the new terms that developed in the 1990s in Azad Jammu and Kashmir to describe displaced Kashmiri peoples' relations with each other, with the state, and with the international community were insufficient and contested. Camp residents, resettled refugees, local residents, government rehabilitation officials, the Urdu media, and translators for foreign representatives used the terms refūjīs (camp refugees), *mutāsirīn* (affectees), and *panāh gazīn* (refuge-seekers) in different ways. None of these terms expressed the social experience and political significance of displacement in ways that generated a broad social consensus and satisfied the people the terms purported to identify.

The Pakistani Urdu-language media applied the Urdu term *panāh gazīn* to the Kashmiri refugees who crossed the LoC after 1990. The term became a part of the popular vocabulary of displacement in Pakistan during the Afghan refugee crisis; international humanitarian organizations had revived the word because it linked the meanings "homeless" or "evacuated" with "in need of protection."[50] Urdu newspapers used the term to refer to flood victims and political refugees in Africa and in reference to Bosnian Muslim refugees during the conflict in Kosovo. In discussions after BBC or Pakistan TV news broadcasts, residents of AJK also used the term when they talked about the people displaced by those humanitarian emergencies, but the term *panāh gazīn* had almost no currency among Kashmiri refūjīs when they spoke about themselves or each other.

When Altaf Lateef said that he and the other residents of Kamsur Camp were "just living like *refūjīs*," he was pointing to a problem of recognition, acknowledgment, and value. He was involved in the internal social, political, and economic life of the camp, and his work with the Camp Welfare Committee meant that he was personally involved in the political work of parties, the policy goals of AJK institutions, and the organizational work of militant organizations. By refusing to identify the act of leaving his home as taking refuge, Altaf Lateef rejected the implication that he was unable or unwilling to intervene directly in the political processes and conditions that had led to his displacement. He was also rejecting a definition of Kashmiri displaced people that reduced them to victims, objects of aid, or supplicants with no claims on others besides an appeal for charity. Some people saw him living like a refūjī, but in his view he and his sons were "fighting for the liberation of occupied Kashmir."

Other residents of the refugee camps in AJK expressed similar objections to the term *panāh gazīn*. Abdul-Wadud was a refugee elder who had been displaced from a village in the Baramullah district in 1990. I met him in Ambore Camp, where he had served for several years as a member of the Camp Welfare Committee. He had met many foreign delegations when they visited the camp, and he worked closely with members of militant organizations to arrange marriages and handle disputes. The first time I met him, the representative from the Department of Refugees and Rehabilitation who accompanied me introduced the camp's residents as "Kashmiri *panāh gazīn*." Abdul-Wadud did not directly contradict the officer, but as we talked about his life in the camp, he made it clear that the term was misleading and objectionable:

> After the [Indian] army came and burned our houses and took the men to the school grounds where many were tortured, we were planning on going to the hills for a little while to protect our sons and preserve the honor of our daughters. . . . We were not seeking *panāh* [refuge]. But then we found ourselves [in Azad Kashmir] where we were met by the [Pakistan] Army. And so we said—it is ok, we will stay for a week and take some rest. But we could not go back, and now we are guests *[mehmān]* here. Even though it is my own *mulk* [county], even so I am a guest here for a while and we have become temporary residents in this *mahfūz jagah* [safe place]. But we are not here looking for *panāh* but for a place to organize the liberation of our properties and families.

Abdul-Wadud invoked the same ethic that I had encountered in my conversations with Shafiq, the young mujāhid who said that his mother had told her sons, "One accrues blessings for feeding a guest or sheltering a traveler who asks for *panāh*, [but] you receive no blessing for offering food to these *muhājarīn*. It is your *farz* [duty] to feed them and it is their *haqq* [right] to eat this corn." In one sense, Shafiq's mother and Abdul-Wadud espoused the idea that muhājarīn have a right to a shared space and livelihood. For Abdul-Wadud, this idea arose from the nationalist value of "one country," while for Shafiq's mother it was an Islamic value of "religious duty."

But Abdul-Wadud's objection went further. In regional cultural understanding and sociopolitical discourse, the term *panāh* refers to a kind of refuge that conveys the social recognition and political authority of acting morally on the one who offers protection, not on the one who seeks it. The implication is that the need for protection results from the political (criminality) or social (rejection by the family) failing of the person seeking refuge. The one who offers refuge, therefore, does so not out of moral obligation but out of his own liberality and pity, his character of open-heartedness, and his superior position of power that allows him to act as a protector and to guarantee asylum.[51] To seek *panāh* was thus not only to abdicate one's claim on the spiritual rewards of moral conduct, but it was also to forgo social recognition for action and to disempower oneself politically. The continuing importance of the concept of hijarat and the rejection of the terms *mutāsirīn* and *panāh gazīn* by the very people these terms were supposed to describe reveals the problem with the apolitical concept of refuge.

A new distinction emerged between women and men refūjīs; women more easily fit the global representational forms that made them recognizable as "victim-refugees." This gendered distinction produced a victim-refugee for the international community, but it also produced a victim-warrior. Refūjī men as a gendered group—and young men as a generational group—became more available for militant mobilization as it became progressively more difficult for them to claim the hijarat as a valued political practice. In everyday speech, when referring to the residents of refugee camps, the term refūjī came to refer to women and children and mujāhid to male youths and adults. Jihād was becoming an important way of remaining a political person and expressing a connection to the ongoing conflict in Jammu and Kashmir.

"But the Camp Is Not Just for Refūjīs—You Can See That There Are Men There with the Women and Children"

The contradictions of this split between male and female refūjīs are still being worked out in social practice and produce a significant amount of practical confusion in AJK. Over the years, I have had many discussions with residents of Azad Kashmir who themselves could not entirely agree on the terms to best describe the residents of the refugee camps.

One example was a conversation that I both instigated and observed between Afroze Begum and her husband during the Kargil War. I had been visiting them at their home outside of Muzaffarabad, and they were driving me back to my residence. As we drove past Manikpian Camp, Afroze Begum turned around in her seat and gestured toward the camp. "That is where the *mujāhidīn* from the Kashmir Valley live," she said. "Since you are researching what is happening in Kashmir, you should talk to them about the abuses in the Valley."

Her husband disagreed with her characterization of the people living in the camp: "No, those are not *mujāhidīn* living there—that is a camp for *refūjīs.*" Afroze Begum was not convinced. "It is not just for *refūjīs*—you can see that there are men there with the women and children," she said. Her husband replied, "They are *refūjīs* too." Afroze Begum was quiet for a long moment. Then she said, "Well, some of them have suffered torture, but after having brought their women here for safety, they go back [to the Valley] and participate in the *jihād*. So why do you say *refūjīs* now when we both know that they are *mujāhidīn*?" Her husband acquiesced to some extent. "Well, some do go there as *mujāhidīn*, but they are in other camps," he said. "These camps are for *refūjīs* and it is best to call them that."

When I visited the camp later that summer, I found that in fact many of the men were or had recently been active members of militant organizations, and quite a few had moved to the camp from independent living quarters after marrying a refūjī woman. After visiting Manikpian for the first time, I referred to the residents of the camp in a casual conversation as "*refūjīs* and *mujāhidīn*." Ehsan Naveed, a resident of Muzaffarabad's old city, quickly corrected me. "Why do you call them *mujāhidīn*? They are not *mujāhids*! A person cannot just say 'I am a *mujāhid*.' Did those rascals tell you that, that they are *mujāhids*?" I was a bit abashed, feeling that I had gotten the categories wrong, and I didn't want my mistake attributed to the residents of the camp. I answered, "Well, no. No one said 'I am a *mujāhid*,' but when I was talking with people living there about how they came here and about living in the camps, I thought that many of them had only recently come to live in the camp. I thought that they go back and forth [across the LoC] a lot." Ehsan Naveed seemed to relax, explaining, "You misunderstood because you do not know what a *mujāhid* is. A real *mujāhid* would not come to sit in a

refugee camp with women and children. Those boys there walk around saying 'I am a *mujāhid*,' but they spend their days worried about how to find a
wife. We see that all the time."

Refūjīs, Mujāhids, and the Problem of Living
a Politically Qualified Life

International observers have reported since the early 1990s that refugee
camps in AJK were places of sanctuary for women and that men returned to
the valley of Kashmir to participate in the armed struggle. These observations
were gleaned during official visits, when there was a predominance of women,
children, and the elderly in the camps, and the resulting reports portrayed
the camps as isolated and unchanging.[52] Life in the camps, though, changes
cyclically and over time, and the social worlds of refūjīs are not limited to the
refugee camps. While a large proportion of refūjī men are registered members
of militant organizations, most of them have spent relatively short periods
of time engaged in militant activities on the Indian side of the LoC and
relatively longer periods of time supporting their families in Pakistan.

Refūjīs must remain registered in their assigned camps in order to continue
receiving relief stipends, but camp residence is an administrative category, not
always a social fact. Many residents spend significant periods of time living
in other places, and refūjī men who live as well as reside in the camps work
as laborers for private contractors in the construction and mining industries,
as domestic workers in private homes, and for local landholders during the
labor-intensive harvest season. Those who don't have regular positions hire
on as daily or weekly labor to local residents. In AJK, refūjīs use the ration
card issued by the Department of Refugees and Rehabilitation as an identity
document for all of the listed family members. It is not a legal form of identity documentation, and it does not technically allow travel or employment,
but the local authorities do not impose travel or employment restrictions
on camp residents. In Pakistan, however, undocumented refūjī men cannot
travel or get work on the basis of the ration card, and to carry such a card
with them would deprive their family members in the camp, including other
dependent men, of their documentation and ration allotments. Still, refūjī
men routinely go to cities of the northern Punjab, especially Rawalpindi and
Islamabad, where they work at the edges of legality. They cannot take jobs
that require identity documentation or professional certification of any kind,
so they work as day laborers and private taxi drivers.

Militant organizations, especially those affiliated with formal political parties, provide refūjīs with a vital link to social networks and political institutions outside the refugee camps. They provide a quasi-institutional structure that is able to mediate what Itty Abraham and Willem van Schendel have called "licit" social arrangements that circumvent the formal criminality of those compelled to operate outside the law.[53] Kashmiri refūjī men who travel in Pakistan explained to me that Pakistani authorities accepted their *tanzīm* membership cards as a form of identification. On a number of occasions I observed that a refūjī man, by showing a *tanzīm* membership card, avoided detention. It was not possible to speak with the police officers or soldiers who accepted this form of documentation, and I therefore cannot explain the mechanism by which they learned which *tanzīms* offered acceptable sanction. In AJK, political party–allied militant organizations established themselves in refūjī social relations by providing a kind of women's welfare through marriage brokering and the provision of dowries; by ensuring employment opportunities; by acting as advocates for men in public spaces; and by guaranteeing secure relations with agents of the state.[54] Charities run by political parties have also been conduits for direct aid from domestic and international donors, but the support that *tanzīms* provide is not primarily material. More significantly, political parties have provided a vital link to local residents, and the Camp Welfare Committees perform much of their work by connecting with political parties through their militant wings.

Refūjīs I met were committed to the work of human rights documentation undertaken in the camps. They expected it would lead to an international response that would change the situation that had led to their displacement. Many were also committed to facilitating the end of their exile by fighting for what they considered the liberation of their homes. Yet neither of these commitments could hold back the imperative to get on with the business of living. Militant refūjī men came back to the camps before the mountain passes became impassable so that they could be with their families over the winter. New babies were born, young people came of age, and marriages were arranged. People died of illness or old age or were killed in the conflict. The camps were just another kind of social space where living took place. For the displaced people who lived in refugee camps, their lives became a struggle to have a "place in the world which makes opinions significant and actions effective,"[55] a struggle not to live politically but to live a politically qualified life.

*"Only We Can Make Sure That Kashmiris Are
Here to Struggle for Their Rights"*

A year after I first met them in Manikpian Camp, Abdul Majid and his wife Naseema Bibi sought me out when I was doing interviews in a labor colony near Islamabad. They were temporarily living in the *kacchī ābādī*, and Abdul Majid was working as a taxi driver. His wife had heard about a woman researcher coming to the colony to talk to Kashmiri muhājirs and had asked him to look for me. He invited me to visit her at their shack the next day, and over the next year I met them both many times.

One day, when Abdul Majid was driving me home, I raised a topic that I had not previously discussed with him. I had known for quite a while that he was a mujāhid and a registered member of a *tanzīm,* because his wife and sister had discussed that with me in a very matter-of-fact way. But he had not referred to himself that way in my presence. He, my research assistant, and I were alone in the taxi, and I hoped that since I was asking him the question in a place that was not public (and where there was no state surveillance or social audience), he would feel comfortable answering the question (or not) as he chose. I asked him about Manikpian Camp and whether people living there were refūjīs or mujāhids. He met my eyes in the rear-view mirror. Then he looked back at the road and lit a cigarette.

After a while, he said, "Most of us men are *mujāhids.* I keep going across the LoC [to the Valley], and until now I keep coming back. My wife and daughter are in the camp living as *refūjīs,* and I come back for them." Since he had answered my question, I decided to tread further into sensitive topics. (As an unmarried woman, not young exactly by Kashmiri standards but still of marriageable age, talking with men about matters related to sexuality was more risqué than asking about jihadist organizations.) I forged on, "May I have your permission to ask a difficult question?" He agreed, and I said, "You know many people say a *mujāhid* should not get married?" He inclined his head in acknowledgement, and I said, "But I noticed that in the camp many *mujāhids* are married to *refūjī* women. Is it possible to be a *mujāhid* and to be a good husband?" My research assistant immediately put his head back and closed his eyes; he seemed to want nothing to do with this conversation. Abdul Majid, however, answered without hesitating: "Well, when people make this criticism, we just say to them 'we have to marry and have children to keep our families going. If this struggle is not successful now, only we can make sure that Kashmiris are here to struggle for their rights.' But really, it is not a problem in the camps. It is only a big problem when some boy wants to marry a *muhājir* or a local *[qaumī bāshindah]* girl. Then there has to be some agreement about where they will live. Often her family says it is not possible."

On another occasion, I asked him how he came to be living in Pakistan and whether the *tanzīm* had given him permission to leave Azad Kashmir or whether he had retired. Abdul Majid explained that leaving a militant organization is not a problem—he had been the member of several different *tanzīms* since 1991. Being a mujāhid he said, had to do with his intentions, not with his membership in a particular organization:

> Well, you can't be there [in Indian Kashmir] all the time. It is too much for a man to bear. All my family is here [in Azad Kashmir]. The rest of my family have been murdered or martyred. Of course I keep going back [to the Valley], and I also keep doing other kinds of work for the *tanzīms*. I go when I get that intention *[nīyat]* which says "now I have to take action."

PART THREE

Body of Victim, Body of Warrior

FIVE

Human Rights and Jihād

VICTIMIZATION AND THE SOVEREIGNTY
OF THE BODY

IN MARCH 2000, delegates of the All Party Hurriyat Conference in Pakistan organized a public protest in conjunction with a mass strike in the Indian Kashmir Valley. The delegates, who were all members of the most influential transnational Kashmiri political parties, planned the march to publicize the arrest of several prominent political leaders in Srinagar and to demand their release. On the day of the demonstration, protesters marched through the international business district of Islamabad and past the Pakistan parliamentary buildings on their way to the diplomatic enclave (figure 4). The marchers carried banners identifying their political parties and associations. Most of the banners did not focus on the recent detentions but rather referred to the ongoing human rights crisis in Indian Jammu and Kashmir State. The banners also addressed themselves not to the government of India but to a broader, although perhaps merely desired, international audience. They asked, "Why world conscious [sic] is silent on violation of human rights in occupied Kashmir?" Others asked why Jammu and Kashmir was not worthy of an international humanitarian intervention, such as one that read "Mr. Kofi Annan, 70 thousand killed in Kashmir. You not bothered. But two hundred killed in East Timour [sic]. You bothered!" The procession was led by a Toyota pick-up filled with men in traditional dress, worn in the style common for mujāhidīn, with loose trousers hitched above their ankles and their beards trimmed in the iconic style of the Lashkar-e-Tayyiba and Al-Badr jihadist organizations. They held posters, handwritten in English and slung over the sides of the truck that read "Kashmiris demand the right of self-determination!" and "Who defends the human rights of Kashmiris?" (figure 5). One mujāhid, chanting into a megaphone, repeated in Urdu "**We** will **demand** our rights. **We** will **defend** our rights . . . **We** will **demand** our rights. **We** will **defend** our rights."

FIGURE 4. Protesters marching (Islamabad, 2000).

Human rights discourses are now a part of how jihād is legitimated and organized in Azad Jammu and Kashmir and among Kashmiri refugee communities in Pakistan. The integration of appeals to human rights into how Islamist militant organizations and jihadist groups attempt to claim social legitimacy is not exclusively a South Asian phenomenon. While scholars and policy analysts have recognized these claims, they dismiss them analytically as a superficial propaganda ploy or denigrate them as a perversion of human rights ideals.[1] However, this dismissal fails to heed a powerful critique inherent in the integration of human rights discourse with the legitimating mechanisms of paramilitary organizations, including Islamic militant groups. For people living in many parts of the world, humanitarian projects have always been recognized as political because such efforts have been carried out as part of geopolitical ideologies that tangibly affect the political conditions of peoples' lives. What the human rights ideal promised them was not a space outside of power politics. Instead, it proposed that the international community intervene to limit the power of states over people rather than furthering the interests of a specific domestic security state or of interventionist foreign powers. Indeed, after the end of the Cold War, human rights became a lever for mobilizing military intervention through the discourse of humanitarianism.[2]

Questions about why some human rights crises became the object of international pressure or intervention while others did not are not new. When I was studying Urdu in Lahore in 1993, many people asked me whether my country knew what was happening to Muslim people in Indian Kashmir. I remember on one occasion watching Pakistan Television news footage

FIGURE 5. Mujāhidīn leading protest march (Islamabad, 2000).

of a funeral procession in Srinagar. The funeral was for several young men whose mutilated bodies had been recovered days after their arrest by military personnel. Witnesses interviewed on TV showed photographs of the youths before they had been killed and told how their dead bodies bore evidence of prolonged torture, no matter the official story of how they had died. One of the young women in the family I was visiting became so distraught that her brother-in-law escorted her out of the room. She was in university at the time, and during her following years as a student she helped organize fundraising events in support of the refujīs and war orphans living in the Azad Jammu and Kashmir (AJK) camps. By the late 1990s, people no longer routinely asked me whether my country knew what was happening to people in Jammu and Kashmir. Instead, many people that I met in Pakistan and among Kashmiri communities asked me, and each other, whether the fact that they were Muslim made them less important to the international community.

International human rights activists, transregional Kashmiri political parties, and Kashmiri, Pakistani, and Indian journalists, and refugees themselves have engaged in human rights documentation and advocacy since the beginning of the armed insurgency against the Indian state in 1989. They have used the language of human rights to appeal to the international community, and, at first, they made extensive use of visual images, particularly photographs, documenting victims of human rights abuses and depicting refugees as victims of those abuses. This reliance demonstrated faith in the possibility of locating an exemplary victim who might speak to and motivate an international audience.[3] Over time, however, it became clear that neither the photographic evidence nor the physical wounds that they documented were seen to point to one absolute truth behind human rights abuses. The people who saw these photographs drew different conclusions about what they were evidence of.[4] Public support for militant groups who claimed to be motivated to defend Kashmiri Muslims against human rights abuses by the state grew from a belief that the international community is, at best, ill equipped to respond to the abject violation of its own ideals or, at worst, unwilling to use its influence and its institutions to enforce those ideals in opposition to other vested political or economic interests.

The discursive use of the term human rights by militant organizations as a mode of legitimating violence distresses international human rights activists, who approach human rights as a coherent (although historically emergent) set of normative values, legal provisions, and regulatory practices. Scholars, activists, and policy analysts alike have had a tendency to write off militant claims on the human rights paradigm, because those claims violate the assumed liberal and humanist orientation of human rights. However, the localization of human rights has become a global social, political, and cultural phenomenon. As Sally Merry has argued, this reality requires shifting evaluation and analysis of human rights from the law to how human rights ideals, interpretations, and practices manifest themselves in local contexts.[5]

One aspect of localization is that the human rights project is taken up unevenly. In the context of Jammu and Kashmir, local human rights advocates have been primarily concerned with human rights abuses that deal with the most violent violations of the body—including torture, extrajudicial execution, and rape. They have been less focused on questions that fall broadly under the purview of civil and political rights. As a matter of international law, human rights promotes a hierarchy of principles, distinguishing between the rights that can never be abrogated and those that can be temporarily suspended under emergency conditions. In transnational Kashmiri political discourse, however, the term *insānī haqūq* (human rights) refers primarily to those nonderogable rights, such as protection of life and prohibitions against torture, which cannot be repudiated even during emergencies. International human rights activists see this as a conceptually thin notion of rights. But in both Pakistan and India, Kashmiri peoples have experienced long histories of exceptional legal regimes and what they call "black laws," which have periodically provided for the legal abrogation of civil and political rights or for the suspension of civil oversight and judicial review.[6] The concept of *insānī haqūq* makes it possible to imagine a political space in which the violation of the body is never legal or legitimate.

THE WORK OF DOCUMENTATION AND A NEW LANGUAGE OF RIGHTS

Refugee camps in AJK became sites where Kashmiri Muslims, displaced from the Indian Kashmir Valley in the 1990s, sought to make themselves visible to the international community as refugees. They did this in part by participating in the work of documenting human rights violations. Diplomats, international human rights investigators, and journalists visited the camps frequently. They left the camps with testimonials and photographs, taken during these official visits, of destitute women, orphaned children, and scarred men. They also left the camps and meetings with political and human rights activists in AJK, with photographs of disfigured corpses and tortured bodies that had been smuggled out of India through refūjī networks expressly to be given to representatives of the international community.[7] Some of these photographs were taken by activist journalists and photographers; others were taken by family members of victims, often at the behest of political organizations in the Kashmir Valley. These photographs came to figure prominently in the reports written about Kashmiri refūjīs that circulated internationally, joining a large body of documentary evidence of human rights violations in Indian Jammu and Kashmir.

This documentary evidence had a different political and social impact than was intended by those who produced it. Photographic and testimonial evidence of political violence was reproduced by multiple domestic and international organizations for public circulation. Publications of political parties and cultural associations used such photos and transcripts, as did the print media, human rights nongovernmental organizations (NGOs) and international nongovernmental organizations (INGOs), and the United Nations High Commission for Refugees (UNHCR) meetings, for which such documentation was originally produced.[8] The photographs, media reports, and testimonials illustrated and cited in each of these contexts was widely cross-referential. Many of the same photographs, for example, appeared in multiple publications, pressed into service in support of divergent political purposes or ideological positions. Human

FIGURE 6. Cover flap of a political card (circulated in Pakistan, 1999).

rights reports also circulated back to refugee camps, where they became part of presentations to visitors, who were sometimes shown pictures of foreign diplomats looking at human rights reports while visiting refugee camps. The visits of especially prominent diplomats and visitors, meeting with Kashmiri refūjīs and examining displays of documentary photographs and human rights reports in the camps, also became the topic of news coverage, aired on Pak TV and reported in the AJK editions of newspapers and magazines.

Recirculation of this documentary evidence through refugee camps and Kashmiri refugee communities (both refūjī and muhājir) in AJK and Pakistan developed another meaning as well. It became testimony to a condition of insecurity created not only by ongoing political violence in the Kashmir region, but also by the inaction of an international community whose own reportage repeatedly proved ongoing human rights abuses by a state against a resident population. The United Nations and the international community, it could be said, already knew about the systematic human rights violations in Indian Kashmir, making differences in the international community's response to mass human rights violations based not on unequal knowledge of those situations, but rather on unequal will to care for some victims.

One of scores of graveyards of Kashmiri freedom fighters killed by Indian army. Since 1988 over 70,000 Kashmiris have been killed, tens of thousands subjected to worst kind of persecution and prosecution, thousands incapacitated in the process and property worth billions destroyed by Indian army.

FIGURE 7. Inside flap of a political card (circulated in Pakistan, 1999).

A political advertisement, circulated in Pakistan by the Jammu & Kashmir Liberation Front (JKLF) political wing as a millennium New Year's greeting card, spoke to this issue. Its cover flap showed India and Pakistan fighting over the bleeding body of a Kashmiri while the world (embodied by a globe with a calculating expression and a slight sneer) looked on (figure 6). The interior of the card read "Happy New Year from Bleeding Kashmir" and pictured a martyr's graveyard set against the mountains of the Kashmir Valley (figure 7). Like the question, "Why world conscious is silent on human rights violations in Kashmir?" asked in English on a protest banner in Islamabad, the JKLF New Year's card was directed at transnational publics constituted by the fact and the shared knowledge of ongoing human rights abuses by the state. These kinds of messages appealed to two sets of institutions and two corresponding sets of claims to the legitimate use of violence: the international political community, which might supersede the excesses of the state; and substate militant networks (like the militant wing of the JLKF), which might subvert the excesses of the state.

The language of human rights, it turned out, could be used to mobilize different political projects and produced no stable progressive or liberatory position against the excesses of state violence. As human rights documentation circulated through different public spaces, it was employed by different publics to legitimate contradictory political movements. More importantly, it accumulated new meanings; discussions of how such documentation had been used or not used by others became a part of how communities evaluated that same documentation. India, Pakistan, and international human rights organizations tried to stabilize the meanings of human rights documentation, with human rights groups seeking to restrict the application of the term human rights to its internationally regulated legal interpretations. Transnational militant groups moved from participating in documenting human rights violations to positioning themselves as the protectors of oppressed (Kashmiri) people in the absence of a significant international response.

"There Is Only One Jihād to Protect the Human Rights of Kashmiris"

Those who documented human rights conditions in the early 1990s, including Kashmiri refugees, were not unsuccessful in arousing international attention. This attention shaped India's institutional response, because India was concerned with its reputation as a modern democratic state; the formation of the Indian Commission of Human Rights in 1993 had been timed in part to forestall the UN Human Rights Commission from passing a resolution reprimanding the Government of India for human rights violations in the valley of Kashmir.[9] While international representatives were meeting at the Human Rights Commission in Geneva, the leader of the Jamaat-e-Islami-e-Kashmir political party issued a statement deploring the Indian human rights record in the Kashmir Valley,[10] and a wing commander of the Jamaat's militant organization, the Hizb-ul-Mujahideen, organized a photographic exhibition for international journalists and diplomats to document human rights abuses, with the stated aim of "[getting] India declared a terrorist state."[11] This attempt to reorient the designation "terrorist" away from the militants fighting against the Indian State, and those they saw as its agents and supporters, appeared early in the Kashmir insurgency.

By the late 1990s, claims that India was a "terrorist state" had become a trope indicting India's practices of violence as a policy of terrorizing a subject population rather than a justified program of counterinsurgency. This trope underwrote a series of conferences in Islamabad that focused on Pakistan's Kashmir policy. It also became a part of a public discourse on the Kashmir problem that argued the difference between jihād and terrorism (understood as antistate violence) and that proposed jihād as a practice necessitated by the illegitimate and excessive deployment of violence by a state against a people.[12]

In AJK and Pakistan, *jihādī tanzīms* and the militant wings of political parties circulated human rights documents through refugee camps and Kashmiri refugee communities. These organizations kept lending libraries of published human rights reports, copies of photographs, and video footage, which they used as recruitment materials. They also referred to the international human rights reports in their own publications, available in the open market and from the groups' lending libraries. Publications such as *Jihād-e-Kashmīr* (the Kashmir Jihad) and *Urūf* (Identification) regularly printed photographs from prominent international human rights reports paired with requests for funding. Others, such as *al-Da'wat* (Invitation) and *Monthlī Mujāhid* (The Islamic Warrior Monthly), did not commonly reprint human rights reports or images, but the articles assumed audience familiarity with the reports in circulation. These groups and publications focused on the nonresponse of the UN and the international community and advocated the practice of jihād as a form of redress.

Becoming a mujāhid and fighting a jihād were articulated very early in the Kashmir insurgency as acts that a person must undertake after becoming aware of the violation of Kashmiri rights. The obligation especially invoked the victimization of women, who were presented as either one's actual kin or "like kin." This self-image of the *mujāhid-e-kashmīr* as the defender of victimized women is evident in one of the earliest published memoirs of a self-proclaimed Kashmiri mujāhid.[13] It was also taken up by the major jihād publications such as *Jihād-e-Kashmīr* and *al-Da'wat,* which also published the final requests *(wazīyat)* of martyrs *(shahīd)* in letters that declared their motives and intentions in becoming a mujāhid.[14]

As Kashmiri refugee communities became aware of international affirmation of human rights abuses on the Indian side of the LoC, militant organizations appealed to this knowledge explicitly in their recruitment materials. For example, one recruitment poster for a Hizb-ul-Mujahideen training camp displayed in Muzaffarabad, Mirpur, Rawalpindi, and Lahore in the summer of 2000 exhorted viewers to "take commando training!" A partial verse of the Surat-ul-Anfāl (Qur'an 8:60) read in small script, "and prepare yourself for them, reserve your strength and power and collect your mounts." (That verse continues, "that from these, you will strike fear into the hearts of those who are enemies of God.") Twentieth-century Islamists commonly invoked this verse in support of modern jihād declarations. However, its

FIGURE 8. Jihād training camp recruitment poster (northern Pakistan, 2000).

invocation was not the poster's advertising for the training camp. That came in larger lettering above the photograph: "*Kashmīr kī mazlūm māoṅ bahenoṅ aur betīyoṅ kī dādrasī ke liyē . . . kamāndoz trening hāsal kareṅ* [For the just redress of the vicitimized mothers, sisters, and daughters of Kashmir . . . take commando training!]" (figure 8). Here, the word *dādrasī* (redress) united the concepts of rights and justice, implying that the victimization of Kashmiri women was well known and demanded a response.

When I spoke with Kashmiri men about why they had joined a *tanzīm*, they were clear about why they felt compelled to participate in the armed struggle but much less concerned about which organization they fought with. While the *tanzīm* leaderships expressed clear ideological and doctrinal positions, I found that young men often joined *tanzīms* for reasons that had nothing to do with those positions. Indeed, many Kashmiri members of militant organizations said that they had intended to seek out a particular organization but had become members of another instead. For some, it had been easier to locate one organization than another. Others had family or friends who were already members of an organization. Even after joining, the new recruits often did not consider various *tanzīms'* ideological orientations significant. Indeed, the young men were usually perplexed by my attempt to clarify how they had become connected to one group and not another. As Tahir, a young man from a Kashmiri muhājir family living in Karachi, told me shortly after joining Al-Badr:

> I was very nervous and excited because after many years of asking my parents for their permission, they have finally given their permission and I was able to take up this *farz* [duty] of *jihād*. . . . I arrived at the bus depot in Muzaffarabad on the first bus in the morning. I had instructions on finding the office [of the Hizb-ul-Mujahideen] but I had never been to Muzaffarabad and I got confused in the rush at the bus depot. I turned a corner at the back of the depot and I was standing in front of the office of Al-Badr, so I went in and told them I am here for training. . . . What does it matter that I did not go to the Hizb-ul-Mujahideen? There is only one *jihād* to protect the human rights of Kashmiris—if your *nīyat* [intentions] are pure then the *tanzīm* makes no difference.

RIGHTS, DUTIES, AND THE GREATER OF LESSER JIHĀDS

For Kashmiri refugee communities in AJK and Pakistan, the legitimization, organization, and practice of jihād as an "armed struggle" is characterized by the connection between human rights *(insānī haqūq)* and the individual's religious duty *(farz)* to others. This concept of *haqūq* is not theologically connected to the armed struggle, "the lesser jihād," as an object of juridical and doctrinal regulation, and Kashmiri refugees almost never discussed the doctrinal basis of declaring an armed jihād or imposing limitations on its practice. Instead, they talked about jihād as a continuum that included a civic jihād as well as spiritual and militant forms. The terms they used for this civic jihād were *jihād-e-zabān* or *jihād-e-qalm*—jihad "of the tongue" or "of the pen"—and its took form in practices of documenting of human rights abuses in Indian Kashmir and disseminating that evidence to global audiences.

The concept of human rights *(insānī haqūq)* as formulated in practice among Kashmiri refugees suggests that the weighing and ordering of obligations and duties became referential to the practice of documenting violations of international human rights. The term *insānī haqūq* referenced the international community and purported to be a simple translation of "human rights" as represented by the treaties and institutions consolidated in the UN system. But it was actually a hybrid concept that drew on the Islamicate idea of the *haqūqul-abād* (rights of human beings), in which rights are embedded in the obligations that people owe to others.[15]

The question of the relationship between Islam and human rights, and of human rights in Islamicate political cultures, is a vexing one. Most contemporary scholarship on Islam and human rights has argued that Islam has no inherent concept of rights and that, "in Islam, what matters is duty rather than rights, [and] whatever rights do exist arise as a consequence of one's status or actions, not from the simple fact that one is a human being."[16] As such, the argument goes, there is no traditional form of human rights in Islam—no set of absolute titles and claims that have priority even over the interests of society and the state.[17] Instead, an historically new concept of rights was created from the foundational Islamicate concept of human dignity.[18] The counterargument is that, while the language and terminology of rights is not traceable to Islamic scripture, the very idea of such rights is the essence of Islamic doctrine. This position was established by the political scientist Majid Khadduri in the immediate post–World War II period when international human rights and humanitarian law was being codified.[19] Modernist and Islamist thinkers and political leaders carried this argument into the realm of political discourse—that Islamic formulations of human rights precede those founded in international law.[20]

There is, however, no natural cultural ownership—Islamic or otherwise—over the modern concept of human rights. In the Kashmir region, as elsewhere in the world, the concept of human rights has developed in tandem with the rise of modern nation-states and their corresponding institutions and technologies of violence.[21] Human rights are thus neither grounded in scripture nor properly understood as a notion of "human dignity." Instead, human rights represent a "cross cultural overlapping consensus on normative standards," a global formation that Muslim societies have participated in shaping.[22] The question that should be examined in any historical location is how human rights are configured and what they mean in relation to other political ideas, values, and practices.

The Lesser and Greater Jihāds

The Islamicate concept of jihād encompasses great moral value in part because it does not exclusively, or even primarily, refer to religiously sanctioned warfare for political ends. Islam's doctrinal traditions and the orthodox schools of Islamic law, both Sunni and Shia'a, distinguish between a "greater" and a "lesser" jihād. The greater jihād (jihād-e-kabīr or jihād kabīra) involves a spiritual transformation and moral reformation of the believer; jihād as a form of warfare constitutes a lesser jihād (jihād-e-saghīr or jihād saghīra).[23] The greater moral value of the spiritual jihād over worldly struggles, including those that use technologies of violence, is most profoundly delineated in the Sufic philosophical traditions, which declare that the only true jihād is an internal struggle with nafs (the passions, desire) on the battleground of the self.[24]

The practice and legitimacy of jihād among Kashmiri refugee communities, and now in AJK more broadly, links the greater and lesser jihāds on a continuum (rather than marking a stark split between the battlefield of the self as the true spiritual struggle versus the worldly practice of sanctioned war-making). In this formulation, the greater jihād precedes the lesser jihād, and it is through the mujāhid's claim to have undertaken a spiritual jihād that the practice of jihād as war-making secures its legitimacy. This transformation moves individuals through states of knowing that gradually creates greater and greater obligations to act on behalf of the good of the larger community. Thus, Kashmiri mujāhids from muhājir settlements discuss their involvement in armed struggle and their membership in militant organizations in terms of progressing through jihād's spiritual, civic, and finally militant phases.

When Kashmiri refugees who had joined militant organizations spoke to me about the meaning of jihād, they often claimed that the first stage of becoming a "true mujāhid" was engaging in jihād-e-nafs (jihād against desire), a struggle to rectify one's internal moral orientation by turning away from the unmediated pursuit of desire fulfillment. When I asked what forms jihād-e-nafs had taken in their lives, the fasting month of Ramadan was a common example, cited by many young men as their first experience of, and failure with, the struggle against desire. A humorous story recounted by many Kashmiris goes like this: The young boy, not yet of age at which fasting is required, demands to keep the fast for the first time. His mother sends him to school with a lunch "just in case" . . . and he devours it on the way to school. I at first took this to be a morality tale, but I have actually seen this story play out during Ramadan several times. Children aspire to fast years before they are religiously mandated to do so and well before their mothers think they are ready. Mothers compare notes about how many hours it took them to cajole a tearful child to eat—praising the child's intentions on the one hand and laughing on the other, because it is so hard for adults to conquer their desires and it takes years to cultivate the discipline to fast for one day, and much more so for a full month.

Young men described *jihād-e-nafs* as a struggle to see what was going on in the world around them, rather than enjoying films or spending time in the market with their friends (a phrase that often hinted at slightly risqué behavior, as the market is a place where a chance meeting with a girl might be arranged). As many young militants told me, once they had "understood the truth" about the human rights violations in the Kashmir Valley, they became very emotional *(jazbātī)* about joining the jihād. This emotion in turn required its own *jihād-e-nafs;* young men told me that their elders accused them of "burning with the heat of youth" or of not being capable of distinguishing a true jihād from common revenge *(badal).*

After *jihād-e-nafs,* the second stage of becoming a true mujāhid involves *jihād-e-zabān* (jihād of the word or jihād of the tongue), which represents the struggle to rectify injustice by making knowledge of it public and inspiring the reaffirmation of practices of justice in society. Many of my interlocutors in Kashmiri refugee communities used the term *jihād-e-qalm* (jihād of the pen) to describe this stage. Both the jihād of the tongue and that of the pen seek to establish public knowledge and acknowledgment through "the word"—communication, education, or publicity more generally. Some of the young men I spoke with used the terms interchangeably, but others made a slight distinction, the struggle of the tongue referring to local (face to face) efforts at consciousness-raising and the struggle of the pen referring to international (print medium) communities. Some spoke as if these were separate stages, the struggle of the tongue preceding that of the pen. Most, however, employed one of the terms to describe all their activities to seek redress through knowledge and acknowledgment of wrongdoing. These activities most commonly involved compiling or distributing documentation of human rights violations, posting flyers, organizing fund-raising events, or going door-to-door collecting charitable donations. Finally, these young men said, they took up *jihād-e-talwār* (jihad of the sword) as the last stage—the use of violence to forcefully reestablish a just society.

Human Rights, the Rights of Human Beings, and a Civic Jihād

Cultivating proper intention and a capacity for discernment were general concerns of Islamic reformist movements in South Asia, and the reformist doctrines emphasized that knowledge itself and disciplined practice could bring about an internal conversion that would eventually enable the individual's struggle against injustice and the reestablishment of the values that ensure a just society. However, Kashmiri refugees interpreted individual knowledge as only one part of cultivating public awareness and consensus about the practices that produce a just society. Their emphasis on *haqūqul-abād* lays out an ethics of social justice that is guaranteed by the obligations that people owe to other people. This concept of the rights of human beings is one pole in a pair of obligations/rights in Islamic philosophy that distinguish between rights of human beings *(haqūqul-abād)* and the rights of God *(haqūqul-khudā)*. The abrogation of ethics is external to the *haqūqul-abād* category; those transgressions that fall within its opposite, the *haqūqul-khudā* category, can be forgiven and ritually purified, but those things that violate the rights of others must be addressed in the temporal mundane world, usually through a combination of public acknowledgment and a process of rectification. Civic jihād is the struggle to rectify wrongs by making knowledge of them public and inspiring a reaffirmation of practices of justice in society.

This concern with the social could be seen as deriving from the Islamist turn in political discourse in Pakistan; since the 1970s, both populist and authoritarian leaders have used rhetorical appeals to Islam to legitimate their regimes. Another aspect of the Islamist turn, however, has been that civic groups motivated by Islam as an ethical project have played an increased role in welfare provision through social volunteerism. Both nonpolitical groups, such as the Tablighi Jamaat, and political parties have used the concept of jihād to describe the connection between national reform and cultivation of proper Islamic values and their group's social service activities.[25] These groups are active in AJK and in the urban centers of Pakistan where Kashmiri refugees have settled, and their interest in social work *(khidmat)* as a form of religious engagement may be a part of refugees' underlying ideas about public service as a form of jihād.

When Kashmiri refugees talked to each other about rights violations, they asked whether the transgression of rights occurred without intention *(nīyat)* or proper discernment *('aql)* between right and wrong. When the conclusion was "yes," then people focused on the moral development of the wrongdoer. When the conclusion was that the rights of human beings had been violated knowingly, or that a public acknowledgment of the wrong did not bring about a reform of the practice, people began talking about the need for intervention. People expressed an idea of rights as manifest in the reciprocity of relationships and secured by evaluating the quality of people's knowledge and intentions—how they act based on what they know and the effects of their actions.

The Rights of Human Beings and Debts Owed to Others

The concept of *haqūqul-abād* represents more than an ethical ideal. In Kashmiri refugee communities, considerations about *haqūqul-abād* provide a foundation for some of the most essential Islamic religious rituals. Evaluating *haqūqul-abād* even precedes ritual practices such as burial rites and the *janāzah,* Islamic prayers for the dead. For example, one man described a funeral in which the ritual preparations of the body were conducted only after the rights of other human beings had been satisfied or forgiven. Only then came the intimate rites of washing the body of worldly impurities and the social rites of saying the burial prayers, in which people publicly asked on behalf of the deceased for divine forgiveness for the transgressions of those things that are God's rights—including the scriptural injunctions at the core of Islam, such as professions of faith and obedience, prayer, fasting, and pilgrimage.

Jamil was a young man from a refugee resettlement village who worked in Rawalpindi. In the autumn of 2000, he was called upon to help return the body of a man to his village in AJK. The man had died in Islamabad, where he had been taken for treatment of a serious illness. When he returned from the funeral, Jamil told me the following story:

> The funeral was delayed because [the deceased's] family had to finish paying his debts. They were thinking, "is there somebody else to whom he owes an obligation that we have not paid?" Actually, in reality, they could not pay

his debts, for the family is very poor and now he has left young children, but they borrowed money and went to the homes of the people who he owed and they offered that money, but at every house the person said, "No, the debt is forgiven. Keep that money for his children." Everyone in the village forgave the debts and every family sent a woman to cry over the body and comfort his old mother and a man to say the prayers. So no one can say that he has even in death eaten any other person's right *[haqq]* and having resolved the debts, we all said his prayers and asked God to grant him forgiveness for any other matter.

Jamil also related a morality tale, a story he remembered having been told many times as a child and that he used to explain why washing the body and burial had been delayed until after the man's debts had been settled:

The elders in my village remind us always of a funeral many years ago. The man who died was not a good man: he was not good to his wife; he cheated people; he ate the rice that was rightly destined to other people. When he died his family offered a big prayer, and they fed everyone in the village. The men took his body to the graveyard in order to offer the prayers, but when it was time to throw dirt in the grave, a black poisonous snake came out of the winding sheet and everyone ran away. The elders tell us, "it is possible to ask forgiveness for sins against God, and God in his greatness will grant mercy, but when you eat someone else's rights you must ask them for forgiveness, and unlike God, not all people are merciful."

Such stories reveal how profoundly considerations of *haqūqul-abād* shape people's experiences of the rituals through which individual Muslims encounter God.

I had known Khalid Rizwan for several years when he had the opportunity to go on the Hajj, the ritual pilgrimage to Mecca. Khalid Rizwan ran a successful business in Muzaffarabad, and I had been a guest in his home many times. One day, he approached me formally and asked my forgiveness for his "transgressions" against me. I was confused and a little embarrassed, and I assured him enthusiastically that he had never offended me and that, in any case, I forgave him. But he was not satisfied and asked me to consider more carefully:

You say that you do not understand for why I am asking your forgiveness and you are giving it blindly. But this is not a social formality; it is a very serious matter, and you should give due consideration. If I have done anything other than treat you as a sister, or if I have done anything to give offense or belittle you, if I have failed in any way to fulfill my obligations to you, you have the right to say that thing to me, and I will satisfy you if possible, or ask your forgiveness if it is not. You must understand, I am going on Hajj and it is said that the person who goes on Hajj when he completes all the rituals receives the full grace of God. But I cannot approach Mecca in a white cloth if I have left the rightful claims of even a single human being unsatisfied.

He insisted that I think for a day about his request, and it was only the following day that he was satisfied by my assurances that I did not hold any complaint in my heart. At the time I did not fully understand Khalid Rizwan's distress or his unwillingness to accept my quick forgiveness for possible transgressions. Much public attention focuses on the Hajj camp as the site where groups of pilgrims receive education and training in proper behavior and conduct while on the pilgrimage. It turned out that Khalid Rizwan's mother, who I also knew, did not agree with some of these guidelines; she had insisted that her son not only repay debts and offer restitution for wrongs he knew he had done to others but also offer others the opportunity to inform him if he had unintentionally wronged them.

When I asked religious scholars to explain the concept of *haqūqul-abād* to me, they spoke about individual rights and obligations. However, in rituals and interpersonal negotiations, Kashmiri refugees used the concept *haqūqul-abād* to talk about social justice and collective responsibility and to describe the obligations that the individual owes to others and that those others can demand as a right. The first step to rectifying the violation of these rights was making them known and establishing public affirmation of the wrong. Wrongs that were then deemed to have been knowingly perpetrated demanded the intervention of others who recognized the transgression. These rights of human beings are linked to social justice because the act of upholding them is what binds a society together; they are linked to concept of individual rights because individuals can publicly demand that their society recognize and respect these rights.

The Greater of Lesser Jihāds

Kashmiri communities' formulation of the relationship between rights and duties encouraged witnesses to the violations of rights to become directly involved in processes of rectification. It also accommodated the idea that people could participate in the jihād in different ways. One could participate in human rights awareness campaigns, for example. One could also provide support to the militant organizations fighting "in defense of the oppressed

FIGURE 9. Collection box for charitable donations to the Kashmir Jihad (northern Pakistan, 2001).

Kashmiris." Collections boxes for spare change, requesting "charity" for the Kashmiri mujāhidīn could be found in small shops and in the open markets (figure 9), and for a number of years, Eid donations of sacrificial hides were made in great numbers to groups like the Lashkar-e-Tayyiba, which exhorted "Participate in the Kashmir Jihad! Give the sacrificial hides to the Lashkar-e-Tayyiba!" (figure 10).

Though in theory the Kashmir Jihad moved people through stages of spiritual, civic, and finally militant forms of jihad, the actual progression young men experienced was much less linear. The Kashmiri muhājir men who first joined militant organizations in the early 1990s considered the

FIGURE 10. Collection tent for sacrificial hides (northern Pakistan, 2000).

jihād-e-zabān a prerequisite to armed struggle, because they linked the legitimacy of that armed struggle to the international community's refusal to acknowledge and act on human rights abuses by the Indian state and to its failure to bring about a resolution to the historical Kashmir problem. Young men who joined militant organizations in the mid-1990s, talked about the *jihād-e-zabān,* but when I asked them how they had participated in practices of consciousness-raising or human rights educational work, it became clear that they had been recruited through such work. That is, by the mid-1990s knowledge of torture and sexual violence in the Kashmir conflict was so widespread that there was a consensus that a generalized state of violence existed. This recognition then secured the general principle that conditions existed that could justify a jihād as a struggle against injustice and oppression, even for young men who had not personally engaged in the practice of raising the consciousness of others.

On the other hand, by the late 1990s, I had met a number of young men who were members of jihādī organizations but who had never fired a weapon except in a training camp. They were involved in disseminating human rights abuse information, fund-raising, and recruiting among Kashmiri refugee communities in various cities in Pakistan or overseas in the United Kingdom. For them, being a mujāhid no longer necessarily meant carrying a gun.

"I Do Not Need to March with Any Party"

Two days before the protest march on the Indian embassy, described at the start of this chapter, I was visiting with Shi'a Kashmiri refugees living in the *kacchī ābādī* near Islamabad. We were in the courtyard of the community's religious leader *(maulvī)*. Unless it was raining, Maulvi Ghulam-Hussain and his visitors always sat outside because his family lived in a single-room shack. On this occasion, many people were in the courtyard, making final arrangements for the march, and the atmosphere among the men was jovial. The maulvi's wife and daughters were busy making and serving many rounds of tea, and they were not enjoying the day to the same extent as the men. The younger men were finishing work on protest signs, prepared in Urdu and English. One asked me if the English on a banner was correct, as he hoped that people in my country would see it on TV. A group of older men sat around a table in the center of the courtyard. They listed off the names of male residents of the colony and agreed upon who would walk with the banners of various political parties. Every now and again, one of the men said that a particular resident would not attend the march but would send another male family member to represent him. Occasionally the men decided that one group or another required more or fewer participants, and they began counting off the names again in a different arrangement.

I was confused by the discussion. It seemed driven by a need for proportional representation of parties, rather than by any adherence to the principles of a particular group. I asked Maulvi Ghulam-Hussain about this several times while we sipped tea, and after a while he became frustrated with me. He motioned me to follow him, and we went into the shack where he unlocked his storage cabinet. He indicated that I should sit down on the room's one *chārpai* (a woven rope bed), and he took a briefcase out of the cabinet and placed it in front of me:

> I am the leader of many people in this community, and they expect that when there is some problem, I can get it resolved. If some person has trouble with the police, I have to speak with the superintendent; if there is a problem with any young child going to school, I have to speak with the director. If they do not satisfy us, then I have to go to our representative, and I say, "I have given you votes, and you must now intervene to resolve this problem." There are ways of convincing people like that to help, but we are poor people, and we are refugees, and it is very difficult to oppose a ruling party.

He snapped open the briefcase and pulled a stack of cards that he explained were *jamā'at* (political party) and *tanzīm* (militant organization) membership cards. These he arrayed in front of me and explained each one's particular usefulness vis-à-vis political authorities and social constituencies:

> So, this card shows that I am a member of the Muslim League. I have this card from the years that Nawaz Sharif was in power. This card shows that I am a member of the People's Party, and I have that card from when Benazir [Bhutto] was in power. The representatives from Azad Kashmir come here and make promises, but they cannot make the [Pakistani state utility companies] connect our water or run an electric line! But I also have a lot of things that have to get done in Azad Kashmir, and so this card shows that I am a supporter of the All Jammu and Kashmir Muslim Conference, and this one that I am a supporter of the Azad Kashmir People's Party. I formed our local unit of the Tehrik-e-Jafria [a sectarian Shi'a militia] after the Sepeha-e-Sahaba [a sectarian Sunni militia] started coming here. It is important that they know that we are active and that there can be no mischief here.

As he spoke, I reached out and picked up the various cards one after the other. By the time he had finished listing several of the parties represented in the All Party Hurriyat Conference (APHC), as well as the Pakistani and AJK political parties, I was holding a full hand of cards.

I prepared to ask him about the different cards, particularly the three different *tanzīm* membership cards I found myself holding. The cards astonished me: one was issued by the militant wing of the JKLF (a secular nationalist party); another was issued by the Hizb-ul-Mujahideen (the militant wing of an Islamist political party) that had killed many JKLF members between 1992 and 1994); another was issued by the Lashkar-e-Tayyiba (a militant group that was not directly allied with any political party and that was decidedly fundamentalist). But apparently I had not yet grasped the point he wished to make. He plucked them out of my hand and threw them dismissively into the briefcase:

> But then the bulldozers come to destroy our houses because the government wants a new colony for the rich politicians. Then I do not call any party or representative. Then I call some journalist and I say, "come write a report about how government of Pakistan treats the refugees of Kashmir" and we stand in front of the bulldozers and until this day they had to delay the bulldozing. But any day they may come and we have to be vigilant.... Tomorrow I do not need to march with any party, so we just divide the men up and one holds this sign and one holds that sign and then this community has sent some representative to those parties. Tomorrow I am marching as a Kashmiri. My father's sister has died in that firing by the Indian army and I do not need any card to burn the [Indian] flag.

He motioned me outside again, where he walked around, approving banners. He gave his daughter an instruction, and she held out a plastic bag. He pulled out an Indian flag and draped it over his stool. Then, he placed one foot on it. He told me to take his picture, and he waited while I got my camera. In the picture, he is resting his elbow on his bent knee, leaning toward the camera, and smiling.

THE SOVEREIGNTY OF THE BODY
AND THE KASHMIR JIHĀD

The idea that jihād is a practice that young men are obligated to undertake after becoming aware of the victimization of Kashmiri people emerged early in the armed conflict in Indian Jammu and Kashmir State. Militant groups *(tanzīms)*, and their associated political parties *(jama'āt)*, accommodated the self-proclaimed mujāhids who came to them. But it was the jihadist organizations, which were not linked to political parties, that most successfully incorporated the mobility and ephemeral loyalties of mujāhids, who felt morally obligated to fight a state oppressor of people to whom they felt intimately connected but who were not necessarily committed to the ideological goals of any particular political party or religious group. Thus, their involvement in these groups shaped the formal organization of what they called *jihād-e-kashmīr* (the Kashmir Jihad). On a conceptual level, the Muslim body, rather than Islamic territory *(dārul-islām)*, became the site of sovereign regulation and sovereign exception.

Kashmiri refugees have had a profound impact on the institutional organization of violence in the current conflict because jihadist organizations appealed to human rights ideals in their fund-raising materials and because they accommodated this concept of jihād among their Kashmiri recruits. From 1989 to 1993, antistate violence in Indian Jammu and Kashmir State was organized by militant organizations with clear hierarchical command structures that paralleled allied political parties. Two of the largest of these were the secular Jammu and Kashmir Liberation Front, which had both militant and political wings, and the Islamist party Jamaat-e-Islami-e-Kashmir and its associated militant organization the Hizb-ul-Mujahideen. Both of these organizations were organized transnationally among Kashmiri communities in Pakistan as well as in India. The political wings of the insurgent parties allied in 1993 in the APHC.[26] Its purpose was to negotiate with India as political representatives of militant organizations and to collectively represent the antistate insurgency to the international community as a struggle to secure a popular referendum regarding the future of Jammu and Kashmir.

By the mid-1990s, a number of organizations that had no direct links to political parties and no explicit political platform other than jihād had become prominent in the struggle; these were the *jihādī tanzīms*. For some of these groups, the *jihād-e-kashmīr* was part of a network of global struggles of Muslim peoples against the oppression of non-Islamic states and would presumably not end with the liberation of Jammu and Kashmir but would continue in other places such as Somalia, Bosnia, and Chechnya. For others, the *jihād-e-kashmīr* was a defensive war against the oppression of Kashmiri Muslims specifically. These groups united in 1996 within the umbrella organization Muttahida Jihad Mahaz (United Jihad Front), also known as the United Jihad Council (UJC).[27] In 1999, the UJC launched the Kargil offensive, and in the summer of 2000, the largest UJC organization declared a short-lived unilateral cease-fire. The APHC correctly recognized the threat of the UJC as not only potentially destabilizing to their referendum agenda but, more importantly, as asserting the right to represent Kashmiri political aspirations based on the capacity to mobilize violence. Several of the APHC political parties began to discuss remobilizing or augmenting their militant wings. *Jihādī tanzīms* had become prominent enough to challenge the political parties that had first directed the armed insurgency; they also recruited members and conducted fund-raising campaigns transnationally using the hybrid notion of rights that had emerged in the Kashmiri refugee community in AJK and Pakistan.

The Islamicate concept of jihād linked the sovereignty of the Muslim community—conceived of as *dār* (sovereign territory) or *dawla* (state) in the classical and modernist Islamic traditions—to the religious obligations (*farz*) of members of that community to uphold its integrity. Kashmiri refūjīs and muhājirs forged a connection between religious obligation and a Muslim community as well, but they paired *farz* not with *dār* but with human rights (*insānī haqūq*). Their understanding of human rights drew on a Islamicate concept of the rights of human beings (*haqūqul-abād*), which articulated rights as a set of constraints that individual members of a community could demand from each other and from their rulers. It also drew on modern conceptions of sovereignty that circulated globally with human rights discourse. From the end of the eighteenth century, sovereignty—previously conceived as unified authority exercising the right of ritual death over subjects in clearly defined territories—became democratized through the language of universal rights unlimited by territorial distinction. Life itself became "the point of indistinction between violence and law, the threshold on which violence passes over into law and law passes over into violence."[28] The practice of sovereignty revealed itself on the terrain of rights, because "life—which with the declarations of rights, had as such been invested with the principle of sovereignty—now [became] the place of sovereign decision."[29] As a *sunnat* (model of behavior), jihād remains a concept that articulates limits on the experience and the use of political violence, but the bodies of Muslim people, rather than the territory of Islam or the Islamic state, became the site of contestation and struggle. Under conditions of generalized political violence widely documented within Kashmiri refugee communities as a human rights crisis, the Kashmir Jihad became a legitimate practice in the absence of an international intervention to limit that transgression.

Kashmiri refugees have long maintained simultaneous affiliations with multiple political parties in Pakistan and AJK as well as with parties in Indian Jammu and Kashmir State and with parties that operate on both sides of the LoC. Maulvi Ghulam-Hussain's briefcase full of membership cards for regional, national, and transnational political parties, sectarian militias active in Pakistan, and militant organizations fighting in Indian Kashmir was the most extreme example of this practice that I encountered during my fieldwork, but it was a common practice. Kashmiri men who had been involved in the militant struggle for more than a short time had almost always been active with several different organizations. This was true for *refūjīs* who resided in the camps in AJK when they weren't on a mission with a *tanzīm* as well as for muhājirs from resettlement villages. An individual mujāhid's formal affiliation might change for any number of reasons. When national or international pressure restricted one group's ability to function, its members often shifted to another group. Organizations also divided and re-formed with leadership struggles, and sometimes one organization merged with another or split factions reunified. Even when a young man expressed an orientation toward a specific group, this preference did not necessarily correspond with the first he joined. Tahir, for example, had joined the group of the first recruitment office he found on his arrival in a strange city. I met many youths who had intended to join a specific organization but joined another for reasons that were coincidental. The experience of the militant training camps, where the meaning of jihād is neither contained nor exhausted by the *tanzīms'* ideological positions, political or sectarian, can create significant discomfort. Differences in how various members are bodily and conceptually incorporated into *jihādi tanzīms* are not widely acknowledged, but they reveal that the *tanzīms* have had to accommodate Kashmiri refugees' concept of the Kashmir Jihad.

"We Cannot, Meeting with These Kashmiris, Walk the Path of Jihād"

Hamid was a non-Kashmiri Pakistani citizen and an active mujāhid who had crossed the LoC into the Indian Jammu and Kashmir State many times. When we met, he was a member of the Lashkar-e-Tayyiba, but he had changed his *tanzīm* affiliation several times, because he did not consider the practices of the Kashmiris in the training camps appropriate for maintaining the bodily and spiritual purity that he insisted must precede the actual practice of jihād:

> There are over 27 or 29 organizations in Pakistan now [2001], some whose names even I do not know, but the biggest are Hizb-ul-Mujahideen, Al-Badr, Lashkar-e-Tayyiba, Harkat-ul-Islam, Harkat-ul-Mujahideen, and Al-Barq. Those are the main and biggest organizations. The Hizb-ul-Mujahideen and Al-Badr used to be one organization. They separated for this reason: those Kashmiri companions, because of their unfairness. Us Pakistanis got together and made Al-Badr. We said to each other, "We cannot, meeting with these Kashmiris, walk on the path of *jihād*." Why could [the Kashmiris and the Pakistanis] not get along? Because those Kashmiri brothers had among the leadership a big majority, and they treated them[selves] well—the Kashmiris, but not the Pakistanis. . . . If they got some good thing for eating or drinking, the Kashmiris were served first and received extra, there were no restrictions on them if they wanted to smoke—so they smoked—and took chewing tobacco—absolutely no restrictions. Besides that, when it was exercise time, if they wanted to or not, well guess what, no restrictions. And then there were situations too, when those Kashmiri companions who came for *jihād*, well, they begin thinking about girls, and then there is for them some arranged marriage. For this reason, when the Pakistani boys saw what is all happening here, they began their own organization in the name of Al-Badr.

The *tanzīms* Hamid listed are all considered Islamist or fundamentalist. All, with the exception of the Hizb-ul-Mujahideen, which has a long association with the Jamaat-e-Islami-e-Kashmir political party, are *jihādī* organizations. None of them espouses a nationalist perspective on the armed conflict and all are ideologically committed to the universal confessional community of Islam. This makes Hamid's description of ethnic affinities, all the more striking.

Hamid complained about the Kashmiri boys' unregulated behavior and their reliance on their personal conscience to determine the parameters of right conduct in the Kashmir Jihad. Indeed, this self-reflective relationship to jihād was mirrored by Hamid's own behavior. By his account, he and others in the camp left the organization to form their own because they disagreed with the personal behaviors of people claiming to be mujāhids. He did not attribute that decision to an edict given by a religious teacher or party leader. Hamid went so far as to attribute the fracture of one of the largest Kashmiri militant groups and the proliferation of militant organizations in Pakistan to disjunctures between Kashmiri militants' bodily practices and the regulated bodily discipline expected of and by militants doctrinally trained in Pakistan.

"The Tanzīm Makes No Difference"

It is not possible to say, based solely on the fact of membership, that the members of a militant organization are "pro-Pakistan" or "pro-Independence," or even that they are fundamentalists or Islamists. One former training camp supervisor for the militant wing of the Jammu Kashmir Liberation Front explained that it was common practice for a *tanzīm* that had become less active to send an aspiring fighter to another organization for training, even after registering him as a member:

> JKLF doesn't have the strength anymore to help people cross the LoC or even to give them their own weapons. They can buy their own weapon on the open market, and we will train them. But when any person arrives at our camp and wants to go fight for his home or his family, then we take his name and tell him the location of another camp.

I'd known the organizer as a refugee politician for several years when he revealed to me that he had been a training camp supervisor for his party's militant wing for much of the 1990s. He had been involved with the JKLF since it was founded, and I was prepared for a pragmatic explanation for sending potential recruits on to other organizations. However, I was surprised to learn that the leadership of the militant wing of the party didn't think it mattered which organizations those were:

> We used to send them to Hizb-ul-Mujahideen, now the Lashkar-e-Tayyiba is very active so we send them to the Lashkar, sometimes we sent them to Al-Badr, sometimes to Harkarul-Mujahideen. It does not matter because we

have taken that boy's name and we know that he has come first to our camp. If we cannot help him fight to protect his sisters or keep his home safe, then we will help him find another organization.

Even with the multiplicity of Kashmiri refugees' political affiliations, it's quite something to claim, as so many Kashmiri militants did, that "the organization doesn't matter." Kashmiri refugees had always maintained multiple affiliations because they *did* make a difference, either in their daily lives or for their political futures. But when it came to the *jihād-e-kashmīr*, many refugee men came to the conclusion that Tahir expressed: "There is only one *jihād* to protect the *insānī haqūq* of Kashmiris—if your intentions are pure then the *tanzīm* makes no difference."

VIOLATED BODIES AND THE POLITICAL LIVES OF THE DEAD

One afternoon, I accompanied a woman to the home of her neighbors who had relatives visiting from Srinagar. The rare visit was a community affair. My hostess, whose husband had stood for election to the AJK legislative assembly, had made it clear that neither she nor her husband did any work with militant organizations, but at gatherings like this, conflicting political sympathies were densely intertwined with networks of kinship relations, social obligations, and party memberships. When we arrived at Adil Karim's home, the assembled guests were drinking green tea and watching a video of a funeral at the martyrs' graveyard in Srinagar that the visitor from Srinagar had brought with her.

Farooq, the young man who was being buried in the video, was Adil Karim's maternal cousin's son. His family had recovered Farooq's body several days after his arrest by Indian security forces in 1998. The visitor from Srinagar sat on a low platform bed at the back of the room, talking with the other women and then weeping and raising cries of lament as she watched the funeral footage. Women were sitting on the bed and on the carpet beside it, alternately comforting her and asking questions about the funeral, the other people in the video, conditions of daily life, and news of people they hoped she might know. Adil Karim invited me to sit with the men on a chair near the door and selected some photographs that showed Farooq's body as it had been found and before it was washed and prepared for burial. As I looked at them, Adil Karim and his guest Rafay Muzeeb commented on the body's condition and told me what kinds of torture caused such injuries. They showed me only close-ups of the boy's face and back, and then they motioned for me to bring the photographs to the women sitting on the other side of the room. I asked about the other photographs, but Adil Karim said that they were only "documentary evidence" and were not appropriate to show to women.

At first, I knew only that both the visitor from Srinagar and Farooq were Adil Karim's relatives. After some time, Adil Karim told me:

> [Farooq] arrived in the neighborhood and asked directions to the house. When I came home, he greeted me saying, "Uncle, do you not recognize your sister's son?". . . We had seen pictures of him and the video from his cousin's wedding, but it is hard to recognize the face of someone you have never met, and many young Kashmiri-speaking boys arrive here having crossed the LoC. We don't always receive word that they are coming.

As Adil Karim spoke, it became clear that he had served as a liaison between the political and the militant wings of one of the pan–Jammu and Kashmir nationalist parties involved in the armed fighting in Indian Kashmir. Young men from the Indian side of the LoC who had been recruited by the party had arrived at his home on many occasions. He let them rest and gave them bed and board before sending them on to a militant training camp.

Adil Karim said that he had not wanted to let Farooq leave his house, but that Farooq, like so many young men, was very "emotional" and could not be prevailed upon to stay in AJK:

> He told us he wanted to take militant training, and I tried to convince him to stay here with us for a while, because I wanted to know this sister's son that I had not known in his childhood. But he said that his friends are dying and that he cannot leave his mother and young brother and he came only with the intention to take training and go back. So we told him that the party does not run a *tanzīm* any more, but we will send you to another group.

After he had completed his training with Harkat-ul-Mujahideen, Farooq had spent several months with his relatives before crossing back into the Valley the following summer. Adil Karim said that he and his family had to be very careful not to mention meeting Farooq; for the safety of relatives in Srinagar, they could not ask Farooq's family if he had made it back. A year after they had last seen him, the video had arrived; they now knew that he had been killed within a month of going back across the LoC.

Adil Karim didn't identify which political party he worked with, but it was clear that it was one of the nationalist parties that did not contest elections in AJK because its candidates would not sign the pro-Pakistan affidavit. I did not understand why he had sent Farooq and other young men to the Harkat-ul-Mujahideen, which was connected to an Islamist political group. Adil Karim was matter-of-fact:

> Our *jamā'at* [political party] is banned here, so we are members of one party in Pakistan and another one in Azad Kashmir and we have no *tanzīm* but we still do all the work of a political organization and we make sure that the world does not forget about the struggle of the Kashmiri people for freedom, or their terrible suffering and sacrifices.

In fact, the men told me that they would send the video and the photographs back to their party's office in Rawalpindi with Rafay Muzeeb, who worked there as a district organizer with the party.

Rafay Muzeeb would take copies of the video and still photographs to a human rights reporting agency in Islamabad. The originals would stay with their own party's records and would become part of the party's documentary collection on human rights violations on the Indian side of the LoC. As Rafay Muzeeb told me, the members of his party maintained formal membership in several AJK and Pakistani political parties. Like Adil Karim, Rafay Muzeeb was not concerned that Farooq had been recruited by one organization, trained by another, and a member of both:

> He may have been the member of a *jihādī tanzīm,* but the video will stay with our party records. We will always know that he was *hurriyāt pasand* [a freedom fighter] and we will always know about the sacrifice of this martyr.

SIX

The Mujāhid as Family-Man

SEX, DEATH, AND THE WARRIOR'S (IM)PURE BODY

ONE DAY IN MURREE, I was walking home with Farida Begum after meeting with a group of resettled Kashmiri refugees. The town has become a tourist destination, and in the main market street we passed restaurants roasting cuts of meat over open fires and shops selling nuts and dried apricots, carved woodcrafts, and heavily embroidered cloth. The town's historical centrality as a transit point for people and goods between the Punjab, the North West Frontier Provinces, and the Kashmir territories made Murree a marketplace for Kashmiri luxury craft items. It also became a recruiting site for Kashmiri militant organizations in the 1990s, and many young men from the Indian side of the LoC funded their purchases of military hardware by bringing embroidered shawls from the Kashmir Valley and selling them to traders in Murree. Other youths, having left the refugee camps in Azad Jammu and Kashmir (AJK), established themselves though marriage and participation in craft communities as muhājirs rather than as active mujāhids.

On a side street, Farida Begum grabbed my arm and pulled me close and with a grin offered to show me something funny. For a moment we stood huddled like that—my head bent toward hers. Then she directed my attention to a young man with a full beard and his ankles showing between his sneakers and the bottom of his *shalwār* (loose drawstring pants worn with a long tunic shirt). He was cradling an infant and walking carefully up a steep path at the side of a woman wrapped in a black *burqa* (a long veil that covers the head and body). The woman appeared tired, and she paused every few steps. The couple neither spoke nor touched, but I had an impression of a great tenderness in the man's care to keep her slow pace.

As they passed, I saw that the infant had a black string tied on each of its wrists, and its eyes were lined with dark kohl, both protections against the evil eye. Farida Begum giggled and looked at me expectantly. I felt sure that the joke was visual. Thinking of the contradiction between the couple's style of dress (the woman's full *burqa* and the man's cut of beard and *shalwār* showing his ankles, signs of a fundamentalist orientation) and the black kohl on the infant's eyes and strings on its wrist (fundamentalists reject devotional practices that place intermediaries between the faithful and God), I guessed, "They have been to the *mazār* (saint's shrine)?"

In a soft voice still touched with laughter, Farida Begum expressed her amazement that I did not understand: "Do you not see who she married? Look! He came from the [Kashmir] Valley to take militant training and become a *mujāhid,* but now he has a wife and a baby too. . . . Come on, you must understand. . . . How can someone who claims to be a *mujāhid* get married?" At the time I did not, in fact, understand what she found so amusing, other than perhaps a generalized juxtaposition of sex and death (since a mujāhid, presumably, might be martyred at any time). I did not understand whether the joke was that, as a husband and father, he claimed to be a mujāhid, or that as a mujāhid he had a sexual relationship with a woman. I asked Farida Begum several more times to explain what was funny, but she became more elusive each time I asked.

The last time I asked was one evening at her house while she was making tea. She quickly hushed me and pointed her chin toward the dining room where her husband was sitting with their daughter. I understood that I had touched on an inappropriate matter, one that she did not want either her husband or daughter to overhear us discussing. Since both she and her husband had spoken frankly with me about the activities of mujāhidīn in Murree, the fact that she had acknowledged the presence of a specific mujāhid on the street seemed unlikely to be the issue. Apparently, her joke was risqué and not to be repeated in gender- or generation-mixed company.

The ethnographic research experience is like that—some things remain unknown or unresolved. Sometimes, the ethnographer knows such moments are important but is only later able to offer a satisfactory interpretation. When Zahid, the "tiger chief," lied about being a mujāhid (as related in chapter 2), I knew that his lie was significant. That ethnographic interaction attuned me to the deep tension in Kashmiri refugee communities between making meaning of histories of political violence and forced displacement as the prelude to a practice of hijarat as opposed to making meaning of those histories as a prelude to a practice of jihād. At other times, those moments pass by because they seem unimportant. I made note of Farida Begum's joke and my misunderstanding in my field journal because I have an interest in the history of local shrines and because I felt embarrassed by my inability to get the joke, not because I understood its importance at the time.

Luckily, long-term field research gives an ethnographer many opportunities to be embarrassed and to observe the embarrassment of others. I heard many such jokes, and arguments, over the years that revolved around how to talk about a mujāhid as someone who is also a husband and a father. Farida Begum's joke pointed to tension in the public evaluation of the real intentions and the conduct of those who participate in the Kashmir Jihad. This tension was inherent in Zahid's lie about being a mujāhid and Hamid's complaint that for the Kashmiri youths who trained with him in a militant camp that "for them there is some arranged marriage." For Kashmiri militants, entry into a militant organization was not the end point of separating young men from the family.

As formulated by Kashmiri refugees in AJK and Pakistan, the status of the armed conflict in the Jammu and Kashmir region as a jihad does not depend on a formal declaration by a religious or political authority. It depends instead on people's conclusion that human rights violations by Indian state forces constitute a transgression of the sovereignty of the Muslim community. It also depends on their acceptance of the idea that they, as members of that community, have an obligation to intervene directly to change the political situation. Intervention does not have to be violent; it can take the form of doing the work of documentation and international public advocacy—as in the case of the practice of civic jihād. But in the absence of a significant effort by the international community to end the conflict, many refugees concluded that an armed struggle was not only just, but also utterly necessary. Men living in the refugee camps and youths from resettlement villages spoke about defending human rights through armed struggle as a religious duty (farz), and they sponsored and joined militant organizations that accepted or tolerated their understanding of jihad.

In their discussion of jihād as farz, Kashmiri mujāhids claimed the status of witnesses who had taken up the burden of fighting to reestablish a sociopolitical order in which living peacefully as a Muslim would again be possible. Their practices of evaluating the relationship between rights and duty shifted the regulation of jihād—and the ability to recognize a combatant as having the moral status of a mujāhid—away from religious groups or even political parties toward individuals. Mujāhids' discussions about their own practices focus on spiritual reform and bodily disciplining, and thus on an internalization and externalization of value and behavior that mutually reinforce each other. But Kashmiri refugee mujāhids were not able to untether themselves from issues of public evaluation and legitimation, because the bodies of both the mujāhid who fights and the *shahīd* (martyr) who dies are public bodies that testify to the conditions that require an armed struggle in the first place. Mujāhids depend on the refugee family to establish their armed struggle as an extension of social relationships and enduring obligations to others. The family mediates the production of these subjects by evaluating and making judgments about the individual mujāhid's faculty of discernment and the intention behind his actions—that is, through judgments about his capacity to subjugate his own natural desires and to weigh the contradictory obligations and motivations that underlie peoples' behavior.

In Kashmiri refugee communities, becoming a mujāhid is therefore founded on a paradox; it requires developing discernment *('aql)* by harnessing the passions *(nafs)* and putting them to the service of the family. At the same time, the mujāhid's close association with those who inspire strong attachments of love and physical desire, especially children and wives, continually threatens to destabilize the state of generalized sacrifice and physical purity required of the living warrior, who must always be prepared to become a *shahīd*. For Kashmiri refugees, the challenge of being a mujāhid is not dying like a martyr, but living like one.

THE MUJĀHID AS FAMILY-MAN

A preponderance of culturally oriented analysis of violence and masculinity in Muslim societies emphasizes that Muslim men's exercise of violence fashions honor and heroism and that being a victim of violence leads to a loss of face and honor.[1] Such accounts are unable to explain how being the recipient of violence might elevate the moral evaluations and social standing of Muslim men. For Kashmiri Muslim men, displaced into AJK and Pakistan over decades of conflict, living with violence enabled them to transform the experiences that led to their forced displacement into a source of ethical, social, and political worth. Their formulation of jihād now reveals a similar orientation, and it also relies on a sacrificial relationship connected to the public recognition of men as recipients of violence.

Kashmiri muhājirs have long expressed a notion of political authority that extends from care, or undertaking responsibility for others, as a form of sacrifice. The definition of their migration as a hijarat was not secured by a religious finding based on the status of the territory they had left. They claimed to have done hijarat through the intentional labor of reestablishing a proper domestic life in the place of exile. In social practice, the authority of interpreting the causes and effects of the violent conditions that led to displacement, and evaluating legitimate mode(s) of redress, was earned through the sacrifices entailed in ensuring the reproduction of the family and the moral community in exile. This concept of sacrifice for the family applied to both men and women. It distinguished the moral status of individuals based on the extent to which a person had harnessed his or her desirous self and put it at the service of the family by caring for others. It recognized the potential for a cultivated humanity from which all members of the family, over time, had the potential to claim authority over others.

The systematic use of sexual tortures as part of a state counterinsurgency program on the Indian side of the Line of Control (LoC), which began in 1989, introduced a challenge to this mode of recuperating violence. In fundamental ways, it threatened men's ability to imagine themselves as having a place in the relational paradigm of sacrifice as a husband to a wife or as a father to a child. Two experiences figure prominently in many young men's accounts of why they joined militant organizations. The first is witnessing or coming to know of the rape or molestation of a female family member and the second is having been tortured, using techniques that focus on the genitals. Refūjī women's narration of men's bodily injuries produced a public knowledge about the intimate physical injuries associated with interrogation and torture while preserving masculine values of modesty and stoic suffering. Men's accounts linked that experience of bodily suffering to the need to defend their Kashmiri "sisters" from violation. But the brother–sister relationship did not supplant the husband–wife and parent–child relationships in the relational paradigm of sacrifice.

Within Kashmiri refugee communities, it was not enough that the mujāhid had endured suffering himself or claimed to recognize the suffering of others. The mujāhid had to be seen as having achieved a state of internal moral reform sufficient to allow him to personally evaluate the relationship between sovereignty and obligation that makes the armed struggle in the Kashmir region a "jihād." Therefore, for Kashmiri refugees, becoming a mujāhid requires maintaining the intimate ties of kinship, because it is the sexual nature of the marital bond that brings human emotion and bodily desire into service for others through right intent and channeled conduct.

Cultivating Discernment and Evaluating Conduct

Islamic philosophy conceives of the human self (*shakhs*) as having several aspects: these include the *jism* (body), *nafs* (desire), *'aql* (intellect), and *rū* (spirit). In very broad terms, *jism* and *rū* represent two poles of personhood and *nafs* and *'aql* represent the capacity, unique to human beings, to cultivate, transform, or perfect the self. The concept of *nafs* encompasses a range of phenomenological and psychological experiences, and Islamic philosophical systems have not emphasized conquering desire but rather channeling it to social and spiritual ends. In the most illustrative form of *nafs*—sexual desire—Islamic traditions have emphasized the importance of experiencing pleasure in (religiously) sanctioned relationships rather than exploring concepts of abstinence, the suppression of desire, or the denial of pleasure.[2] The concept of *'aql* represents the human faculty for rational discernment; it is what facilitates the development of habits that bring innate human passions and pleasures to the service of God and the confessional community by channeling desire through proper conduct.[3] These Islamicate concepts are referenced in a wide range of actual social practices and cultural values, but there is nothing inherent in the Islamic concept of the self or the existential challenges of human experience that predetermines how societies configure these ideas in practice.[4]

Comparative ethnography of Muslim societies has widely documented that mainstream Muslim conceptions of human nature emphasize the development of balance between *nafs* and *'aql* by making *nafs* useful to social ends.[5] It also reveals that people attribute moral superiority to those members of society who have a perceived greater capacity for *'aql*. The social recognition of a person's capacity for rational discernment lends that person's understanding of the world social and political credibility. Indeed, the recognition of *'aql* is ultimately a form of "bargaining over which person's view will be used to describe a particular circumstance."[6] The concepts of *nafs* and *'aql* thus provide a terminology for evaluating a person's worthiness without relying on categories of status, identity, or descent.[7] This attribution creates its own hierarchical distinctions between categories of people as moral subjects by associating certain categories of people with behavior motivated by the *nafs* and attributing to others greater abilities to cultivate *'aql*.

Ethnographers have noted that *nafs* and *'aql* are often invoked as gendered qualities. In the Middle East and northern Africa, men's natural sexuality is thought of as inherently weaker than women's, and this belief effectively naturalizes women as less capable of achieving *'aql* than men (in part because women's supposed greater sexual desires prevent them from cultivating cultural values and exercising social restraints without external enforcement).[8] Lawrence Rosen argued that *'aql* is considered something that only men have a capacity to develop, but that it has to be cultivated; the power of religious education lies precisely in its ability to guide reason over passion.[9] On the other hand, Islamic reformist movements have enabled women to engage in bodily discipline as performances of piety, making correct ritual behavior a vehicle for spiritual development.[10] In Southeast Asia, James Siegel's work showed that *'aql* is thought of as a capacity that cannot be taught but that increases with age and experience. He agreed that it was thought of as primarily as male capacity, because *'aql* develops primarily through a person's removal from the household, thus "conceptualizing the ability of men to leave family identification behind and unite as Muslims [and] represent[ing] [men's] ability to transcend family identifications."[11] Michael Peletz's work, however, demonstrates that the recognition of men's innate desires is a central existential problem and that their social recognition as morally realized subjects cannot be attained by controlling women or by escaping the household.[12] Suzanne Brenner has revealed that the expansion of the global market economy, as a site of unrestricted exchange and capitalist desire, has increased the importance of the domestic sphere as a site of cultural cultivation and therefore of women's social recognition as moral subjects capable of restraint and as the actual source of men's moral development.[13]

In the South Asian context, there is also a great variation in how these terms are used to express gendered differences. Several ethnographers working in Pakistan have noted that hierarchical differences that seem gendered, actually describe ethnic differences between different groups of Muslims; groups distinguish themselves by claiming superior qualities of personal discipline and by defining the ethnic other as wild, childlike, feminine, or uneducated.[14] In general, women and men alike are recognized as having the capacity to cultivate *'aql*, in part because of the regional influence of Islamic revivalist and reform movements of the late colonial and postcolonial periods, in which scholars and missionaries emphasized the development of both men and women as Muslim subjects. In this moral transformation, bodily practices were a vehicle for interior moral transformation and an external sign of an interior state; one both developed proper conduct *(salūk)* and also cultivated right intentions *(nīyat).*[15]

One of the comparative points of variation in how Muslim societies conceptualize the relationship between the *nafs* and *aql* is in their relation to conduct *(salūk)* and intent *(nīyat).* Rosen described Moroccan conceptions of intentionality as being available for direct evaluation through observation of behaviors, so that there was very little consideration or discussion of interior states but only of conduct and action.[16] Siegel emphasized that by linking social evaluations of people's actions to the concepts of *'aql* and *nafs,* Indonesian Muslims are able "to conceptualize interior nature and social experience in the same terms."[17]

Kashmiri refugees in AJK and in Pakistan, however, discuss the question of *nīyat* extensively in their evaluations of other people's behavior. *Salūk,* which appears to be externally available to human regulation and judgment, can in fact be deceiving to others. Those who are meticulous in their behavior, from the full performance of obligatory prayers to demonstrating modesty in interactions with others, are appreciated. However, people do not presume that this automatically indicates a cultivated and moral interior state. Discussions within families and peer groups, as well as political and religious public addresses, emphasize that human beings can be fooled by others' behavior, revealing another central human problem: while the impeccable behavior of a pretender will not fool God, it may fool people, who might unknowingly be misled. For this reason, Kashmiris consider *nīyat* an important indication of an interior state that might not be otherwise evident in a person's conduct. People may do things that seem incorrect or wrong to others, but they may simply have made a mistake or have acted on incomplete information. Someone who has developed the capacity of discernment will be able to constantly adjust their conduct to adapt to new knowledge, distinguish correct motivations, and bring their interior emotional state into compliance with them. They are also more able to evaluate how their own and others' conduct relates to consciously formulated intentions to respond to social and political conditions.

The Intimacy of Cultivating Discernment

In AJK and among Kashmiri refugee communities in Pakistan, the extent to which people are seen to encounter the world and to understand it through their innate *nafs* or through a developed capacity for *'aql* is understood neither as inherently gendered nor as ultimately generational. Both men and women are innately capable of developing *'aql* and becoming *'aqlmand* (wise, having the capacity of discernment), and as a person is recognized by others as *'aqlmand*, he or she acquires greater influence. However, *'aql* does not merely accrue with time, and neither men nor women are considered *'aqlmand* merely because they are older. *'Aql* has to be cultivated.

The cultivation of discernment is grounded in an ethic of care; individuals gain the wisdom and discernment required for political authority through the practice of controlling or disciplining individual mental and bodily desires and fulfilling obligations to significant social others, paradigmatically spouses, children, and parents. For refugees, *'aql* is not accorded to those who have learning, either religious or secular, and the term is distinct from "intelligence" or "cleverness"—words often used to describe people who are good at negotiations in the market or getting bureaucratic work accomplished. For example, a young man with an engineering degree might be both intelligent and clever but have no *'aql*. Memorizing the Qur'an accords the title and acclaim of being a *hafiz-e-qur'an* (literally, protector of Qur'an), but it does not make the youth *'aqlmand*. Instead, becoming *'aqlmand* is intimate; it requires channeling desire toward a social good (spoken of first as the good of the family).

Rubina Begum's experience during the fasting month of Ramadan is illustrative. She was pregnant with her first child, and pregnant women, like travelers and those who are ill, are not required to fast with other adult members of the Muslim community. The blood associated with menstruation and childbirth makes women ritually impure and unable to carry out certain obligations, such as praying or fasting. However, her pregnancy made it possible for her to fast a full 28 to 30 days (depending on moon sightings), something her menstrual cycle had never permitted:

> This is my opportunity to fast for the full cycle of Ramadan and accrue the full benefits of this fasting and of all the special prayers. My doctor kept saying to me that I am not obligated to fast in pregnancy, but I see this as an opportunity that I have never had before. I am only concerned that my body not overcomes me vomiting, and that is why [my husband] is preparing *iftār* [food for the breaking the day's fast].

The fact of her sexual relations with her husband, evidenced by her pregnancy, did not decrease her ability to accrue the spiritual benefits of the ritual month; rather, the fact of her pregnancy actually eliminated a source of bodily impurity (menstruation) that was entirely biological and outside her control. Indeed, the problem of bodily impurity is as pressing for men as it is for women; any blood let unintentionally makes men also ritually impure, and the other polluting bodily substances (including semen, feces, and vomit) also make it ritually ineffectual for a man to approach a mosque, pray, or fast without conducting the full ablutions, known as *ghusl*.[18] (The lesser impurities, such as urine, can be purified with the lesser ablutions known as *wazū*.)

As Kashmiri refugees use the concept, *nafs* is an aspect of human nature, a part of how people experience the world, the gift of pleasure, and a central challenge to the cultivation of interior morality. Rubina Begum, like many refugee women and men, thus approached bodily impurity and desires of all kinds as an impediment to certain kinds of ritual value production but not as a sign of a natural inability to cultivate *'aql* over *nafs:*

> It is my *nīyat* to keep this full fast, and I confirm my resolve every morning before the sun comes up. It is hard when I feel ill, but Ramadan is always difficult in some way. That is why we say it is a *jihād-e-nafs* [struggle with desire]; there is always some temptation, even some way that small deception or lie would make the day easier or some angry word that indulges the lesser spirit might bring a moment of pleasure. Ramadan is the time to be conscious of and exercise control over all these bodily *[jismānī]* and psychological *[nafsiyātī]* desires that we don't think about all the time.

The topic of *'aql* comes up in daily life in utterly mundane and routine ways, for example, in the context of arranging marriages for young people. Salima Begum lived most of the year with her daughters in a Kashmiri refugee resettlement village. Her husband and her son both had wage jobs in Rawalpindi, where they lived most of the year. I had met her and her family many times when she and her married daughters recruited me to help convince her son Rafiq to agree (in principal) to get married. They had been looking for a suitable match for him, and they had a number of girls in mind, but they did not want to officially arrange the match until he had agreed to marry. His sisters wanted him to marry because their mother was getting older and needed a daughter-in-law to help with the work of the house. Salima Begum was less concerned about that, but she was lonely; she wanted company and grandchildren. And she was worried that her son was becoming *āwārah* (loose and unrestricted):

> The only wealth in a house is honor, and his father and I have always told [our son] that you are only permitted that which you earn through honest labor and demonstrated to him the correct behaviors and proper conduct. When he comes to the village he is wearing his *shalwār-qamīz,* but here in the city he roams about in jeans and fancy collar shirts as if he thinks he is some film actor. All this concern for image and fashion, as if he were *āwārah,* when his

old mother is doing all the housework and there is no daughter-in-law to keep her company and no descendants [on the male line] in our house.

More and more, Salima Begum worried that Rafiq was indulging his impulses and giving in to his desires in small ways that might indicate a more profound abandonment of the moral ideals and guidelines she and her husband had sought to instill in him.

In the abstract, concerns about a young man's conduct and moral compass might be addressed in several ways. He could be encouraged to become active in a religious society that regulates the behavior of its members or his family could require him to live with extended family members rather than share a room with other young men working in the city. Salima Begum, however, did not consider those options. For her, the solution was for Rafiq to marry; a wife would remind him of his duty to his family.

Describing a person as *āwārah* implies considerable condemnation, but such behavior is generally expected of young men and is somewhat tolerated. Those who are considered too unrestricted, too unconstrained, however, become the subject not of disparaging indulgence but of deep concern. Kashmiri refugees use the word *āwārah* (an adjective, also used as a verb *āwārah honā*) to suggest a "loose person," acting outside the constraint of the household and indulging impulsive individual desires. Homelessness is a state in which a person is subject to one's own desires, deprived of the opportunity of subjugating those passions to the needs of others and thus from the mechanisms of cultivating true wisdom.

I heard many mothers lament the waywardness of their unmarried sons. But Safia Begum's complaint about her own son first made me aware of the distinct way that Kashmiri refugee families think about the problem of being *āwārah*. As she said of her son, Asad, one afternoon, waiting (and waiting) for him to return from the market with the chicken she would cook for dinner:

> Really, he has become so *āwārah* and completely undependable, but what other behavior can I expect? This is what happens when boys become youths. They find excuses to go to the market, and then return late without that thing you sent them for. But, you know, you cannot expect a young man to find his mother and sisters as interesting as his friends and the happenings of the market. I am looking for a wife for him, and when I bring a bride for him to our house you will see, he will be taking his afternoon tea at home.

Safia Begum's comments struck me as strange because by many measures, and certainly in comparison to his peers, Asad was not *āwārah*. He had been the primary financial support for his family since he was seventeen years old, when his father had retired on a small government pension. Asad's labor had supported the family while his younger brothers stayed in school and his younger sisters acquired advanced degrees and made what were considered excellent marriages. The family lived in Muzaffarabad, and Asad had a government position and had been promoted many times. His secure employment and his contacts with highly placed government officials enabled him to assist others in securing coveted government employment. In fact, in the arsenal of political tools people often told me were essential to negotiating the political landscape of Muzaffarabad's civil bureaucracy—*rishtā* (kinship and connections), *rishwat* (bribery, also blackmail), and *safārish* (recommendation and advocacy)—Asad was an acknowledged source of effective *safārish*. On several occasions, I observed a neighbor appeal to him to settle the employment issues of a relative, and twice I observed him effectively resolve these concerns by meeting with political party leaders or government ministers. In short, it was clear to me that Asad was politically savvy and that he had dedicated his resources to the collective family benefit.

His support of his elderly father and younger siblings, however, conferred almost no social recognition. During dinner at the house of a friend, Khalid Rizwan's mother (who frequently visited with Asad's mother) berated him in front of the assembled guests: "Why haven't you married yet? You are from a respectable family, yet you are running about causing mischief and grief to your mother! Being *āwārah* like this is not proper behavior! You are completely irresponsible and entirely without *'aql*!" She then accused Asad of making his mother cry, and he hung his head and nodded seriously until his friend ushered her from the room.

For Safia Begum, like Salima Begum and other elders of Kashmiri refugee communities, it was important to bind young men to the family though a conjugal tie because it is that tie that puts sexual desire in service to the family. By harnessing young men's (natural) desire within the home, young men become socially recognized and valued as responsible moral actors. And in the estimation of Kashmiri refugees, the cultivation of a young man's moral self requires a wife to harness that desire.

"We Will Make a Hijra Out of You," and *"The Soldiers Run Amuck"*

Some of forms of political violence practiced by the Indian state during years of counterinsurgency operations directly challenged young men's ability to participate in this kind of sacrificial relationship with the family. Ishfaq was a student at the University of Kashmir in Srinagar when he gave an interview to the BBC about a mass rape that took place in his hometown in 1993.[19] Immediately after the interview, he was detained, interrogated, and tortured. The torture techniques used on him included the nearly ubiquitous practice of applying electric shocks to the penis via a wire inserted into the urethra. Despite the excruciating bodily pain of the electric shocks applied to his genitals and the weeks of pain that followed (urination irritates the swollen tissues until they heal), he did not describe the experience of torture as a purely physical experience. Rather, he saw the electrocution through the stated social and political aims of his torturers—as a practice intended to render him impotent:

> They [the interrogators] kept saying to me "Why did you make that report?" They said that I had been to Pakistan, and they asked me if I was married. When they attached the wires they said to me "We are going to a make a *hijra*[20] out of you." They kept me for a week like that, saying "You have been to Pakistan," and saying "Now you are unworthy of marriage." But by the grace of God their work was unsuccessful and after some time I became all right.

Like that of numerous young men who were detained and interrogated before being either released or formally arrested, Ishfaq's conceptual experience of torture was part of the torture itself; he believed that he would become incapable of being a good husband, who could satisfy his wife sexually, or of becoming a father.

What his account—and that of many of the men who told me about how they had first joined a militant organization *after* being detained, interrogated, and tortured by Indian security forces—illustrates is that there is nothing precultural about pain, because pain is an experience that requires conceptual as well as physical interpretation. This means that people experience the same kinds of political violence in very different ways, even through certain practices, such as techniques of torture, have a global circulation.[22] Elaine Scarry, in her comparative analysis of accounts of modern torture practices, argued that the near-universal use of everyday objects—a chair, a stove, a tire iron, an electric wire—to implement pain has the effect of suffusing the daily life of survivors with the signs of political authorities and their power over individuals. Thus, she argued, the work that modern torture does is the "unmaking of the world."[23] But the transformative power of pain emanates from the fact that the physical body is also always a social body.[21] People are continually involved in the making and the remaking of their worlds. In that process, they reclaim pain in ways that transform cultural meanings and social formations.[23]

In narratives of displacement that circulate in refugee camps and refugee communities, men who survived interrogation sessions in which electric shocks were applied to their genitals expressed this form of sexual torture as political in both intent and effect. Kashmiri refugees described these practices as genocidal acts *(nasl kushī);* male sexual torture was specifically described as a state program to cause impotence and end the Kashmiri descent lines, therefore rendering the territory of Jammu and Kashmir available for final colonization by (Indian) non-Kashmiris. International reporting also placed sexual torture of men firmly within the Indian state's interrogation techniques and forms of political violence, although it did not use the terminology "genocide" or "ethnic cleansing."

On the other hand, the rape and molestation of women in the home was discussed as an apolitical event, and an apolitical form of violence. As Ishfaq and I continued to talk, he told me about a conversation with a childhood friend who had been raped:

> After a crackdown, an old friend of mine was crying. We were neighbors and we had been to school together. I asked her what was wrong and she began to tell me about some [sexual] misbehavior of the soldiers. I grabbed her by both shoulders and shook her very hard and slapped her. I told her to be quiet—I told her it would ruin her and that she should never tell anyone.

His remembrance caught my attention because, although he had forcibly silenced his friend, he considered his own acts "not violent," and he had told me about them with pride.[23] He believed that he had saved her from the social consequences of being raped, such as being considered unpure and unmarriageable.

The configuration of sexual violation of women in Jammu and Kashmir as apolitical was not limited to popular discourse. The explanatory phase, "the soldiers ran amuck" recurred in official reports and essentially attributed acts of sexual violence against women to the idea that Indian soldiers succumb to their desires if unconstrained by external regulations on behavior. This explanation was even a part of the reporting practices of regional and international human rights groups. Regional reports characterized the sexual violation of Kashmiri women as a consequence of men's unconstrained but natural desires for women.[23] International commissions and INGOs reinforced this discourse by emphasizing that assault, molestation, and mass rapes have taken place during crackdowns when women were separated from their male family members; international groups have thus recommended that India institute procedural changes, such as keeping enlisted soldiers (as opposed to "disciplined" officers) out of houses and increasing the number of female personnel in operations that involve civilians.[27] After more than a decade of insurgency and counterinsurgency in Jammu and Kashmir State, reports at the highest levels of the Indian judiciary still conclude that, in the rape of Kashmiri women, the "selection of victims is arbitrary, [and] like other civilians who are assaulted or killed, [these women were] in the wrong place at the wrong time."[28]

The Warrior Brother and the Victimized Sister

Knowledge about sexual violence circulated among refugees in several different ways, and there were some important differences between how refūjīs and muhājirs incorporated this knowledge into their understanding of what their ongoing obligations were to their community and how they should best fulfill them.

In the refugee camps in AJK, sexual tortures of both men and women were simultaneously the most enshrouded by personal silence and the most publicly acknowledged in refūjīs' accounts of the experiences that precipitated their decisions to leave their homes. Refūjī men linked their own experiences of being tortured to their ability to understand that the widespread molestation of women required them to undertake an armed struggle for the defense of the community. Their stories suggest that young men's cultivation of discernment, previously attainable primarily by advancing generationally through the family structure and by taking on the burden of caring for others, might be reformulated as attainable through withstanding suffering in their own bodies for a collective cause.[29] In effect, these two conclusions introduced the brother–sister relationship into the paradigm of sacrifice for the family in a way that had the potential to supplant it. Indeed, *jihādī tanzīms* recruited mujāhids by accommodating their self-presentation as defenders of women victimized by the Indian state, especially women who have special claims to protection within the family structure—sisters, most especially, and also mothers, and daughters.

The "victimized sister" did not, however, replace wives and children in the sets of relationships through which Kashmiri refugees thought about people as developing the discernment required to make the complex evaluations required of a mujāhid. One reason for this was that refūjī men needed women to tell the stories of what had happened to their bodies in order to claim the spiritual merit accorded to them by having suffered for others; it was only by withholding accounts of suffering that young men demonstrated that they were not ruled by their passions (or pains). They therefore needed woman to make public the details of what happened to men under interrogation and to render accounts of the fear, grief, and anger that they felt on seeing what had happened to men's bodies.[30] As the primary sources of social testimony about the suffering of men and as key interpreters of their interior states, women paradoxically became the epicenter of knowledge about the violation of the body and practices of political violence, even as their own experiences were depoliticized.

Another reason was that the vast majority of those who supported and joined *tanzīms* were from muhājir families resettled in AJK or Pakistan. In those communities, the physical and emotional suffering of political violence had been historically reworked as a charter for protective migration for men and for women, and sacrifice was expressed as a form of *khidmat* (service). *Khidmat* refers to service performed by people in nonegalitarian social relationships for one another, often in intimate and mundane ways, and to social work. As a public practice it is connected to collective causes in which people who stand in nonegalitarian hierarchical relations to each other can contribute to a group effort. For example, in donating to a mosque or to the poor, the amount given is unimportant—all givers stand in relation to each other as supporters of a common cause.[31] For muhājirs, resettling and reestablishing the refugee family had involved performing *khidmat* in both of those senses; such sacrifice bound the passions to reason and produced both sincere *(haqīqī)* emotions and the capacity of discernment.[32]

The concept of jihād as a struggle for rights as forged in Kashmiri refugee communities linked the greater and lesser jihāds on a continuum through spiritual, civic, and militant phases. This offered young men several ways of engaging in jihād, but it also meant that without social recognition as a person who had developed his capacity for *'aql*, men could not claim to be sufficiently qualified to evaluate whether or not jihād was a duty they had to undertake or how to contribute to jihād. For muhājir youths, preparing to take up the role of mujāhid required settling worldly debts, offering restitutions for wrongs, and fulfilling one's ongoing social obligations, requirements that often meant that the youths who joined militant groups and who saw themselves as mujāhids could not actually serve as active warriors. In

Kashmiri muhājir communities, it became a common practice to secure permission from one's parents to join a *tanzīm*. Even if a young man was not the primary support, present or future, of his parents and family, people generally thought that he could participate in jihād only with the knowledge and consent of his family, and the secretaries of *tanzīms* claimed that they required that young men sign an oath that stated that they had their parents' permission to take militant training. In cases in which the youth was an only son, they would not accept him. I know of several instances in which a young man joined such an organization without his parents' permission; when an elder relative testified to the *tanzīm* authorities about the nonconsent of the mother and father, the young man was sent home with his relative on the basis that jihād was not permitted under such circumstances. The process of becoming a mujāhid involved several cycles of individual ritual purification, social evaluations of motivation, and often, the withholding of legitimization.

Underlying these sometimes conflicting requirements and the different conclusions that people came to is an argument about the nature of *farz* that I never heard incorporated into these debates; that is whether the Kashmir Jihad is an individual duty *(farzul-ʿayn)* or a collective duty *(farzul-kafāya)*. Although those doctrinal terms were not used in the many arguments that I observed or was told about, muhājir parents and sisters made arguments that seemed to withhold legitimizing young men's participation in militant jihād based on the belief that their duty to the community was better fulfilled through other forms of social and political engagement or that his family's needs precluded his participation in jihād. In such situations, a young man's insistence that he had an overriding individual obligation to take up arms was seen as a sign of his failure to develop the necessary capacity for discernment that would allow him to distinguish his own desires for revenge or personal aggrandizement from the principles of justice and rights of others that connected the defense of human rights to the integrity of the Muslim community. At the same time, refūjī men who had found it difficult to claim muhājir status in the context of the current conflict, discovered that their recognition as mujāhids depended on the same formulations of moral social and political being that characterized being a muhājir.

"No Boy Becomes a Man by Caring for His Sister!"

Naseema Bibi claimed that her husband, Abdul Majid had never told her how he had gotten the scars on his body. Instead, she had asked his sister Yasmeen

Begum, who had eventually told her how he had gotten those scars. One day, I was sitting with Yasmeen Begum and a group of refūjī women from the Manikpian Camp and the Ambore Camp who were visiting with each other in Rawalpindi. It was late Thursday afternoon, and the men had left for a local shrine. I asked Yasmeen Begum, who I knew was a widow, how she had lost her husband. Instead, she told me about her brother, Abdul Majid:

> The BSF [Border Security Force (Indian)] came to our village. They were looking for some boys, including our maternal cousin, who were members of a *tanzīm*. My father was not in favor of those organizations, and he had told my brother that he could not join one. But when they came to our house, we had to feed them. Then the BSF came. When they were unable to locate our cousin, they took my brother instead. They took him to the camp, and we could not get him out because we didn't have any money.

I asked whether they would have been able to get him out if there had been some money:

> There is a list that all the women keep in their head—how much it costs to keep from burning, how much it costs to keep from beating, how much it costs to keep from having the "telephone" attached [electric wires to the genitals]. Some boys they say, "Pay to stop the telephone, but I can bear the beatings." But in those days [mid-1990], only the real *mujāhids* were able to pay—that is, the *tanzīm* gave money to the family. The regular boys had to bear it. That was why no one knew where that cousin was, because they would have told when the torture started. . . . Twice our old mother went to that camp and asked to see her son, and twice she was sent away. Then some boys came carrying his body. Mother began to wail, and then the other women came out to mourn with her. The boys said that [my brother] was not dead, and they brought him into the house. His back was burned and he was bleeding from all the parts of his body. Everyone began to pray, and he got slowly better. He said to his mother, "It was just a little beating," but I was sitting there in that room, and I had washed his body when he was unconscious, so I know what happened to him.

The women sitting around the room nodded and murmured. She continued:

> There were some arguments with my father about joining the JKLF after that. My father wanted my brother to take up work as a truck driver and go out of Kashmir, but he said, "I can still defend my sisters." There were a lot of crackdowns in those days, and no one wanted their daughters to go out because the army soldiers would misbehave with the girls if they got any opportunity and no one could stop them. My brother went to Pakistan to get

training. When he came back to our village, he learned about how the army came and took his old father and tied him to a tree and then they shot him. They took my children's father to the camp and he never came back and I was not given a body to bury. But I have seen the other bodies that came out of that camp.

Yasmeen Begum said that after her husband was killed, Abdul Majid brought her and her children to AJK, while he continued to go back to the Kashmir Valley:

He kept going first with the JKLF, and then with some other *tanzīm,* and then with some other. At first, he refused to take a wife, saying, "I have a duty to my sisters, so first we will liberate Kashmir. Then having returned home, I will bring a daughter-in-law to the house, if God is willing."

I asked her how she had convinced her brother to marry Naseema Bibi. That's when one of the other women began to laugh: "He might be a *mujāhid,* but what is a man without a wife? He was coming and going, with one organization and then later with another. We told the camp committee—you must find a wife for that boy. . . . They all say that 'torture has ruined me,' but God is great and does not allow the genocide *(nasl kushī)* to be successful." Yasmeen Begum interjected, "He is a good brother, he is my head of household and he has raised his nieces and nephew because his brother-in-law was martyred."

The woman sitting next to her slapped her on the thigh with a loud "thump" and with a grin on her face said, "No boy becomes a man by caring for his sister!"

THE MUJĀHID'S (IM)PURE BODY

In Kashmiri refugee communities, the mujāhid—in life and death alike—is enmeshed in relationships and subject to ongoing social evaluation about the significance and value of his intentions and actions. The sacrifice of the Kashmiri mujāhid does not necessary require that he die, but rather that he live in a way that allows him to socially validate his ability to bear violence in the name of abstract principles that have social value, such as the integrity of the community and the rights of Kashmiri people. But a mujāhid is also supposed to meet death in a conscious state of spiritual and bodily ritual purity, so as a living person, he must manage ongoing cleanliness and uncleanliness, produced not only by his own inherent human bodilyness but also by living in the world of the family. That world is associated with semen and menstrual blood, substances that ritually threaten the mujāhid's outward signs of purity and symbolically represent the ongoing social relations that constantly create challenges of desire, affect, and intention.

In Pakistani communities, becoming a fully recognized mujāhid involves renouncing family ties, especially reproductive relations. A mujāhid cannot be a husband or a father, because to take up the responsibility for a generalized community one must first have satisfied all of the specific claims that people have a right to expect one to fulfill. While a young man can potentially fulfill his responsibility to his parents by providing for them before joining a *jihādī tanzīm,* or by having a brother who agrees to undertake full responsibility for them, wives and children have durable and significant claims on men that exceed financial obligations, and few married men can assert a claim to being a mujāhid that will be socially recognized. The announcement of a Pakistani mujāhid's formal entrance into a *tanzīm* is publicized as a wedding, and the contract he signs is called a *nikah,* an Islamic marriage contract. The family members of the young man, including sisters and female cousins, are expected to distribute sweets, wear wedding clothes, and decorate their hands with henna.[33] In becoming a mujāhid, the young man renounces reproductive relations and cuts off nearly all relations with his family, who are told they will be informed when the mujāhid becomes a *shahīd* (martyr). In effect, the mujāhid is transformed into a living *shahīd* through symbolic exclusion from the social bonds that motivate human emotions and desires.[34]

Kashmiri muhājir and refūjī families have not ceded the formal evaluation of death to militant organizations or to the space of the militant training camp. For them, it is the funeral, not a wedding, that produces the mujāhid. Final evaluations of the mujāhid's motivations occur after his death, in the burial rituals through which communities uphold or cast doubt on the deceased's status as a *shahīd.* When a family either mourns the death of a loved one and prays for forgiveness of his transgressions or celebrates his eternal life as a *shahīd,* they are effectively declaring either approval or condemnation of the actions, intentions, and effects of the mujāhid's use of violence. Death's meaning is not predetermined; rather, it is subject to ongoing and changing conditions of evaluation.[35] Even the behavior of others after a mujāhid's death affects the meaning of that death. Taking revenge, for example, for a death of a declared *shahīd* removes that death from the moral domain of jihad and puts violence back into a domain of retribution. People recognize and accept revenge as a powerful human emotion, linked to codes of honor and shame, which may even be considered just, but it can not be the basis of a jihād.[36] The refugee family is intimately linked to the processes of legitimation by which young men become mujāhids. By evaluating the political conditions of death, as well as life, the family became more and more integrally linked to the production of the *jihād-e-kashmīr*.

Intimate Absolutions and the Body of the Martyr

The Islamic doctrinal traditions distinguish between two categories of martyrs: the "battlefield martyrs," who are *shahīd* in this world and the next and those who are *shahīd* in the next world only. The burial rites for the battlefield martyr, who has performed his own *ghusl* and thus ritually purified himself, differ from that for other Muslims in three major ways. First, his body is not washed. Second, his body is buried in its bloodstained clothing as a sign of martyrdom. Finally, the funeral prayers *(namāz-e-janāzah)* are not offered in request for forgiveness of his sins. Because martyrs are "everliving" and therefore cannot be considered ritually dead, there is no need to ask for intercessions; martyrdom by definition absolves the martyr of sins.[37] But between the death of civilians, called *shahīd* after only after burial, and the death of mujāhidīn declared to be *shahīd* by other members of *jihādī tanzīms,* is a vast space of social practice that contradicts the ideological certainty of religious discourse.

The term *shahīd* has some other applications in the context of the armed struggle in Indian Jammu and Kashmir State and in the mobilization of dissent within transborder political communities. While generally translated as "martyr," in its broadest use, a *shahīd* is a witness constituted by death, someone whose death itself, as known first through the presence of the dead body and then through the absence of a person in social life, bears witness to a state of violence or the dissolution of a state of justice. The term *shahīd* is most often applied to people, and in this usage it can describe deaths that in and of themselves create a state of recognition in those who come to see or know of the death. Self-knowledge or the intention of martyrdom is not required, and so this term can be applied to children who have not yet developed the capacity for moral discernment as well as to inanimate things, like mosques, that are not supposed to be dismantled by human actions. The word *shahīd* is also applied to a person killed while fulfilling a *farz* to their family or community, if the person died in the context of a broader political dispute that is considered a violation of the proper moral order. In cases such as these, a person killed by violent events is named a *shahīd* after death; the rites of mourning are observed and his or her body is purified. It is the dead body itself that testifies to the state of improper order by which such a death occurred.

During the Kargil War in the summer of 1999, mujāhidīn and Pakistani soldiers traveled through the streets of Muzaffarabad city, heading toward the LoC. The shrill alarms of ambulances sounded regularly and became a part of daily life that summer, as wounded civilians and soldiers came back from the LoC. As the fear of an imminent Indian invasion led more people to make war contingency plans, the status of those declared *shahīd* by the Pakistani government, *jihādī tanzīms,* and local communities was part of daily conversation. Discussions about the treatment and state of the bodies often reflected tension about the status of the conflict.

The residents of one village in Athmuqam near the LoC, set aside a new section of the graveyard for the people who became *shahīd* that summer. Yacoob Haroon recalled to me some of the people he had helped bury there that summer. One was a woman who went out at dusk to fetch water; another was a man who was taking his turn sweeping the mosque; another was a child who was hit by shrapnel that flew through a window. Each of the funerals were held at night, their final and most intimate ablutions having been performed by their families and their nakedness wrapped in a simple white cloth. The men of the village performed the special prayers for the dead, standing behind the graves and facing Mecca.

Several times, members of a jihadist organization brought the dead body of one of their companions to the village, instructing that he be buried in the martyrs' graveyard. This, said Yacoob Haroon, is what it means to become a mujāhid:

> It is the angels of heaven who perform the final prayers and wash the dirt and blood of battle from the body of the *shahīd*. He must pay all his debts and offer restitution to anyone he has offended, and then only he can go out [into the world], having bound the winding cloth to his own head *[nikalnā, kafan band kar sir pe]*. He has taken leave of his family who await only the news that he has indeed received his heavenly reward.

Yacoob Haroon said that he and the other men still resident in his village buried the young men according to the strict instructions of the *jihādī tanzīms;* they absolved the physical body of none of its possible and probable impurities, they did not wash blood or urine or feces from the body, they did not remove the clothes or even the shoes of the dead man. They placed him in the grave and covered his body with dirt, asking no blessings and offering no prayers.

Qasif Mutasim, a resident of another village near the LoC in the Bagh district, provided a similar account of how the members of his village treated the bodies of mujāhidīn and jihādīs:

> We find sometimes in the hills the bodies of *mujāhidīn* who have died in the attempt to cross the LoC. We take those boys and bury them where we find them. We know that they do not need the full burial because they have tied the cloth to their foreheads, and this means that on that day that he has fully washed and purified his body and done his prayers and went knowingly to his death. So we bury the body as we find it.

Indeed, I was told many times that the graves of true *shahīd* should go unmarked and unvisited, as the *shahīd* remain a part of the living world, giving testimony to their righteous struggle.

Both Yacoob Haroon and Qasif Mutasim talked first in an undifferentiated way about the mujāhidīn who died in their attempts to cross the LoC into the Indian-administered territory. But during longer discussions, small differences began to emerge. Qasif Mutasim was critical of the "brothers" of the mujāhids and jihādīs who died crossing the LoC. He expressed concern that they would leave the bodies of their colleagues out in the open, subject to the elements and scavenging by wild animals. He also said that by leaving the bodies behind, the mujāhidīn and jihādīs were putting local villagers like himself at risk of becoming *shahīd* as well when they tried to retrieve the bodies.

I asked him why the villagers buried the bodies rather than allowing them to be scavenged. At the time, I was trying to work out what I saw as the contradictions between his claim that the bodies don't need burial, from a ritual perspective, and his statement that the members of his village risked their lives to bury them. Qasif Mutasim was utterly horrified by my question. He ran through a list of responses—such as that the bodies smell and attract wild animals, that it is not safe to have animals that have tasted human flesh near a village—until his wife dismissively commented, "They are someone's sons."

Yacoob Haroon got to that point more immediately. In the presence of a group of men at the local tea stall, he spoke exclusively about fact that the true mujāhid has prepared his own body and soul for burial before going out onto the battlefield. However, when I met with him in the home of a relative he talked about the efforts that he and the villagers made to return the bodies to their families. Most of the bodies they had buried in the village martyrs' graveyard were the bodies of Pakistani or Afghan members of jihād organizations. But when a Kashmiri mujāhid died, he said that the other Kashmiri mujāhidīn in their organization returned the body to the family:

> We have buried only one Kashmiri *mujāhid*. That boy was from Annatnag [in the southwest of the Indian Kashmir Valley] and no one in our village or any other knew any of his family. We have read the *namāz-e-janāzah* [burial prayers] for that son of the soil.

The treatment of the bodies of mujāhids from Kashmiri refugee communities in AJK and Pakistan who died fighting, whether their families and communities received their bodies or not, often contradicted the public ideological positions of *jihādī tanzīms*. The joy commonly attributed to families who receive the "congratulatory news" of a mujāhid's martyrdom was often contradicted by the actual practices of mourning and ritual prayer that accompanied the news such a death. Families evaluated and even critiqued the practice of jihād by publicly evaluating and questioning the moral status of its warriors.

Living in the Body of the Martyr, Becoming Jihādī

For Kashmiri refugee men who claim to be a mujāhid, the social problem is not dying like a martyr, but living like one. There is no single ritual of becoming that produces a person as a mujāhid. And there is no transformative moment that makes a person, in effect, a living *shahīd,* someone capable of bearing witness to violence through his (living) body. Living like a *shahīd*—serving perpetually as a living testimony to the need for an armed struggle—is a social impossibility. Among refugee families in AJK and Pakistan, becoming a mujāhid depends on a man's embodied and affective link to the reproductive work of the family. At the same time, mujāhids' close association with children and wives creates a tension between the self-regulation and generalized sacrifice required of a mujāhid and these attachments of love and physical desire.

The resulting jokes, misunderstandings, and arguments marked points of ambiguity, dissension, and discomfort between Kashmiri mujāhids and non-Kashmiri members of *jihādī tanzīms* and, more significantly, deep conflicts within Kashmiri refugee communities. I saw the beginning of that in 1998, when Farida Begum laughed about the young mujāhid holding his infant child. In the summer of 1999, I made note that Ehsan Naveed referred to some militants as jihādīs when he wanted to acknowledge them as members of *tanzīms* and cast aspersions on their understanding of jihād at the same time. The word jihādī appeared in my notes more often in the spring of 2000, and in the recordings of interviews I conducted that fall (when the members of *tanzīms* come back to AJK for the winter), speakers made clear distinctions between mujāhids and jihādīs. They used the words to mark different kinds of distinctions, but use of one or the other term mostly indicated disapproval or suspicion about jihādīs as people who have a different relationship to jihād than mujāhids. Through field visits to Pakistan and AJK in 2003 and 2005, that distinction held, and jihādī remained a semi-pejorative term in Kashmiri refugee communities. During that time, I never heard a mujāhid refer to himself as jihādī. Indeed, people deployed the term in contentious disagreements as a pejorative reference to Kashmiri members of *jihādī tanzīms* who moved between different organizations or who claimed the status of a mujāhid when engaged in activities other than fighting. It marked intense social anxiety about the political potential, unpredictability, and ambiguity of the idea of jihād as formulated by Kashmiri mujāhids who had use for the organizations they joined, but were in not committed their ideological goals.

DEAD BODIES AND THE POLITICS OF RELIGIOUS DOUBT

The ritual preparations of the body through which mujāhids and jihādīs claim preparation for death and lay claim to a moral authority does not preclude social doubt or speculation about the judgments of the ultimate authority in such matters. Those doubts also have multiple political meanings, making it difficult for the state to institutionalize their sacrifices or harness their violence within a national Islamist framework.

During one prominent AJK state burial in the city of Muzaffarabad, a group of young women watching the ceremonies on television told me about a martyr who had been buried in the same state graveyard in the early 1990s:

> He wrote in his letter of intentions and last requests *[wasīyet]* that his body would only accept burial when he returned to his own home and was buried in that soil of the valley. He said "I am a son of the soil and my body will return to that soil only." So when he became *shahīd,* he was given the shallow temporary grave only, and his family said, "When Kashmir is liberated and we return to our homes, we will take his body with us."

As Noorin Bibi spoke, the other women nodded solemnly. It wasn't clear to me at first whether they shared a memory of this event or whether they agreed that the body would not decay until it was laid to rest in "liberated" soil. I asked this question, and Noorin Bibi answered quickly that there was no doubt that the body of a *shahīd* would not decay until the Kashmir Jihad was successful. She looked around the room at the other women until they nodded again.

After a few moments, however, her cousin Khalilah Bibi admitted that she had some serious doubts about the physical bodies of state-recognized *shahīd:*

> They say that the bodies of the martyrs stay pure even after death. I know that it is possible because even the worms and the insects do not touch the bodies of the saints in life or in death. But then I think—that would only be true of a real *mujāhid.* And we can only think that his *nīyat* was pure or it was not pure, but if he was really a pious *[nek]* person, that is known only to God. It is difficult to hide your heart from your own mother, but you cannot hide your heart from God.

Khalilah Bibi's comments opened up the conversation. No one expressed doubt about any specific declared *shahīd,* but they did talk about how to distinguish a real mujāhid from a person who participated in the Kashmir Jihad but did not have the moral status of a true mujāhid. As Khalilah Bibi said, "It is a great struggle to walk the path of a mujāhid."

That there can be a link between the moral state of the living and the state of the mortal body after death is not an idea limited to the mujāhid. The holy men associated with many shrines in AJK, including that of Sain Saheli Sarkar in the center of the capital city, include in their hagiographies attributions of the continuing purity, and in some cases enhanced beauty and divine fragrance, of the body after death, among the other outwardly manifestations of a state of divine grace, such as healing, which are commonly associated with Muslim saints in South Asia.[38] Indeed, a person in a state of heightened grace sometime becomes known only through the unusual state of his or her body after death.

Such was the case of an unnamed holy man who "humbled the Pakistan army" and whose shrine, as reported to me several times, had become a surreptitious stopping point for Kashmiri mujāhids and jihādīs as they made their way toward the LoC. The shrine is located on the Srinagar Highway. Much of that road that runs along a sharp precipice between the Jhelum river-bank and steep mountains, but the mountains open occasionally into valleys where rice paddies are terraced into the hillsides beside the river. Near the town of Gahri Dupatta, the road makes a sharp curve, edging past a high tree-covered mound marked by green flags and brightly colored strips of cloth hanging from tree branches beside knotted black cords and women's glass bangles. These are familiar signs of the burial place of a Muslim saint, or the place where a holy man had completed a period of aesthetic observance. So I was not surprised that the road passed around it; what I did not notice at first was that the road literally split, with the hill shrine like an island in the center, so that vehicles coming from the other direction also made the same sharp jaunt to the left.

A steep path led directly to the top of the mound over dirt steps set between the thick roots of a tree that formed a canopy overhead. Ibrahim Hanif, who had escorted me here, stood for a moment there with his hands cupped and then made the sweeping motions with his palms that signaled the end of his brief prayer. Then he laughed and said that he enjoyed his moments at this shrine because it was the shrine of a man who had humbled the Pakistan Army:

> No one knows who is buried here. In fact, no one even knew that this site was the burial site of a holy man until the Pakistan Army began widening and repaving the road [as an access route for military supplies at the border with India]. The troops working on the road awakened each morning for days to find that the trough they had dug for the new roadbed was filled in at the point where their work had disturbed the ground around the old tree's roots, so the [army regulars] continued their work on the other side of the hill. Finally, some officers and the Army Engineers had to come to the site to oversee the completion of the road by connecting its two ends, but they had the same difficulty. One of the officers decided to examine the tree more closely, and dug a small tunnel between its roots. At the heart of a cupped root ball, he found the body of a man, long dead but completely untouched by worms or decay, whose body though obviously human had not returned to dust like that of most men after death. The officer proclaimed that this was the resting site of a holy man. He said, "It is clear that this holy man's burial was not carried out by human beings, his final prayers have surely been done by angels themselves and his intact body was marked and protected by this tree."

That the pronouncement that the body testified to a holy man's state of grace was attributed to an officer in the Pakistan Army, representative of rationality and authority, indicates a narrative resolution to the modernist and fundamentalist critique of faith in intermediaries between the individual and God.[39] When mujāhids or jihādīs stopped at this particular shrine, appealing to a man whose state of grace was evidenced by his body's ability to foil the Pakistan Army, it was in effect a critical nod back to the state of Pakistan even as they headed off to confront India.

From Muhājir to Mujāhid to Jihādī in the Global Order of Things

Kashmiri refugees have shaped the organization of violence in one of the world's most volatile and contentious borderlands in foundational ways, but the history of forced mass migration in the Jammu and Kashmir region has largely gone unexamined. This is in part because they occupy an indeterminate geographical and political space between India and Pakistan, and in part because they disappear before analytical lenses that are focused on formal institutions, geopolitical security, and the nation-building projects of postcolonial states.

People displaced within and from the former Princely State of Jammu and Kashmir have made claims on political belonging grounded in rights rather than in culture, and this rights-bearing form of being Kashmiri has both a history and a historicity. Its history is grounded in the development of the hereditary state subject as a political identity though which the people of the Princely State struggled to define and enforce limits on monarchical sovereignty. The past, however, leaves many different traces on the present, and the salience of the people of the state *(awām-e-riyāsat)* or people of Kashmir *(awām-e-kashmīr)* as a political form could have dissipated after the end of the monarchical rule against which it first developed. Instead, during the Partition, displaced state subjects became a distinct governmental category within the South Asian refugee regime. In Pakistan, refugees of Jammu and Kashmir *(muhājir-e-jammū-o-kashmīr)* did a tremendous amount of social and political work to preserve and extend their rights by maintaining their claims to property in the former Princely State. Under the provisions that provided for their temporary resettlement, Kashmiri refugees acquired citizenship privileges and protections by documenting and maintaining their status as categorical refugees. The ultimate failure to either hold a plebiscite or by abrogating the UN resolutions on Jammu and Kashmir made possible the institutionalization of this new political form as a electoral çonstituency for the state of Azad Jammu and Kashmir (AJK). There is nothing inherently unalterable about the legal provisions that created the presumption of return for Kashmiri refugees—the law is made and shaped by people, and laws and legal systems change and develop. In the modern state, the law is an object and a tool of social struggles because it links the regulatory and bureaucratic functions of the state to systems of cultural order and recognition. However, this rights-bearing form of being Kashmiri also has a historicity in the sense that it was reinscribed as a part of the historical consciousness of Kashmiri refugees for whom the right of return is configured as a return to specific homes and properties, not a repatriation to a generalized homeland. It exists alongside, and sometimes in conflict with, cultural claims on national belonging that became politically important in the postcolonial context.

Muslim refugees from Jammu and Kashmir also drew on the Islamicate concept of hijarat (protective migration) in making meaning of their experiences. This understanding of being a refugee allowed people to acknowledge the violence that led to their displacement and the suffering of loss and exile without making those the source of political value per se. Instead, muhājirs used their displacement experiences as a source of moral and social worth by cultivating a domestic sphere, nurturing the family, and working to reestablish the confessional community. Muhājirs recaptured their personal histories of violence-related forced displacement as a hijarat through their conduct after being displaced, not by any formal declaration by a religious authority or through ritualized preparations to flee their homes. And both men and women contributed to the re-creation of the refugee family; the form of their contributions were determined in part by their gender identities, but the work of resettlement was a collective project that began in the domestic sphere and generated political value.

That political value, however, had no singular expression in forms of political power, because no state—be it Azad Jammu and Kashmir or Jammu and Kashmir State or Pakistan or India—was able to claim the legitimacy of representing the rights of Kashmiri refugees without engaging with actual displaced subjects who had their own clear ideas about the nature of those rights. These ideas sometimes subverted and sometimes extended state political projects. The idea of the Kashmir Problem (mas'alah-e-kashmīr) as a trope of political discourse, for example, reconfigured the Kashmir Dispute as a peoples' struggle that did not end with the dissolution of monarchical control, rather than as a territorial conflict between India and Pakistan. For decades, Kashmiri refugees and people living in the borderlands transgressed the Line of Control (LoC) as an irrelevant social boundary. As it became harder to cross, some made crossing a public political act, but many others resisted both politicization and criminalization by practicing clandestine crossing, movements that are written into the family histories of those who live in the borderlands. Their historical consciousness posits a link between the individual and corporate identity of Kashmiri refugees and a territorial state that no longer exists and does not yet exist. In the interim, the integrity of the State of Jammu and Kashmir *(riyāsat-e-jammū-o-kashmīr)* is maintained through the property claims and in the bodies of its dispersed people.

At the same time, there are many contradictions between formal legal documentation, political recognition, social inclusion, and cultural attachment that reveal ambivalence about what it means to be a Kashmiri refugee over six decades after the dissolution of the Princely State. Arguments and disagreements about who qualifies as Kashmiri or as a refugee erupt in daily life around numerous political and economic issues, like eligibility for employment or elections, the receipt of government aid, the allocation of reserved seats in higher education, and the transfer of property rights. Other conflicts arise around marriage negotiations, which include elaborate considerations of the possible future constellations of visiting networks, before and after a projected resolution of the Kashmir dispute. These arguments and debates tie manifestly public issues to the affective life of the family. They also make that social ambivalence a source of political power, because it reinscribes the importance of maintaining the Kashmiri refugee identity even through interactions in which the authenticity of any person's specific claim is brought into question.

In the early 1990s, the epistemological principles and historical experiences that organized what it meant to be a Kashmiri refugee in AJK and Pakistan came into conflict with the principles of recognition articulated by the international refugee regime. The regional context of this shift was multifaceted: the immediate precipitating event was the beginning of an armed conflict on the Indian side of the LoC, which displaced new people into AJK. In Indian Jammu and Kashmir State, the forms of violence used by the state in its counterinsurgency campaigns were the objects of collective efforts to bring international attention to the Kashmir issue. These efforts did not focus on the potential for regional instability between India and Pakistan, but rather on the claims of Kashmiri subjects to be protected as human beings from the practices of violence that qualify as human rights abuses—including practices of torture during interrogation and disappearances suspected to be executions—and to claim that protection from the international community if they could not get it as citizens of a state. In Pakistan, practices of refugee administration had begun to change in the 1980s because of changes in the political economy of international aid, relief, and development that emerged in camps for Afghan refugees.

The refugee camps established by the AJK government in the 1990s aimed to render displaced people from Indian Jammu and Kashmir visible to the international community as "refugees" instead of "immigrants," a distinction that was ambiguous in the political and social identity "muhājir." In the camps established after 1989, refūjīs—as social actors and as symbolic representatives of a claim for international recognition—were both the agents and the objects of efforts to resolve the fundamental differences between the constructions of refugee subjectivity in the South Asian refugee regime and in the international refugee regime. Their efforts to make displaced Kashmiri people recognizably global humanitarian subjects involved producing, collecting, and distributing documentation of human rights abuses as evidence of their status as victims of political violence. It also required depoliticizing the refugee as a political subject. This was accomplished in part by a focus on refūjī women as innocent victims of state excesses, but this new order of displacement and refugee recognition challenged the cultural and political order that was marked by the historically constituted legal rights and social value accorded to the practice of hijarat as claimed by previous groups of Kashmiri muhājirs. Many refūjī men participated in militant activities, but they spent relatively more time in AJK or Pakistan taking care of their families. Under different conditions, they might have become a new group of resettled muhājirs, like those who had preceded them in other times of war. In the increasingly gendered dichotomy of producing refūjīs as humanitarian subjects, however, refūjī men found it difficult to gain social or political recognition as contributors to their community as participants in domestic life.

This shift in the social value accorded to hijarat and a growing focus on jihād as a valued form of political engagement was most profoundly evident among Kashmiri muhājirs living in formerly resettled communities throughout AJK and Pakistan. As evidence of both human rights abuses and of the international community's knowledge of those practices circulated through refugee communities, refūjīs and muhājirs increasingly talked about the conflict in Indian Jammu and Kashmir as a jihād. But their ideas about what they called the Kashmir Jihad were not primarily defined by Islamic doctrine or by fundamentalist or Islamist ideology. In Kashmiri communities, the term jihād accommodated multiple political aspirations within an Islamicate terminology, including nationalist ideals such as self-determination *(khudirādīyat)* and independence *(āzādī)*. As the conflict continued, and as refugees and mujāhids continued the work of documenting the human rights crisis and advocating for a coordinated international intervention, public support for militant organizations fighting in Kashmir took the material forms of charitable donations to and enlistment in such organizations.

This public support was based not on a disavowal of the moral order indicated by international human rights and humanitarian ideals; nor was it based on a clash of cultural values. Instead, as formulated by Kashmiri refugee communities in Azad Jammu and Kashmir and Pakistan, the legitimization, organization, and practice of jihād as an armed struggle was characterized by the connection between duty *(farz)* and rights, specifically human rights *(insānī haqūq)*—not between duty and sovereign territory *(dār)* (as in both classical and modernist juridical and doctrinal traditions), or between duty and the Islamic order *(nizām-e-islāmī)* or the state *(dawla)* (as formulated by Islamist ideologues). Jihadist organizations accommodated the image of the mujāhid as the defender of victimized Kashmiri women, but self-proclaimed mujāhids joined multiple organizations and frequently left one for another. They needed the infrastructural support that jihadist organizations offered, but were not constrained by the ideological and bodily disciplining of religious institutions. In evaluating the extent and limits of their duties, Kashmiri mujāhids emphasized the importance of their personal experiences, their understanding of those experiences in the broader political context, and their conscious evaluations of their obligations to their families and their society. Their concept of rights was a hybrid of Islamicate and global political ideas, and it shifted the terrain of struggle from sovereign territory to the sovereign body.

Even though this formulation was coherent and persuasive for Kashmiri refugee communities, mujāhids did not receive unqualified public support. Parents and community elders often worked very hard to keep young men out of jihadist organizations, even if they agreed that the Kashmir conflict had the status of a jihād and even when they were very critical of the international community for its refusal to make serious, visible efforts to end the human rights crisis and bring about a final resolution to the Kashmir issue. Debates about the moral status of individual mujāhids created a space for public debate about the conduct of the Kashmir Jihad, even as they established the family as an important mediator of men's incorporation into jihadists organizations as organizers, fund-raisers, or as fighters. Indeed, the term jihādī, when it came into use in the later 1990s to early 2000s, emerged as an oppositional term to mujāhid. It appeared in complaints and arguments about how individual members of jihadist organizations managed the balance between caring for family and contributing to the material practices of the Kashmir Jihad. What underlay these discontents was not always or only a disagreement about how these young men conducted themselves, but also an implicit recognition of a profound shift in how jihād was incorporated into social and political life.

DETERRITORIALIZED JIHĀD, THE SOVEREIGNTY OF THE BODY, AND POLITICAL ISLAM

Many scholars have noted the connection between increasingly deterritorialized Islam and the rise of a global jihadist movement. The case of Kashmiri refuges suggests that this rise may be an interpretable, if unsettling, consequence of the way that the body has became a site of political contestation in late modern political forms of rule.

The connection between refugee recognition and the documentation of a human rights crisis was not invented in Kashmiri refugee camps; it was part of a global reconfiguring of conventional refugee subjects connected to the practice of offering temporary protection to people collectively affected by political turmoil. Although humanitarian projects had always been part of the politics of establishing hierarchical relations between states, the emergence of humanitarian refugee as a global category, and that category's reliance on a doctrine of rights, depended on the shift in focus to human rights and the liberties of individuals as a fix for the loss of ideological oppositions occasioned by the decline of clear Cold War divisions in the global political community. The end of the Cold War also shifted a focus to the problem of the so-called new wars, fought within states—the reliance on victims and human rights that functionally replaced the state and borders in the recognition of refugees. This corresponded to a shift in an array of domains, including the social sciences and policy studies, that made the institutional state a subsidiary unit of political analysis to other categories of political organization, such as, for example, "ethnicity" or "civil society."

Placed in this global context, the praxis of jihād among Kashmiri refugees is revealed as a legible and coherent rethinking of the relationship between Muslim people and late modern conceptions of sovereignty and practices of violence. This "loss of ideology," or loosening of ideological control, is not an exclusively South Asian phenomenon,[1] and "human rights" are a part of jihād formulations in other contexts as well.[2] But in many ways, Kashmiri refugees were in an excellent historical position to forge this link. Their historical subject formation linked their political identities to a territorial polity and embodied that polity in the bodies of displaced people through their property claims. As refugees, they were incorporated into the postcolonial order as transnational subjects, but were also integrated into several international and global political and cultural regimes. The politicization of Islam in the Kashmir region occurred through the integration of these Muslim people into global political regimes—including systems of representation, moral evaluation, administration, and violence—rather than through an inherent clash of ideology or a resurgence of timeless or universal religious ideals. And the point of intersection between these processes is "the refugee" as a political subject who embodies and condenses local, national, and international social forms and symbolic orders.

And, "Humanitarian Jihād"

An earthquake quite literally changed the landscape of northeast Pakistan in October 2005. It had its epicenter near Muzaffarabad, where houses, schools, hospitals, and government buildings collapsed, and in mountainous areas entire villages were buried in landslides. The earthquake killed over eighty thousand people, injured approximately one hundred thousand, and rendered three million others homeless; half of those deaths and losses occurred in Azad Jammu and Kashmir (AJK), primarily in the Muzaffarabad district. This natural disaster brought numerous state institutions, international agencies, and voluntary organizations together in a vast humanitarian relief project. In the immediate postdisaster context, members of jihadist organizations worked with international humanitarian organizations, the Pakistan army and security services, global Islamic charities, and Pakistani domestic and transnational civil society groups, all of whom came to AJK to provide emergency relief.

For the international community, an area that had long been a site of global humanitarian refusal became an acceptable terrain of humanitarian work because the disaster was "natural." The new administrative and institutional practices that came with billions of dollars of international aid and development funds opened the region to international investment and observation and initiated a period of intense privatization and the reemergence of a domestic tourist industry. For Pakistani voluntary organizations, four years into the War on Terror, AJK became a place in which Pakistani society's capacity for self-organization and self-care could be mobilized against the images of Pakistan as a place of perpetual crisis and institutionalized disorder, on the one hand, and as the object of militarized humanitarian interventions on the other. For the members of *jihādī tanzīms,* it became a domain of governance, in which welfare could be articulated as a form of state security provision that would continue to compete for funds and recognition with the border security concerns; this vision shaped the reconstruction of AJK in formal and informal ways.

Pakistani state security policy in Kashmir has long treated security primarily as the military defense of borders, but after the earthquake, members of the *jihādī tanzīms* demonstrated that they had a broader concept of security. Kashmiri jihādīs declared a temporary stop to the armed activities in order to engage in the labor of relief work. Those whom I met in the relief operations described their involvement in the relief work as a part of their practice of jihād—a practice they called "humanitarian jihād."[1] They imported emergency supplies such as all-weather tents from storehouses located throughout Pakistan and they constructed well-run, secure, and hygienic camps for the homeless. They put their satellite communications technology to use locating people trapped in the mountains, and carried the injured out of isolated villages on their backs. They also established the first working field hospital with surgical capacity (including mobile x-ray and microbial analysis machines). It was operating thirty-six hours after the earthquake. By comparison, Turkey had an operational field hospital running five days later, the United States eight days later. Five weeks after the earthquake, when I was escorted on an official visit to a Pakistan military field hospital on the Line of Control near Chakothi, the Pakistani army's model civilian field hospital consisted of a tent, two chairs, and a table with a display of bandages, analgesics, and antimalarials.

A commonly told tale in those first months went like this: the Pakistani army troops, redeployed from the Punjab, showed up in AJK and then marched to the LoC to protect it from military adventurism by Indian troops. Alternatively, troops arrived at a collapsed school with weapons, but no heavy equipment suitable for extracting survivors from beneath the slabs of concrete and iron rods that are the construction norm in the area. A trope of complaint was "the army showed up with bayonets, not shovels, and tanks, not bulldozers." Many in AJK attributed this to Pakistan's interest in "Kashmir, not Kashmiris," but it must be said that the same complaint was made in Islamabad, where two of the luxury apartment towers in the Margala complex had collapsed.

Years later, many who lived through the earthquake still begin their recollections of the first days after the quake that *jihādīs* brought the first help they received in the form of excavating survivors, or the delivery of food and water to people unable to make their way through the rubble of the urban neighborhoods. They also stayed in those neighborhoods and villages to bury the dead. As one man I've known for many years said to me, stating his shame and declaring his gratitude:

> Cabeiri, my children's mother was carrying my three sons, my brother and uncle and I carried father and grandfather out on a *chārpai* [a cord bed]. In the end, I looked at the dead and then I walked over their bodies. When we came back, in each of those spots where there had been a body there was a flag with a number, and a notation of the burial ground where each of those bodies had been properly buried. I failed my neighbors, but in the end, the *jihādis* kept a list of the person's age and what they were wearing, and every family could find their loved ones in the ground where they had been laid to rest, and the funeral prayers had been said in their name.

In the early days and weeks after the earthquake, they were widely regarded by Azad Kashmiri citizens to be the most responsive and effective relief aid workers. Indeed, they had organized themselves into informal brigades, which in the first weeks morphed and re-formed, as new tasks were required until they were settled in organized service societies with assigned tasks in the month after the quake. The point I want to emphasize here is not that the members of *jihādi tanzīms* jumped into the task of caring for the displaced, the injured, and the dead, although they did. Nor that they carried mobile x-rays and centrifuges on their backs and on pack mules when the roads from Kohalla and Mansera were blocked and no trucks could get through. Nor that they set up tented relief camps that were so well guarded that men felt comfortable leaving their women and young children there. Rather, the point is that the jihadist groups had stores of such equipment stashed in various locations around Pakistan, which their members *could* deploy during an emergency.

As the resident surgeon of the Jamaat ul Dawa camp and field hospital complex said to me: "We know if there is some invasion or disaster, the common people suffer most, so we have to plan and be prepared for their safety. Our closest storehouse was in Balakot, but that was destroyed, so we had the supplies brought from Peshawar and Lahore." He himself had been working in a free medical clinic in Lahore run by the Jamaat ul Dawa until he was asked to oversee the field hospital in Muzaffarabad. Even the United Nations High Commission for Refugees (UNHCR), which normally maintains large stores of tents and other supplies in Pakistan for its Afghan refugee operations, was unable to meet the need so quickly, as they had depleted their regional supplies during the relief work that followed the Indian Ocean Tsunami earlier in the year. When delegates of formal international humanitarian organizations like the International Committee of the Red Cross (ICRC) and UNHCR established a presence on the ground in Azad Jammu and Kashmir, they found themselves working side by side with international volunteers who had arrived with extraction and mountain-climbing equipment, with solders from many national armies, including two Cuban army doctors who had, lacking their own transport, hitched a ride to Muzaffarabad in an American black-hawk helicopter, and with *jihādīs* from several organizations on a number of states' designated terrorist organization lists.

The *jihādī tanzīms* had also adopted an institutional structure for their practices of "humanitarian jihād." They turned to the religious institutions with which they were loosely affiliated and used their charity wings to establish welfare projects to support and sustain their relief work. At the top level of organizational hierarchy, the association was quite direct—the Jamaat ul Dawa was connected to the Lashkar-e-Tayyiba, the Al Rehmat Trust to the Jaish-e-Mohammad, and the Al Safa Foundation to Al-Badr. But in the field, the connection was much looser. Individual jihādīs moved between projects and organization; setting up a school for children in a Jamaat ul Dawa camp and then one in an Al Safa camp. Or alternatively, purchasing commodities and keeping the ration accounts for three different camps that were engaging in collective bargaining with shops in the Rawalpindi bulk market. They also had to follow orders in their assigned tasks, but were quite able to move on if they tired of an assignment.

The task of separating the *jihādī tanzīms* from the international humanitarian project was undertaken in the reconstruction and rehabilitation phase, which began in March 2006. The UN emerged as the coordinator of a five-year Rehabilitation and Reconstruction Project (originally scheduled to conclude in 2011, it is now extended for an additional 3 years) called "Build Back Better" that represented a form of development humanitarianism. It had the great advantage of conceiving of humanitarian work as a long-term process to rebuild sustainable civil infrastructure and build local capacity and expertise, but it distrusted government officials and institutions as corrupt and preferred to foster private initiatives and support private contractors. While members of *jihādī tanzīms,* Islamist nongovernmental organizations (NGOs), government militaries, and international humanitarian organizations worked together throughout the relief phase, the UN-led recovery project also sought to insulate itself from all forms of interaction with the Islamist charities in all the reconstruction work.[2]

In AJK after 2006, the separation took institutional form by the establishment of two new agencies/departments—the Earthquake Reconstruction and Rehabilitation Agency (ERRA) by the Government of Pakistan, and the Camp Management Organization by the Government of AJK.[3] The AJK Camp Management Organization was established as the site through which the humanitarian workers on the ground maintained claims to be accountable to local populations and supportive of civil society initiatives while isolating themselves from the organizations that spearheaded many initiatives during the relief phase. ERRA became a site through with the international community moved its substantial aid and reconstruction funds, and established principles of transparency in funding and expenditure. In practice, this transparency was apparent for the institutional funders, but local communities and the AJK government officials did not understand the total picture of how money was spent. They did not understand, for example, why funds were spent importing raw materials from Turkey for the rebuilt campus of the University of Azad Kashmir, or why a team of Turkish engineers, all collecting overseas and hazard pay, were running the project when Kashmiri engineers were unemployed.

Once the Camp Management Organization took over the refugee camps, the service societies began to work on other projects funded by the charities. I found that by a year after the earthquake, the main organizations affiliates were these service committees *(khidmat-e-khalq)* and allied charitable funds which no longer reflected the pre–October 2005 militant affiliations of the members. By following up on specific relief workers, I discovered that the service committees were then made up of former members of many different militant organizations and that individual workers had moved at will between different committee groups. By 2006, these activists no longer identified themselves by the militant organization to which they previously belonged—maintaining a self-identification simply as jihādīs. Members of the service societies and Islamic charities took up central roles in supporting the initiatives of local civic groups, and they received support from multiple charities, which had become competitors with international aid agencies for philanthropic donations from Muslim communities around the world in times when those agencies were facing lower-than-needed contributions and were worried about the problem of donor fatigue.[4] Their initiative might be termed "Build Back Different;" it involved projects such as establishing free, well-staffed schools and health clinics in outlying areas and the development of very small-scale hydroelectric power projects to bring power to isolated mountain communities. The presence of numerous UN and INGO projects and foreign aid workers, in a region that had been closely surveilled and though which financial regulation had been under tight Pakistani government control, established new flows of capital that were not controlled by the government as a form of patronage. The project thus protected the space that the religious *khidmat-e-khalqs* had opened up in the months after the earthquake, but fostered a diverse array of civil society groups, which for the first time in AJK's postcolonial history could withstand the political suspicion of the state security agencies and command resources that are not wholly dependent on a supplicant relationship with Pakistani national elites.

Many Kashmiri members of *jihādī tanzīms* stayed in their demobilized service circles and became formal members of the government and INGO reconstruction effort. They did not renounce their commitment to the Kashmir Jihad, and they consider themselves still actively engaged in the work of humanitarian jihād. In 2006, I was visiting a school-building project in one of the neighborhoods in Muzaffarabad that had been completely destroyed by the earthquake. Ehsan Naveed motioned to a middle-aged man in a military-style vest over his *shalwār-qamīz* who was holding a clipboard and supervising the unloading of construction supplies from the back of a pick-up displaying the prominent logo of a major humanitarian INGO and two new AJK-based NGOs. Ehsan Naveed said to me "he's a *jihādī*," and the man looked at me and nodded.

NOTES

PREFACE

1. See, for example, the January 4–11, 2008 cover of *The Economist*.

2. *Hijarat* is more properly translated as "flight" or simply "migration", while *jihād* literally means "a great effort" or "struggle." "Protective migration" and "armed struggle" reflect the terms' predominant usage among Kashmiri Muslim refugees living in Pakistan. I discuss these terms in detail at the beginning of chapter 2.

3. See Robinson (2012).

4. Sluka (2000a, p. 35). This principle corresponds to an increasing reliance on addressing individual trauma as a model for accountability in the political process (Hayner 2001; Winter and Sivan 1999).

5. Metcalf (2002); see also, Smith (2007).

6. Mahmood (1996), McKenna (1998), Nordstrom (1997, 2004); Nordstrom and Martin (1992), Nordstrom and Robben (1995), and Sluka (2000b).

7. Taussig (1999); see also, Ferme (2001).

INTRODUCTION

1. When the last full census was conducted in 1998, the total resident population of AJK was 2.9 million, including approximately one million resettled refugees; its Pakistan-resident refugee population was 2.5 million (Azad Government of the State of Jammu & Kashmir 1999, 2009; Government of Pakistan 1998). The 2008 census was not conducted because the state administration was focused on reconstruction after the earthquake of October 2005. The AJK government's estimated population for 2008, based on an education sector census and statistical growth projection, was a resident population of 3.77 million.

2. Devji (2005, pp. vii–xvii).

3. Abu-Lughod (2002) and Hirshkind and Mahmood (2002) made scathing critiques of invoking the protection of Muslim women from (fundamentalist) Muslim men to legitimize military intervention in Afghanistan. Mamdani (2002) offered a wider critique of the Cold War logic that made Muslim religious warriors anticommunist allies and that led to international support for nondemocratic, authoritarian and military regimes in Muslim-majority societies. These culturally legitimated forms of political and military intervention were not the sole purview of the "Great Game" players. Hegghammer's (2010) analysis of Saudi Arabian state and societal support for the Afghan Jihad in the 1980s and 1990s shows that participation in resistance struggles abroad came to be seen domestically as a form of altruism (pp. 1–37).

4. Jansen (1993), Khadduri (1997), and Peters (1979).

5. Diverse scholars such as Burgat (2003), Juergensmeyer (2000), Kepel (2002), and Lewis (2002) posited a direct link between Islamic theology and political radicalism. Others argued the inherent modernity of Islamic fundamentalism and Islamist movements, yet still accepted the premise that an unmediated Islamic/Arab past is the cultural source for critiques of modernity in the Muslim world (Barber 2001; Roy 1994).

6. Mamdani (2002).

7. For a discussion and bibliographies, see Esposito (1997).

8. See Tibi (2002a, pp. xiii–xxx) for a personal reflection on this point, Jalal (2008, pp. 1–19, 314) for an analytical defense, and Mamdani (2004) for a critique of its political uses. As an analytical orientation, it mirrors an empirical one—many traditionally trained Islamic scholars ('ulemah) have blamed secularly trained Muslim intellectuals for distorting or misusing classical Islamic concepts.

9. A notable exception is Devji's (2005) discussion of the hermeneutics of jihadist discourses in the global public sphere.

10. For a full discussion, see Volpi (2010).

11. For an excellent recent example, see Firestone (1999), who examines the interpretive processes though which the classical doctrinal positions on jihād were forged in the Sunni traditions. Bonney (2004) presents a synthetic overview of the uses of the concept as a form of just war around the Muslim world to argue that jihāds are always mobilized in historically contingent ways. On the other hand, several studies, such as those by Bonner (2006) and Cook (2005), have been redeployed within reductionist culturalist frameworks as an a priori explanation for the social phenomenon of religiously legitimated political violence, because they suggest that familiarity with classical Islamic texts in and of itself connects Muslims to jihadist radicalism.

12. See, for example, Jalal's (2008) study of jihād movements in colonial and post-colonial South Asia; also Hadler's (2008) study of resistance against the Dutch on the island of Sumatra (Indonesia) and Haroon's (2009) study of the struggle for regional autonomy from the British on the Afghan frontier.

13. See, for example, Juergensmeyer (2008) and Sageman (2004). There is a crossover here with counterterrorism scholars such as Brachman (2009), who rely on open source intelligence (which often means websites and print publications of jihadist organizations).

14. Noteworthy exceptions to this dearth of ethnographic studies of jihād include Edwards (2002) and McKenna (1998). Other sociologically oriented scholars have undertaken to explain changes in the organization of a specific jihād over time; see Roy (1986), Hasan (2005), Hegghammer (2010), and Rougier (2007).

15. Asad (1993, 2003); see also, Green and Searle-Chatterjee (2008).

16. Sontag (2003, pp. 38–40).

17. For examples and bibliographies, see Haqqani (2005a, 2005b), Kumar (2001), Shafqat (2002), Sikand (2007), and Swami (2008).

18. Bose (2003), Ganguly, R. (2003), Ganguly, S. (1997), Lamb (1991), Puri (1993), and Wirsing (1994).

19. Jamal (2009) examines this in detail. Indian human rights groups have documented this extensively since 1991.

20. This paradoxical relationship with modernity has led to debates about whether fundamentalism and Islamism are modern, premodern, or antimodern phenomena. For an overview, see Euben's (1999) analysis of the modernity of fundamentalism as a philosophical orientation and as an expression of an "alternative modernity." On fundamentalism and Islamism as modern movements, see also Beinin and Stork (1997), Eickelman (2000), Hefner (1998), Lapidus (1983), Lawrence (1989), Salvatore (1997) and Turner (1994). While it is important to engage fundamentalists' and Islamists' own explanations for their movements, interpretations of fundamentalism and Islamism too often conflate the arguments of Islamic scholars and Muslim public intellectuals about how Muslim societies should be organized with explanations of actual sociopolitical movements in those societies. For examples of this problem, see Burgat (2003), Kepel (2002), Lewis (2002), and Roy (1994).

21. See Lawrence (2000), Hefner (2005), and Nasr (2001, 2008). Marty and Appleby's fundamentalisms project, on the other hand, treated Islamic fundamentalism and Islamism together. This had the advantage of emphasizing their mutual emergence from the eighteenth- and nineteenth-century reformist movements and also their debates with each other (see Ahmad 1991; Arjomand 1995; Sachedina 1991; Voll 1991), but did not sufficiently distinguish between the groups that took society as their object and those that became focused on formal politics and the state.

22. Euben (1999, pp.16–19, 154–167) and Voll (1991, p. 347).

23. The term in Arabic is *al-nizām al-islāmī*. Both Abu A'la Maududi and Sayyid Qutb (of the Muslim Brotherhood), as significant articulators of this position, were influenced by fundamentalist thinkers (Maududi's own first works are philosophically fundamentalist, and he argued against the formation of the state of Pakistan) as well as by each other (see Adams 1983; Bonney 2004, pp. 199–223; Haddadd 1983; Osman 2003).

24. Tibi (2002a, p. 99).

25. Mitchell (1993) and Nasr (1994, 2001).

26. In Urdu, the words for these divisions are, respectively, *jamā'at* (party), *khalq* (service society, literally "circle"), and *tanzīm* (militant organization, literally "organization").

27. Brenner (1998), Çınar (2005), Deeb (2006), Iqtidar (2011), Mahmood (2005), and Navaro-Yashin (2002).

28. The influence of service provision and political activists (rather than ideologies) on the social impact of such organizations has been the topic of recent studies. See Ahmad (2009), Hegghammer (2010), Norton (2007), Roy (2011), Wickham (2002), and Wiktorowicz (2001). See also, Meijer (2009) and Wiktorowicz (2004) for comparative rethinking of Islamist organizations as social movements.

29. Ahmad (2009), Fischer and Abedi (1990), Hefner (2000), McKenna (1998), Osanloo (2009), Peletz (2002), and White (2002).

30. Evans (2008) and Ellis and Khan (2003).

31. Khan, B.A. (2000), Madan (1998), Sikand (2001) and Varshney (1992).

32. Bakewell (2008), Lanz (2008), and Polzer and Hammond (2008).

33. See Terry (2002).

34. See Hathaway (1991) for analysis of refugee juridical status and Chimni and United Nations High Commissioner for Refugees (2000) for a critical legal studies perspective on "refugee" as a legal category.

35. For a critical legal studies perspective on the distinction between "migrants" and "refugees" in South Asia, see Chari et al. (2003), Chimni (1998), Oberoi (2006), and Samaddar (2003).

36. Mazower (2004, p. 380).

37. Chimni and United Nations High Commissioner for Refugees (2000, p. 4).

38. Kamenka (1989).

39. Malkki (1995b), Zolberg (1983), and Zolberg et al. (1989). See Harrell-Bond and Voutria (1992) and Skran and Daughtry (2007) for a discussion of how these perspectives have contributed to the emergence of the interdisciplinary field of "refugee studies."

40. Estimates based on surveys of refugee camps place the numbers lower, between 8 million and 10 million, while estimates based on comparisons between the 1941 and 1951 national censuses put the estimate as high as 14 million (Government of India 1948; National Documentation Center 1993; Rao 1967). Between 500,000 and a million people were killed in the first year of the Partition process, and family members reported more than 100,000 women abducted. The Partition ended by bilateral agreement in 1951, but cross-border movements and forced displacements continued through the 1960s, especially on the Bengal border.

41. Zamindar (2007). Several scholars have recently examined the importance of refugees as central, rather than liminal, postcolonial subjects, most importantly Zamindar has argued that refugees were the subjects around which the state attempted to resolve the contradictions of Indian colonial nationalisms and that the postcolonial citizenship regimes of India and Pakistan were constructed through attempts to eliminate the "bothness" of refugee political and cultural identification. Ansari (2005) has taken up the same problem with a focus on the divided region of Sindh. Khan (2007) has put the study of refugee displacement back into the normative history of modern South Asia by synthesizing Partition with the study

of institutional and party politics of South Asian decolonization and postcolonial state formation.

42. See Feldman (2008a) and Peterson (2008). Liisa Malkki's analysis of the international refugee regime emerged from the African context in the 1970s and 1980s and described the depoliticization of national subjects into refugees as an outcome of the cultural processes of (de)territorialization and (de)nationalization in global political culture (Malkki 1992, 1995a).

43. Bayefsky and Fitzpatrick (2000), Ferris (1993), and Shue (1989). For a discussion of the relationship between humanitarianism and rights, see also, Barnett and Weiss (2008a), Calhoun (2004), and Wilson and Brown (2009). These practices of depoliticized care for refugees now contribute to the development of "antipolitical" forms of governance (Ticktin 2011).

44. Benthall (1993) and Chandler (2001).

45. Moore (1994, p. 63).

46. For a discussion of the Eastern Europe context of the early 1990s, see Borneman (1998), Korac (1994), and Stiglmayer (1994). On rape as a normalized practice of warfare, see Littlewood (1997), Nordstrom (1996), and Weitsman (2008).

47. Moser and Clark (2001, p. 5).

48. Research on women's roles in modern insurgencies has focused on domestic activities as emancipatory political activism (Werbner 1999) or the use of domestic spaces in the service of public militant politics (Aretxaga 1997, 2001; Peteet 1991, 1997). See also, Manchandra's (2001) effort to highlight examples of women's militant activism in the Kashmir insurgency.

49. Ahmed (1992).

50. Chatterjee (1989, 1995).

51 Aggarwal (2004), Brenner (1998), Hansen (2001), Joseph (1997), Peteet (2005), Ring (2006), and Verkaaik (2004).

52. Arendt (1951, p. 296).

53. At the time of publication, AJK is divided into eight administrative districts: Rawalakot District has been divided into the districts of Poonch and Sudhnoti; the northern *tehsil* of Athmuqam in Muzaffarabad District has become Neelum District.

54. For the history and legal structure of the administrative separation of AJK and the Northern Areas, see Raman (2004). For an overview of the postcolonial emergence of political movements in those regions, see Sökefeld (2005). In 1993, the Muzaffarabad High Court found that Pakistan had failed to safeguard the fundamental political rights of the people living in the Northern Areas and ordered AJK to extend representative government to that region (Azad Government of the State of Jammu & Kashmir 1993). Pakistan's 2010 Constitutional Amendment provided instead for political integration with Pakistan.

55. This ministry has been renamed several times since it was established in 1949 as the Ministry of Kashmir Affairs. Most recently, it was the "Ministry of Kashmir Affairs and Northern Areas," until it was renamed in 2010. For simplicity, I hereafter call it the "Ministry of Kashmir Affairs"—the colloquial designation used by AJK politicians.

56. See, for example, Dasgupta (1968), Rose (1992), Puri (2010), and Singh (1995).

57. Mahmud (2006), Puri (2010), Rose (1992), and Snedden (2001).

58. The Pakistani civil administrative services played a central role in the consolidation of the Pakistani state (Burki 1969; Sayeed 1958), and the deliberate exclusion of the Pakistan Civil Service from AJK was an explicit provision of the 1974 constitution.

59. Schools in which English is the language of instruction. In Urdu medium schools, Urdu is the language of instruction, and English is taught as a second language.

60. Five reserved seats are for women, one is for a religious scholar, and one for a technocrat. See Government of Azad Jammu and Kashmir Legislative Assembly, http://www.ajkassembly.gok.pk/AJK_Interim_Constitution_Act_1974.pdf. The seat for overseas state-subjects was included in the 7th Amendment Act (II) of 1986. The representatives for this seat have been elected from the members of Kashmiri political parties active in the United Kingdom. The seat usually goes to a representative from Birmingham or Manchester, where the South Asian diaspora is primarily comprised of people displaced from Mirpur District by the building of the Mangla Dam and the subsequent submersion of Mirpur town in the 1950s.

61. Lamb (1991) and Wirsing (1994).

62. The Kashmir Council is made up of the Prime Minister of Pakistan (Chairperson), the President of AJK (vice-Chairperson), five appointed members (federal ministers or members of the Pakistan National Assembly), and six members elected by the AJK Legislative Assembly. The Minister of Kashmir Affairs participates as an ex officio member. Fifty-two subjects are the exclusive domain of the council, including collecting most forms of revenue, which makes the Legislative Assembly fiscally beholden to the council even in matters within its portfolio. In addition, the government of Pakistan deputes officers from the Pakistan Civil Services as "lent officers." These include the Accountant General, Inspector General of Police, and the Chief Secretary. See Section 21 of the AJK Interim Constitution Act, 1974. For an enumerated list of subjects, see Section 31(2), Schedule Three.

63. See, for example, Human Rights Watch (2006).

CHAPTER 1

1. Focusing on borderlands rather than borders emphasizes the social struggles that take place in divided regions and offers a corrective to historical narratives that naturalize the territoriality of the modern state (Baud and van Schendel 1997; Sahlins 1989; van Schendel 2005; Wilson and Donnan 1998). On Jammu and Kashmir as a borderland, see Zutshi (2009). See also Aggarwal (2004), Bhan (2008), and Sökefeld (1998) on the Kargil, Ladakh, and Baltistan regions of the Jammu and Kashmir borderlands.

2. The origins of the territorial dispute are said to be the Hindu Maharaja's contested accession to India—contested because his state was Muslim majority and shared borders with Pakistan, which claimed to represent Muslims of the Indian

subcontinent. See Bose (2003), Ganguly (1997), Hewitt (1995), and Wirsing (1994) for scholarly accounts of this history, and Schofield (1996) and Whitehead (2007) for excellent journalistic ones.

3. Zamindar (2007).

4. In 1947, there were over five hundred Native States of India that comprised approximately forty-five percent of the territories and twenty-four percent of the population of British India (Shastry 1941). Per the Instrument of Accession for Indian Princely States mandated by the Office of Indian States, the acceding Prince State conceded control over defense, international affairs, currency, and communications to the national state of either India or Pakistan. Further conditions of accession depended on the specific agreements that each monarch made for his state; see Menon (1956) for India and Wilcox (1963) for Pakistan.

5. Bhagavan (2009) and Ramusack (2004, pp. 8–11). See also, Jalal's (1985) now-classic analysis of the changing historical meaning of "Pakistan".

6. One side of the debate focuses on the histories of specific states and on the differences between political, social, and economic developments within the Princely States and those of colonial India (Jeffrey 1978; Ramusack 2004). Another emphasizes the colonial practices of governance in the history of the states, focusing on the inability of the princes to assert sovereignty in the imperial context (Copland 1982; Dirks 1987). From this latter perspective, elite ideologues and popular forms of resistance in British India were the primary influences on the emergence of political movements in the Indian States (Copland 2005; Ernst and Pati 2007).

7. McLeod (1999).

8. Bhagavan (2003), Cohen (2007), Mayaram (1997), Rai (2004), and Ramusack (2004). For analysis of the politics of the Chamber of Princes, and its relationship with the colonial Office of Indian States and the All India States' Peoples Conference, see Copland (1997) and Ramusack (1978). See also Handa's (1968) discussion of the All India States' Peoples Conventions.

9. Bhagavan (2003) and Rai (2004).

10. Rai (2004) and Zutshi (2003).

11. See Jammu and Kashmir State (1935).

12. One envoy traveling from Punjab to Lhasa in 1845 described the journey from Muzaffarabad to Srinagar as an almost daily progression through the territories of independent Sultans, Rajas, and Khans (von Hugel 1976 [1845], pp. 75–174).

13. Rai (2004); see also, Panikkar (1953) and Lawrence (1967 [1895]).

14. See Sökefeld (2005).

15. The system constituted a relationship of authority over people rather than simple territorial domination (Habib 1963; Neale 1969).

16. See Bamzai (1987).

17. Lawrence(1967 [1895], p. 251) and Saraf (1977a, pp. 295–298).

18. For detailed discussions of the agrarian system in the Princely State and the process of land settlement, see Kak (2007) and Hangloo (1995).

19. For a discussion of the practice of *bēgār,* see MacDonald (1998) and Sökefeld (2005, pp. 953–955).

20. The British colonial government attempted to exert control over the internal administration of the state as it became progressively interested in securing the northern borders of the Frontier Ilaqas, particularly the feudatories of Chitral, Gilgit, and Hunza. See Dani (1989) and Yasin (1984).

21. Frykenberg(1969), Neale (1962), and Wink (1986).

22. Lawrence (1967 [1895], pp. 399–453).

23. The first political parties in the State were the communist Kashmir Kisan Mazdoor Party and the antimonarchist Dogra Party, both founded in 1905. They were outlawed several years later.

24. Bamzai (1962, pp. 702–704), Khan (1980, pp. 101–103), and Saraf (1977a, pp. 344).

25. Neither Gujars nor Bakerwals were initially recognized under the 1912 national provisions. Sedentary Gujars were included in the 1927 provisions, but nomadic and migratory Gujars and Bakerwals were recognized only after 1931, when they mobilized to demand state-subject status (Rao 1999, p. 10).

26. Dates on Princely State legal documents follow the Vikram Samvat calendar *(smavat),* which began in 57 B.C.E.

27. Jammu and Kashmir Government (1971b, pp. 677–680). See also, the State Subject Definition Notification No. 1-L/1984 (1927 C.E.) and Notification No. 13-L/1989 (1932 C.E.]. The dates refer to the years preceding the founding of the Princely State (1847 C.E.) and the year in which the Maharaja's Council changed the court language from Persian to Urdu (1889 C.E.), which excluded the Sanskrit and Persian educated classes from state patronage and led to the in-migration of Urdu educated administrators from the Punjab and Bengal (Bamzai 1962, p. 701).

28. For example, under the *rehdārī* system, the Customs Act of 1958 (1901 C.E.) restricted the importation of newspapers over the borders of the state in the name of preventing sedition (Jammu and Kashmir Government 1971a, p. 40). After 1932, the Jammu and Kashmir State Press and Publications Act of 1989 (1932 C.E.) restricted the possession and distribution of books, newspapers, and documents within the state (Jammu and Kashmir Government 1971b, pp. 737–749).

29. These riots are not per se signifiers of communal identification in Princely State popular politics. In Mirpur District, where the proprietary rights claimed by the state extended to religious trusts *(waqf),* struggles for proprietary rights, tax protests, and demands for recognition of Muslim communities were often connected. In the Kashmir Valley, public discourses on religious difference focused on dissensions between Muslims communities. The Maharaja accommodated demand for control over the properties, funds, and resources of religious sites by ceding the administrative power of specific mosques and shrines to the community to which the site belonged. The process of registering a site and assigning a permanent caretaker and speaker led to disputes over the rights to speak at shrines and the division of mosques and shrines between Islamic schools (Bazaz 1987 [1941], pp. 137–218; Saraf 1977a, pp. 371–500).

30. Document Number 52 in Teng, Bhatt, and Kaul (1977).

31. See Jammu and Kashmir State (1935). Class I Subjects were hereditary state subjects, as previously defined. Class II Subjects were persons who settled in the state

after 1846 and 1911 and who had acquired immovable property there before 1911 C.E. The Maharaja reserved his right to create new subjects by instituting land grants through the category of Class III Subjects, persons who resided permanently in the state and were issued an *ijāzatnāmah* (document of permission) for the purchase of property. Later notices elaborated on these definitions and provided for the recognition of future state subjects (the provisions mixed standards of *jus sanguinis* and *jus solis*). Descendants of state subjects acquired the class distinction of their parents, with preference for the male line. A woman who married a non–state subject, however, did not lose her class status, and her children inherited it. Emigrants from Jammu and Kashmir born outside the State would be recognized as state subjects— and enjoy the right of ownership of immovable property—for two generations.

32. See Council Order No. 1234-C of 1939 (Jammu and Kashmir Government 1971C, pp. 514–515).

33. For discussion of political party development in the Princely State between 1905 and 1946, see Bamzai (1962), Bazaz (1954), Khan, G.H. (2000), Saraf (1977a), and Sikand (2002). There was no two-party dominance of Jammu and Kashmir politics until the division of Jammu and Kashmir between 1947 and 1949 and the subsequent periods of party rule by the AJKNC and the AJKMC, respectively, on the Indian and Pakistani sides of the LoC (Khan 1980, pp. 49–115).

34. Among the ideological influences in Jammu and Kashmir, socialist thinking was the strongest (Whitehead 2010).

35. See Taseer (1973, pp. 29, 310–383).

36. Bhatt (1984, pp. 104–107).

37. Bazaz (1950).

38. The declaration's notion of abrogation was so influential that the treaty has since been referred to as the *farocht-e-kashmīr* (Sale of Kashmir).

39. Bhatt and Bhargava (2005, pp. 114–115). The Quit Kashmir slogan echoed the Quit India demands of the anticolonial movement in British India (1942–1947), but Sheikh Abdullah's public speeches between 1944 and 1947 indicate that he also saw a shared interest with the All India State People's Conference and the antimonarchist movements in other Indian Princely States. See Documents Number 99, 101, and 103 in Teng, Bhatt, and Kaul (1977).

40. See Bazaz (1954, pp. 414–417). Exiled Muslim Conference party leaders and Kashmir refugee politicians helped found transborder nationalist parties in AJK in later decades, and this historical antagonism explains why Kashmiri nationalist politics in AJK and in Pakistan have not allied with the National Conference. Even when Sheikh Abdullah began to explicitly criticize Indian policies in Jammu and Kashmir State after 1956 and became associated in the Kashmir Valley with demands for Kashmiri independence, transregional nationalist parties allied across the LoC through the Plebiscite Front (which was critical of the National Conference) and the Liberation League (Bamzai 1962, pp. 785–804; Bazaz 1954, pp. 172–194; Puri 1981, pp. 42–89).

41. As described in contemporary accounts and political memoirs, see Hafizullah (1948), Birdwood (1956, pp. 49–51), Khan (1965, pp. 49–75), and Symonds (2001, p. 80).

42. There are two distinct perspectives on the Poonch revolt. Some see the Poonch uprising as ethno-religious and the violence of this period as largely unorganized rioting inspired by communal rioting in Punjab (Hewitt 1995, p. 74). Others link the Poonch uprising to the Poonchis' history of service in the British Army in the world wars (Bazaz 1987 [1941], p. 200). Poonchi soldiers who served in the British Indian Army before 1947 became members of the Pakistan Army when Pakistan became independent, because while the Kashmir Court had restricted the recruitment of state subjects into the British Indian Army, Poonchis had been at liberty to serve under the rules of the Jagir.

43. *Civil and Military Gazette,* October 7, 1947.

44. Sardar Mohammad Ibrahim Khan. 1947. *Civil and Military Gazette,* October 29, 1947.

45. Quoted in Hafizullah (1948, pp. 103–105).

46. Whitehead (2007) integrates oral history reflections on the incursion with contemporary media accounts.

47. This division of power was preserved by Article 370 of the Indian Constitution and Presidential Order (Application to Jammu and Kashmir) of 1950. Other Indian States were fully integrated into the Indian Union by constitutional amendment in 1956, at which time their "protected subjects" became Indian citizens with no separate status.

48. See Documents Number 117 and 118 in Teng, Bhatt, and Kaul (1977) and Abdullah (1948). The National Conference functioned as a one-party government until the Jammu and Kashmir Constitutional Convention ratified a new constitution in 1956.

49. For a contemporary account of the civil militias mobilized against the Pathans and the Pakistani Army, including the Peace Brigade, the Kashmir Women's Militia, and the Children's Militia, see Bamzai (1948).

50. (Robinson n.d.-b). See also, Rey-Schyrr (1998), and, for contemporary accounts, Korbel (1954), Marti (1950), and Symonds (2001).

51. The UNCIP reports, upon which the Security Council resolutions were based, referred to the Azad Kashmir Government as the local authority that would administer the Azad Jammu and Kashmir part of the Princely State until the UN plebiscite determined its integration into one of the postcolonial dominions. Under these agreements, Azad Kashmir was neither a sovereign state nor a province of Pakistan (Rose 1992, pp. 236–237).

52. See Sheikh Abdullah's 1952 speech in the Constituent Assembly of Kashmir (Noorani 1964, pp. 95–109) and also Abdullah (1948).

53. Azad Kashmir Government 1948a, 1948b).

54. The Dixon Report of 1950 was rejected by the governments of India and Pakistan. It advocated a limited plebiscite for the Kashmir Valley and a partition of the rest of the state on (religious) majoritarian grounds, roughly following the 1949 Ceasefire Line. This settlement proposal has been resurrected several times, most recently in 2000 during bilateral talks between India and Pakistan. The Graham Report of 1951 followed the UN principle of referendum for the entire state as it had

existed in 1946. Its proposal for a Kashmir settlement failed in part because India refused to recognize the Azad Kashmir Government, insisting that it be dissolved before a plebiscite could be arranged, and in part because the convening of the All Jammu and Kashmir Constituent Assembly in Srinagar in 1952 raised the possibility that a new democratic constitution might obviate the need for a plebiscite.

55. Dasgupta (1968, p. 173).

56. See Gilani (2008), Anand (1994), Bhatt (1984), and Gilani (1988).

57. The 1952 Delhi Agreement was a compromise in which Indian Prime Minister Jawaharlal Nehru agreed that the state constitution would recognize the separate status of Jammu and Kashmir state subjects. Until then, the state subjects of Jammu and Kashmir had the status in India of "protected subjects."

58. For the full text of the speech, see Noorani (1964, pp. 95–109).

59. Jammu and Kashmir State Constitution of 1956 (part iii, section 6) (Jammu and Kashmir Government, 1971d). This has remained a constitutional provision to the present day. See the Jammu and Kashmir Constitution (Twenty-Eighth Amendment Act) of 2000 (section 6), Official website of the General Administration Department, Government of Jammu and Kashmir, available at http://jkgad .nic.in/statutory/Rules-Costitution-of-J&K.pdf

60. See Anand (1994, pp. 261–264) and Bhatt (1984, pp. 201–203).

61. See the Jammu and Kashmir State Constitution of 1956 (part i, section . 28a). This territorial definition was also used in Article 370 of the Indian constitution (1950) and the Delhi Agreement (1952).

62. See the Jammu and Kashmir State Constitution of 1956 (part i, section 28b). This preservation of seats also remains a constitutional provision, See the Jammu and Kashmir Constitution (Twenty-Eighth Amendment Act) of 2000 (section 48).

63. Their argument was that although India had assured the UN Security Council that democratic representation within the Indian framework would be a temporary measure until the mandated plebiscite could be conducted, constitutional formation in Jammu and Kashmir State (1952–1956) was retroactively claimed to have obviated the need for a statewide referendum (A. Khan 1970; S.M.I. Khan 1965; S.M.A.Q. Khan 1992).

64. Khan (1992, p. 137).

65. Saraf (1977b, p. 1368).

66. By adoption of the Azad Jammu and Kashmir Refugees Registration and Representation Act of 1960 (Azad Government of the State of Jammu & Kashmir 1984b, pp. 42–43).

67. By adoption of the Azad Jammu and Kashmir Electoral Rolls Ordinance of 1970 (Azad Government of the State of Jammu & Kashmir 1984a, p. 396).

68. In the nineteenth century, the British Colonial Government of India recorded the social geography of the Princely State, noting the east–west routes of trade, travel, and military access that followed mountain ridges and riverbeds and connected the state's administrative divisions. The region was ethnically and linguistically diverse; languages spoken included Punjabi, Dogri, Hindko, Gojiri, Chibhali, Koshûr (Kashmiri), and Pahari. Many people spoke multiple languages

out of necessity—the language of the home and the language of the market (Bates 1990 [1873], pp. 409–504; Drew 1971 [1875], pp. 527–544). See also, G.W.E Atkinson's *Map of Kashmir,* Published in 1873 by the Great Trigonometrical Survey of India, Dehra Dune (circulated with Bates's [1873] *A Gazetteer of Kashmir*), Lawrence (1985 [1909]), and the district maps in Government of India, Census Commissioner, Jammu and Kashmir State (1943) and Jammu and Kashmir Government, Superintendent of Census Operations Jammu and Kashmir (1966a).

69. Government of India, Census Commissioner, Jammu and Kashmir State (1943); Korbel (1954, pp. 153, 199); Marti (1950).

70. Per the 1941 State of Jammu and Kashmir Census, the areas that became AJK had a minority population of twelve percent (Government of India, Census Commissioner 1943). The UNCIP estimated two percent in 1950 (Korbel 1954, p. 199); and by 1951, the Azad Government's state census showed a minority population of 1.8% (Azad Kashmir Government 1952, pp. 12–14).

71. This work of "minority evacuation" was carried out by the ICRC and the Indian and Pakistani Red Cross Societies (Rey-Schyrr 1998).

72. See Chatta (2009). It is not possible to extrapolate from comparison of census data how many people were killed as opposed to displaced from the Jammu Province because no district-level census was conducted in Indian or Pakistani-administered Jammu and Kashmir in 1951. The census commissioner of the 1961 census of Jammu and Kashmir State explained noticeable changes in proportions of populations in the border districts by citing redistricting and the loss of territory to Pakistan (AJK), rather than forced migration or deaths related to political violence (see Jammu and Kashmir Government and Kamili 1966b, 1966c, 1966d).

73. Minutes of the 15th-20th meeting of the Pak. Punjab Joint Refugees Council held at Lahore (March 1948) (National Documentation Center 1993, pp. 54–55).

74. Telegram (Indian Post and Telegraph Department) from President Muslim Conference Jammu to President Muslim Conference Sialkot, dated October 22, 1947; telegram (Indian Post and Telegraph Department) from President Muslim Conference Jammu to Mohammad Ali Jinnah, dated October 23, 1947; telegram (Indian Post and Telegraph Department) to Mohammad Ali Jinnah, dated October 24, 1947; telegram (Indian Post and Telegraph Department) from Faizullah Khan to Mohammad Ali Jinnah, dated October 28, 1947; memo requesting evacuation of Muslims of Jammu, Muslim Conference Sialkot to Mohammad Ali Jinnah (DY.No. 408-GG/47), dated November 6, 1947. MAJ F-118(2)GG/47(ii), National Archives of Pakistan (NAP).

75. See Symonds (2001, pp. 67–75).

76. Marti (1950). The ICRC survey further found that, of the Jammu and Kashmir refugees in Pakistan, only 100,000 were in formal refugee camps in Pakistan and 5,000 in Azad Kashmir; the rest were in informal accommodations or squatting on government land. These figures support the January 1949 UNICP's estimates as reported in Korbel (1954, p. 153).

77. Azad Kashmir Government (1952); see also, Korbel (1954, p. 199).

78. AJK Government Department of Refugees and Rehabilitation, Departmental Report. The Details of Refugees Coming from the Indian Occupied Kashmir (1998).

79. AJK Government Department of Refugees and Rehabilitation, Departmental Reports. Muhājirīn Amadah Maqbooza Jammu-o-Kashmir 1990-31/8/2000 (Refugee Arrivals from Occupied Jammu and Kashmir from 1990-8/31/2000); The Details of Refugees Coming from Indian Occupied Kashmir (2000).

80. Patterns of political violence by Indian state forces in the 1990s have been well documented by human rights NGOs (see Amnesty International 1993, 1995; Human Rights Watch/Asia and Physicians for Human Rights 1993a, 1993b; Physicians for Human Rights and Asia Watch 1993).

81. See Birdwood (1956, p. 80) for a description.

82. See Dasgupta (1968) and Hussain (1998).

83. Nehru (1951, p. 195).

84. For a critique of this policy formulation, see Noorani (1993).

85. See for example, Khan (1952).

86. The two-nation theory was a political claim advanced by the Muslim League during the Independence movement that the Muslims and Hindus of India constitute two nations. Jalal (1985) has argued that the demand was symbolic and intended to guarantee concessions for protections of minorities within a federated system of central state-provincial relations (see also Esposito 1996; Jaffrelot 2002; Hasan 1997; Malik 1997; Metcalf 2004; Nasr 2008; Pasha 1992; Weiss 1986).

87. Government of Pakistan, Ministry of Foreign Affaris (1977, p. 1).

88. For an analysis of revolutionary ideology in writing about the *mas'alah-e-kashmīr,* see Robinson (n.d.-a).

89. For discussions of the Kashmir Problem as an issue of the incomplete realization of Kashmiri rights, see Akhtar (1963), Gimmi (1963), and Kushfi (n.d.). For those rights expressed as the "right of self-determination," see Ahmad (1970), Bat (1980), Irfani (1997), Khan (1991), and Shibli (1977).

90. The limited political analysis that exists on the politics of AJK suggests that regional ethnic differences influence political affiliation (see Madan 1995; Mahmud 2006; Rose 1992).

91. For details of such action by AJK presidents K.H. Khurshid (1959–1964) and Abdul Hamid Khan (1964–1968), see Dasgupta (1968, pp. 184–248).

92. Shaheen (2000).

CHAPTER 2

1. Hodgson (1974, p. 59).

2. These schools *(mazhabs)* are the Hanifi, the Hanbali, the Malaki, and the Shafi'i.

3. Said (2002). Esposito's (1987) and Esposito et al.'s (2008) work on "Asian Islam" emphasized that regional traditions are best understood in terms of the lineages of interpretation, institutional sites of authority, and forms of piety that have shaped the practice of Islam and people's consciousness of what it means to be Muslim, rather than as aberrations of Middle Eastern Arab or Persianate Islamic

traditions (see also, Eickelman and Piscatori 1996; Gilmartin and Lawrence 2000; Metcalf 1984b).

4. See Brown (1996) for a discussion of how classically trained scholars invoked reform *(islah)* and revival *(tajdīd)*. See also Geertz (1968) and Metcalf (1984b) for discussions of historical pressures to purify Muslims of "unIslamic" cultural influences.

5. See Rosen (1984) for an overview.

6. Eickelman and Piscatori (1990a, p. 18).

7. See Zaman (2002) for an overview of this issue and a close analysis of this tension in the Sunni Hanifi school of Islam, which is prominent in South Asia and Egypt in the Middle East. See also, Volpi and Turner (2007) for a discussion of the theoretical challenges this tension poses the analytic categories of the social sciences.

8. The most widely cited examples come from the Afghan context. Oliver Roy (1986) reported that Afghan mujāhidīn told him "those who believed and left their homes *[hijarat]* and strove *[jihād]* for the cause of Allah ... these are the believers in truth" (p. 165). Centlievres and Centlievres-Dumont (1988a) reported that refugees in Pakistani refugee camps asserted "those who believe and have emigrated *[hijarat]*, and have struggled *[jihād]* in the way of God with their possessions and their selves are mightier in rank than God; and they are triumphant" (p. 73).

9. Centlievres and Centlievres-Dumont (1988b, p. 146); see also, Anderson and Dupree (1990), Masud (1990), Shahrani (1995), Terry (2002), and Weinbaum (1989).

10. Eickelman and Piscatori (1990b).

11. Discussion of *hijarat* as an Islamic religious term is based on Andrews (1993), Ansari (1990, 1993), Firestone (1999, pp. 115–117), Masud (1990), and Watt (1971, 1993).

12. The discussion of *jihād* as an Islamic religious term is based on Abou El Fadl (1990), Firestone (1999), Jansen (1993), Khadduri (1955), Peters (1977), and Tyan (1965).

13. Some scholars claim that the distinction between *jihād* as religiously sanctioned warfare and warfare in general is post-Qur'anic and developed to deal with the reality of armed conflict between independent Muslim states in the second and third Islamic centuries (Ali 1977; see also, Tyan 1965).

14. Masud (1990, p. 32).

15. Eickelman and Piscatori (1990a, p. 14).

16. Masud (1990); Tibi (2002b).

17. Johnson (1997, p. 25).

18. Lawrence (2000, pp. 181–182).

19. See Firestone (1999), Johnson and Kelsay (1990), Kelsay and Johnson (1991), Khadduri (1955), and Peters (1979). For discussion of the history of "holy war" in the Judeo-Christian tradition and its misapplication as a translation for *jihād* in Islamic political philosophy and theology, see Bainton (1960), Johnson (1997), and von Rad (1991 [1958]).

20. Firestone (1999) cites the Hadith literature as the basis for this restriction; on several occasions the prophet Mohammad forbade "anyone who had not

consummated his marriage, finished building his own house, or seen the offspring of his own flocks" from going into battle (pp. 99–104); on another occasion, the prophet denied permission to a young man who had requested permission to engage in *jihād* saying, "Strive on behalf of [your parents]" (pp. 163–164).

21. Ansari (1990, p. 9).

22. Some religious scholars and the spiritual heads of several north Indian Sufi shrines declared British India *dārul-harb* and encouraged the Muslims of al-Hind (India) to conduct hijarat as a political protest against the British Empire. This led to migrations from the Punjab, NWFP, Sindh, and Uttar Pradesh to Afghanistan, which was not under British control. On the whole, these movements were unsuccessful; muhājarīn were not welcomed and returned to their home territories within a matter of years (Ansari 1992; Minault 1982). Other anticolonial resistance was organized under the rubric of jihād (see Aziz 1964; Bannerji 2001; Nichols 2001; Reetz 1998).

23. Firestone (1999), Karpat (1990), Khaddurī (1955), Masud (1990), and Peters (1977, 1979). For comparative studies and bibliographies about the wide variety of anticolonial jihāds, see Bonner (2006, pp. 157–165), Bonney (2004, pp. 172–199), Cook (2005, pp. 73–92), and Peters (1979).

24. For some key writings by influential Islamic reformers, modernists, and Islamists, see Euben and Zaman (2009), Kurzman (2002), and Moaddel and Talattof (2000).

25. Masud (1990, pp. 44–45); see also, Hashmi (2002).

26. Bonney (2004, pp. 199–223). Abu A'la Maududi, Hassan al Banna, and Sayyid Qutb first articulated a doctrine of jihād for the modern state. They were in dialogue with each other and were influenced by Muslim modernist thinkers like Rashid Rida and European nationalist philosophers like Earnst Renan and Johann Herder, in addition to drawing tremendous influence from the Marxist–Leninist tradition. Maududi's and Qutb's later writings articulated defensive jihad as a form of resistance against a ruler, even a nominally Muslim ruler, who failed to govern according to Islamic principles (Adams 1983; Euben 1999; Haddadd 1983; Mitchell 1993; Nasr 1994; Osman 2003).

27. Abedi and Legenhausen (1986), Bonner (2006), Jansen (1993), Kohlberg (1997), and Peters (1997).

28. See Jalal (2000), Metcalf (1982), Wickham (2002), Nasr (1996), and Robinson (2002).

29. See Brenner (1996), Brown (1997), Hegland (1998), Mahmood (2001), Metcalf (1994), and Werbner (1996).

30. See Gilmartin (1984, 1988), Lelyveld (1996), Mahmood (2001), Malik (1996), Metcalf (1998), Nasr (1994), and Zaman (2002).

31. See Aziz (1964), Bannerji (2001), Edwards (2002), Haroon (2009), and Reetz (1998). This focus on jihad as a set of ethical concerns—corrupted, she argues, by political pragmatism—is the focus of Jalal's (2008) study of jihād in South Asia.

32. See Brenner (1996), Esposito (1984, 1997), Esposito and Burgat (2003), Horstmann (2007), Kepel (1985), Kurz and Tal (1997), Lawrence (2000), Lorimer (1997), Martin (1987), and McKenna (1998).

33. Lawrence (2000, p. 157); see also, Lincoln (2003).

34. The term mytho-history refers to historical thinking that is concerned with order in a cosmological or theological sense, with "the ordering and reordering of social and political categories, with the defining of self in distinction to other, [and] with good and evil" (Malkki 1995a, pp. 54–55). Its anthropological meaning derives from Claude Lévi-Strauss's (1966, 1995) distinction between dynamic and static ways that societies explain the relationship between their past times and their present times. *Mythic* conceptions of a society's past focus on explaining how patterns of repetition reenact an original sociopolitical order or cosmological truths. *Historical* conceptions of a society's past times are concerned with discerning how patterns of cause and effect result in the transformation of an original sociopolitical order. In this sense, myth is not a historical but is rather a specific symbolic language through which people integrate the past and the present (Barthes 1972). Similarly, historical conceptions of past times require the "invention of tradition" (Hobsbawm and Ranger 1983) to secure the authenticity of the past as a source of continuity, against which changes can be evaluated.

35. Brown (1996).

36. Ironically, this is also the Orientalist construction of Islam. Thus, the self-legitimating "culture talk" about Islam that was so useful for the European and Western colonial and imperialist agendas (Mamdani 2000, 2002) also had uses for those wanting to articulate a modern Islamic ideology that could compete with ideologies of the colonial and postcolonial powers (such as nationalism and capitalism). For an excellent discussion of this point, see Ayoob (2008, pp. 1–23).

37. Mauss (1935, 1960).

38. Foucault (1979, 1990).

39. Feldman (1991, p. 8).

40. Mahmood (2005).

41. The South Asian metric degree, based on the British system basic educational system, is the degree awarded at the completion of ten years of primary and secondary schooling.

42. "Sher Khan" has been the nômme de guerre of several Kashmiri mujāhids.

CHAPTER 3

1. Bem (2004, p. 622).

2. Vernant (1953, pp. 735–769); see also, Henderson (1953) and Stoessinger (1956, p. 159).

3. Mazower (2006, 2009) and Malkki (1994).

4. Bem (2004, pp. 613, 621–622) and Loescher (2001, pp. 92–95).

5. See Robinson (2012).

6. Oberoi (2001, pp. 38, 43–44).

7. The Protocols removed date and geographical limitations on refugee recognition that many of the dissenting representatives had critiqued as precluding a truly

universal definition for the international community. See Bem (2004), Loescher (2001), and Mazower (2004) for discussion of the processes by which exclusions were removed.

8. Cohen (2008). See Malkki (1996) for examples of the consolidation of these projects by the late 1980s.

9. Barnett and Weiss (2008a) and Calhoun (2008).

10. Cohen (2008, p. 439).

11. Humanitarian ideals shaped the practice of international relief on the ground. In general, human welfare and social rehabilitation were landmark concepts of postwar humanitarian ideology (Cohen 2008, p. 443). These concepts drew on middle-class models of social work and family reform (Borgwardt 2005; Zahra 2009) and on faith traditions and norms of charity (Feldman 2007; Benthall and Bellion-Jourdan 2003).

12. Cohen (2006, p. 125).

13. Publicity Department, Ministry of the Interior. Annexure V: Regarding foreign publicity for the Quaid-i-Azam's Relief Fund (No. F.8/R.F/47-P.D.) by M. Arshad Hussain, October 6, 1947. MAJ F-80.GG/47, vol.1, p. 38, NAP.

14. Pakistan Red Cross Society, An Enterprise in the Service of Humanity, Transcript of the Inaugural Meeting of the Pakistan Red Cross Society, March 15, 1948, http://www.pakistan.gov.pk/Quaid/speech28.htm.

15. Rey-Schyrr (1998).

16. Refugees have been subjects of state surveillance and suspicion, families are divided across boundaries, and people have been excluded from the postcolonial national citizenship regimes (Zamindar 2007). See Gilmartin (1998) for a discussion of the problem of the two-nation theory for the idea of a singular national belonging.

17. See, for example, Butalia (1998), Menon and Bhasin (1998), Kaul (2001), Kamra (2002), and Tan and Kudaisya (2000). For a discussion of the influence of this approach in South Asian studies, see Pandey (2001) and Saikia (2011).

18. Rao (1967, pp. 229).

19. West Punjab Government, Legislative Assembly (1948, pp. 19–25).

20. Appeal to the Nation of Pakistan, Text of radio speech delivered by Mohammad Ali Jinnah, September 12, 1947. MAJ F-80.GG/47, vol.1, NAP.

21. The formation of a QARF Provincial Committee in East Bengal was delayed because of confusion about whether relief monies could be made available to non-Muslim refugees; it began its work after the QARF Central Committee clarified that they would be. Telegram from Secretary Quaid-ie-Azam's Relief Fund to Governor East Bengal (QARF/15), September 26, 1947. MAJ F-80.GG/47, vol.1, NAP.

22. Government of India (1948).

23. Government of Pakistan (1949, pp. 391–396).

24. The greatest dissension concerned whether property exchanges should be directly negotiated between individual refugees and evacuees or whether the state should undertake the purchase of all evacuee property and its reallocation. The question was not resolved until 1949, when the parties agreed that only recognized refugees would be permitted to occupy evacuee property and that "the duty of

preserving [the evacuee's] property and safeguarding his rights shall be entrusted by the government concerned to the Custodian of the Province where the property is located." Appendix I: Decisions of the Inter-Dominion Conference Held at Karachi on the 10th-13th January 1949 on the Draft Scheme for Inter-Dominion Evacuee Property Agreement, unsigned and undated. MAJ F-283-GG/47, NAP.

25. Many of those refugees were seeking relief not from mass communal rioting but from widespread famine associated with Partition-related changes in the political economy (Chatterji 2007).

26. The question of linking land reform and redistribution to refugee resettlement came up many times in the West Punjab (Pakistan) Legislative Assembly through the 1950s, primarily when representatives objected to some refugees receiving numerous large allotments while other refugees received none. Assembly members against land reform argued that the issue was a separate one from refugee allotments, which were based entirely on the value of property lost or left behind and that, as a process established by international agreement, was nonnegotiable on the provincial level (see West Punjab Government 1952, p. 661). For similar debates in India, see Chatterji (2001) and Kudaisya (1995).

27. For a review of recent scholarship on this topic, see Robinson (2010).

28. For a discussion of Bengal refugees and the rise of left political parties in India, see Chatterji (2001) and Chakrabarti (1999). In Pakistan, the refugee political rights movement produced the "mohajir" ethnic identity decades after the partition in response to political controversies within the postcolonial state, specifically controversy over language recognition, state patronage, and urban space in the Sindh province (Ansari 2005; Seiler 1988; Tambiah 1996; Verkaaik 1994) and in refugee groups' support of (West) Pakistan during the 1971 war, in the case of Bangladesh (Ghosh 1998; Hasan 1998).

29. See Government of Pakistan (1949) and Goyal (1964).

30. Pakistan-West Punjab Joint Refugees and Rehabilitation Council, Note on the Statistics of the Refugee Problem, by R.F. Mudie, undated—circa October 1947; Note on Evacuee Property I, by R.F. Mudie, undated—circa October 1947; Note on Evacuee Property II, by R.F. Mudie, undated—circa October 1947; Note on Rehabilitation, by R.F. Mudie, undated—circa October 1947. MAJ F-803, NAP.

31. Board of Economic Inquiry, West Punjab, A Note on the Statistics of the Refugees and Evacuees' Problem, by H. Hassan, undated—circa November 1947. MAJ F-803, NAP.

32. Note on Evacuee Property I.

33. Note on Rehabilitation. The numbers in the original document are listed in lakhs (1 lakh = 100,000).

34. Note on the Statistics of the Refugee Problem.

35. Note on Evacuee Property I.

36. Note on Evacuee Property II.

37. Pakistan Administration of Evacuee Property Ordinance, 1949 (Government of Pakistan 1949, pp. 378–391); see also, Indian Administration of Evacuee Property Act, 1950, and Evacuee Interest (Separation) Act, 1951 (Goyal 1964).

38. New refugees were created by this corporate refugee definition when members of a joint family, who had remained in either Pakistan or India, found their home declared "evacuee property" because another member of the family had taken a refugee allotment in the other dominion (Zamindar 2007, pp. 119–135).

39. See Robinson (n.d.-b) for a full discussion.

40. The correspondence, collections receipts, and banking records for the QARF are in the Mohammad Ali Jinnah (MAJ) files F-80.GG/47, vol.1, F-80(10) GG/47, and F-80(12)GG/47, NAP.

41. Draft Appeal to the Nation of Pakistan, approved September 12, 1947 and Text of radio speech delivered by Mohammad Ali Jinnah, September 12, 1947. MAJ F-80.GG/47, vol. 1, NAP.

42. Publicity Department, Ministry of the Interior Anexure V: Regarding foreign publicity for the Quaid-i-Azam's Relief Fund (No. F.8/R.F./47-P.D) by Joint-Secretary M. Arshad Hussain, October 6, 1947. MAJ F-80.GG/47, vol. I, NAP.

43. The letters and receipts of collections for the Pakistan Red Cross and the United Nations Appeal for Children can be found in the National Archives of Pakistan Mohtarma Fatima Jinnah (MFJ) files F-316 and F-1017.

44. Agreement between the Secretary-General of the United Nations and the Pakistan National Committee of the United Nations Appeal for Children (Schedule "A"), signed by Fatima Jinnah and Assistant Secretary-General of the United Nations, August 10, 1948. MFJ F-1017, NAP.

45. Letter from Manfred Simon, Acting Director of the UNAC, to Fatima Jinnah (ref. no. 650-9-76/EO), October 15, 1948; letter from Fatima Jinnah to General Secretary, UNAC, January 1, 1949. MFJ F-1017, NAP.

46. Pakistan Red Cross Society, Agenda for the Meeting of the Managing Body of the Pakistan Red Cross Society on 11 December (no. PRCS/5/A), November 24, 1948; Notes on the Agenda for the Meeting of the Managing Body of the Pakistan Red Cross Society on 11 December, 24 November 1948; Letter from Ltd. General Thomson, Commissioner, British Red Cross Society, to Fatima Jinnah, Chairman, Pakistan Red Cross Society, November 24, 1948. MFJ F-1017, NAP.

47. A Note on the Statistics of the Refugees and Evacuees' Problem. The West Punjab refugee census (1948) reported two hundred fifty thousand refugees from the Princely State of Jammu and Kashmir in government-run camps in West Punjab. In June 1949, the ICRC estimated the Kashmir refugee population in Pakistan (excluding AJK) at three hundred eighty thousand, of whom only one hundred thousand were accommodated in formal refugee camps in Pakistan (Marti 1950).

48. Confidential Dispatch 2680 from Chief of Staff to Mohammad Ali Jinnah, July 17, 1948, Telegram Grade C from Foreign Secretary to Mohammad Ali Jinnah, July 17, 1948, Confidential Dispatch 3182 from Z. A. Khan, Secretary Quaid-e-Azad Relief Fund to Chief of Staff, Military Head Quarters, July 18, 1948, and Confidential Dispatch 2746 from Mohammad Ali Jinnah to Chief of Staff, July 21, 1948. MAJ F-80(10)GG/47, NAP.

49. Minutes of the 25th-27th meeting of the Pak. Punjab Joint Refugees Council held at Lahore, September 1948 (as reproduced in National Documentation Center 1993, pp. 78–88).

50. The letters and receipts of collections for the "Miss Fatima Jinnah (Kashmir Fund)," the "Women's Relief Committee Kashmir Mujahideen Fund," and the "Bomber's Fund," as well as bank deposit statements and shipping records, can be found in the National Archives of Pakistan MFJ files F-310, F-312, F-316, F-736, and F-1017 and in the MAJ files F80(12)GG/47.

51. This organization is sometimes confused with the Pakistan Voluntary Service for Refugee Relief (PVS), which was not a PML organization. The Women's Relief Committee (WRC) developed as a subcommittee of the Punjab Muslim League Women's Committee (PMLWC). In 1948, the WRC split off from the PMLWC and merged with the women's group of the national Red Cross society (Virdee 2009).

52. Letter from G. S. Ahmed, Deputy Assistant Military Accountant General, to Syed Yaqub Shah Sahib, Auditor General of Pakistan, (No.Cor/64 Office of the Account General Military, Rawalpindi), December 14, 1948, MFJ F-310; letter from Captain M.S. Durrani to Begum Abdul Qadir (D.O. No.4040/24/MO General Headquarters, Rawalpindi), February 5, 1949. MFJ F-316, NAP.

53. Letter from Women's Relief Committee, Karachi, to Fatima Jinnah, undated. MFJ F-310, NAP.

54. Draft appeal for Kashmiri refugee relief by Fatima Jinnah, September 29, 1948. MFJ F-572, NAP.

55. Press release for Kashmiri mujahideen by Fatima Jinnah, October 12, 1948. MFJ F-80(12)GG/47, NAP.

56. *Dawn,* November 10, 1948. The following day, the paper published a photograph labeled "Ladies of Karachi packing parcels for Kashmir Mujahideen" (*Dawn,* November 11, 1948). The WRC members in the photograph included Begum Raana Liaquat Ali Khan, wife of Pakistan's Prime Minister.

57. The UNCIP mission assumed that refugees from the Princely State of Jammu and Kashmir would participate in the UN-mandated plebiscite after returning to their homes (see Korbel 1954). British relief workers drew the same conclusion from meetings with the leaders of Jammu and Kashmir political parties (see Symonds 2001).

58. Rey-Schyrr (1998, pp. 42–44).

59. See Korbel (1954, p. 153). See also Marti (1950) for the ICRC summary report.

60. Security Council Resolution 47 (1948) of April 21, 1948. S/RES/47 (1948): Section B. 14.a. Section A.1.b and Section B. 12 refer to "subject(s) of the State" or "subjects(s) of the State of Jammu and Kashmir."

61. Resolution of the United Nations Commission on India and Pakistan of January 5, 1949, Section 6(a) (Korbel 1954:Appendix III).

62. The ICRC's transregional survey of Jammu and Kashmir refugees (June 1949) found that only 5,000 refugees of an estimated total of 155,000 in AJK territories were in refugee camps (Marti 1950).

63. The KRCRC's founding members included Chaudhry Ghulam Abbass, who founded the AJKMC in Jammu in 1932; Mohammad Yousaf Shah, the Mir Waiz of the Kashmir Valley; and Sardar Mohammad Ibrahim Khan and Sardar Mohammad

Abdul Qayyum Khan, both Muslim Conference organizers from the Poonch and Rajouri regions of Azad Kashmir.

64. Letter from Ghulam Abbass to Mohammad Ali Jinnah, dated April 4, 1948. MAJ F-80(10)GG/47, NAP.

65. Letter from Mohammad Ali Jinnah to Ghulam Abbass, dated April 8, 1948. MAJ F-80(10)GG/47, NAP.

66. Interview with Abdul Qayyum Khan at the AJKMC (Qayyum faction) Headquarters, Rawalpindi, February 2001. Abdul Qayyum Khan was one of the members of the KRCRC. He has served as both the President and the Prime Minister of AJK and as President of the AJKMC.

67. Dispatch no. 276 from the Office of the Kashmir Refugees Central Relief Committee to Khawaja Nizimuddin, Governor General of Pakistan, April 7, 1949. MAJ F-80(10)GG/47, NAP.

68. Letter from Z. A. Khan, Sec. Quaid-i-Azam Relief Fund, to Kashmir Refugees Central Relief Committee (D.O. No.QARF/II(ii)), November 11, 1949; letter from Ghulam Abbass, Chairman KRCRC, to Z. A. Khan, Sec. QARF, November 14, 1949; Draft minutes of the meeting of the Kashmir Refugees Central Relief Committee 4-5 January 1950, dated January 5, 1950; letter from Z. A. Khan, Sec. Quaid-i-Azam Relief Fund, to Kashmir Refugees Central Relief Committee (Ref. No. 263-GG/50), January 26,1950. MAJ F-80(10)GG/47, NAP.

69. Notice of the establishment of the "Kashmir Fund," Ministry of Kashmir Affairs, by Z. A. Khan, Sec. QARF (ref. no. QARF/12), June 29, 1950. MAJ F-80(10) GG/47, NAP.

70. For an overview, see Gilani (1988).

71. The initial formulation of the category of the refugee of Jammu and Kashmir with reference to the hereditary state subject and the temporary nature of all allotments to Kashmir refugees can be found in the following acts of law: in AJK, the Azad Kashmir Protection of Evacuee Property Act, 1950 and the Azad Kashmir Administration of Evacuee Property Rules, 1957 (Azad Government of the State of Jammu & Kashmir 1984b, pp. 144–149); in Jammu and Kashmir State (India), the Jammu and Kashmir State Evacuees (Administration of Property) Act, 2006 [1949 C.E.], Cabinet Order No. 913-C of 1951, Allotment of Land to Displaced Persons Rules, 1954 and Cabinet Order No. 578-C of 1954 (Jammu and Kashmir Government 1971b, pp. 451–452, 460, 548–551; 1971a, pp. 23–53). The definition of "displaced persons" in the first Jammu and Kashmir State provisions paralleled the legal category "refugees" in AJK's laws.

72. The refugee provisions generally did not recognize internal displacement within territories administered by each of the respective successor governments. On the Indian side of the LoC, there were some provisions for relocation within Jammu and Kashmir State. Thus, by Cabinet Order No. 1184-C of 1951, Muslims living near the border, or in places where a Muslim population had ceased to exist, were permitted to apply for lands in villages other than their own. See Jammu and Kashmir Government (1971cp.460).

73. Azad Government of the State of Jammu & Kashmir (1984b, pp. 42–44).

74. Azad Government of the State of Jammu & Kashmir (1984b, pp. 84–93).

75. Azad Government of the State of Jammu & Kashmir (1984a, p. 396; 1984c, pp. 62–63). The migration of state subject landholders from AJK to Pakistan created administrative confusion about the relationship between migration to Pakistan and family landholdings in AJK. The first Legislative Assembly of AJK clarified through the 1971 amendment ordinance that the property of state subjects who left the territory of AJK for Pakistan after 1947 could not be declared evacuee property.

76. The AJKMC held this position of prominence for a number of reasons. The party claimed to have organized the armed "liberation" movement in 1946 and to have functioned as the Azad Kashmir War Council from 1946 to 1948. It thus articulated a liberation ideology within a spectrum of antimonarchist, anticolonialist, and emergent nationalist sentiments (Robinson n.d.-a). There were also close personal links between the leaders of the Muslim Conference and the All India Muslim League, which in 1947 took up the reins of government in Pakistan. This factor is often overestimated, however; there were several shifts in party leadership that did not singularly result from changes in the patronage of Pakistan's political elites for their ideological allies. Instead, kinship affiliation began to determine political party affiliation in AJK politics as political elites forged alliances with social elites in AJK as a region no longer on the margins of the Princely State's political centers. The first AJKMC leadership was predominantly comprised of leaders from the Indian side of the LoC; Ghulam Abbass, Hamidullah Khan, and the Mirwaiz Yusef Shah were political exiles and refugees from Jammu city and Srinagar. Mohammad Ibrahim Khan's and Abdul Qayyum Khan's struggle for control over AJKMC leadership in the 1950s was related to changes in the kin-based and descent group politics of the Sudhans and Abassis of Poonch (Bazaz 1954, pp. 633–636; Saraf 1977b, pp. 1290–1294, 1367). Finally, the AJKMC established a base among people displaced from Jammu and Kashmir. This support was the result of the party's unique position as patrons of Jammu and Kashmir refugees and as the public representatives of Kashmiri refugee causes during the war and in the early 1950s (Robinson n.d.-b).

77. These institutional developments should be seen as indicating Pakistan's recognition of its failure to govern through AJK political parties—even those with overtly pro-Pakistan manifestos, like the AJKMC—and not as Pakistan's complete control over the AJK government. Cf. Rose (1992) for a critique of the Ministry of Kashmir Affairs as exercising nearly complete control in Azad Jammu and Kashmir after 1953.

78. The state's foundational legal structure was a hybrid of the legal codes of the Princely state and the 1949 West Punjab Law codes. For an overview, see Gilani (1988).

79. Bhat et al. (1955), Jammu and Kashmir Muslim Conference (1998).

80. Letter from Ghulam Abbass, Chairman of the KRCRC, to Khawaja Nazam-ud-din, Governor General of Pakistan (Office of the Chairman of the Kashmir Refugees Relief Committee D.O. No. 1175-80/c), October 9, 1948. MAJ F-80(10)GG/47, NAP.

81. Letter from Ghulam Abbass to Mohammad Ali Jinnah, dated April 4, 1948. MAJ F-80(10)GG/47, NAP.

82. Letter from Ghulam Abbass to Mohammad Ali, Prime Minister of Pakistan, dated July 17, 1954. MFJ F-648, NAP.

83. By Cabinet Order No. 574-C of 1954, evacuees who returned under a permit issued by the Jammu and Kashmir State government from "the enemy-occupied territory" were to be restored possession of their lands and houses, with the only restriction being that they were not to be restored more land than permitted under the socialist land reform provisions of the Big Landed Estates Abolition Act, 2007 [1950 C.E.] (Jammu and Kashmir Government 1971a, pp. 461–462). The difficulty of actually acquiring such a permit, and the complications of the implications for recognition of Indian citizenship, made it extremely difficult to return across the LoC. This was one of the reasons for the Refugee Resettlement Bill of 1980, which authorized the Jammu and Kashmir State administration to issue permits of return for refugees who had left their homes between 1947 and 1949, without going through the Indian government's central administration. The Jammu and Kashmir Legislative Assembly passed this bill in 1982, but the central government of India objected, citing national security risk. See Ganguly (1997, pp. 78–79) and Singh (1992, p. 158). In AJK, the provisions for refugee return were secured within the resettlement acts.

84. The following discussion is based on records of the Department of Refugees and Rehabilitation, Ministry of Kashmir Affairs (1950–1971), held in the National Archives of Pakistan. The records contain ration logbooks, ration cards, movements transfer orders, and land acquisition records.

85. Proceedings of the All Pakistan Muhajir Convention held in Lahore, Pakistan, January 12 and 13, 1957. FJ F-448, NAP.

86. See The Azad Kashmir Administration of Evacuee Property Rules of 1957 (Azad Government of the State of Jammu & Kashmir 1984b, pp. 144–149).

87. The governments of AJK and Jammu and Kashmir State both levied explicit provisions for expelling non–state subjects from property, and for preventing them from deriving proprietary rights from the fact of occupancy, and thus state residency and citizenship status, because non–state subject refugees did in fact occupy properties, especially in the cities and municipal areas. See especially the Government Order No. 25/60, Office of the Secretary General, Azad Jammu and Kashmir 11/1/60, the Azad Jammu & Kashmir Evacuee Property (Multiple Allotments) Act, 1961, and Government Order No. Reh-371 of 1971.

88. See Gilani (2008).

89. Husain (1990), Saraf (1977b).

90. Khan (1965, p. 113).

91. Azad Government of the State of Jammu & Kashmir (1984a, pp. 106–110).

92. In Pakistan, provincial domicile certificates are required to compete for reserved positions based on provincial affiliations. See Waseem (1997).

CHAPTER 4

1. Bayefsky and Fitzpatrick (2000), Ferris (1993), and Shue (1989); see also, Calhoun (2004), Fassin and D'Halluin (2005), and Wilson and Brown (2009).

2. Chandler (2001) and Leader (1998).

3. de Waal (1997).

4. Duffield (2001). For an overview of these changes in the UNHCR specifically, see Loescher (2001, pp. 140–200).

5. Weiss (1999a).

6. Barnett (2001), Hyndman (2000), and Weiss (1999b). See also, Cohen (2006) for a discussion of the IDP category in the post-WWII years.

7. Chandler (2001).

8. Zolberg et al. (1989a, pp. 30–31); see also, Bayefsky and Fitzpatrick (2000).

9. Brauman (1998), Burgerman (2001), Chandler (2001), Terry (2002), and Weiss (1999a). Médecins Sans Frontièrs (MSF), for example, was founded by doctors who rejected the working modes of the ICRC and criticized the very idea of neutrality. MSF identifies its mission as responding to the needs of victims and considers a part of its responsibility to publicize the structural inequalities and political situations that cause emergencies (Fox 1995; Redfield 2005; Tanguay 1999).

10. Loescher (2001, pp. 140–246).

11. Regional legal norms also reflect the changing nature of the international regime. For example, Central American countries adopted the Cartagena Declaration on Refugees in 1984; its definition of refugees includes not only those recognized by the 1951 Convention and 1967 Protocols but also those who have left their countries because of "a massive violation of human rights" (Article iii(a)). The European Union developed standards for temporary protection rather than working towards refugee asylum and practiced repatriation rather than granting new citizenship (see European Commission 1995b). The UN's official statement at the end of the cold war described the reformulation of UN development activities as "rights advocacy" (see United Nations 1995).

12. Frelick (2002).

13. Calhoun (2008); see also, Barnett and Weiss (2008b).

14. Ogata (1999) and Warner (1999); see also, European Commission (1995a).

15. Kaldor (1999).

16. Goodwin-Gill (1999, p. 3).

17. This corresponds with a shift from policies and practices of refugee resettlement and integration to refugee repatriation (Hathaway 1997; Zieck 1997). This shift was so profound that the international refugee regime is "now best described as one of return, rather than asylum" (Duffield 2001, p. 4).

18. Malkki (1995b).

19. Benthall (1993); see also, Chandler (2001).

20. Kennedy (2009), Haskell (1985), (Hopgood 2008), and (Rieff (1996).

21. *Cf.* Ong (2003), Fassin and D'Halluin (2005), and Redfield (2005) on interactions between refugees and medical professionals that shape the refugee as a biopolitical subject of the international community.

22. The symbolic nakedness of refugees, created by their having been stripped of political and cultural recognition, and the concept of human rights as that which cannot be "stripped away" are linked to the establishment of the nation-state as the preeminent organization of modern political and economic power (Arendt 1951).

Foucault's (1979) analysis of the micropolitics of power identified this privileging of natural life as the marker of the beginning of the modern biopolitical form of politics; Agamben (1998) argued that the refugee camp in all its forms serves as the "nomos of the modern" (p. 174) and that the refugee is the quintessential modern subject who renders the biopolitical foundations and working of the modern state visible (1995, 1998, pp. 131–134).

23. Malkki (1995a, pp. 385–390).

24. Warner (1999, p. 109).

25. Terry (2002, p. 19).

26. Refugee camps in India accommodated more than 10 million refugees during the 1971 war. The first agency assigned to deal with refugees in India was the United Nations East Pakistan Relief Organization (UNEPRO). It was widely denounced as a political organization and suspended, after which the UNHCR became the central coordinator for refugee relief in India (Gottlieb 1972; see also. Sisson and Rose 1990, pp. 177–190).

27. As the UN High Commissioner for Refugees from 1965 to 1977, Prince Sadruddin Aga Khan expanded the UNHCR mandate to focus on the spirit of the 1951 Refugee Convention instead of its strict legal limits. He opened offices in Asia and Latin America, extended assistance to internally displaced people, and allowed petitions for assistance to come from nonstate agencies (Loescher 2001, pp. 140–200).

28. Gottlieb (1972), Loescher (2001, pp. 155–162), and Sisson and Rose (1990, pp. 177–190).

29. See Bose (2000), Chakraborty (1998), Chimni (1998), and Hans and Suhrke (1997).

30. From the mid-1980s through the early 1990s, between 2 million and 4 million Afghan refugees were registered by the Pakistan government and recognized as prima facie refugees by the UNHCR. In 1992, more than 350 Refugee Tented Villages (RTVs), were spread across northern Pakistan (United Nations High Commissioner for Refugees 2000a, pp. 34, 48).

31. Government of Pakistan (1985); see also, U.S. Committee on Foreign Affairs (1981, pp. 71–88).

32. Brauman (1998), Centlievres and Centlievres-Dumont (1988b), and Weinbaum (1989); see also United Nations High Commissioner for Refugees 2000b).

33. Kattak (2003); see also, Government of Pakistan (1984).

34. Centlievres and Centlievres-Dumont (1988a), Terry (2002), and Weinbaum (1989).

35. Matinuddin (1990) and Shahrani (1995).

36. Zolberg et al. (1989, pp. 126-154). *Cf.* Ahmed (1986) and Kattak (2003).

37. Falk (1989), Merriam (1987), and Yousaf and Adkin (1992).

38. Edwards (2002) and Roy (1986).

39. Falk (1989) and Terry (2002, p. 222).

40. Kattak (2003).

41. Kronenfeld (2008). .

42. I use the word militarization here in the anthropological sense, meaning a process by which the institutions and practices of society are re-orientated to serve military ends deMel (2007), Enloe (1983), and Lutz (2001).

43. Terry (2002) and Zolberg et al. (1989).

44. Dupree (1990) and Mayotte (1992, pp. 128–216).

45. Mayotte (1992, p. 156).

46. Many other refugee communities are likewise committed to documenting human rights documentation in their home places and contributed to the global spread of human rights networks (see Loescher 2001, p. 165).

47. Malkki (1995a) and Turner (2005)

48. Peteet 1991, (2005) and Ballinger (2003).

49. Brauman (1998), Feldman (2008b), Harrell-Bond et al. (1992), Hyndman (2000), Sorensen (2008), and Voutira and Harrell-Bond (1995).

50. The word first gained currency in Pakistan as a Persian word for Palestinian refugees—*"panāhandāh-i-falastīnī"* and *"āwārahgān-i-falastīnī."* In addition, *panāhandāh,* meaning "a person seeking protection or political asylum," and *āwārahgān,* meaning "an evacuee or homeless person," were already used in Pakistan to refer to people displaced by political violence and natural disasters in other parts of the world (Shahrani 1995, p. 189).

51. Ahmed (1980), Barth (1959), Boesen (1990), Grima (1993), Knudsen (2009), Lindholm (1982), and Werbner (1991).

52. For example, see Newberg (1995).

53. Abraham and Schendel (2005)

54. These are typical activities for Islamist organizations, which usually provide forms of social welfare and security when and to whom the state does not (Meijer 2009; Norton 2007; Rougier 2007; Wickham 2002; Wiktorowicz 2001).

55. Arendt (1951, p. 296).

CHAPTER 5

1. See Burr and Collins (2006).

2. Cambell and Weiss (1991) and Macrae and Leader (2001). The R2P (Right to Protect) Agreement signed at the UN level in 2006 negotiated guidelines for humanitarian intervention that had been developing since the NATO intervention in Kosovo in 1999.

3. Malkki (1996).

4. See Feldman (1994, 1997) and Sontag (2003).

5. Merry (2006).

6. In Pakistan, these include martial rule orders, antiterrorism ordinances, and the Antiterrorism Act (ATA). In India, the Terrorism and Disruptive Activities Act (TADA), the Public Security Act (PSA), and the Preventions of Terrorism Act (POTA) legalized long periods of preventive detention, without effective judicial review for cause or evidence. See Kennedy (2004) and Singh (2007) for discussions.

7. After 2003, digital cameras in cell phones and cellular connectivity in the mountainous regions of AJK changed how such photographs circulate.

8. For publications of cultural associations and political parties, see Jammu & Kashmir Action Committee (1992), Kashmir Liberation Cell (1997, 1999), and Jammu and Kashmir Liberation Front (1997). For Kashmiri NGO human rights reporting, see Jammu & Kashmir Human Rights Awareness and Documentation Center (1995, 1996, 1997, 1998a, 1998b), Institute of Kashmir Studies (1993, 1994), and Institute of Kashmir Studies, Human Rights Division (1993, 1994a, 1994b, 1994c, 1997). For INGO human rights reporting, see also Amnesty International (1993, 1995), Human Rights Watch/Asia and Physicians for Human Rights (1993a, 1993b), International Commission of Jurists (1995), and Physicians for Human Rights and Asia Watch (1993a). Official complaints submitted to the UNHCR reference all these sources, as do consciousness-raising publications issued and circulated by advocacy groups (see Government of Pakistan n.d.).

9. Khurshid (1994, pp. 105–126).

10. Sayed Ali Shah Geleeni, quoted in Sharma and Sharma (1998, p. 426).

11. Mohammad Safi, quoted in Sharma and Sharma (1998, p. 428).

12. See, for example, Kahn, I. (2000) and Siddiqui (2000).

13. Gardeezi (1991).

14. See especially the bimonthly magazine *al-Da'wat* (1995–2001) for examples of such death requests and motivation letters. *Al-Da'wat* is a publication of the Lashkar-e-Tayyiba.

15. *Insānī haqūq* was also distinct from *insānyat,* which derives from *insān* (human being) and can be translated as "humanity." The word *insāniyat* is used to invoke the idea of human dignity and compassion, as in the concept of humanitarianism. See also Saikia's (2011, pp. 13, 20–26) discussion of the concept *insān* as an evolved person in contrast to *bashar* (of the human species).

16. Donnelly (1989, p. 52). Islamic law recognizes obligations between rulers and divine authority, which impose limits on the legitimate powers of rule over Muslim subjects, but the "essential characteristic of human rights in Islam is that they constitute obligations connected with the Divine and derive their force from this connection" (Said 1979, p. 63).

17. Donnelly (1989, pp. 7–46).

18. An-Na'im (1990, 2001), Bielefeldt (1995), Donnelly (1985, pp. 50–52), Dwyer (1991), Freeman (2004), and Wilson (1997b).

19. Khadduri (1946, 1955).

20. Khadduri (1946) established Islamic precedence by citing the five rights of man recognized by Islam: rights to personal safety, rights that respect personal reputation, and the rights of equality, brotherhood, and justice (pp. 76–78). Abu A'la Maududi, the founder of the Jamaat-e-Islami, argued that "Islam has laid down some universal fundamental rights for humanity as a whole, which are to be observed and respected. . . . [These are] fundamental rights for every man by virtue of his status as a human being" (Maudoodi 1976, p. 10).

21. Donnelly (1989) and Wilson (1997a).

22. Bielefeldt (2000, p. 114). Bielefeldt's current position revises his earlier writings, which found no notion of "rights" but only of "human dignity" in Muslim societies (Bielefeldt 1995).

23. Johnson (1997) and Tyan (1965).

24. Tyan (1965). In the battle with the self, it is not necessary to defeat desire, but to harness the natural desires and to seek the pleasure of their fulfillment as a celebration of the divine (Bouhdiba 1998).

25. Metcalf (1987). See also, Ahmad (1991) and Iqtidar (2011).

26. The APHC Executive Committee member parties were the Awami Action Committee (associated militant wing, Al-Ummar Mujahideen), Ittihad-ul-Muslimeen (Hizb-ul-Momineen), Jamaat-e-Islami-e-Kashmir (Hizb-ul-Mujahideen), Jammu and Kashmir Liberation Front (National Students Front, JKLF, and Kashmir Liberation Army), All Jammu and Kashmir Muslim Conference (Tareek-e-Jihad), Jammu and Kashmir People's Conference (Al-Barq), and the People's League (Al-Jihad and Al Fateh Force). Other General Body members were the Jammu and Kashmir Muslim League (Hizb-ullah), Jamiat-e-Ahl-e-Sunnat (Jamiat-ul-Mujahadeen), Jamiat-e-Ahl-e-Hadith (Jamiat-ul-Mujahadeen), People's Democratic Forum (Muslim Janbaz Force), and the Jamiat-ul-Ulema-e-Islam (Harkat-e-Jihad-e-Islami, Harkat-ul-Mujahideen, Harkul-ul-Ansar). My sources include Amin (1995) and Ganguly (1997), Baweja (1995), reports in *Dawn,* the *Herald, India Today, Jang, Outlook,* the *Pakistan Times* (1995–2003); and interviews conducted in New Delhi, Islamabad, London, Muzaffarabad, and New York (1998–2005).

27. In 1996, declared UJC members included the Lashkar-e-Tayyiba (connected to the Markaz Da'wa wal Irshad of the Ahl-e-Hadith seminary), the Harkat-ul-Islam and Harkat-ul-Mujahideen (both associated with the Deobandi Ulama and the Jamiat-ul-Ulema-e-Islam, but joined independently after splitting from the Harkul-ul-Ansar). In 1998, Al-Badr and Hizb-ul-Mujahideen announced their membership. After splitting from the Hizb-ul-Mujahideen of the Jamaat-e-Islami-e-Kashmir, (which maintained its membership in the APHC), Al-Badr was loosely connected to the Jamaat-e-Islami-e-Pakistan. It was not the same Al-Badr that was prominent in the Kashmir insurgency in 1990. Al-Badr in 1990 was a Kashmiri regiment of the Hizb-ul-Mujahideen (the militant wing of the Pakistan political party the Jamaat-e-Islami), which served as a vehicle to bring Kashmiris fighting in Afghanistan back to Jammu and Kashmir; it merged with the Hizb-ul-Mujahideen of the Kashmiri party in 1990. The Jaish-e-Mohammad declared its membership in 2000 as an independent jihadist group. Between 1996 and 2001, other organizations were sometimes listed as members by journalists and government reports, but there is a great deal of contradiction in such reports. My sources include Jane's Intelligence Backgrounder (2001), Rana (2002), Abbas (2000), Khan (1998), reports in *Dawn,* the *Herald, India Today, Jang, Outlook,* the *Pakistan Times* (1995–2003), and interviews conducted in New Delhi, Islamabad, London, Muzaffarabad, and New York (1998–2005).

28. Agamben (1998, p. 32).

29. Agamben (1998, p. 142).

CHAPTER 6

1. Abu-Lughod (1986), Ewing (2008), Gilsenan (1996), Knudsen (2002), Lavie (1990), Lindholm (1982, 1996), and Ouzgane (2006). Scholars of South Asian studies have also emphasized that masculine paradigms of honor shape the postcolonial public through intercommunal competition (Das 1995b; Gupta 2002; Hansen 1996; Jayawardena and Alwis 1996; Verkaaik 2004).

2. Bouhdiba (1998); see also, Mernissi (1975).

3. Lapidus (1984). See also Metcalf (1984a) on how South Asian reformist scholars employed theological writing on *'aql* to invoke it as a source of reason and discipline in the reform tradition.

4. Mernissi (1975, 1992).

5. Peletz (1996), Ring (2006), Rosen (1984), and Siegel (1969).

6. Rosen (1984, p. 47).

7. Siegel (1969, p. 252).

8. Abu-Lughod (1986), Lavie (1990, pp. 119–145), and Rosen (1984, pp. 18–59).

9. Rosen (1984, p. 49). This created a social hierarchy as teachers refused to provide women with religious training, because they already "conceptualized women as morally weak and irresponsible [and] lacking the spiritual and mental strength of men, [and therefore] regarded [women] as neither fit nor equipped for public tasks" (Wikan 1982, p. 56).

10. Brenner (1996), Hegland (1998), and Mahmood (2001a, 2001b).

11. Siegel (1969, p. 196).

12. Peletz (1993b, 1996); see also, Brenner (1998, pp. 144–170), and Ong and Peletz (1993b).

13. Brenner (1996, 1998), Ong and Peletz (1993a), and Peletz (1993a).

14. Kurin (1984, 1988), Ring (2006, pp. 109–113), and Verkaaik (2004, pp. 51–53).

15. Ahmad (1991), Metcalf (1982, 1998), and Sanyal (1996).

16. Rosen (1984).

17. Siegel (1969, p. 252).

18. See Khuri (2001, pp. 49–88) for a discussion of the *sunnats* that deal with how the prophet handled his body in ritual and intimate relations.

19. The Army fired on a protest demonstration, killing thirty-three people by the official Indian count. The public rapes that followed during a period of curfew and crackdowns are reported by human rights organizations but denied by the Indian government (Amnesty International 1993, 1995; Human Rights Watch/Asia and Physicians for Human Rights 1993a, 1993b; Physicians for Human Rights and Asia Watch 1993).

20. A *hijra* is a man who dresses in women's clothing and fulfills female social roles, and many *hijras* earn their living as (female) prostitutes.

21. This point is extensively elaborated in anthropological studies of the role of violence in religious rituals and rites of initiation (Bloch 1992; George 1996; Gluckman 1963; Rosaldo 1980; Turner 1967). See also Mahmood (1996), McCoy (1999), Peteet (1994), and Rejali (1994) on the transformation of the meanings of political violence through its reinterpretation as invested with ritual meanings.

22. Torture is a topic of scientific research to maximize its efficiency; certain techniques have developed to maximize the spectacle of harm to the body, and others to make it possible deny its practice. See Rejali (2007) for a detailed discussion of the scientific research behind the practice of torture by modern states. These techniques also produce truth effects that have political uses; that is, while the intelligence and juridical value of information extracted from people interrogated using torture techniques is dubious at best, it does have the effect of producing confessions that legitimate the violent practices of the state as necessary and rational (Abrahamian 1999; Danner 2004; Gregory 2007; Lazreg 2008).

23. Scarry (1985).

24. On this point, I disagree with scholars who argue that militant diasporas develop because people become culturally reinterpolated through the circulation and distribution of the body as a spectacle of violence. Writing about torture and militancy in Ireland, Allen Feldman (1991) argued, "political power increasingly becomes a matter of regimenting the circulation of bodies in time and space in a manner analogous to the circulation of things. ... [An] entity violently expelled from the social order is transformed into an emissary, a cultural donor and bearer of seminal political messages" (p. 8). Instead, the most useful perspectives on the transformative effects of political violence emphasize the social aspects of managing the experience of living under conditions of violence (Aretxaga 1997; Das 2007; Hansen 2001; Klima 2002; Mahmood 1996; Taussig 1987; Zulaika and Douglass 1996), rather than the rupture of symbolic systems and cultural meaning (Axel 2001; Daniel 1996; Das et al. 2000; Martinez 1993).

25. In this relationship between the physical body and the social body, particular histories and languages can also be a part of denying violence (Das 1995a, 1996).

26. Institute of Kashmir Studies (1994).

27. International Commission of Jurists (1995, pp. 62–65).

28. Walikhanna (2004, p. 104).

29. Young Palestinian men's bodily experiences as victims of state violence during the Intifatah shifted traditional community leadership away from elder men toward younger ones. Elder men developed 'aql through their generational relationships as fathers and grandfathers; they exercised 'aql in their roles as leaders of the family, lineage, and community. Disclosures about the violation of the body did not diminish young Muslim men's moral worth and social standing, despite the problematic aspects of public collaboration on matters of the body. The testimonials of suffering did not subvert the qualities of constraint and modesty that are signs of a moral person (Jean-Klein 2000). Young men were able to claim their bodily suffering as sacrificial suffering and thus a manifestation of 'aql through which they could assert themselves as decision makers and community leaders (Peteet 1994, 1997).

30. See also Jean-Klein (1997, 2000) on this intersubjective narration between sisters and brothers in the Palestinian Intifada and Joseph (1994) on the importance of the brother–sister relationship to legitimating violence in Lebanon.

31. Werbner (1990) has argued that *khidmat* is one form that sacrifice takes in South Asian Muslim practice (pp. 103, 151–171, 227–258).

32. Emotion *(jazbāt)* can be both sincere *(haqīqī)* and fake *(naqlī)*. As Verkaaik (1994) argued regarding sectarian and ethnic militancy in Pakistan, sincere emotions are thought to provide a spiritual power that is capable of overturning existing power relations, "a true sacrifice is [therefore] perceived as a matter of passion" (pp. 51–53).

33. Abou Zahab (2007) and Haq (2007).

34. Rosen (2000) attributes this idea to the Islamic legal injunction that a *shāhid* (witness) cannot give testimony against an enemy. The words *shahīd* (martyr) and *shāhid* (a juridical witness) are both derived from the Arabic root word for "testimony" or "attestation."

35. See also Klima (2002), Sermetakis (1991), and Verdery (1999) on the moral evaluation of the body post-mortem in non-Muslim societies.

36. See McKenna (1998, 2000) for a discussion of how these processes manifest in the Islamic-nationalist violence in the Philippines, and Edwards (2002) for a discussion of the connection between social, philosophical, and doctrinal interpretations of jihād practice in the Afghan context.

37. There is significant doctrinal divergence on this point. The Malakis and the Shafi'is are adamant that funeral prayers should not be offered, but some Hanifi scholars accepted that prayers should be made on the martyr's behalf (Abedi and Legenhausen 1986; Jansen 1993; Kohlberg 1997; Peters 1997).

38. See Ayubi (1991) and Ewing (1997).

39. See Ewing (1997) for a discussion of the ways in which the philosophical and political debate is replicated in expressions of piety and devotion.

CONCLUSION

1. Devji (2008) has suggested that the influence of the Kashmir formulation of human rights can be seen in the current configuration of "global jihadism." Hafez (2010) and Paz (2009) have described this influence in the Middle Eastern context.

2. See Allen (2009), Kirchner (2007), and Ochs (2006).

POSTSCRIPT

1. This was first discussed as a policy issue by the International Crisis Group (2006) in their first report on the impact of the earthquake. Other commentators predicted that this would have far reaching social and political impacts in AJK (Bamforth and Qureshi 2007; Qureshi 2006).

2. Many scholarly and policy perspectives currently see Islamic charities as a thin propaganda cover for transfers of funds to terrorist organizations, and therefore

approach Islamic philanthropy as a problem (Burr and Collins 2006; Sageman 2004), but Islamic charities have such a great impact on their societies that it is imperative to work with them (Benthall 2007; van Beuinessen 2007).

3. See Government of Pakistan, Earthquake Reconstruction and Rehabilitation Authority, and United Nations System in Pakistan (2006); see also, Azad Government of the State of Jammu & Kashmir, Planning and Development Department (2006), and Oxfam International (2006).

4. See Pappas and Hicks (2006), Rehman and Kalra (2006), and. U.S. Committee on Foreign Relations (2005).

GLOSSARY

'AQL Wisdom, or discernment.

AWĀM-E-KASHMĪR People of Kashmir.

ĀWĀRAH Unrestricted, unconstrained, homeless.

BĀSHINDAH Resident.

BĒGAR Forced labor as a form of taxation rather than share in agricultural product.

DĀR Sovereign territory.

DĀRUL-ISLĀM The land of peace/faith.

DĀRUL-HARB The land of war dissent.

FARZ Obligation or duty.

FARZUL-'AYN Individual duty.

FARZUL-KAFĀYA Collective duty.

HAQŪQ Rights (singular, *haqq*).

HIJARAT Migration, flight; also, protective migration.

JĀGĪR Heredity estates in which the land revenue accrued to the holder.

JĀGĪRDĀRĪ The system of administering local rule over designated estates.

JAMĀ'AT Political party.

JIHĀD A struggle, great effort; sometimes, an armed struggle.

JIHĀD-E-KASHMĪR The Kashmir Jihad.

JIHĀDĪ An Urdu neologism commonly used in English media and policy documents to refer to someone engaged in the "global jihad." In Kashmir and Pakistan, refers to someone connected with a *jihādī tanzīm*.

JIHĀDĪ TANZĪM An Islamic militant organization not connected with a political party.

KASHMĪRĪYAT A claim on political rights based on the cultural history of the Kashmir Valley.

KHĀLSAH Government property.

KHIDMAT Service, social work.

LASHKAR Army, militia. In South Asia refers to irregular militias mobilized under the authority of descent group chiefs or Sufi brotherhood leaders.

MAS'ALAH-E-KASHMĪR The Kashmir Problem

MUHĀJIR Person who has done *hijarat,* a refugee or migrant.

MUHĀJIRĪN Proper grammatical plural of *muhājir* (immigrant/ refugee). This text makes use of the English plural *muhājirs* to distinguish a multiplicity of refugees from refugees as a social collective (*muhājirīn*).

MUHĀJIR-E-KASHMĪR Kashmiri refugee.

MUHĀJIR-E-RIYĀSAT-E-JAMMŪ-O-KASHMĪR Refugee of the State of Jammu and Kashmir.

MUJĀHID Person engaged in the practice of jihād, a warrior.

MUJĀHIDĪN Proper grammatical plural of *mujāhid.* This text makes use of the English plural *mujāhids* to distinguish a Multiplicity of warriors from a group from refugees as a social collective rather than members of the same militant organization.

MULKĪ "[the people] of the land"; A legal category that defined a monarchical Hereditary State Subject.

MUTĀSIRĪN "Affectees"; in contemporary AJK, firing-line displaced people.

MUTAHIDAH JIHĀD MAHĀZ United Jihad Council.

NAFS The passions, desire, natural instincts.

NĪYAT Intention.

PANĀH Refuge.

PANĀH GAZĪN Refuge-seekers.

REFŪJĪ An English loan word for "refugee"; in AJK, a displaced person who lives in a refugee camp.

RIYĀSAT State, rule.

SHAHĪD Martyr.

SUNNAT Habit, customary practices; model for behavior or bodily practice in daily life, as demonstrated by the prophets.

TANZĪM Literally, "organization"; refers to a militant organization allied with a particular political party, religious organization, or social group.

TEHSIL District; an administrative division and tax assessment unit.

'ULEMAH Scholars trained in the traditional Islamic sciences.

UMMAH The Muslim political community.

WASĪYAT A command, bequest, or last testament.

BIBLIOGRAPHY

Abbas, Zaffar. 2000. A Who's Who of Kashmir Militancy. *Herald*, August, pp. 29–32.

Abdullah, Sheikh Mohammad. 1948. *Kashmir: Appeal to World Conscience*. Delhi: Government of Jammu and Kashmir.

Abedi, Mehdi, and Gary Legenhausen. 1986. Introduction. In *Jihad and Shahadat: Struggle and Martyrdom in Islam*, M. Abedi and G. Legenhausen, eds. Houston: Institute for Research and Islamic Studies.

Abou El Fadl, Khaled. 1990. Ahkam Al-Bughat: Irregular Warfare and the Law of Rebellion in Islam. In *Cross, Crescent, and Sword: The Justification and Limitation of War in Western and Islamic Tradition*, J. T. Johnson and J. Kelsay, eds. New York: Greenwood Press.

Abou Zahab, Miriam. 2007. "I Will Be Waiting for You at the Door of Paradise": The Pakistani Martyrs of Lashkar-e-Taiba. In *The Practice of War: Production, Reproduction and Communication of Armed Violence*, A. Rao et al., eds. New York: Berghahn Books.

Abraham, Itty, and Willem van Schendel. 2005. Introduction: The Making of Illicitness. In *Illicit Flows and Criminal Things: States, Borders, and the Other Side of Globalization*, W. von Schendel and I. Abraham, eds. Bloomington: Indiana University Press.

Abrahamian, Ervand. 1999. *Tortured Confessions: Prisons and Public Recantations in Modern Iran*. Berkeley: University of California Press.

Abu-Lughod, Lila. 1986. *Veiled Sentiments: Honor and Poetry in a Bedouin Society*. Berkeley: University of California Press.

———. 2002. Do Muslim Women Really Need Saving? Anthropological Reflections on Cultural Relativism and Its Others. *American Anthropologist* 104(3):783–790.

Adams, Charles J. 1983. Mawdudi and the Islamic State. In *Voices of Resurgent Islam*, J. L. Esposito, ed. New York: Oxford University Press.

Agamben, Giorgio. 1995. We Refugeés. *Symposium* 49(2):114–119.

———. 1998. *Homo Sacer: Sovereign Power and Bare Life*. Stanford, CA: Stanford University Press.

Aggarwal, Ravina. 2004. *Beyond Lines of Control: Performance and Politics on the Disputed Borders of Ladakh, India*. Durham, NC: Duke University Press.

Ahmad, Irfan. 2009. *Islamism and Democracy in India: The Transformation of Jamaat-e-Islami*. Princeton, NJ: Princeton University Press.

Ahmad, Mumtaz. 1970. *Mas'alah-e-Kashmir: Tarikhi, Siyasi, Aur Qanooni Mutala'ah* [The Kashmir Problem: Historical, Political, and Legal Perspectives]. Lahore, Pakistan: al-Mahrāb.

————. 1991. Islamic Fundamentalism in South Asia: The Jamaat-e-Islami and the Tablighi Jamaat of South Asia. In *Fundamentalisms Observed*, M. E. Marty and R. S. Appleby, eds. Chicago: University of Chicago Press.

Ahmed, Akbar S. 1980. *Pukhtun Economy and Society*. Boston: Routledge.

————. 1986. The Afghan Refugees. In *Pakistan Society: Islam, Ethnicity, and Leadership in South Asia*. Karachi, Pakistan: Oxford University Press.

Ahmed, Leila. 1992. *Women and Gender in Islam: Historical Roots of a Modern Debate*. New Haven, CT: Yale University Press.

Akhtar, Kalim. 1963. *Sher-e-Kashmir: Sheikh Mohammad Abdullah* [The Lion of Kashmir: Sheikh Mohammad Abdullah]. Lahore, Pakistan: Istqilal Press.

Ali, Maulvi Cherágh. 1977. *A Critical Exposition of the Popular "Jihád."* Karachi, Pakistan: Karimsons.

Allen, Lori A. 2009. Martyr Bodies in the Media: Human Rights, Aesthetics, and the Politics of Immediation in the Palestinian Intifada. *American Ethnologist* 36(1):161–180.

Amin, Tahir. 1995. *Mass Resistance in Kashmir: Origins, Evolution, Options*. Islamabad: Institute of Policy Studies.

Amnesty International. 1993. *India, an Unnatural Fate: Disappearances and Impunity in the Indian States of Jammu and Kashmir and Punjab*. New York: Amnesty International USA.

————. 1995. *India, Torture and Deaths in Custody in Jammu and Kashmir*. New York: Amnesty International USA.

An-Na'im, Abdullahi. 1990. *Toward an Islamic Reformation: Civil Liberties, Human Rights, and International Law*. Syracuse, NY: Syracuse University Press.

————. 2001. Human Rights in the Arab World. *Human Rights Quarterly* 23:701–732.

Anand, Justice Adarsh Sein. 1994. *The Constitution of Jammu and Kashmir: Its Development & Comments*. Delhi: Universal Book Traders.

Anderson, Ewan W., and Nancy Hatch Dupree, eds. 1990. *The Cultural Basis of Afghan Nationalism*. New York: Pinter.

Andrews, P.A. 1993. Muhadjir. In *The Encyclopedia of Islam*, Second Edition, Vol. VII, C.E. Bosworth et al., eds. Leiden, The Netherlands: E.J. Brill.

Ansari, Sarah. 1992. *Sufi Saints and State Power: The Pirs of Sind, 1843–1947*. New York: Cambridge University Press.

————. 1993. Muhadjir. In *The Encyclopedia of Islam*, Second Edition, Vol. VII, C.E. Bosworth et al., eds. Leiden, The Netherlands: E.J. Brill.

————. 2005. *Life after Partition: Migration, Community and Strife in Sindh, 1947–1962*. Karachi, Pakistan: Oxford University Press.

Ansari, Zafar Ishaq. 1990. Hijrah in the Islamic Tradition. In *The Cultural Basis of Afghan Nationalism*, E. W. Anderson and N. H. Dupree, eds. New York: Pinter.

Arendt, Hannah. 1951. The Decline of the Nation-State and the End of the Rights of Man. In *The Origins of Totalitarianism*. New York: Harvest.

Aretxaga, Begona. 1997. *Shattering Silence: Women, Nationalism, and Political Subjectivity in Northern Ireland*. Princeton, NJ: Princeton University Press.

————. 2001. The Sexual Games of the Body Politic: Fantasy and State Violence in Northern Ireland. *Culture, Medicine, and Psychiatry* 25:1–27.

Arjomand, Said Amir. 1995. Unity and Diversity in Islamic Fundamentalism. In *Fundamentalisms Comprehended*, M. E. Marty and R. S. Appleby, eds. Chicago: University of Chicago Press.

Asad, Talal. 1993. *Genealogies of Religion: Discipline and Reasons of Power in Christianity and Islam*. Baltimore: Johns Hopkins University Press.

————. 2003. *Formations of the Secular: Christianity, Islam, Modernity*. Stanford, CA: Stanford University Press.

Axel, Brian Keith. 2001. *The Nation's Tortured Body: Violence, Representation, and the Formation of a Sikh "Diaspora."* Durham, NC: Duke University Press.

Ayoob, Mohammed. 2008. *The Many Faces of Political Islam: Religion and Politics in the Muslim World*. Ann Arbor: University of Michigan Press.

Ayubi, Nazih N. M. 1991. *Political Islam: Religion and Politics in the Arab World*. New York: Routledge.

Azad Government of the State of Jammu & Kashmir, High Court of Judicature. 1993. *Verdict on Gilgit and Baltistan (Northern Areas)*. Mirpur: Kashmir Human Rights Forum.

Azad Government of the State of Jammu & Kashmir, Law and Parlimentary Affairs Department. 1984a. *The Azad Jammu and Kashmir Laws*. Vol. III (1957–1962). Muzaffarabad: Government Printing Press.

————. 1984b. *The Azad Jammu and Kashmir Laws*. Vol. IV (1963–1970). Muzaffarabad: Government Printing Press.

————. 1984c. *The Azad Jammu and Kashmir Laws Code*. Vol. V (1971–73). Muzaffarabad: Government Printing Press.

Azad Government of the State of Jammu & Kashmir, Planning and Development Department. 1999. *Statistical Handbook of Azad Jammu and Kashmir*. Muzaffarabad: Government Printing Press.

————. 2006. *An Overview of Development & Reconstruction in AJK: Text of a Slideshow Presentation for Briefing of Journalists, Foreign Dignitaries, and Relief Agencies on August 9, 2006*.

————. 2009. *Azad Kashmir at a Glance, 2008*. Official Website of Planning and Development Department, AJK. Available at http://www.pndajk.gov.pk /psdp.asp

Azad Kashmir Government. 1948a. *Behind the Iron Curtain in Kashmir*. Rawalpindi: Department of Public Relations.

————. 1948b. *Kashmir's Fight for Freedom*. Rawalpindi: Department of Public Relations.

Azad Kashmir Government, and Iftikhar Ahmad. 1952. *The Census of Azad Kashmir, 1951*. Rawalpindi: Government Printing Press.

Aziz, Ahmad. 1964. *Studies in Islamic Culture in the Indian Environment*. Oxford, United Kingdom: Clarendon Press.

Bainton, Roland Herbert. 1960. *Christian Attitudes toward War and Peace: a Historical Survey and Critical Re-Evaluation*. New York: Abingdon Press.

Bakewell, Oliver. 2008. Research Beyond the Categories: The Importance of Policy Irrelevant Research into Forced Migration. *Journal of Refugee Studies* 21(4):432–453.

Ballinger, Pamela. 2003. *History in Exile: Memory and Identity at the Borders of the Balkans*. Princeton, NJ: Princeton University Press.

Bamforth, Thomas, and Jawad Hussain Qureshi. 2007. Political Complexities of Humanitarian Intervention in the Pakistan Earthquake. *Journal of Humanitarian Assistance*, January 16. Available at http://sites.tufts.edu/jha/archives/12

Bamzai, K.N. 1948. *Kashmir Defends Democracy*. New Delhi: Kashmir Bureau of Information.

Bamzai, Prithvi Nath Kaul. 1962. *A History of Kashmir: Political, Social, Cultural*. New Delhi: Metropolitan Book.

————. 1987. *Socio-Economic History of Kashmir, 1846–1925*. New Delhi: Metropolitan Book.

Bannerji, Mukulika. 2001. *The Pathan Unarmed: Opposition and Memory in the North West Frontier*. Sante Fe: School of American Research Press.

Barber, Benjamin R. 2001. *Jihad versus McWorld*. New York: Ballantine Books.

Barnett, Michael. 2001. Humanitarianism with a Sovereign Face: UNHCR in the Global Undertow. *International Migration Review* 35(1):244–277.

Barnett, Michael N., and Thomas George Weiss. 2008a. Humanitarianism: A Brief History of the Present. In *Humanitarianism in Question: Politics, Power, Ethics*, M. N. Barnett and T. G. Weiss, eds. Ithaca, NY: Cornell University Press.

————, eds. 2008b. *Humanitarianism in Question: Politics, Power, Ethics*. Ithaca, NY: Cornell University Press.

Barth, Fredrik. 1959. *Political Leadership among Swat Pathans*. London: Athlone Press.

Barthes, Roland. 1972. Mythologies. New York: Hill and Wang.

Bat, Sana'ullah. 1980. *Kashmir: 1947 Se 1977 Tak* [Kashmir: From 1947 to 1977]. Jammu Masjid, Delhi: Islamic Publications.

Bates, Charles Ellison. 1990 [1873]. *A Gazetteer of Kashmir and the Adjacent Districts of Kishtawar, Badrawar, Jammu, Naoshera, Punch, and the Valley of the Kishan Ganga: Compiled for Political and Military Reference*. New Delhi: Light and Life.

Baud, Michiel, and Willem van Schendel. 1997. Toward a Comparative History of Borderlands. *Journal of World History* 8(2):211–242.

Baweja, Harinder. 1995. Who's Who of Militancy. *India Today*, September 15, p. 24.

Bayefsky, Anne, and Joan Fitzpatrick. 2000. *Human Rights and Forced Displacement*. The Hague: Martinus Nijhoff.

Bazaz, Prem Nath. 1950. *Azad Kashmir: A Democratic Socialist Conception*. Lahore, Pakistan: Ferozsons.

—————. 1954. *The History of Struggle for Freedom in Kashmir, Cultural and Political, from the Earliest Times to the Present Day*. New Delhi: Kashmir Publishing.

—————. 1987 [1941]. *Inside Kashmir*. Mirpur, Azad Kashmir: Verinag.

Beinin, Joel, and Joe Stork. 1997. On the Modernity, Historical Specificity, and International Context of Political Islam. In *Political Islam: Essays from Middle East Report*, J. Beinin and J. Stork, eds. Berkeley: University of California Press.

Bem, Kazimierz. 2004. The Coming of a "Blank Cheque"—Europe, the 1951 Convention, and the 1967 Protocol. *International Journal of Refugee Law* 16(4):609–627.

Benthall, Jonathan. 1993. *Disasters, Relief and the Media*. New York: I.B. Tauris.

—————. 2007. The Overreaction against Islamic Charities. *ISIM Review* 20:6–7.

Benthall, Jonathan, and Jerome Bellion-Jourdan. 2003. *The Charitable Crescent: The Politics of Aid in the Muslim World*. London: I. B. Tauris.

Bhagavan, Manu Belur. 2003. *Sovereign Spheres: Princes, Education and Empire in Colonial India*. New Delhi: Oxford University Press.

—————. 2009. Princely States and the Making of Modern India: Internationalism, Constitutionalism and the Postcolonial Moment. *Indian Economic & Social History Review* 46(3):427–456.

Bhan, Mona. 2008. Border Practices: Labour and Nationalism among Brogpas of Ladakh. *Contemporary South Asia* 16 (2):139–157.

Bhat, Sanullah, et al. 1955. *A Humble Appeal to the Members of the Constituent Assembly of Pakistan*. Rawalpindi: Noor Art Press.

Bhatt, Ram Krishen Kaul. 1984. *Political and Constitutional Development of Jammu and Kashmir State*. Delhi: Seema.

Bhatt, S.C., and Gopal K. Bhargava, eds. 2005. *Land and People of Indian States and Union Territories*. Vol. 11: Jammu and Kashmir. Delhi: Kalpaz.

Bielefeldt, Heiner. 1995. Human Rights in the Arab World. *Human Rights Quarterly* 17(4):701–732.

—————. 2000. Positioning Rights in a Multicultural World: "Western" Versus "Islamic" Human Rights Conceptions? A Critique of Cultural Essentialism in the Discussion on Human Rights. *Political Theory* 28(1):90–121.

Birdwood, Lord Christopher. 1956. *Two Nations and Kashmir*. London: Hale Press.

Bloch, Maurice. 1992. *Prey into Hunter: The Politics of Religious Experience*. New York: Cambridge University Press.

Boesen, I.W. 1990. Honor in Exile: Continuity and Change among Afghan Refugees. In *The Cultural Basis of Afghan Nationalism*, E. W. Anderson and N. H. Dupree, eds. New York: Pinter.

Bonner, Michael David. 2006. *Jihad in Islamic History: Doctrines and Practice*. Princeton, NJ: Princeton University Press.

Bonney, Richard. 2004. *Jihad: From Qur'an to Bin Laden*. New York: Palgrave Macmillan.

Borgwardt, Elizabeth. 2005. *A New Deal for the World: America's Vision for Human Rights*. Cambridge, MA: Belknap Press of Harvard University Press.

Borneman, John. 1998. Toward a Theory of Ethnic Cleansing: Territorial Sovereignty, Heterosexuality, and Europe. In *Subversions of International Order: Studies in the Political Anthropology Culture*. Albany: State University of New York Press.

Bose, Sumantra. 2003. *Kashmir: Roots of Conflict, Paths to Peace*. Cambridge, MA: Harvard University Press.

Bose, Tapan K. 2000. *Protection of Refugees in South Asia: Need for a Legal Framework*. Kathmandu: South Asia Forum for Human Rights.

Bouhdiba, Abdelwahab. 1998. *Sexuality in Islam,* A. Sheridan, trans. London: Saqi Books.

Brachman, Jarret. 2009. *Global Jihadism: Theory and Practice*. New York: Routledge.

Brauman, Rony. 1998. Refugee Camps, Population Transfers, and Ngos. In *Hard Choices: Moral Dilemmas in Humanitarian Intervention*, J. Moore, ed. Lanham, MD: Rowman and Littlefield.

Brenner, Suzanne. 1996. Reconstructing Self and Society: Javanese Muslim Women and "the Veil." *American Anthropologist* 23(4):673–697.

———. 1998. *The Domestication of Desire: Women, Wealth, and Modernity in Java*. Princeton, NJ: Princeton University Press.

Brown, Daniel W. 1996. *Rethinking Tradition in Modern Islamic Thought*. New York: Cambridge University Press.

———. 1997. Islamic Modernism in South Asia. *The Muslim World* 87(3–4):258–271.

Burgat, François. 2003. *Face to Face with Political Islam*. New York: Palgrave Macmillan.

Burgerman, Susan. 2001. *Moral Victories: How Activists Provoke Multilateral Action*. Ithaca, NY: Cornell University Press.

Burki, Shahid Javed. 1969. Twenty Years of the Civil Service of Pakistan: A Reevaluation. *Asian Survey* 9(4):239–254.

Burr, Millard, and Robert O. Collins. 2006. *Alms for Jihad: Charity and Terrorism in the Islamic World*. New York: Cambridge University Press.

Butalia, Urvashi. 1998. *The Other Side of Silence: Voices from the Partition of India*. New Delhi: Viking.

Calhoun, Craig. 2004. A World of Emergencies: Fear, Intervention, and the Limits of Cosmopolitanism. *Canadian Review of Sociology and Anthropology* 41(4):375–395.

———. 2008. The Imperative to Reduce Suffering: Charity, Progress, and Emergencies in the Field of Humanitarian Action. In *Humanitarianism in Question: Politics, Power, Ethics*, M. N. Barnett and T. G. Weiss, eds. Ithaca. NY: Cornell University Press.

Cambell, Kurt M., and Thomas G. Weiss. 1991. Military Humanitarianism. *Survival* 33 (5):451–465.

Centlievres, Piere, and Micheline Centlievres-Dumont. 1988a. The Afghan Refugees in Pakistan: A Nation in Exile. *Current Sociology* 36(2):71–92.

———. 1988b. The Afghan Refugees in Pakistan: An Ambiguous Identity. *Journal of Refugee Studies* 1(2):141–152.

Chakrabarti, Prafullah. 1999. *The Marginal Men: The Refugees and the Left Political Syndrome in West Bengal.* Calcutta: Naya Udyog.

Chakraborty, Manik. 1998. *Human Rights and Refugees: Problems, Laws and Practices in India.* New Delhi: Deep & Deep.

Chandler, David. 2001. The Road to Military Humanitarianism: How the Human Rights NGOs Shaped a New Humanitarian Agenda. *Human Rights Quarterly* 23(3):678–700.

Chari, P. R., Mallika Joseph, and D. Suba Chandran, et al., eds. 2003. *Missing Boundaries: Refugees, Migrants, Stateless and Internally Displaced Persons in South Asia.* New Delhi: Manohar.

Chatta, Illays. 2009. Terrible Fate: "Ethnic Cleansing" of Jammu Muslims in 1947. *Pakistan Vision* 10(1):117–140.

Chatterjee, Partha. 1989. Colonialism, Nationalism, and Colonized Women: The Contest in India. *American Ethnologist* 16(4):622–633.

———. 1995. *The Nation and Its Fragments: Colonial and Postcolonial Histories.* Delhi: Oxford University Press.

Chatterji, Joya. 2001. Right or Charity? The Debate over Relief and Rehabilitation in West Bengal, 1947–50. In *Partitions of Memory*, S. Kaul, ed. Delhi: Permanent Black.

———. 2007. *The Spoils of Partition: Bengal and India, 1947–1967.* New York: Cambridge University Press.

Chimni, B. S. 1998. *The Law and Politics of Regional Solution of the Refugee Problem: The Case of South Asia.* Colombo Sri Lanka: Regional Centre for Strategic Studies.

Chimni, B. S., and United Nations High Commissioner for Refugees, eds. 2000. *International Refugee Law.* London: Sage.

Çinar, Alev. 2005. *Modernity, Islam, and Secularism in Turkey: Bodies, Places, and Time.* Minneapolis: University of Minnesota Press.

Cohen, Benjamin B. 2007. *Kingship and Colonialism in India's Deccan, 1850–1948.* New York: Palgrave Macmillan.

Cohen, G. Daniel. 2006. The Politics of Recognition: Jewish Refugees in Relief Policies and Human Rights Debates, 1945–1950 *Immigrants and Minorities* 24(2):125–143.

———. 2008. Between Relief and Politics: Refugee Humanitarianism in Occupied Germany 1945–1946. *Journal of Contemporary History* 43(3):437–449.

Cook, David. 2005. *Understanding Jihad.* Berkeley: University of California Press.

Copland, Ian. 1982. *The British Raj and the Indian Princes: Paramountcy in Western India, 1857–1930.* Bombay: Orient Longman.

———. 1997. *The Princes of India in the Endgame of Empire, 1917–1947.* Cambridge, United Kingdom: Cambridge University Press.

———. 2005. *State, Community, and Neighbourhood in Princely North India, C. 1900–1950.* New York: Palgrave Macmillan.

Dani, A.H. 1989. *History of the Northern Areas of Pakistan.* Islamabad: National Institute of Historical and Cultural Research.

Daniel, E. Valentine. 1996. *Charred Lullabies: Chapters in an Anthropography of Violence.* Princeton, NJ: Princeton University Press.

Danner, Mark. 2004. *Torture and Truth: America, Abu Ghraib, and the War on Terror.* New York: New York Review of Books.

Das, Veena. 1995a. *Critical Events: An Anthropological Perspective on Contemporary India.* Delhi: Oxford University Press.

———. 1995b. National Honor and Practical Kinship: Unwanted Women and Children. In *Conceiving the New World Order: The Global Politics of Reproduction,* F. D. Ginsburg and R. Rapp, eds. Berkeley: University of California Press.

———. 1996. Language and the Body: Transactions in the Construction of Pain. *Daedalus* 125(1):67–92.

———. 2007. *Life and Words: Violence and the Descent into the Ordinary.* Berkeley: University of California Press.

Das, Veena, et al., eds. 2000. *Violence and Subjectivity.* Berkeley: University of California Press.

Dasgupta, Jyotibhusan. 1968. *Jammu and Kashmir.* The Hague: Martinus Nijhoff.

de Waal, Alexander. 1997. *Famine Crimes: Politics & the Disaster Relief Industry in Africa.* Bloomington: Indiana University Press.

Deeb, Lara. 2006. *An Enchanted Modern: Gender and Public Piety in Shi'i Lebanon.* Princeton, NJ: Princeton University Press.

deMel, Neloufer. 2007. *Militarizing Sri Lanka: Popular Culture, Memory, and Narrative in the Armed Conflict.* New Delhi: Sage.

Devji, Faisal. 2005. *Landscapes of the Jihad: Militancy, Morality, Modernity.* Ithaca, NY: Cornell University Press.

———. 2008. *The Terrorist in Search of Humanity: Militant Islam and Global Politics.* New York: Columbia University Press.

Dirks, Nicholas. 1987. *The Hollow Crown: Ethnohistory of an Indian Kingdom.* New York: Cambridge University Press.

Donnelly, Jack. 1985. *The Concept of Human Rights.* New York: St. Martin's Press.

———. 1989. *Universal Human Rights in Theory and Practice.* Ithaca: Cornell University Press.

Drew, Fredric. 1971 [1875]. *The Jammoo and Kashmir Territories: A Geographical Account.* Delhi: Oriental.

Duffield, Mark. 2001. *Global Governance in the New Wars: The Merging of Development and Security.* New York: Zed Books.

Dupree, Nancy Hatch. 1990. A Socio-Cultural Dimension: Afghan Women Refugees in Pakistan. In *The Cultural Basis of Afghan Nationalism,* E. W. Anderson and N. H. Dupree, eds. New York: Pinter.

Dwyer, Kevin. 1991. *Arab Voices: The Human Rights Debate in the Middle East.* Berkeley: University of California Press.

Edwards, David B. 2002. *Before Taliban: Genealogies of the Afghan Jihad.* Berkeley: University of California Press.

Eickelman, Dale F. 2000. Islam and the Languages of Modernity. *Daedalus* 129(1):119–135.

Eickelman, Dale F., and James P. Piscatori. 1990a. Social Theory in the Study of Muslim Societies. In *Muslim Travelers: Pilgrimage, Migration, and the Religious Imagination*, D. Eickleman and J. Piscatori, eds. Berkeley: University of California Press.

———, eds. 1990b. *Muslim Travelers: Pilgrimage, Migration, and the Religious Imagination*. Berkeley: University of California Press.

———, eds. 1996. *Muslim Politics*. Princeton, NJ: Princeton University Press.

Ellis, Patricia, and Zafar Khan. 2003. Kashmiri Displacement and the Impact on Kashmiriyat. *Contemporary South Asia* 12(4):523–538.

Enloe, Cynthia H. 1983. *Does Khaki Become You? The Militarisation of Women's Lives*. London: Pluto Press.

Ernst, Waltraud, and Biswamoy Pati, eds. 2007. *India's Princely States: People, Princes, and Colonialism*. New York: Routledge.

Esposito, John L. 1984. *Islam and Politics*. Syracuse, NY: Syracuse University Press.

———. 1996. Islam: Ideology and Politics in Pakistan. In *The State, Religion, and Ethnic Politics: Afghanistan, Iran, and Pakistan*, A. Banuazizi and M. Weiner, eds. Syracuse, NY: Syracuse University Press.

———, ed. 1987. *Islam in Asia: Religion, Politics, and Society*. New York: Oxford University Press.

———, ed. 1997. *Political Islam: Revolution, Radicalism, or Reform?* Boulder, CO: Lynne Rienner.

Esposito, John L., and François Burgat, eds. 2003. *Modernizing Islam: Religion in the Public Sphere in the Middle East and Europe*. New Brunswick, NJ: Rutgers University Press.

Esposito, John L., John Voll, and Osman Bakar, eds. 2008. *Asian Islam in the 21st Century*. New York: Oxford University Press.

Euben, Roxanne Leslie. 1999. *Enemy in the Mirror: Islamic Fundamentalism and the Limits of Modern Rationalism*. Princeton, NJ: Princeton University Press.

Euben, Roxanne Leslie, and Muhammad Qasim Zaman, eds. 2009. *Princeton Readings in Islamist Thought: Texts and Contexts from Al-Banna to Bin Laden*. Princeton, NJ: Princeton University Press.

European Commission, ed. 1995a. *Law in Humanitarian Crises: How Can International Humanitarian Law Be Made Effective in Armed Conflicts?* Vol. I. Luxembourg: Office for Official Publications of the European Communities.

———, ed. 1995b. *Law in Humanitarian Crisis: Access to Victims-- Right to Intervene or Right to Receive Humanitarian Assistance?* Vol. II. Luxembourg: Office for Official Publications of the European Communities.

Evans, Alexander. 2008. Kashmiri Exceptionalism. In *The Valley of Kashmir*, A. Rao, ed. New Delhi: Manohar.

Ewing, Katherine Pratt. 1997. *Arguing Sainthood: Modernity, Psychoanalysis, and Islam*. Durham, NC: Duke University Press.

_____. 2008. *Stolen Honor: Stigmatizing Muslim Men in Berlin*. Stanford, CA: Stanford University Press.

Falk, Richard. 1989. The Afghanistan "Settlement" and the Future of World Politics. In *Soviet Withdrawal from Afghanistan*, A. Saikal and W. Maley , eds. Cambridge, United Kingdom: Cambridge University Press.

Fassin, Didier, and Estelle D'Halluin. 2005. The Truth from the Body: Medical Certificates as Ultimate Evidence for Asylum Seekers. *American Anthropologist* 107(4):597–608.

Feldman, Alan. 1991. *Formations of Violence: The Narrative of the Body and Political Terror in Northern Ireland*. Chicago: University of Chicago Press.

_____. 1994. On Cultural Anesthesia: From Desert Storm to Rodney King. *American Ethnologist* 21:404–418.

_____. 1997. Violence and Vision: The Prosthetics and Aesthetics of Terror. *Public Culture* 10(1):281–304.

Feldman, Ilana. 2007. The Quaker Way: Ethical Labor and Humanitarian Relief. *American Ethnologist* 34(4):689–705.

_____. 2008a. *Governing Gaza: Bureaucracy, Authority, and the Work of Rule, 1917–1967*. Durham, NC: Duke University Press.

_____. 2008b. Refusing Invisibility: Documentation and Memorialization in Palestinian Refugee Claims. *Journal of Refugee Studies* 21(4):498–516.

Ferme, Mariane C. 2001. *The Underneath of Things: Violence, History, and the Everyday in Sierra Leone*. Berkeley: University of California Press.

Ferris, Elizabeth G. 1993. *Beyond Borders: Refugees, Migrants, and Human Rights in the Post-Cold War Era*. Geneva: World Council of Churches.

Firestone, Reuven. 1999. *Jihad: The Origin of Holy War in Islam*. New York: Oxford University Press.

Fischer, Michael M. J., and Mehdi Abedi. 1990. *Debating Muslims: Cultural Dialogues in Postmodernity and Tradition*. Madison: University of Wisconsin Press.

Foucault, Michel. 1979. *Discipline and Punish: The Birth of the Prison,* A. Sheridan, trans. New York: Vintage Books.

_____. 1990. *The History of Sexuality: An Introduction,* R. Hurley, trans. New York: Vintage Books.

Fox, Renee. 1995. Medical Humanitarianism and Human Rights: Reflections on Doctors without Borders and Doctors of the World. *Social Science and Medicine* 41(12):1607–1616.

Freeman, Michael. 2004. The Problem of Secularism in Human Rights Theory. *Human Rights Quarterly* 26:375–400.

Frelick, Bill. 2002. *The U.S. Refugee Admissions Program: Starting Over*. Testimony of Mr. Bill Frelick, Subcommittee on Immigration, Senate Judiciary Committee, February 12. United States Senate Committee on the Judiciary, Hearings and Meetings. Available at http://www.judiciary.senate.gov/hearings /testimony.cfm?id=4f1e0899533f7680e78d03281fdbeacd&wit_id=4f1e089953 3f7680e78d03281fdbeacd-2-3

Frykenberg, Robert Eric, ed. 1969. *Land Control and Social Structure in Indian History*. Madison: University of Wisconsin Press.

Ganguly, Rajat. 2003. From Jang to Jihad: Continuity and Change in Pakistan's Kashmir Policy, 1947–2002. In *Terrorism and Low Intensity Conflict in South Asia Region*, O. Misra and S. Chosh, eds. New Delhi: Manak.

Ganguly, Sumit. 1997. *The Crisis in Kashmir: Portents of War, Hopes for Peace*. Cambridge, MA: Cambridge University Press.

Gardeezi, Saleem. 1991. *Mai Ne Kashmir Jelte Dekha* [I Saw Kashmir Burning]. Lahore, Pakistan: Jang.

Geertz, Clifford. 1968. *Islam Observed: Religious Development in Morocco and Indonesia*. New Haven, CT: Yale University Press.

George, Kenneth. 1996. *Showing Signs of Violence: The Cultural Politics of a Twentieth-Century Headhunting Ritual*. Berkeley: University of California Press.

Ghosh, Papiya. 1998. Partitions Biharis. In *Islam, Communities, and the Nation: Muslim Identities in South Asia and Beyond*, M. Hasan, ed. New Delhi: Manohar.

Gilani, Syed Manzoor H. 1988. *Constitutional Development in Azad Jammu & Kashmir*. Lahore, Pakistan: National Book Depot.

———. 2008. *The Constitution of Azad Jammu and Kashmir: The Historical Backdrop with Corresponding Pakistan, India & Occupied Jammu and Kashmir Constitutions*. Islamabad: National Book Foundation.

Gilmartin, David. 1984. Shrines, Succession, and Sources of Moral Authority. In *Moral Conduct and Authority: The Place of Adab in South Asian Islam*, B. Metcalf, ed. Berkeley: University of California Press.

———. 1988. *Empire and Islam: Punjab and the Making of Pakistan*. Berkeley: University of California Press.

———. 1998. Partition, Pakistan, and South Asian History: In Search of a Narrative. *Journal of Asian Studies* 57(4):1068–1095.

Gilmartin, David, and Bruce B. Lawrence. 2000. *Beyond Turk and Hindu: Rethinking Religious Identities in Islamicate South Asia*. Gainesville: University Press of Florida.

Gilsenan, Michael. 1996. *Lords of the Lebanese Marches: Violence and Narrative in an Arab Society*. New York: Tauris.

Gimmi, Salim Khan. 1963. *Kashmir: Adab-o-Saqafat*. Karachi, Pakistan: International Press.

Gluckman, Max. 1963. *Custom and Conflict in Africa*. Oxford, United Kingdom: Blackwell.

Goodwin-Gill, Guy S. 1999. Refugees and Security. *International Journal of Refugee Law* 11(1):1–5.

Gottlieb, Gidon. 1972. The United Nations and Emergency Humanitarian Assistance in India-Pakistan. *American Journal of International Law* 66(2):362–365.

Government of India, Census Commissioner, Jammu and Kashmir State. 1943. *Census of India, 1941. Vol. 22, Jammu & Kashmir State; Parts I & II—Essay and Tables*. Jammu: Ranbir Government Press.

Government of India, Ministry of Information and Broadcasting. 1948. *After Partition*. Delhi: Publications Division, Ministry of Information and Broadcasting.

Government of Pakistan. 1984. Handbook on Management of Afghan Refugees in Pakistan. Islamabad: Government of Pakistan.

Government of Pakistan, Directorate General of Films and Publications. n.d. *Kashmir Bleeding and Burning*. Islamabad: Ministry of Information.

Government of Pakistan, Earthquake Reconstruction and Rehabilitation Authority, and United Nations System in Pakistan. 2006. *E.R.R.A.-U.N. Early Recovery Plan*. Islamabad, Pakistan. Available at http://www.unicef.org/pakistan /partners_1622.htm

Government of Pakistan, High Court of Judicature. 1949. *The All-Pakistan Legal Decisions*. Vol. II. Lahore: Punjab Educational Press.

Government of Pakistan, Ministry of Foreign Affairs. 1977. *White Paper on Jammu and Kashmir Dispute*. Islamabad: Government of Pakistan.

Government of Pakistan, Population Census Organization. 1998. *Population and Housing Census of Azad State of Jammu and Kashmir and Northern Areas*. Islamabad: Statistics Division.

Government of Pakistan, States and Frontier Regions Division. 1985. *Memorandum on Relief Assistance for Afghan Refugees in Pakistan 1985–1986*. Islamabad: Government Printing Press.

Goyal, Hukamchand. 1964. *The Administration of Evacuee Property Act, 1950 and Evacuee Interest (Separation) Act, 1951*. Allahabad, India: Ram Narain Lal Beni Madho Law.

Green, Nile, and Mary Searle-Chatterjee. 2008. *Religion, Language, and Power*. New York: Routledge.

Gregory, Derek. 2007. Vanishing Points: Law Violence and Exception in the Global War Prison. In *Violent Geographies: Fear, Terror, and Political Violence*, D. Gregory and A. Pred, eds. New York: Routledge.

Grima, Benedict. 1993. *The Performance of Emotion among Paxtun Women: "The Misfortunes Which Have Befallen Me."* Karachi, Pakistan: Oxford University Press.

Gupta, Charu. 2002. *Sexuality, Obscenity, Community: Women, Muslims, and the Hindu Public in Colonial India*. New York: Palgrave.

Habib, Irfan. 1963. *The Agrarian System of Mughal India, 1556–1707*. New York: Asia Publishing House.

Haddadd, Yvonne Y. 1983. Sayyid Qutb: Ideologue of Islamic Revival. In *Voices of Resurgent Islam*, J. L. Esposito, ed. New York: Oxford University Press.

Hadler, Jeffrey. 2008. *Muslims and Matriarchs: Cultural Resilience in Indonesia through Jihad and Colonialism*. Ithaca, NY: Cornell University Press.

Hafez, Mohammed M. 2010. The Alchemy of Martyrdom: Jihadi Salafism and Debates over Suicide Bombings in the Muslim World. *Asian Journal of Social Science* 38(3):364–378.

Hafizullah, Mohammad. 1948. *Towards Azad Kashmir*. Lahore, Pakistan: Bazam-i-Frogh-i-Abad.

Handa, Rajendra Lal. 1968. *History of Freedom Struggle in Princely States.* New Delhi: Central News Agency.

Hangloo, R. L. 1995. *Agrarian System of Kashmir, 1846–1889.* New Delhi: Commonwealth.

Hans, Asha, and Astri Suhrke. 1997. Responsibility Sharing. In *Reconceiving International Refugee Law,* edited by J. C. Hathaway. The Hague: Martinus Nijhoff.

Hansen, Thomas Blom. 1996. Recuperating Masculinity: Hindu Nationalism, Violence, and the Exorcism of the Muslim "Other." *Critical Anthropology* 16(2):137–172.

———. 2001. *Wages of Violence: Naming and Identity in Post-Colonial Bombay.* Princeton, NJ: Princeton University Press.

Haq, Farhat. 2007. Militarism and Motherhood: The Women of the Lashkar-i-Tayyabia in Pakistan. *Signs* 32(4):1023–1046.

Haqqani, Husain. 2005a. The Ideologies of South Asian Jihadi Groups. *Current Trends in Islamic Ideology* 1:12–26.

———. 2005b. *Pakistan: Between Mosque and Military.* Washington, DC: Carnegie Endowment for International Peace.

Haroon, Sana. 2009. *Frontier of Faith: Islam in the Indo-Afghan Borderland.* New York: Columbia University Press.

Harrell-Bond, Barbera, and Eftihia Voutria. 1992. Anthropology and the Study of Refugees. *Anthropology Today* 8(4):6–10.

Harrell-Bond, Barbera, et al. 1992. Counting the Refugee: Gifts, Givers, Patrons, and Clients. *Journal of Refugee Studies* 5(3/4):205–225.

Hasan, Mushirul, ed. 1997. *Legacy of a Divided Nation: India's Muslims since Independence.* Bolder, CO: Westview Press.

Hasan, Noorhaidi. 2005. *Laskar Jihad; Islam, Militancy, and the Quest for Identity in Post-New Order Indonesia.* Ithaca, NY: Cornell Southeast Asia Program Publications.

Hasan, Taj ul-Islam. 1998. The "Bihari" Minority in Bangladesh: Victims of Nationalisms. In *Islam, Communities, and the Nation: Muslim Identities in South Asia and Beyond,* M. Hasan, ed. New Delhi: Manohar.

Hashmi, Sohail H., ed. 2002. *Islamic Political Ethics: Civil Society, Pluralism, and Conflict.* Princeton, NJ: Princeton University Press.

Haskell, Thomas L. 1985. Capitalism and the Origins of the Humanitarian Sensibility, Part 1. *The American Historical Review* 90(2):339–361

Hathaway, James. 1991. *The Law of Refugee Status.* Torronto, ON: Butterworths.

———. 1997. *Reconceiving International Refugee Law.* The Hague: Martinus Nijhoff.

Hayner, Priscilla B. 2001. *Unspeakable Truths: Confronting State Terror and Atrocity.* New York: Routledge.

Hefner, Robert. 1998. Multiple Modernities: Christianity, Islam, and Hinduism in a Globalizing Age. *Annual Review of Anthropology* 27:83–104.

———. 2000. *Civil Islam: Muslims and Democratization in Indonesia.* Princeton, NJ: Princeton University Press.

_____, ed. 2005. *Remaking Muslim Politics: Pluralism, Contestation, Democratization*. Princeton, NJ: Princeton University Press.

Hegghammer, Thomas. 2010. *Jihad in Saudi Arabia: Violence and Pan-Islamism since 1979*. New York: Cambridge University Press.

Hegland, Mary Elaine. 1998. Flagellation and Fundamentalism: (Trans)Forming Meaning, Identity, and Gender through Pakistani Women's Rituals of Mourning. *American Ethnologist* 25(2):240–266.

Henderson, William. 1953. Refugees in India-Pakistan. *Journal of International Affairs* 7(1):57–65.

Hewitt, Vernon. 1995. *Reclaiming the Past? The Search for Political and Cultural Unity in Contemporary Jammu and Kashmir*. London: Portland Books.

Hirshkind, Charles, and Saba Mahmood. 2002. Feminism, the Taliban, and the Politics of Counter-Insurgency. *Anthropological Quarterly* 75(2):339–354.

Hobsbawm, Eric, and Terence Ranger. 1983. *The Invention of Tradition*. Cambridge, United Kingdom: Cambridge University Press.

Hodgson, Marshall. 1974. *The Venture of Islam; Conscience and History in a World Civilization*. Vol. I: The Classical Age of Islam. Chicago: University of Chicago Press.

Hopgood, Stephen. 2008. Saying No to Wal-Mart? Money and Morality in Professional Humanitarianism. In *Humanitarianism in Question: Politics, Power, Ethics*, M. N. Barnett and T. G. Weiss, eds. Ithaca, NY: Cornell University Press.

Horstmann, Alexander. 2007. The Tablighi Jama'at, Transnational Islam, and the Transformation of the Self between Southern Thailand and South Asia. *Comparative Studies of South Asia, Africa, and the Middle East* 27(1):26–40.

Human Rights Watch. 2006. *"With Friends Like These . . .": Human Rights Violations in Azad Kashmir*. Available at http://www.unhcr.org/refworld/docid /4517b1a14.html

Human Rights Watch/Asia, and Physicians for Human Rights. 1993a. *The Human Rights Crisis in Kashmir: A Pattern of Impunity*. New York: Human Rights Watch.

_____. 1993b. *Rape in Kashmir: A Crime of War*. New York: Human Rights Watch.

Husain, Mirza Shafiq. 1990. *Azad Kashmir, Ek Siyasi Ja'izah: 1947 Tak 1975* [Azad Kashmir, a Political Perspective: 1947 to 1975]. Islamabad: Qaumi Idaaarah baraa'e Tahqeeq-i Taareekh-o-Saqaafat.

Hussain, Ijaz. 1998. *Kashmir Dispute: An International Law Perspective*. Rawalpindi: National Institute of Pakistan Studies.

Hyndman, Jennifer. 2000. *Managing Displacement: Refugees and the Politics of Humanitarianism*. Minneapolis: University of Minnesota Press.

Institute of Kashmir Studies. 1993. *Repression in Kashmir Moves On*. Srinagar: Institute of Kashmir Studies.

_____. 1994. *The Siege and the Massacre*. Srinagar: Institute of Kashmir Studies.

Institute of Kashmir Studies, Human Rights Division. 1993. *"Catch and Kill": A Pattern of Genocide in Kashmir: A Bestial Method of Breaking the Will of a People*. Srinagar: Jammu & Kashmir Awareness and Documentation Center.

_____. 1994a. *Massacres in Kashmir: A Special Report on Three Massacres at Bijbehara, Sopore and Kupware in Kashmir by Indian Forces.* Srinagar: Institute of Kashmir Studies, Human Rights Division.

_____. 1994b. *Tearful Summer in Kashmir: June & July, 1993, Report.* Srinagar: Institute of Kashmir Studies, Human Rights Division.

_____. 1994c. *Turbulence in Kashmir: A Report on Human Rights Violations Committed by the Indian Forces During the Month of August 1993.* Srinagar: Institute of Kashmir Studies, Human Rights Division.

_____. 1997. *Trials and Tribulations in Kashmir: A Report on Human Rights Violations Committed by the Indian Forces during the Months of October, November and December, 1996.* Srinagar: Jammu & Kashmir Awareness and Documentation Center.

International Commission of Jurists. 1995. *Human Rights in Kashmir: Report of a Mission.* Geneva, Switzerland: International Commission of Jurists.

International Crisis Group. 2006. Pakistan: Political Impact of the Earthquake. *Asia Briefing* 46 (Islamabad/ Brussels, 15 March 2006): [electronic document]. Available at http://www.crisisgroup.org/library/documents/asia/south_asia /b046_pakistan_political_impact_of_the_earthquake.pdf

Iqtidar, Humeira. 2011. *Secularizing Islamists? Jama'at-e-Islami and Jama'at-ud-Da'wa in Urban Pakistan.* Chicago: University of Chicago Press.

Irfani, Suroosh, ed. 1997. *Fifty Years of the Kashmir Dispute: Proceeding of an International Seminar.* Muzaffarabad, AJK: University of Azad Jammu and Kashmir Press.

Jaffrelot, Christopher, ed. 2002. *Nationalism without a Nation.* New York: Zed Books.

Jalal, Ayesha. 1985. *The Sole Spokesman: Jinnah, the Muslim League, and the Demand for Pakistan.* Cambridge, United Kingdom: Cambridge University Press.

_____. 2000. *Self and Sovereignty: Individual and Community in South Asian Islam since 1950.* New York: Routledge.

_____. 2008. *Partisans of Allah: Jihad in South Asia.* Cambridge, MA: Harvard University Press.

Jamal, Arif. 2009. *Shadow War: The Untold Story of Jihad in Kashmir.* Brooklyn, NY: Melville House.

Jammu & Kashmir Action Committee. 1992. *Atrocities & Violation of Human Rights in Jammu & Kashmir.* Karachi, Pakistan: Jammu and Kashmir Action Committee.

Jammu & Kashmir Human Rights Awareness and Documentation Centre. 1995. *Heaven on Fire: A Report on Human Rights Violations Committed by the Indian Forces During the Months of Jan., Feb., and March 1995.* Srinagar: Institute of Kashmir Studies Srinagar, Human Rights Division.

_____. 1996. *Carnage in Kashmir: A Report on Human Rights Violations Committed by the Indian Forces During the Months of October and November, 1995.* Srinagar: Institute of Kashmir Studies Srinagar, Human Rights Division.

_____. 1997. *Kashmir: A Paradise Outraged: A Report on Human Rights Violations Committed by the Indian Forces During the Months of January,*

February and March, 1997. Srinagar: Institute of Kashmir Studies Srinagar, Human Rights Division.

————. 1998a. *Rape and Molestation: A Weapon of War in Kashmir.* Srinagar: Institute of Kashmir Studies Srinagar, Human Rights Division.

————. 1998b. *Turbulent Autumn in Kashmir: A Report on Human Rights Violations Committed by the Indian Forces During the Months of October to December 1997.* Srinagar: Institute of Kashmir Studies Srinagar, Human Rights Division.

Jammu and Kashmir Government, Law Department. 1971a. *General Statutory Rules and Orders: Vol. I (Samvat 1945–1977).* Srinagar: Government Printing Press.

————. 1971b. *Laws of Jammu and Kashmir: Vol. I (1888–1920).* Srinagar: Government Printing Press.

————. 1971c. *Laws of Jammu and Kashmir: Vol. II (1920–1933).* Srinagar: Government Printing Press.

————. 1971d. *Laws of Jammu and Kashmir: Vol. III (1933–1947).* Srinagar: Government Printing Press.

————. 1971e. *Laws of Jammu and Kashmir: Vol. IV (1948–1959).* Srinagar: Government Printing Press.

Jammu and Kashmir Government, Superintendent of Census Operations Jammu and Kashmir, and M. H. Kamili. 1966a. *District Census Handbook, Jammu & Kashmir.* Srinagar: Government Printing Press.

————. 1966b. *District Census Handbook, Jammu & Kashmir 3: Baramulla District.* Vol. III. Srinagar: Government Printing Press.

————. 1966c. *District Census Handbook, Jammu & Kashmir 7: Jammu District.* Vol. VII. Srinagar: Government Printing Press.

————. 1966d. *District Census Handbook, Jammu & Kashmir 9: Poonch District.* Vol. IX. Srinagar: Government Printing Press.

Jammu and Kashmir Liberation Front. 1997. *Twenty Years (1977–1997) of JKLF.* Rawalpindi: Jammu and Kashmir Liberation Front.

Jammu and Kashmir Muslim Conference. 1998. Memorandum on Azad Kashmir. In *Kashmir through the Ages, Vol. IV: Kashmir and the World,* S. Sharma and U. Sharma, eds. New Delhi: Deep & Deep.

Jammu and Kashmir State. 1935. Definition of State Subject: A Historical Review. *The Ranbir Weekly.*

Jane's Intelligence Backgrounder. 2001. *Kashmir: An Insurgency Wedged between Two Nuclear Powers.* Surrey, United Kingdom: Jane's Information Group.

Jansen, J.J.G. 1993. Mudjahid. In *The Encyclopedia of Islam,* Second Edition, Vol. VII, C.E. Bosworth et al., eds. Leiden, The Netherlands: E.J. Brill.

Jayawardena, Kumari, and Malathi de Alwis, eds. 1996. *Embodied Violence: Communalizing Women's Sexuality in South Asia.* New Delhi: Kali for Women.

Jean-Klein, Iris. 1997. Palestinian Militancy, Martyrdom, and Nationalist Communities in the West Bank Occupied Territories During the Intifada. In *Martyrdom and National Resistance Movements: Essays on Asia and Europe,* J. J. M. Pettigrew, ed. Amsterdam: VU University Press.

_____. 2000. Mothercraft, Statecraft, and Subjectivity in the Palestinian Intifada. *American Ethnologist* 27(1):100–127.

Jeffrey, Robin, ed. 1978. *People, Princes, and Paramount Power: Society and Politics in the Indian Princely States*. Delhi: Oxford University Press.

Johnson, James Turner. 1997. *The Holy War Idea in Western and Islamic Traditions*. University Park: Pennsylvania State University Press.

Johnson, James Turner, and John Kelsay, eds. 1990. *Cross, Crescent, and Sword: The Justification and Limitation of War in Western and Islamic Tradition*. New York: Greenwood Press.

Joseph, Suad. 1994. Brother-Sister Relationships: Connectivity, Love, and Power in the Reproduction of Patriarchy in Lebanon. *American Ethnologist* 21(1):31–34.

_____. 1997. The Public/Private—the Imagined Boundary in the Imagined Nation/State/Community: The Lebanese Case. *Feminist Review* 57:73–92.

Juergensmeyer, Mark. 2000. *Terror in the Mind of God: The Global Rise of Religious Violence*. Berkeley: University of California Press.

_____. 2008. *Global Rebellion: Religious Challenges to the Secular State, from Christian Militias to Al Qaeda*. Berkeley: University of California Press.

Kak, Shakti. 2007. The Agrarian System of the Princely State of Jammu and Kashmir: A Study of Colonial Settlement Policies, 1960–1905. In *India's Princely States: People, Princes, and Colonialism*, W. Ernst and B. Pati, eds. New York: Routledge.

Kaldor, Mary. 1999. *New and Old Wars: Organized Violence in a Global Era*. Stanford, CA: Stanford University Press.

Kamenka, Eugene. 1989. On Being a Refugee. In *Refugees in the Modern World*, E. Kamenka, ed. Canberra: Australian National University Press.

Kamra, Sukeshi. 2002. *Bearing Witness: Partition, Independence, and the End of the Raj*. Calgary, AB: University of Calgary Press.

Karpat, Kemal H. 1990. The Hijra from Russia and the Balkans: The Process of Self-Definition in the Late Ottoman State. In *Muslim Travelers: Pilgrimage, Migration, and the Religious Imagination*, D. Eickleman and J. Piscatori, eds. Berkeley: University of California Press.

Kashmir Liberation Cell. 1997. *Kashmir: Battered Bodies and Shattered Souls*. Rawalpindi: Kashmir Liberation Cell.

_____. 1999. *Religious, Medical & Journalistic Rights Violations in Kashmir*. Muzaffarabad: Kashmir Liberation Cell.

Kattak, Saba Gul. 2003. In/Security: Afghan Refugees and Politics in Pakistan. *Critical Asian Studies* 35(2):195–208.

Kaul, Suvil, ed. 2001. *Partitions of Memory*. Delhi: Permanent Black.

Kelsay, John, and James Turner Johnson, eds. 1991. *Just War and Jihad: Historical and Theoretical Perspectives on War and Peace in Western and Islamic Traditions*. New York: Greenwood Press.

Kennedy, Charles H. 2004. The Creation and Development of Pakistan's Anti-Terrorism Regime, 1997–2002 In *Religious Radicalism and Security in South Asia*, S. P. Limaya, et al., eds. Honolulu: Asia-Pacific Center for Security Studies.

Kennedy, Dennis. 2009. Selling the Distant Other: Humanitarianism and Imagery. *Journal of Humanitarian Assistance*, February 28. Available at http://sites.tufts.edu/jha/archives/411

Kepel, Gilles. 1985. *Muslim Extremism in Egypt*. Berkeley: University of California Press.

———. 2002. *Jihad: The Trail of Political Islam*. Cambridge, MA: Belknap Press of Harvard University Press.

Khadduri, Majid. 1946. Human Rights in Islam. *The Annals* 243(January):77–81.

———. 1955. *War and Peace in the Law of Islam*. Baltimore: Johns Hopkins University Press.

———. 1997. Jihad as a Concept of Just War. In *Justice and Human Rights in Islamic Law*, G. Lampe, ed. Washington, DC: International Law Institute.

Khan, Amanullah. 1970. *Free Kashmir*. Karachi: Central Printing Press.

———. 1991. *Nazariyyah-i-Khudmukhtar Kashmir* [The Ideology of Independent Kashmir]. Rawalpindi: Jammu and Kashmir Liberation Front.

Khan, Bashir Ahmad. 2000. The Ahl-e-Hadith: A Socio-Religious Reform Movement in Kashmir. *The Muslim World* 90(1&2):133–157.

Khan, G.H. 1980. *Freedom Movement in Kashmir: 1931–1940*. Jammu: Light & Life.

———. 2000. *The Ideological Foundation of the Freedom Movement in Jammu & Kashmir: 1931–1947*. Delhi: Bhavan Prakashan.

Khan, Ismail, 2000. Terrorists or Crusaders? *Newsline*, February, pp. 23–25.

Khan, Liaquat Ali. 1952. *Kashmir and Inter-Dominion Relations*. Karachi: Ministry of Advertising, Films, and Publications.

Khan, Sardar Mohammad Ibrahim. 1965. *The Kashmir Saga*. Lahore, Pakistan: Ripon.

Khan, Sardar Muhammad Abdul Qayyum. 1992. *The Kashmir Case*. Rawalpindi: Al-Mujahid Academy.

Khan, Yasmin. 2007. *The Great Partition: The Making of India and Pakistan*. New Haven, CT: Yale University Press.

Khan, Zaigham. 1998. Allah's Army. *Herald Annual*, January, pp. 123–133.

Khuri, Fuad I. 2001. *The Body in Islamic Culture*. London: Saqi Books.

Khurshid, Salman. 1994. *Beyond Terrorism*. New Delhi: UBS.

Kirchner, Henner. 2007. Martyrs, Victims, Friends, and Foes: Internet Representations by Palestinian Islamists. In *The Practice of War: Production, Reproduction and Communication of Armed Violence*, A. Rao et al.,, eds. New York: Berghahn Books.

Klima, Alan. 2002. *The Funeral Casino: Mediation, Massacre, and Exchange with the Dead in Thailand*. Princeton, NJ: Princeton University Press.

Knudsen, Are J. 2002. *Political Islam in South Asia*. Bergen, Norway: Chr. Michelsen Institute, Development Studies and Human Rights.

———. 2009. *Violence and Belonging: Land, Love, and Lethal Conflict in the Northwest-Frontier Province of Pakistan*. Copenhagen: NAIS Press.

Kohlberg, E. 1997. Shahid. In *The Encyclopedia of Islam*, Second Edition, Vol. IX, C.E. Bosworthet al., eds. Leiden, The Netherlands: E.J. Brill.

Korac, M. 1994. Representations of Mass Rape in Ethnic Conflicts in What Was Yugoslavia. *Sociologija* 36(4):495–514.

Korbel, Josef. 1954. *Danger in Kashmir*. Princeton, NJ: Princeton University Press.

Kronenfeld, Daniel A. 2008. Afghan Refugees in Pakistan: Not All Refugees, Not Always in Pakistan, Not Necessarily Afghan? *Journal of Refugee Studies* 21(1):43–63.

Kudaisya, Gyanesh. 1995. The Demographic Upheaval of Partition: Refugees and Agricultural Resettlement in India. *South Asia: Journal of South Asian Studies* XVIII(Special Issue):73–94.

Kumar, Sumita. 2001. Pakistan's Jihadi Apparatus: Goals and Methods. *Strategic Analysis* XXIV(12).

Kurin, Richard. 1984. Morality, Personhood, and the Exemplary Life: Popular Conceptions of Muslims in Paradise. In *Moral Conduct and Authority: The Place of Adab in South Asian Islam*, B. Metcalf, ed. Berkeley: University of California Press.

———. 1988. The Culture of Ethnicity in Pakistan. In *Shari'at and Ambiguity in South Asian Islam*, K. P. Ewing, ed. Berkeley: University of California Press.

Kurz, Anat, and Nahman Tal. 1997. *Hamas: Radical Islam in a National Struggle*. Tel Aviv: Jaffee Center for Strategic Studies, Tel Aviv University.

Kurzman, Charles, ed. 2002. *Modernist Islam, 1840–1940: A Sourcebook*. New York: Oxford University Press.

Kushfi, Mir Ghulam Ahmad. n.d. *Kashmir Humara Hai*. Lahore, Pakistan: Classic.

Lamb, Alistair. 1991. *Kashmir: A Disputed Legacy 1846–1990*. Hetfordshire, England: Roxford Books.

Lanz, David. 2008. Subversion or Reinvention? Dilemmas and Debates in the Context of UNHCR's Increasing Involvement with IDPs. *Journal of Refugee Studies* 21(2):192–209.

Lapidus, Ira M. 1983. *Contemporary Islamic Movements in Historical Perspective*. Berkeley: Institute of International Studies, University of California, Berkeley.

———. 1984. Knowledge, Virtue, and Action: The Calssical Muslim Conception of Adab and the Nature of Religious Fulfillment in Islam. In *Moral Conduct and Authority: The Place of Adab in South Asian Islam*, B. Metcalf, ed. Berkeley: University of California Press.

Lavie, Smadar. 1990. *The Poetics of Military Occupation: Mzeina Allegories of Bedouin Identity under Israeli and Egyptian Rule*. Berkeley: University of California Press.

Lawrence, Bruce B. 1989. *Defenders of God: The Fundamentalist Revolt against the Modern Age*. San Francisco: Harper & Row.

———. 2000. *Shattering the Myth: Islam Beyond Violence*. Karachi, Pakistan: Oxford University Press.

Lawrence, Walter. 1967 [1895]. *The Valley of Kashmir*. Srinagar: Kesar.

———. 1985 [1909]. *Provincial Gazetteer of Kashmir*. New Delhi: Rima.

Lazreg, Marnia. 2008. *Torture and the Twilight of Empire: From Algiers to Baghdad*. Princeton, NJ: Princeton University Press.

Leader, Nicholas. 1998. Proliferating Principles, or How to Sup with the Devil without Getting Eaten. *International Journal of Human Rights* 2(4):1–27.

Lelyveld, David. 1996. *Aligarh's First Generation: Muslim Solidarity in British India*. Delhi: Oxford University Press.

Lévi-Strauss, Claude. 1966. History and Dialectic. In *The Savage Mind*. Chicago: University of Chicago Press.

———. 1995. *Myth and Meaning*. New York: Schocken Books.

Lewis, Bernard. 2002. *What Went Wrong? Western Impact and Middle Eastern Response*. New York: Oxford University Press.

Lincoln, Bruce. 2003. *Holy Terrors: Thinking About Religion after September 11*. Chicago: University of Chicago Press.

Lindholm, Charles. 1982. *Generosity and Jealousy: The Swat Pukhtun of Northern Pakistan*. New York: Columbia University Press.

———. 1996. *Frontier Perspectives*. Oxford, United Kingdom: Oxford University Press.

Littlewood, Roland. 1997. Military Rape. *Anthropology Today* 12(2):7–16.

Loescher, Gil. 2001. *The UNHCR and World Politics: A Perilous Path*. New York: Oxford University Press.

Lorimer, Roman. 1997. *Islamic Reform and Political Change in Northern Nigeria*. Evanston, IL: Northwestern University Press.

Lutz, Catherine. 2001. *Homefront: A Military City and the American Twentieth Century*. Boston: Beacon Press.

MacDonald, Kenneth Iain. 1998. Push and Shove: Spatial History and the Construction of a Portering Economy in Northern Pakistan. *Comparative Studies in Society and History* 40(2):287–317.

Macrae, Joanna, and Nicholas Leader. 2001. Apples, Pears and Porridge: The Origins and Impact of the Search for 'Coherence' between Humanitarian and Political Responses to Chronic Political Emergencies. *Disasters* 25(4):290–307.

Madan, T.N. 1995. Kashmir Crisis: View from Mirpur. In *Need for Sub-Continental Political Initiative*, G. M. Wani, ed. New Delhi: Ashish.

———. 1998. Coping with Ethnicity in South Asia: Bangladesh, Punjab, and Kashmir Compared. *Ethnic and Racial Studies* 21(5):969.

Mahmood, Cynthia Keppley. 1996. *Fighting for Faith and Nation: Dialogues with Sikh Militants*. Philadelphia: University of Pennsylvania Press.

Mahmood, Saba. 2001a. Feminist Theory, Embodiment, and the Docile Agent: Some Reflections on the Egyptian Islamic Revival. *Cultural Anthropology* 16(2):202–236.

———. 2001b. Rehearsed Spontaneity and the Conventionality of Ritual: Disciplines of Salat. *American Ethnologist* 28(4):827–853.

———. 2005. *The Politics of Piety: The Islamic Revival and the Feminist Subject*. Princeton, NJ: Princeton University Press.

Mahmud, Ershad. 2006. Status of AJK in Political Milieu. *Policy Perspectives* 3(2). Available at http://www.ips.org.pk/pakistanaffairs/education/1115-status-of-ajk-in-political-milieu.html

Malik, Iftikhar H. 1997. *State and Civil Society in Pakistan: Politics of Authority, Ideology, and Ethnicity*. Oxford, United Kingdom: MacMillan.

Malik, Jamal. 1996. *Colonialization of Islam: Dissolution of Traditional Institutions in Pakistan*. New Delhi: Monohar Books.

Malkki, Liisa. 1992. National Geographic: The Rooting of Peoples and the Territorialization of National Identity among Scholars and Refugees. *Cultural Anthropology* 7(1):24–44.

———. 1994. Citizens of Humanity: Internationalism and the Imagined Community of Nations. *Diaspora* 3(1):41–68.

———. 1995a. *Purity and Exile: Violence, Memory, and National Cosmology among Hutu Refugees in Tanzania*. Chicago: University of Chicago Press.

———. 1995b. Refugees and Exile: From "Refugee Studies" to the National Order of Things. *Annual Review of Anthropology* 24:495–523.

———. 1996. Speechless Emissaries: Refugees, Humanitarianism, and Dehistoricization. *Cultural Anthropology* 11(3):377–404.

Mamdani, Mahmood. 2000. Introduction. In *Beyond Rights Talk and Culture Talk: Comparative Essays on the Politics of Rights and Culture*, M. Mamdani, ed.. New York: St. Martin's Press.

———. 2002. Good Muslim, Bad Muslim: A Political Perspective on Culture and Terrorism. *American Anthropologist* 104(3):766–775.

———. 2004. *Good Muslim, Bad Muslim: America, the Cold War, and the Roots of Terror*. New York: Pantheon Books.

Manchanda, Rita. 2001. Guns and Burqa: Women in the Kashmir Conflict. In *Women, War, and Peace in South Asia: Beyond Victimhood to Agency*, R. Manchanda, ed. London: Sage.

Marti, Roland. 1950. The ICRC in India and Pakistan: The Kashmir Refugees. *Revue Internationale de la Croix-Rouge (Supplement)* III(1):38–42.

Martin, Richard. 1987. Religious Violence in Islam: Towards an Understanding of the Discourse on Jihad in Modern Egypt. In *Contemporary Research on Terrorism*, P. Wilkinson and A. M. Stewart, eds. Aberdeen, United Kingdom: Aberdeen University Press.

Martinez, Renato. 1993. On the Semiotics of Torture: The Case of the Disappeared in Chile. In *Reading the Social Body*, C. B. Burroughs and J. Ehrenreich, eds. Iowa City: University of Iowa Press.

Masud, Muhammad Khalid. 1990. The Obligation to Migrate: The Doctrine of Hijrah in Islamic Law. In *Muslim Travelers: Pilgrimage, Migration, and the Religious Imagination*, D. Eickleman and J. Piscatori, eds. Berkeley: University of California Press.

Matinuddin, Kamal. 1990. Afghan Refugees: The Geostrategic Context. In *The Cultural Basis of Afghan Nationalism*, E. W. Anderson and N. H. Dupree, eds. New York: Pinter.

Maudoodi, Syed Abu A'la. 1976. *Human Rights in Islam*. Leichester, United Kingdom: Islamic Foundation Press.

Mauss, Marcel. 1935. Techniques of the Body. *Economy and Society* 2(1):70–88.

————. 1960. Une Catégorie de l'ésprit Humaine: La Notion de Personne, cell de "Moi." In *Sociologie et Anthropologie*. Paris: Presse Universitaire de France.

Mayaram, Shail. 1997. *Resisting Regimes: Myth, Memory, and the Shaping of a Muslim Identity*. Delhi: Oxford University Press.

Mayotte, Judy A. 1992. *Disposable People? The Plight of Refugees*. New York: Orbis Books.

Mazower, Mark. 2004. The Strange Triumph of Human Rights, 1933–1950. *The Historical Journal* 47(2):379–398.

————. 2006. An International Civilization? Empire, Internationalism and the Crisis of the Mid-Twentieth Century. *Foreign Affairs* 82(3):553–566.

————. 2009. *No Enchanted Palace: The End of Empire and the Ideological Origins of the United Nations*. Princeton, NJ: Princeton University Press.

McCoy, Alfred. 1999. *Closer Than Brothers: Manhood at the Philippine Military Academy*. New Haven, CT: Yale University Press.

McKenna, Thomas M. 1998. *Muslim Rulers and Rebels: Everyday Politics and Armed Separatism in the Southern Philippines*. Berkeley: University of California Press.

————. 2000. Murdered or Martyred? Popular Evaluations of Violent Death in the Muslim Separatist Movement in the Philippines. In *Death Squad: The Anthropology of State Terror*, J. Sluka, ed. Philadelphia: University of Pennsylvania Press.

McLeod, John. 1999. *Sovereignty, Power, Control: Politics in the State of Western India, 1916–1947*. Leiden, The Netherlands: E.J. Brill.

Meijer, Roel, ed. 2009. *Global Salafism: Islam's New Religious Movement*. New York: Columbia University Press.

Menon, Ritu, and Kamla Bhasin. 1998. *Borders & Boundaries: Women in India's Partition*. New Brunswick, NJ: Rutgers University Press.

Menon, V.P. 1956. *The Story of the Integration of the Indian States*. Bombay: Orient Longmans.

Mernissi, Fatima. 1975. *Male-Female Dynamics in a Modern Muslim Society*. Cambridge, MA: Schenkman.

————. 1992. *Women and Islam: A Historical and Theological Enquiry*. Oxford, United Kingdom: Blackwell.

Merriam, John G. 1987. Arms Shipments to the Afghan Resistance. In *Afghan Resistance: The Politics of Survival*, G. M. Farr and J. G. Merriam, eds. Boulder, CO: Westview Press.

Merry, Sally Engle. 2006. *Human Rights and Gender Violence: Translating International Law into Local Justice*. Chicago: University of Chicago Press.

Metcalf, Barbara. 1982. *Islamic Revival in British India: Deoband, 1860–1900*. Princeton, NJ: Princeton University Press.

————. 1984a. Islamic Reform and Islamic Women: Maulana Thanawi's *Jewelry of Paradise*. In *Moral Conduct and Authority: The Place of Adab in South Asian Islam*, B. Metcalf, ed. Berkeley: University of California Press.

————, ed. 1984b. *Moral Conduct and Authority: The Place of Adab in South Asian Islam*. Berkeley: University of California Press.

———. 1987. Islamic Arguments in Contemporary Pakistan. In *Islam and the Political Economy of Meaning: Comparative Studies of Muslim Discourse*. Berkeley: University of California Press.

———. 1994. "Remaking Ourselves" Islamic Self-Fashioning in a Global Movement of Spiritual Renewal. In *Accounting for Fundamentalisms*, M. E. Marty and R. S. Appleby, eds. Chicago: University of Chicago Press.

———. 1998. Women and Men in a Contemporary Pieist Movement: The Case of the Tablighi Jama'at. In *Appropriating Gender: Women's Activism and Politicized Religion in South Asia*, P. Jeffrey and A. Basu, eds. New York: Routledge.

———. 2004. *Islamic Contestations: Essays on Muslims in India and Pakistan*. New Delhi: Oxford University Press.

Metcalf, Peter. 2002. *They Lie, We Lie: Getting on with Anthropology*. New York: Routledge.

Minault, Gail. 1982. *The Khalifat Movement: Religious Symbolism and Political Mobilization in India*. New York: Columbia University Press.

Mitchell, Richard P. 1993. *The Society of the Muslim Brothers*. New York: Oxford University Press.

Moaddel, Mansoor, and Kamran Talattof, eds. 2000. *Modernist and Fundamentalist Debates in Islam: An Anthology of Modernist and Fundamentalist Thought*. New York: St. Martin's Press.

Moore, Henrietta L. 1994. Fantasies of Power and Fantasies of Identity: Gender, Race, and Violence. In *A Passion for Difference: Essays in Anthropology and Gender*. Bloomington: Indiana University Press.

Moser, Caroline O.N., and Fiona C. Clark. 2001. *Victims, Perpetrators or Actors? Gender, Armed Conflict and Political Violence*. New York: Zed Books.

Nasr, Sayyed Vali Reza. 1994. *The Vanguard of the Islamic Revolution: The Jama'at-i-Islami of Pakistan*. Berkeley: University of California Press.

———. 1996. *Mawdudi and the Making of Islamic Revivalism*. Oxford, United Kingdom: Oxford University Press.

———. 2001. *Islamic Leviathan: Islam and the Making of State Power*. New York: Oxford University Press.

———. 2008. Pakistan after Islamization: Mainstream and Militant Islamism in a Changing State. In *Asian Islam in the 21st Century*, J. L. Esposito, et al., eds. New York: Oxford University Press.

National Documentation Center. 1993. *Journey to Pakistan: A Documentation on Refugees of 1947*. Islamabad: Government of Pakistan, Cabinet Secretariat.

Navaro-Yashin, Yael. 2002. *Faces of the State: Secularism and Public Life in Turkey*. Princeton, NJ: Princeton University Press.

Neale, Walter C. 1962. *Economic Change in Rural India: Land Tenure and Reform in Uttar Pradesh, 1800–1955*. New Haven, CT: Yale University Press.

———. 1969. Land is to Rule. In *Land Control and Social Structure in Indian History*, R. E. Frykenberg, ed. Madison: University of Wisconsin Press.

Nehru, Jawaharlal. 1951. *Discovery of India*. London: Meridian Books.

Newberg, Paula. 1995. *Double Betrayal: Repression and Insurgency in Kashmir.* Washington, DC: The Carnegie Endowment.

Nichols, Robert. 2001. *Settling the Frontier: Land, Law, and Society in the Peshawar Valley 1500–1900.* Karachi, Pakistan: Oxford University Press.

Noorani, A.G. 1964. *The Kashmir Question.* Bombay: Manaktalas.

———. 1993. Article 370: Broken Pledges and Flawed Secularism. In *Hindus and Others: The Question of Identity in India Today*, G. Pandey, ed. New Delhi: Viking.

Nordstrom, Carolyn. 1996. Rape: Politics and Theory in War and Peace. *Australian Feminist Studies* 11(23):147–162.

———. 1997. *A Different Kind of War Story.* Philadelphia: University of Pennsylvania Press.

———. 2004. *Shadows of War: Violence, Power, and International Profiteering in the Twenty-First Century.* Berkeley: University of California Press.

Nordstrom, Carolyn, and JoAnn Martin. 1992. *The Paths to Domination, Resistance, and Terror.* Berkeley: University of California Press.

Nordstrom, Carolyn, and Antonius Robben, eds. 1995. *Fieldwork under Fire: Contemporary Studies of Violence and Survival.* Berkeley: University of California Press.

Norton, Augustus R. 2007. *Hezbollah: A Short History.* Princeton, NJ: Princeton University Press.

Oberoi, Pia A. 2001. South Asia and the Creation of the International Refugee Regime. *Refuge* 19(5):36–45.

———. 2006. *Exile and Belonging: Refugees and State Policy in South Asia.* New Delhi: Oxford University Press.

Ochs, Juliana. 2006. The Politics of Victimhood and Its Internal Exegetes: Terror Victims in Israel. *History and Anthropology* 17(4):355–368.

Ogata, Sadako. 1999. The Plight of Refugees: Issues and Problems Affecting Their Humanitarian Needs. In *A Framework for Survival: Health, Human Rights, and Humanitarian Assistance in Conflicts and Disasters*, K. M. Cahill, ed. New York: Routledge.

Ong, Aihwa. 2003. *Buddha Is Hiding: Refugees, Citizenship, the New America.* Berkeley: University of California Press.

Ong, Aihwa, and Michael G. Peletz. 1993a. Introduction. In *Bewitching Women, Pious Men: Gender and Politics in Southeast Asia*, A. Ong and M. G. Peletz, eds. Berkeley: University of California Press.

———, eds. 1993b. *Bewitching Women, Pious Men: Gender and Politics in Southeast Asia.* Berkeley: University of California Press.

Osanloo, Arzoo. 2009. *The Politics of Women's Rights in Iran.* Princeton, NJ: Princeton University Press.

Osman, Fathi. 2003. Mawdudi's Contribution to the Development of Modern Islamic Thinking in the Arabic-Speaking World. *Muslim World* 93(3–4):465–485.

Ouzgane, Lahoucine. 2006. Islamic Masculinities, an Introduction. In *Islamic Masculinities*, L. Ouzgane, ed. London: Zed Books.

Oxfam International. 2006. *Keeping Recovery on Course: Challenges Facing the Pakistan Earthquake Response One Year On.* October 2. Available at http://www.oxfam.org/en/policy/bno610_pakistan_earthquake_oneyear

Pandey, Gyanendra. 2001. *Remembering Partition: Violence, Nationalism, and History in India.* New York: Cambridge University Press.

Panikkar, K. M. 1953. *The Founding of the Kashmir State; a Biography of Maharajah Gulab Singh, 1792–1858.* London: Allen & Unwin Press.

Pappas, Gregory, and Esther K. Hicks. 2006. Coordinating Disaster Relief after the South Asia Earthquake. *Society* 43(5):42–50.

Pasha, Mustapha Kamal. 1992. Islamization, Civil Society, and the Politics of Transition in Pakistan. In *Religion and Political Conflict in South Asia*, D. Allen, ed. London: Greenwood Press.

Paz, Reuven. 2009. Debates within the Family: Jihadi-Salafi Debates on Strategy: Takfir, Extremism, Suicide Bombings, and the Sense of the Apocalypse. In *Global Salafism: Islam's New Religious Movement*, R. Meijer, ed. New York: Columbia University Press.

Peletz, Michael G. 1993a. Neither Reasonable nor Responsible: Contrasting Representations of Masculinity in a Malay Society. In *Bewitching Women, Pious Men: Gender and Politics in Southeast Asia*, edited by A. Ong and M. G. Peletz. Berkeley: University of California Press.

———. 1993b. Sacred Texts and Dangerous Words: The Politics of Law and Cultural Rationalization in Malaysia. *Comparative Studies in Society and History* 35(1):66–109.

———. 1996. *Reason and Passion: Representations of Gender in a Malay Society.* Berkeley: University of California Press.

———. 2002. *Islamic Modern: Religious Courts and Cultural Politics in Malaysia.* Princeton, NJ: Princeton University Press.

Peteet, Julie. 1991. *Gender in Crisis: Women and the Palestinian Resistance Movement.* New York: Columbia University Press.

———. 1994. Male Gender and the Rituals of Resistance in the Palestinian Intifada: A Cultural Politics of Violence. *American Ethnologist* 21(1):31–49.

———. 1997. Icons and Militants: Mothering in a Danger Zone. *Signs: Journal of Women in Culture and Society* 23(1):103–129.

———. 2005. *Landscape of Hope and Despair: Palestinian Refugee Camps.* Philadelphia: University of Pennsylvania Press.

Peters, Rudolph. 1977. *Jihad in Medieval and Modern Islam.* Leiden, The Netherlands: E.J. Brill.

———. 1979. *Islam and Colonialism: The Doctrine of Jihad in Modern History.* New York: Mouton.

———. 1997. Shahid. In *The Encyclopedia of Islam*, Second Edition, Vol. VII, C.E. Bosworth et al., eds. Leiden, The Netherlands: E.J. Brill.

Peterson, Glen. 2008. To Be or Not to Be a Refugee: The International Politics of the Hong Kong Refugee Crisis, 1949–55 *Journal of Imperial and Commonwealth History* 36(2):171–195.

Physicians for Human Rights, and Asia Watch. 1993. *The Crackdown in Kashmir: Torture of Detainees and Assaults on the Medical Community.* Boston: Physicians for Human Rights & Asia Watch.

Polzer, Tara, and Laura Hammond. 2008. Invisible Displacement. *Journal of Refugee Studies* 21(4):417–431.

Puri, Balraj. 1981. *Jammu and Kashmir: Triumph and Tragedy of Indian Federalism.* New Delhi: Sterling.

———. 1993. *Kashmir: Towards Insurgency.* N. Bhattacharya, ed. New Delhi: Orient Longman.

Puri, Luv. 2010. *Across the LoC: Inside Pakistan-Administered Jammu and Kashmir.* New Delhi: Penguin, Viking.

Qureshi, Jawad. 2006. Earthquake Jihad: The Role of Jihadis and Islamist Groups after the October 2005 Earthquake. *Humanitarian Exchange Magazine* 34 (July). Available at http://www.odihpn.org/report.asp?id=2815

Rai, Mridu. 2004. *Hindi Rulers, Muslim Subjects: Islam, Rights, and the History of Kashmir.* Delhi: Permanent Black.

Raman, Anita D. 2004. Of Rivers and Human Rights: The Northern Areas, Pakistan's Forgotten Colony in Jammu and Kashmir *International Journal on Minority and Group Rights* 11:187–228.

Ramusack, Barbara. 1978. *The Princes of India in the Twilight of Empire: Dissolution of a Patron-Client System, 1914–1939.* Columbus: Ohio State University Press.

———. 2004. *The Indian Princes and Their States.* New York: Cambridge University Press.

Rana, Muhammad Amir. 2002. *Jihad-e-Kashmir Aur Afghanistan: Jihadi Tanzeemon Aur Mazahabi Jamaaton Ka Ek Janaza* [The Kashmir Jihad and Afghanistan: An Examination of Jihadist Organizations and Religious Parties]. Lahore, Pakistan: Mashal Books.

Rao, Aparno. 1999. A Tortuous Search for Justice: Notes on the Kashmir Conflict. *Himalayan Research Bulletin* XVIX(1):9–20.

Rao, U. Bhaskar. 1967. *The Story of Rehabilitation.* Faridabad: Ministry of Labor, Employment, and Rehabilitation, Government of India.

Redfield, Peter. 2005. Doctors, Borders, and Life in Crisis. *Cultural Anthropology* 20(3):328–361.

Reetz, Dietrich. 1998. On the Nature of Muslim Political Responses: Islamic Militancy in the Northwest Frontier Provinces. In *Islam, Communities, and the Nation: Muslim Identities in South Asia and Beyond*, M. Hasan, ed. New Delhi: Manohar.

Rehman, Shams, and Virinder S. Kalra. 2006. Transnationalism from Below: Initial Responses by British Kashmiris to the South Asia Earthquake of 2005. *Contemporary South Asia* 15(3):309–323.

Rejali, Darius M. 1994. *Torture and Modernity: Self, Society, and State in Modern Iran.* San Francisco: Westview Press.

———. 2007. *Torture and Democracy.* Princeton, NJ: Princeton University Press.

Rey-Schyrr, Catherine. 1998. The ICRC's Activities on the Indian Subcontinent Following Partition (1947–1949). *International Review of the Red Cross* 323:267–291

Rieff, David. 1996. The Humanitarian Trap. *World Policy Journal* 12(4):1–12.

Ring, Laura A. 2006. *Zenana: Everyday Peace in a Karachi Apartment Building.* Bloomington: Indiana University Press.

Robinson, Cabeiri deBergh. 2010. Review Essay: Partition, Its Refugees, and Post-Colonial State-Making in South Asia. *India Review* 9(1):68–86.

———. 2012. Too Much Nationality: Kashmiri Refugees, the South Asian Refugee Regime, and a Refugee State, 1947–1974. *Journal of Refugee Studies* 25(3):344–365.

———. n.d.-a. Before Islamist Jihad: Revolutionary Violence, Kashmiri Subjectivity, and the Sovereignty of Azad Kashmir. Presented at the 37th Annual Conference of South Asian Studies Madison, WI, October 18, 2008.

———. n.d.-b. Humanitarian Internationalism, the South Asian Refugee Regime, and Funding Kashmiri Refugee Relief in Pakistan, 1947–1951. Presented at the Symposium on New Approaches to the History of Humanitarianism, Stanford University, May 28, 2010.

Robinson, Francis. 2002. *The 'Ulama of Farangi Mahall and Islamic Culture in South Asia.* Lahore, Pakistan: Ferozsons.

Rosaldo, Renato. 1980. *Ilongot Headhunting 1883–1974: A Study in Society and History.* Stanford, CA: Stanford University Press.

Rose, Leo E. 1992. The Politics of Azad Kashmir. In *Perspectives on Kashmir: The Roots of Conflict in South Asia*, R. Thomas, ed. San Francisco: Westview Press.

Rosen, Lawrence. 1984. *Bargaining for Reality: The Construction of Social Relations in a Muslim Community.* Chicago: University of Chicago Press.

———. 2000. *The Justice of Islam.* New York: Oxford University Press.

Rougier, Bernard. 2007. *Everyday Jihad: The Rise of Militant Islam among Palestinians in Lebanon.* P. Ghazaleh, trans. Cambridge, MA: Harvard University Press.

Roy, Olivier. 1986. *Islam and Resistance in Afghanistan.* New York: Cambridge University Press.

———. 1994. *The Failure of Political Islam.* C. Volk, trans. Cambridge, MA: Harvard University Press.

Roy, Sara. 2011. *Hamas and Civil Society in Gaza: Engaging the Islamist Social Sector.* Princeton, NJ: Princeton University Press.

Sachedina, Abdulaziz A. 1991. Activist Shi'ism in Iran, Iraq, and Lebanon. In *Fundamentalisms Observed*, M. E. Marty and R. S. Appleby, eds. Chicago: University of Chicago Press.

Sageman, Marc. 2004. *Understanding Terror Networks.* Philadelphia: University of Pennsylvania Press.

Sahlins, Peter. 1989. *Boundaries: The Making of France and Spain in the Pyrenees.* Berkeley: University of California Press.

Said, Abdul Aziz. 1979. Precept and Practice of Human Rights in Islam. *Univeral Human Rights* 1(1):63–79.

Said, Edward. 2002. Impossible Histories: Why the Many Islams Cannot Be Simplified. *Harper's Magazine*, July, 69–74.

Saikia, Yasmin. 2011. *Women, War, and the Making of Bangladesh: Remembering 1971*. Durham, NC: Duke University Press.

Salvatore, Armando. 1997. *Islam and the Political Discourse of Modernity*. Reading, United Kingdom: Ithaca Press.

Samaddar, Ranabir, ed. 2003. *Refugees and the State: Practices of Asylum and Care in India, 1947–2000*. New Delhi: Sage.

Sanyal, Usha. 1996. *Devotional Islam and Politics in British India*. Delhi: Oxford University Press.

Saraf, Mohammad Yusaf. 1977a. *Kashmiris Fight for Freedom: Volume 1, 1819–1946*. Lahore, Pakistan: Farozsons.

———. 1977b. *Kashmiris Fight for Freedom: Volume 2, 1947–1965*. Lahore, Pakistan: Farozsons.

Sayeed, Khalid B. 1958. The Political Role of Pakistan's Civil Service. *Pacific Affairs* 31(2):131–146.

Scarry, Elaine. 1985. *The Body in Pain: The Making and Unmaking of the World*. New York: Oxford University Press.

Schofield, Victoria. 1996. *Kashmir in the Crossfire*. New York: I.B. Tauris.

Seiler, F. 1988. *Rural-Urban Migration in Pakistan*. Lahore, Pakistan: Vanguard Books.

Sermetakis, C. Nadia. 1991. *The Last Word: Women Death, and Divination in Inner Mani*. Chicago: University of Chicago Press.

Shafqat, Saeed. 2002. From Official Islam to Islamism: The Rise of the Dawat-ul-Irshad and Lashkar-e-Taiba. In *Nationalism without a Nation*, C. Jaffrelot, ed. New York: Zed Books.

Shaheen, Khurshid. 2000. *A Complete Report of Muslim Colony Katchi Abadi & 3 Other Katchi Abadies in Islamabad, 1961–2000*. Islamabad: Kashmir Public Welfare Society.

Shahrani, M. Nazif. 1995. Afghanistan's Muslim "Refugee-Warriors": Politics of Mistrust and Mistrust of Politics. In *Mistrusting Refugees*, E. V. Daniel and J. C. Knusdsen, eds. Berkeley: University of California Press.

Sharma, Suresh, and Usha Sharma, eds. 1998. *Kashmir through the Ages: Kashmir and the World*. Vol. IV. New Delhi: Deep & Deep.

Shastry, K.R.R. 1941. *Indian States*. Allahabad, India: Kitabistan.

Shibli, Abdur Rahim. 1977. *Pakistan Aur Bharat Ke Do Tarafah Ta'alluqat Aur Kashmir* [Kashmir and Pakistan's and India's Bilateral Relations]. Lahore, Pakistan: Intikhab Publications.

Shue, Henry. 1989. Morality, Politics, and Humanitarian Assistance. In *The Moral Nation: Humanitarianism and U.S. Foreign Policy Today*, B. Nichols and G. Loesher, eds. Notre Dame: University of Notre Dame Press.

Siddiqui, Taimur. 2000. There Should be a Distinction Between Jihad and Terrorism. *Newsline*, February, pp. 26–30.

Siegel, James T. 1969. *Rope of God*. Berkeley: University of California Press.

Sikand, Yoginder. 2001. The Changing Course of the Kashmiri Struggle: From National Liberation to Islamist Jihad? *The Muslim World* 91(1&2):229–257.

———. 2002. The Emergence and Development of the Jama'at-I-Islami of Jammu and Kashmir (1940s–1990). *Modern Asian Studies* 36(3):705–751.

———. 2007. Stoking the Flames: Intra-Muslim Rivalries in India and the Saudi Connection. *Comparative Studies of South Asia, Africa, and the Middle East* 27(1):95–108.

Singh, Narinder. 1992. *Political Awakening in Kashmir*. Delhi: H.K. Publications.

Singh, Tavleen. 1995. *Kashmir: A Tragedy of Errors*. New Delhi: Viking.

Singh, Ujjwal Kumar. 2007. *The State, Democracy and Anti-Terror Laws in India*. New Delhi: Sage.

Sisson, Richard, and Leo E. Rose. 1990. *War and Secession: Pakistan, India, and the Creation of Bangladesh*. Berkeley: University of California Press.

Skran, Claudena, and Carla N. Daughtry. 2007. The Study of Refugees before "Refugee Studies." *Refugee Survey Quarterly* 26:15–35.

Sluka, Jeffery. 2000a. Introduction: State Terror and Anthropology. In *Death Squad: The Anthropology of State Terror*, J. Sluka, ed. Philadelphia: University of Pennsylvania Press.

———, ed. 2000b. *Death Squad: The Anthropology of State Terror*. Philadelphia: University of Pennsylvania Press.

Smith, Daniel Jordan. 2007. *A Culture of Corruption: Everyday Deception and Popular Discontent in Nigeria*. Princeton, NJ: Princeton University Press.

Snedden, Christopher. 2001. Paramountcy, Patrimonialism and the Peoples of Jammu and Kashmir, 1947–1991. PhD. dissertation, LaTrobe University, Melbourne, Australia.

Sökefeld, Martin. 1998. High-Country Balawaristan. *Himal* 11(5):28–31.

———. 2005. From Colonialism to Postcolonial Colonialism: Changing Modes of Domination in the Northern Areas of Pakistan. *Journal of Asian Studies* 64(4):939–973.

Sontag, Susan. 2003. *Regarding the Pain of Others*. New York: Farrar Straus and Giroux.

Sorensen, Birgitte Refslund. 2008. Humanitarian Ngos and Mediations of Political Order in Sri Lanka. *Critical Asian Studies* 40(1):113–142.

Stiglmayer, Alexandra, ed. 1994. *Mass Rape: The War against Women in Bosnia-Herzegovenia*. Lincoln: University of Nebraska Press.

Stoessinger, John G. 1956. *The Refugee and the World Community*. Minneapolis: University of Minnesota Press.

Swami, Praveen. 2008. The Well-Tempered Jihad: The Politics and Practice of Post-2002 Islamist Terrorism in India *Contemporary South Asia* 16(3):303–322.

Symonds, Richard. 2001. *In the Margins of Independence: A Relief Worker in Indian and Pakistan, 1942–1949*. Delhi: Oxford University Press.

Tambiah, Stanley J. 1996. *Leveling Crowds: Ethnonationalist Conflicts and Collective Violence in South Asia*. Berkeley: University of California Press.

Tan, Tai Yong, and Gyanesh Kudaisya, eds. 2000. *The Aftermath of Partition in South Asia*. New York: Routledge.

Tanguay, Joelle. 1999. The Medicins Sans Frontiers Experience. In *A Framework for Survival: Health, Human Rights, and Humanitarian Assistance in Conflicts and Disasters*, K. M. Cahill, ed. New York: Routledge.

Taseer, Rasheed. 1973. *Tahreekh-e-Hurriyat-e-Kashmir* [The Kashmiri Freedom Movement]. Vol. 2. Srinagar: Muhafiz.

Taussig, Michael. 1987. *Shamanism, Colonialism, and the Wild Man: A Study in Terror and Healing*. Chicago: University of Chicago Press.

———. 1999. *Defacement: Public Secrecy and the Labor of the Negative*. Stanford, CA: Stanford University Press.

Teng, Mohan Krishen, Ram Krishen Kaul Bhatt, and Santosh Kaul. 1977. *Kashmir Legal Documents,* Jammu: Light & Life.

Terry, Fiona. 2002. *Condemned to Repeat? The Paradox of Humanitarian Action*. Ithaca, NY: Cornell University Press.

Tibi, Bassam. 2002a. *The Challenge of Fundamentalism: Political Islam and the New World Disorder*. Berkeley: University of California Press.

———. 2002b. War and Peace in Islam. In *Islamic Political Ethics: Civil Society, Pluralism, and Conflict*, S. H. Hashmi, ed. Princeton, NJ: Princeton University Press.

Ticktin, Miriam Iris. 2011. *Casualties of Care: Immigration and the Politics of Humanitarianism in France*. Berkeley: University of California Press.

Turner, Bryan S. 1994. *Orientalism, Postmodernism, and Globalism*. New York: Routledge.

Turner, Simon. 2005. Suspended Spaces—Contesting Sovereignties in a Refugee Camp. In *Sovereign Bodies: Citizens, Migrants, and States in the Postcolonial World*, T. B. Hansen and F. Stepputat, eds. Princeton, NJ: Princeton University Press.

Turner, Victor. 1967. *The Forest of Symbols: Aspects of Ndembu Ritual*. Ithaca, NY: Cornell University Press.

Tyan, E. 1965. Djihad. In *The Encyclopedia of Islam*, Second Edition, Vol. II, B. Lewis et al., eds. Leiden, The Netherlands: E.J. Brill.

United Nations. 1995. *The United Nations and Human Rights: 1945–1995*. Vol. VII. New York: United Nations Department of Public Information.

United Nations High Commissioner for Refugees. 2000a. *Refugees and Others of Concern to UNHCR: 1999 Statistical Overview*. Geneva, Switzerland: .

———. 2000b. *The State of the World's Refugees: Fifty Years of Humanitarian Action*. Oxford, United Kingdom: United Nations High Commissioner for Refugees. U.S. Committee on Foreign Relations. 2005. Pakistan Earthquake: International Response and Impact on U.S. Foreign Policies and Programs: Staff Trip Report to the Committee on Foreign Relations, United States Senate, One Hundred Ninth Congress, First Session.: Washington: Government Printing Office.

U.S. Committee on Foreign Affairs. 1981. Reports on Refugee Aid: U.N. High Commissioner for Refugees, Refugees in Somalia, Refugees in Pakistan, Bataan Refugee Processing Center: Reports of Staff Study Missions to the Committee on

Foreign Affairs, U.S. House of Representatives. Washington, DC: Government Printing Office.

van Beuinessen, Martin. 2007. Development and Islamic Charities. *ISIM Review* 20(1):5.

van Schendel, Willem. 2005. *The Bengal Borderland: Beyond State and Nation in South Asia*. London: Anthem.

Varshney, Ashutsh. 1992. Three Compromised Nationalisms: Why Kashmir Has Been a Problem. In *Perspectives on Kashmir: The Roots of Conflict in South Asia*, R. Thomas, ed. San Francisco: Westview Press.

Verdery, Katherine. 1999. *The Politics of Dead Bodies*. New York: Columbia University Press.

Verkaaik, Oskar. 1994. *A People of Migrants: Ethnicity, State, and Religion in Karachi*. Amsterdam: VU University Press.

———. 2004. *Migrants and Militants: Fun and Urban Violence in Pakistan*. Princeton, NJ: Princeton University Press.

Vernant, Jacques. 1953. *The Refugee in the Post-War World*. London: Allen & Unwin Press.

Virdee, Pippa. 2009. Negotiating the Past: Journey through Muslim Women's Experience of Partition and Resettlement in Pakistan. *Cultural and Social History* 6(4):467–483.

Voll, John O. 1991. Fundamentalism in the Sunni Arab World: Egypt and the Sudan. In *Fundamentalisms Observed*, M. E. Marty and R. S. Appleby, eds Chicago: University of Chicago Press.

Volpi, Frederic. 2010. *Political Islam Observed: Disciplinary Perspectives*. New York: Columbia University Press.

Volpi, Frederic, and Bryan S. Turner. 2007. Introduction: Making Islamic Authority Matter. *Theory, Culture & Society* 24(2):1–19.

von Hugel, Baron Charles. 1976 [1845]. *Travels in Kashmir and the Punjab*, T. B. Jervis, trans. Lahore: Qausain.

von Rad, Gerhard. 1991 [1958]. *Holy War in Ancient Israel*, M. J. Dawn, ed. Grand Rapids, MI: Eerdmans.

Voutira, Eftihia, and B.E. Harrell-Bond. 1995. In Search of the Locus of Trust: The Social World of the Refugee Camp. In *Mistrusting Refugees*, E. V. Daniel and J. C. Knusdsen, eds. Berkeley: University of California Press.

Walikhanna, Charu. 2004. *Women Silent Victims in Armed Conflict: An Area Study of Jammu and Kashmir, India*. Delhi: Serials.

Warner, Daniel. 1999. The Politics of the Political/ Humanitarian Divide. *International Review of the Red Cross* 833:109–118.

Waseem, Mohammad. 1997. Affirmative Action Policies in Pakistan. *Ethnic Studies Report* XV(2):223–245.

Watt, W. Montgomery. 1971. Hidjra. In *The Encyclopedia of Islam*, Second Edition, Vol. III, B. Lewis et al., eds. Leiden,The Netherlands: E.J. Brill.

———. 1993. Al-Muhadjirun. In *The Encyclopedia of Islam*, Second Edition, Vol. VII, C.E. Bosworth et al., eds. Leiden, The Netherlands: E.J. Brill.

Weinbaum, Marvin. 1989. The Politics of Afghan Resettlement and Rehabilitation. *Asian Survey* 29(3):287–307.

Weiss, Anita M., ed. 1986. *Islamic Reassertion in Pakistan: The Application of Islamic Laws in a Modern State*. Syracuse, NY: Syracuse University Press.

Weiss, Thomas G. 1999a. Principles, Politics, and Humanitarian Action. *Ethics and International Affairs* 13(1):1–22.

―――. 1999b. Whither International Efforts for Internally Displaced Persons? *Journal of Peace Research* 36(3):363–373.

Weitsman, Patricia A. 2008. The Politics of Identity and Sexual Violence: A Review of Bosnia and Rwanda. *Human Rights Quarterly* 30(3):561–578.

Werbner, Pnina. 1990. *The Migration Process: Capital, Gifts, and Offerings among British Pakistanis*. New York: Berg.

―――. 1991. Factionalism and Violence in British Pakistani Communal Politics. In *Economy and Culture in Pakistan: Migrants and Cities in a Muslim Society*, H. Donnan and P. Werbner, eds. New York: St. Martin's Press.

―――. 1996. Stamping the Earth with the Name of Allah: Zikr and the Sacralizing of Space among British Muslims. *Cultural Anthropology* 11(3):309–338.

―――. 1999. Political Motherhood and the Feminization of Citizenship: Women's Activism and the Transformation of the Public Sphere. In *Women, Citizenship, and Difference*, N. Yuval-Davis and P. Werbner, eds. London: Zed Books.

West Punjab Government, Legislative Assembly. 1948. *Debates: Vol. I (No. 2)*. Lahore, Pakistan: Din Muhammad Press.

―――. 1952. *Debates: Vol. V*. Lahore, Pakistan: Din Muhammad Press.

White, Jenny B. 2002. *Islamist Mobilization in Turkey: A Study in Vernacular Politics*. Seattle: University of Washington Press.

Whitehead, Andrew. 2007. *A Mission in Kashmir*. New Delhi: Penguin.

―――. 2010. The People's Militia: Communists and Kashmiri Nationalism in the 1940s. *Twentieth Century Communism* 2(1):141–168.

Wickham, Carrie Rosefsky. 2002. *Mobilizing Islam: Religion, Activism, and Political Change in Egypt*. New York: Columbia University Press.

Wikan, Unni. 1982. *Behind the Veil in Arabia: Women in Oman*. Chicago: University of Chicago Press.

Wiktorowicz, Quintan. 2001. *The Management of Islamic Activism: Salafis, the Muslim Brotherhood, and State Power in Jordan*. Albany: State University of New York Press.

―――, ed. 2004. *Islamic Activism: A Social Movement Theory Approach*. Bloomington: Indiana University Press.

Wilcox, Wayne Ayres. 1963. *Pakistan; the Consolidation of a Nation*. New York: Columbia University Press.

Wilson, Richard. 1997a. Human Rights Culture and Context: An Introduction. In *Human Rights Culture and Context: Anthropological Perspectives*, R. A. Wilson, ed. Chicago: Pluto Press.

_____. 1997b. Representing Human Rights Violations: Social Contexts and Subjectivities. In *Human Rights Culture and Context: Anthropological Perspectives*, R. A. Wilson, eds. Chicago: Pluto Press.

Wilson, Richard A., and Richard D. Brown, eds. 2009. *Humanitarianism and Suffering: The Mobilization of Empathy*. New York: Cambridge University Press.

Wilson, Thomas M., and Hastings Donnan. 1998. Nation and State at International Frontiers. In *Border Identities: Nation and State at International Frontiers*, T.M. Wilson and H. Donnan, eds. New York: Cambridge University Press.

Wink, Andre. 1986. *Land and Sovereignty in India: Agrarian Society and Politics under the Eighteenth Century Maratha Swarajya*. Cambridge, United Kingdom: Cambridge University Press.

Winter, Jay, and Emmanuel Sivan, eds. 1999. *War and Remembrance in the Twentieth Century*. Cambridge, United Kingdom: Cambridge University Press.

Wirsing, Robert G. 1994. *India, Pakistan, and the Kashmir Dispute: On Regional Conflict and Its Resolution*. Delhi: Rupa.

Yasin, Madhavi. 1984. *British Paramountcy in Kashmir 1876–1894*. New Delhi: Atlantic.

Yousaf, Mohammad, and Mark Adkin. 1992. *The Bear Trap: Afghanistan's Untold Story*. London: Leo Kuper.

Zahra, Tara. 2009. Lost Children: Displacement, Family and Nation in Postwar Europe. *Journal of Modern History* 81:45–86.

Zaman, Muhammad Qasim. 2002. *The Ulama in Contemporary Islam: Custodians of Change*. Princeton, NJ: Princeton University Press.

Zamindar, Vazira Fazila-Yacoobali. 2007. *The Long Partition and the Making of Modern South Asia: Refugees, Boundaries, Histories*. New York: Columbia University Press.

Zieck, Marjoliene. 1997. *UNHCR and Voluntary Repatriation of Refugees: A Legal Analysis*. The Hague: Martinus Nijhoff.

Zolberg, Aristide. 1983. The Formation of New States as a Refugee-Generating Process. *The Annals* 467(1):24–38.

Zolberg, Aristide R, et al. 1989. *Escape from Violence: Conflict and the Refugee Crisis in the Developing World*. New York: Oxford University Press.

Zulaika, Joseba, and William A. Douglass. 1996. *Terror and Taboo: The Follies, Fables, and Faces of Terrorism*. New York: Routledge.

Zutshi, Chitralekha. 2003. *Languages of Belonging: Islam, Regional Identity, and the Making of Kashmir*. New York: Oxford University Press.

_____. 2009. Re-Visioning Princely States in South Asian Historiography: A Review. *Indian Economic & Social History Review* 46(3):301–313.

INDEX

community structure: Islamic laws concerning, 74–75; in refugee camps, 148–60

conduct: in ethnographic research, xviii–xx; Islamic concepts (salūk) of, 206–8

conflict ethnography: categories and taxonomies, 12–16; conduct and confidentiality issues, xviii–xx; Kashmir dispute and, xiii–xv; lies, secrets, and conflicts of, 92–96, xx–xxi; research methodology, 21–25; in war setting, xvi–xxi

Constitution Act of 1934, Princely State of Jammu and Kashmir and, 38–39

Constitution of Jammu and Kashmir State (1956), 44–45, 253nn59–62

Convention Relating to the Status of Refugees (1951). See also Refugee Convention: 13–15, 99–100

culture: humanitarian narrative framed by, 142–43; Kashmiri identity and, 60–66; of Muslim societies, 6, 76

dār (sovereign territory): anticolonial movements and, 74, 256n20; dārul-islām/dārul-harb (land of peace/faith-land of war/dissent) and, 72–74; dārul-sulk/dārul-aman (domains of truce and peace) as modernist forms of, 74–75, Islamic scholarship, and 72–75; hijarat and, 73–75, 78–79; jihād and, 73–75, 79, 194; Kashmir Jihad and, 193; relationship with farz, 73–75, 194

Dawn (publication), 116

death: embodied ideology and, 198–200; mujāhids and, 201–4, 220–25; religious doubt and politics of, 225–27; violated bodies and political lives of the dead, 198–200

Delhi Agreement (1952), 44, 253n57

Deobandis, 74–75, 270n27

depoliticization of refugees: categorization of Kashmiri refugee status and, 15–16, 26, 140, 247n42; humanitarianism and, 140–141, 232–35; victim-refugees and human rights and, 142–43; women and, 16, 146, 216

Details of Refugees Coming from Indian Occupied Kashmir, The, 155–56

development paradigm, refugee policies and, 141–46

De Waal, Alex, 140

discernment: Islamic reform movements and, 185, 'aql and, 186, 206–12, martyrs and, 27, 204, 221–24

Dixon Report of 1950, 252n54

documentation of refugees: in AJK, 151–53; Hereditary State Subject provisions and, 128–30; human rights language and, 175–81; identity documentation, 123–24; landholder permission documents, 37–38; refugee camp social order and, 148–60; victim-refugee documentation, 155–56

Dogra Maharajas, of Princely State of Jammu and Kashmir and, 31–33, 36–40

Dogra Party, 39–40

domicile certificates, 128–30, 158–60

doubt, rituals of dead bodies and politics of, 225–27

Earthquake Reconstruction and Rehabilitation Agency (ERRA), 241–42

Eickelman, Dale, 70

elections: AJK and, 46, 55, 64, 124; Kashmiri refugee electorate and, 46, 127–30; refugee seats and, 19, 61, 121

embodied ideology: jihād and, 75–77; sovereignty of body and, 193–98, 234–35; victimization and body sovereignty, 171–75

Emergency Interim Government of Jammu and Kashmir State, 35, 43–46

emotion: khidmat (service), and 216; militants and, 184, 220, vi; Pakistani concepts of, 273n32

European Union (EU), human rights legal norms in, 266n11

evacuee property: deprivation of, 105–8, 259n24; temporary allotments and resettlements and, 126–27, 261n38, 265n83

Evacuee Property Management Boards, 107–8

family structure: mujāhids and, 204–19; protective migration and preservation of, 78–96; temporary resettlement and, 130–36; victimization of family members, 215–17

Farida Begum, 59–62, 201–3

farz (duty): as a collective duty (*farzul-kafāya*), 73–75, 91–96, hijarat as, 73, 79–80, 84; as an individual duty (*farzul-'ayn*), 73–75, individual *vs.* collective duty, 73, 217; Islamic scholarship, and 72–75; jihāds and, 68, 73–75, 79–80, 88–91, 181–93, 203–4, 233–35; martyrs' fulfillment of, 221–24; relationship with *dār* (sovereign territory), 71, 73–75, 194, relationship with rights, 79, 90, 162, 181–94, 233

Federal Investigation Authority (FIA), 20–21

Feldman, Allen, 272n24

Foucault, Michel, 266n22

freedom movement, Kashmir Problem and LoC and, 57–59

Frelick, Bill, 141

Frontier Ilaquas, 36–40

fundamentalism: defined, 9–10; Islamism and, 9–11, 245n20; jihād and, 4, 6, 27; modernity of, 10, 75, 245n20; Muslim societies and, 69–77; mytho-histories and, 75–77

funeral rituals: of earthquake victims, 222–23; LoC permeability for, 54–55; of martyrs, 198–99, 221–22, 273n37; for mutilated warriors, 172–73, 219–20; mujāhid distinction and, 90–91, 220–21; rights of human beings and, 186–87

gender issues: charitable activities and, 230–35; conflict ethnography and, 22–25, 244n3, xviii–xix; in ethnographic research, xviii–xx; hijarat and, 78–79; Islamic concepts of personhood and, 206–8; protective migration and, 80–87; in refugee camps, 15–16, 26; refūjīs and, 140, 162–64; universal Islamic symbolism and, 16; victim-refugees and, 162–64

Geneva Conference of Plenipotentiaries, 99–101

Ghulam-Hassan, Maulvi, 191–93, 195

Gilgit-Baltistan, 17, 47; renaming of Northern Areas as, 247nn54–55

global jihadism, 273n1

Government of Azad Kashmir, regional autonomy of, 35

Government of Jammu and Kashmir State, regional autonomy of, 35

Graham Report of 1951, 252n54

Gujars, 23, 37, 56, 65, 250n25

Gulab Singh, 36, 38

Hanif, Ibrahim, 227

Harkat-ul-Islam, 196, 270n27

Harkat-ul-Mujahideen, 196, 199–200, 270n27

Haroon, Yacoob, 222–23

Hattian Refugee Camp, 147, 159

Hereditary State Subjects: legal provisions, 32–35, 38–39, 45–46, 250n31; identity documentation and, 128–30; Pakistani refugee recognition based on, 112–16; political recognition of Kashmiri refugees and, 119–30

hijarat (protective migration) 1, 243n2, xv. *See also* muhājirs: bodily practice of, xv–xvi; as duty, 67–68, 73, 79–80; Hadith literature and, 72–73; as historical symbol, 71–73; human rights and, 79–80, 89–96; as Islamicate concept, 26, 69–73, 230–35; jihād and, 1–2, 68–71, 73–75; limits of violence and, 73–75; experiences of, 77–96; mujāhids and, 204–19; multiple meanings of, 69–77; political engagement through, 26; Qur'an and, 71, 256n13, xv; refugee camp social order and, 150–51; social production of jihād and, 1–5; violence and, 4, 7, 67–96; war and, 80–87

Hizb-ul-Mujahideen, 178–80, 192–193, 196–98, 270n27

Hodgson, Marshall, 69–70

"honorary man" concept, in ethnographic research, xviii–xx

humanitarianism: humanitarian jihād, 237–42; international refugee regime and, 140–46; military intervention and, 172–75; post-war refugee regimes and,

101–3; refugee camps and politics of, 143–46; refugee categories and, 15–16, 246nn40–41; refūjī concept and, 137–40; victim-refugees and human rights and, 142–43

human rights. *See also insānī haqūq:* civic jihād and, 185–86; debts owed to others and, 186–88; documentation of in refugee camps, 149, 165, 175–81, 234; in Indian Jammu and Kashmir, violations of, 171–75; jihād and hijarat as protection of, 79–80, 89–96, 171–200; localization of, 173–75; refugee categories and, 15–16, 141–46, 246n40; victim-refugees and, 142–43

Ibrahim, Mohammad, 77, 85–87

identity: documentation of, 123–24, 127–30; in ethnographic research, xviii–xx; of Kashmiris, 59–66; political recognition of Kashmiri refugees and, 119–30; transformation of, 137–67

ijāzatnāmah (landholder permission document), 37–38, 250n31

India: interpretation of Kashmir boundaries by, 55–56; Kashmir local authorities and successor states and, 43–46, 252n54; Kashmiri refugee population in, 50–51, 178–81; Muslim communities in, 74–75; "Native States" of, 249n4; postcolonial historiography of, 33–34; Princely State of Jammu and Kashmir and, 42–43; refugees in, 100–101, 144, 267n26

Indian Administration of Evacuee Property Ordinance of 1949, 107–8

Indian Commission of Human Rights, 178

Indian Constitution and Presidential Order (Application to Jammu and Kashmir) of 1950, 252n47

Indian Kashmir Barrier, 54

Indian National Congress, 31

Indian Princely States. *See also* Princely State of Jammu and Kashmir: autonomy of, 34–35; exemption from British partition, 31–33; hereditary monarchies as, 34–35; Instrument of Accession for, 249n4; state subjects and, 31

India-Pakistan interstate wars: border evacuation and political persecutions and, 52–53; conflict ethnography and, xiii–xv; divided territories of Jammu and Kashmir and, 31–33, 46; protective migration and, 80–87; UN Ceasefire Line following, 46–47; LoC permeability and, 54–55

insānī haqūq (Kashmiri human rights concept): *insānyat* (humanity) compared with, 269n15; in Islamicate political culture, 182–93; jihād and, 194–98, 229–35; *farz* and, 181–82, 233; transnational Kashmiri discourse and, 174–75

insurgency, 53–54; human rights advocacy and, 173–75

Inter-Dominion Agreements, 44; evacuee property and refugee deprivation and, 105–8; Partition and refugee status and, 103–5; refugee relief in Pakistan and, 108–11; territorial status disputes and, 111–12

Inter-Dominion Conferences, 103–5

internal displacement: AJK refugee camps and, 137–40; emergence as category, 141; *mutāsirīn* (firing-line-affected people) category and, 158–60; refugee camps and Azad Kashmir social order and, 146–60; refūjī designation of, 138–40

International Committee of the Red Cross (ICRC), 102–3; Kashmiri refugees and, 116–17, 261n47; Pakistan earthquake relief and, 240–42; refugee crises and, 50–51

International Covenant on Civil and Political Rights, 57

International Crisis Group, 243n1

international nongovernmental organizations (INGOs): Afghan refugees in Pakistan and, 144–46; international refugee regime and, 141–46; sexual violence discourse of, 215

international refugee regime. *See also* refugees: categories of refugees and, 12–16, 99–101; humanitarian space and, 142–43, India and, 144; in late Cold War era, 140–46; refugee camps in AJK and, 137–40; regional legal norms and, 266n11; resettlement *vs.* repatriation policies and, 266n17

refugee resettlement villages and, 87–96, xiv–xvii; rights and duties of, 181–93; social production of, 2–5, xv; sovereignty of body and, 193–98; victim-refugees and, 160–62; violence of contemporary jihadists and, 5–11

Jihād-e-Kashmīr (publication), 179–81

jihādīs, 223, 227; humanitarian jihād, and 240–42; oppositional term as, 4, 234; social distinction from muhajir and, 27, 225, 234

jihadist organizations *(jihādī tanzīm). See also* specific organizations, e.g., Lashkar-e-Tayyiba: bodies of martyrs and, 222–25; earthquake relief and, 237–42; emergence of, 2–5, 193–94, 196–97, xiv; ideology of, 194–98; in refugee resettlement villages, 222; self-determination and, 171–72, 233–35

Jinnah, Fatimah, 110, 114–16

Jinnah, Mohammad Ali, 104, 108–10, 117–18

just war theory, jihād and hijarat and, 73–75

Kaldor, Mary, 142–43

Kamsur Refugee Camp, 147–48, 150–51, 154–55, 161

Karachi Agreement of March 1949, 32–33

Karachi Women's Relief Committee, 115–16

Kargil War, 68, 194; conflict ethnography and, xiii–xv; martyrdom during, 222–24; refugee categorization and, 163

Karim, Adil, 198–200

Kashmir Council, 20, 127–28, 248n62

Kashmir Dispute: APHC and, 63–64; conflict ethnography and, xiii–xv; Indian and Pakistan interpretations of, 55–56; Kashmir Problem reconfiguration of, 56–59, 230–35; legacy of Partition and, 33; LoC and, 56–59, 57–59; nuclear tests and, 53, 159, xiii; refugees' role in, 116–17

Kashmir for Kashmiris, demand for, 37–38

Kashmir Funds, establishment of, 110, 112; dispute over, 118; Muslim Conference and, 115–18; QARF and, 114–16; Women's Relief Committee's Kashmir (Mujahidden) Fund, 115–16

Kashmir Jihad *(jihād-e-kashmīr):* emergence of, 2–5, xv-xvi; ethnographic research on, 24–25; human rights and, 179–81; Kashmir Dispute and, 233–34; Pakistani State and, 8–9; political parties and, 195–98; sovereignty of the body and, 193–98, 217; self-determination and, 233–35

Kashmir Valley: displacement from, 50–51, 53–54, 61; human rights and, 175, 179–81; refugee seats and, 46, 61, 128; 24–25; militants crossing into, 166, 199

Kashmiri identity: classification and taxonomy, 12–16; Kashmiri language and, 61–62, political and cultural paradigms and, 2–5; political recognition of Kashmiri refugees and, 59–66, 119–30; people-of-Kashmir *(awām-e-kashmir)* and, 34–35, 57–59, 229–31; people-of-the-state *(awām-e-riyāsat)* and, 34–40, 57, 229–31

Kashmir Kisan Mazdoor Party, 39–40

Kashmir Mujahideen Bombers Fund, 115–16

Kashmir Refugee Camps, in Pakistan, 125–27

Kashmir Refugees Central Relief Committee (KRCRC), 115–18, 262n63; AJK Rules of Business and, 123–24

Kashmir State Dogra Army, 41–43; hijarat and, 80–87; refugees and, 49–51

Kel Refugee Camp, 147, 159

Khadduri, Majid, 182, 269n20

Khalilah Bibi, 226–27

Khan, Prince Sadruddin Aga, 267n27

Khan, Sardar Mohammad Abdul Qayyum Khan, 134, 262n63, 264n76

Khan, Sardar Mohammad Ibrahim Khan, 42–43, 262n63, 264n76

Khidmat (publication), 40

kinship, refugees and, 52, 152, 154, 82–87, 131–36198–200

Korbel, Joseph, 116–17

labor colonies *(kacchī ābādī),* 22, 67–68, 85–87; Kashmiri rights activism in, 60, 166–67; political activism in, 65–66, 191–93; mujāhids in, 88–91, 157–58

Ladakh Autonomous Hill Province, 17, 47

Lashkar-e-Tayyiba, 171–75, 189, 192,
196–197, 240, 269n14, 270n27
Lateef, Altaf, 150–51, 161
Lawrence, Bruce, 75–77
legal systems: human rights and, 174–75,
269n16; refugee laws and, 142–43,
230–34, 268n6; regional legal norms
and, 266n11
Legislative Assembly of AJK, refugee seats
in, 61–66, 127–30
Lévy-Strauss, Claude, 258n34
liberation struggles: colonial empire and, 35;
homes of refugees, 165; indigenous
movements and, 63; international aspects
of, 194; in Kashmir, 93–96, 157; self-rule
and, 40; *sunnats* regarding, 76–77
lies, conflict ethnography and, 92–96,
202–4, xx–xxi
Line of Control (LoC): border evacuation
and political persecutions and, 52–53;
disputed territory and, 54–56; division
of Princely State of Jammu and
Kashmir by, 46–47; earthquake relief
and, 238–42; firing-line-affected people
(mutāsirīn) and, 158–60; insurgency
and counterinsurgency and, 53–54;;
Kashmir Dispute and, 56–59, 231–35;
kinship and, 54–55, 131–136, 152; refugee
camps in AJK and, 137–40; refugee
migrations across, 49–53; social production of jihād and, 1–5; state political
power and, 150–51
loose conduct *(āwārah)*, Islamic concepts
of, 210–12

Maharaja of Jammu and Kashmir: accession
to India and, 31, 41, 248n2; autonomy of,
34–35; Hari Singh, 38–39, 42–43; Pratap
Singh, 37–38; Ranbir Singh 36
Majid, Abdul, 156–58, 166–67, 217–19
Malkki, Liisa, 14, 143, 247n42
Manikpian Refugee Camp, 147,
156–57, 163, 218
marriage arrangements: for mujāhids,
166–67, 201–4, 217–19; in refugee
camps, 156–57; refugee identification
and documentation process and, 152–53;
temporary resettlements and, 130–36

martyrs *(shahīd)*, 90–91; dead bodies and
politics of doubt, 225–27; intimate
absolutions and body of, 221–24; living
in the body of, 224–25; mujāhids as,
204, 220–25; political lives of, 198–200
Maududi, Abu A'la, 10, 245n23, 257n26,
269n20
Mauss, Marcel, 77
Mazower, Mark, 14
media coverage: of human rights abuses,
172–75; photographic documentation
and, 175–81
Merry, Sally, 174–75
metric degree, in South Asian education,
258n41
militant organizations *(tanzīm)*. See also
jihadist organizations *(jihādī tanzīm)*:
confusion about, 162–63; civic jihād
and, 191–93; defense of family members as recruiting tool, 215–17; earthquake relief and, 237–42; greater of
lesser jihāds and, 189–90; Kashmiri
muhājirs in, 88–91, 93–96, 163–64;
human rights appeals and, 172–75,
179–81; ideological positions of, 181;
membership cards and, 152–53;
mujāhids affiliation with, 196–97;
mujāhids contract with, 220–21;
political affiliations of, 165, 195–98;
refūjī status and, 139–40
militarization of refugee men, 15–16,
244n3, 268n42; Afghan refugees in
Pakistan and, 146; personal accounts of,
87–96; sexual torture as incentive in,
213–15, 272n24
Military Intelligence (MI), 20–21
Ministry of Kashmir Affairs (MKA), 17, 19,
22, 118, 247n55, 246n77; Jammu and
Kashmir state subjects and, 123–24,
127–30
modernity, of politicized Islam, 7, 9–11,
76–77, 182–83, 195, 235, 245n20, xvi
Mohajir Claims-Holder Association,
107–8
Monthlī Mujāhid (publication), 179–81
muhājirs (refugees), 1, xv. See also refugee
resettlement villages *and* refūjīs: All
Parties Hurriyat Conference and,

62–64; Azad Kashmir Government and, 50–52, 64–66, 254n76; border evacuation and political persecutions of, 52–53; categorical confusion about, 160–67; classification and taxonomy, 12–16; disputed territory and, 54–56; evacuee property and, 105–8; humanitarian internationalism and, 101–3; identity documentation in AJK and, 123–24; identity documentation in Pakistan and, 122, 127–130; jihād and, 87–96; Kashmir Dispute and role of, 116–17; Kashmiri identity and, 59–66; social differences among, 111–18, 139–140; local authorities and, 44–46; Kashmir Problem and, 56–59, 230–35; LoC and location of, 46–59; experiences of, 77–96, x; Pakistani recognition of, 112–16; Pakistan relief for, 108–11; Partition and, 103–11; patterns of violence and, 48–52; political identities of, 119–30; distinction from camp refugees and, 138–140, 146–60; ration cards and, 114–16, 125; refugee-warrior status and, 70, 91–96; resettlement villages and, 2, 77, 80–87, 91, 99, 126–27; social order and, 111–18, 229–34, 229–35; social production of jihād and, 1–5; in South Asian refugee law and, 13–15, 100–101, 119–122; temporary resettlement of, 51–52, 124–27, 130–36, 229–230

Muhajir Council of the Pakistan Muslim League, 107–8

mujāhids (warriors) 1, xv: categorical confusion regarding, 162–64; death and, 201–4, 220–25; as family men, 201–27; family structure and, 204–19; Hadith literature and, 256n20; human rights violations and, 179–81; identification and documentation of, 152–53; militant affiliations of, 196–97; politically qualified life of, 164–65; protective migration and evolution of, 80, 87–96; Qur'anic verses and, 70; in refugee camps, 162–64, 166–67; sexuality of, 201–4; social order and, 229–35; social production of, 1–5, 70–77; victimized family members and, 215–17

Munirah Begum, 131–36

Murree, 22, 41; Kashmiri refugees in, 57, 60–62, 117, 201–202

Mutasim, Qasif, 223–24

mutāsirīn (affectees): categorical confusion concerning, 4 160–67; refugee camps and, 147, 158–60

Muttahida Jihad Mahaz. See United Jihad Council

Muzaffarabad: ethnographic research in, 21–23; refugee camps in, 50–51, 53, 147–49, 154–55; resettlement villages in 23, 51, 80–85, 126–27; militant organizations and, 163, 179, 181

Muzeeb, Rafay, 198–200

mytho-history: defined, 258n34; embodied ideology and, 75–77; fundamentalist Islam and, 70, 75–76

Naseema Bibi, 156–58, 166–67, 217–19

Naseer, Fiasal, 159–60

National Archives of Pakistan, 21–22

Naveed, Ehsan, 163–64, 224–25, 242

Nehru, Jawaharlal, 55–56, 253n57

new wars: human rights and, 234; refugee law and, 142–43

nīyat (intention), Islamic concept of, 208; in Kashmiri refugees' accounts, 86–67, 167, 181, 186, 210, 226

Noorin Bibi, 226–27

Northern Areas, 17, 247n54; LoC and establishment of, 46–47; refugees from 54, 65–65 North West Frontier Provinces (NWFP): Jammu and Kashmir and, 17–21, 60, 201; Pathan militias from, 42–43; refugee migrations to, 41, 49–52, 117

Obaid, Arif, 60, 63–64

Organization for the Rehabilitation (Settlement) of Unsettled Refugees of Jammu and Kashmir, 57–59

Oxfam, 141

Pakistan: AJK and, 18–21; boundary interpretations by, 55–56; categorical confusion about refugees in, 160–67; civic jihad and political discourse in, 185–86;

Pakistan *(continued)*: earthquake of 2005 in, 237–42; gendered hierarchical differences in, 207–8; humanitarian aid to, 102–3, 137–40; Kashmiri human rights policy in, 178–81; Kashmiri identity in, 60–66, 260n28; Kashmiri refugees and, 112–18, 229–35; Kashmir Jihad and, 8–9; Kashmir local authorities and successor states and, 43–46, 252n54; legal definitions and political recognition of refugees in, 120–22; mujāhids in, 220–25; politics of humanitarianism in, 143–46; postcolonial historiography of, 33–34; refugees in, 100–101, 108–11, 260n28; social production of jihād and, 2–5; temporary allotments and resettlements in, 125–27

Pakistan Administration of Evacuee Property Ordinance of 1949, 107–8

Pakistan Central Ministry of Refugees, 112–16; census by, 49

Pakistan Kutchi Mohajir Agriculturalis Jamait (Pakistan Party of Refugee Agriculturists from Kutch), 108

Pakistan Muslim League, 31, 107, 115, 192, 255n86, 264n76

Pakistan National Committee of the United Nations Appeal for Children (UNAC), 110–11

Pakistan Red Cross Society, 102–3, 110–11, 116

Pakistan-West Punjab Joint Refugees and Rehabilitation Council, 106–8

Palestinian men, violence against, 272nn29–30

panāh (refuge), cultural concept of, 88, 161–62

panāh gazīn (refuge-seekers): AJK terminology and, 138–39; categorical confusion concerning, 160–67, 268n50; political debate concerning, 4, 138

Partition: humanitarianism and refugees from, 102–3; political and cultural separations in, 33–34; Princely State of Jammu and Kashmir and, 31–33; regional refugee policies and, 3–5, 246nn40–41; social production of jihād and, 1–2; South Asian refugee regime and, 13–15, 100–101, 103–11

Pathan militias *(lashkars)*: Princely State of Jammu and Kashmir and, 42–43; protective migration and, 80–87; violence of, 50–52

Peletz, Michael, 207

personhood: Islamic concepts of, 206–8, 271n1; in Muslim society, 9–11

philanthropy, culture of: humanitarian internationalism and, 101–5; international aid agencies and, 241–42; Kashmiri refugees and, 114–15

Philippines, Islamic nationalist violence in, 273n36

photographic evidence, documentation using, 175–81

place, protective migration and sense of, 78–96

political advertisements, refugee documentation using, 172–75, 191–93

political Islam: current scholarship on, xvi–xvii; defined, 9–11; deterritorialized jihād and, 234–35; emergence of, 11

political life: Islamic concepts of, 212; of mujāhids and refūjīs, 164–65

political parties. *See* specific parties, e.g. Jamaat-e-Islami

Poonch Jagir, 35, 36–38, 40–41, 252n42

Poonch: AJK and, 52–53, 123, 247n53, 262n63, 264n76; refugees and, 51, 60–62, 65, 120–121, 147

Praja Parishad, 39–40

Praja Sabha (legislative assembly), 38–39, 43–46

pregnancy, Islamic rituals concerning, 209–12

Princely State of Jammu and Kashmir: *begār* (corvee labor) and, 36–38; borders and political boundaries of, 35–36, 47; containment and exit permits *(rehdārī)*, 36–37; Customs Act of 1958 and, 250n28; development of political parties in, 39–40, 250n23, 251n33; end of British Empire and, 33–46; founding of, 31–32, 34–40, 250n27; Glancy Commission Report and, 38; government property *(khalsa)* and land rights in, 36–38; Hereditary

State Subjects Order and, 35, 38–39,
250n31; internal *jāgīrs* (hereditary
estates) and internal *wazārats* (vassal
states) and, 34–39; Kashmir Nationals'
Law of 1912, 35, 37–38; land settlement
and *kashmīr mulkī* in, 37–38; LoC and
divided territories of, 46–48; local
authorities and successor states,
43–46; proprietary rights in, 35–40,
250n29; refugees expelled from, 49–52,
100–101; rights of *awām-e-kashmīr*
(people of Kashmir) and, 34–35; rights
of *awām-e-riyāsat* (people-of-the-state)
and, 34–40; Treaty of Amritsar and,
35–36, 40
property rights: evacuee property, 105–8,
126–27, 259n24, 260n26, 261n38,
265n83, 265n87; in Princely State of
Jammu and Kashmir, 35–40; temporary
resettlement and allotments and,
124–27
Proprietary Rights Transfer Order,
121–22
Protocol Relating to the Status of Refugees,
100–101, 143, 258n7
Provisional Revolutionary Government of
Azad Kashmir, 41–43; as Azad Kashmir
War Council, 41, 264n76
politically qualified life, 116, 164–67
public secrecy, conflict ethnography
and, xxi
Punjab: colonial control of, 35–36, 252n42;
Kashmiri refugees in, 51, 112, 119–20,
125; Partition refugees and, 14–15
106–107
Punjab Muslim League Women's
Committee (PMLWC), 115–16, 262n51

Qadir, Sabur, 64–66
Quaid-i-Azam Relief Fund (QARF),
formation of, 108–11, 117–18, 259n21;
Kashmiri refugees and, 114–16;
Quit Kashmir movement, 39–43, 251n39;
Azad Kashmir movement and, 40–43;
New Kashmir Manifesto and, 40;
Quit Kashmir Declaration and, 40,
251n39
Qutb, Sayyid, 245n23, 257n26,

Rafi, Mumtaz, 138–40
rape: accounts of, 89, 174, 212–15, 271n19;
counterinsurgency and, 205; of
Kashmiri women, 155, 205, 214–15
Raru Domishi Camp, 154–55
Rashid, Hajji Mohammad, 79, 94, xiv–xv
Rashitrya Rifles (RR), 92–93
ration cards, refugee status and, 114–16, 125,
145, 153–54, 164
Rawalpindi, 22; allotments for Kashmiri
refugees in, 82, 125–131; displacement
from Jammu and Kashmir into, 49–52;
refugees living in, 57–59, 64–65, 82–83,
186–87, 210–11; refūjīs and, 157–58, 164,
218–19; jihadist organizations and, 93,
179, 200, 240
recruitment posters, jihād training camps,
180–81
refugee camps: administration of, 153–55; in
Azad Kashmir social order, 146–60,
232–35; documentation of human rights
in, 164, 175–81; establishment of, 2, 138,
146; firing-line-affected people
(mutāsirīn) in, 158–60; humanitarianism politicization and, 143–46;
politically qualified life and, 164–65;
politicization of, 142–43
Refugee Convention, 99–100, 141, 143,
266n11, 267n27
Refugee Resettlement Bill of 1980,
265n83
refugee resettlement villages: councils
(*jirgas*) and 80, 154, xiv; hijarat and
settlement practices, 77–87; jihād
practices in, 195–196, xvii; Kashmiri
refugees and, 2, 91, 99, 146; temporary
allotments and, 2, 126–27
refugee. *See also* muhājirs, refūjīs, refugee
camps, *and* refugee resettlement
villages: classification and taxonomy,
12–16; conventional definitions of, 2, 13,
99–101, 234; international refugee
regime and, 137–140 terminology
concerning, 160–61; humanitarian
definitions of, 140–46
refūjīs (camp refugees) 1, xv. *See also* refugee
camps: categorical confusion concern-
ing, 160–67; emergence of, 137–40;

refūjīs (camp refugees) 1, xv. *See also* refugee camps *(continued)*: gender distinctions concerning, 162–64; identification and documentation of, 151–53; insurgency and counterinsurgency and, 53–54; international refugee regime and, 137–40; as laborers, 151, 164–165; mujāhids as protectors of, 204–19; photographic documentation of, 172–75; ration cards and, 153–54, 164; social order of refugee camps and, 148–60; stipends for, 153–55; torture experienced by, 53, 139–140, 161–62, 215–17, 252–53

Rehabilitation and Reconstruction Project, Pakistan earthquake relief and, 241–42

Renan, Earnst, 257n26

Research Analysis Wing (RAW), 139–140

Rida, Rashid, 257n26

rights-based humanitarianism, 141–46

rights of human beings *(haqūqul-abād):* civic jihād and, 185–86; debts and, 186–88; Kashmir Jihad and, 194–98

Rizwan, Khalid, 187–88

Robinson, Nehemiah, 99

Rosen, Lawrence, 207, 271n9

Rubina Begum, 209–12

Rules of Business of Azad Kashmir Government, 123–24

sacrifice: body rituals and, 225–26; brother-sister relationships and, 215–16; *khidmat* as, 116, 273n31; mujāhid paradigm of, 200, 204–5, 219–20, 224–25; refugees and, 103–4, 109

Safia Begum, 211–12

Saleem, Omar, 159–60

Salima Begum, 210–12

Save the Children, 141

Scarry, Elaine, 213

Security Zone, 20–21, 24; refugees and, 54, 138, 152

self-determination: Azad Kashmir movement and, 40–43; Islamicate terminology concerning, 233–35; Kashmir Jihad and, 233; Kashmir Problem and, 57–59, 255n89; jihadist organizations and, 171–72

service *(khidmat):* jihād and, 186, 216–17; Pakistan earthquake relief and, 241–42

sexuality: Islamic concept of, 206; *jism* (body) and, 206, 210; Kashmiri concepts of, 166, 204–5, 209–13; mujāhids and, 27, 201–4; *nafs* (passions) and, 206–12

sexual torture. *See* rape *and* torture

Shah, Yusaf, 42

Sharif, Nawaz, 61–62

Sher-Bakra conflict, 41–43

Shia'a Islam, lesser and greater jihāds in, 183–85

Shireen Begum, 77, 83–85, 130–31

Siegel, James, 207

Sikh state: colonial policies and, 36–40; formation of Princely State of Jammu and Kashmir and, 31–33, 36–40

Simla Agreement of 1972, 46–47

social justice: civic jihād and, 185–86; rights of human beings *(haqūqul-abād)* and, 186

social order: Kashmiri refugee differences and, 111–18; protective migration and preservation of, 78–96; refugee-to-mujāhid-to-jihādī and, 229–35; refugee camps in Azad Kashmir and, 146–60;

social production of jihad: current scholarship and, 5–8; Kashmir Jihad and, 1–5, 221, xxi; religious symbols and, 7, 10, 70–77; September 2001 and, xvi

Sohail, Arshad, 57–59

Sontag, Susan, 7–8

South Asian refugee regime: development of, 13–15, 103–8; humanitarian internationalism and, 101–3; human rights discourse and, 172; Indian Princely States and, 34–35; international refugee regime *vs.,* 16; Jammu and Kashmir refugee policies and, 119; Kashmiri refugees within, 26; Partition and, 103–11, 229–30; politics of humanitarianism in, 143–46; refugee resettlement villages and, 99–136

sovereignty: body sovereignty, 171–75, 234–35; Islamic scholarship concerning,

72–75; in Kashmiri political culture, xv; Kashmir Jihad and, 194–98

spirit *(rū),* Islamic concept of, 206–8

state boundaries, Kashmiri identity and, 59–66

Sufism: anticolonial resistance and, 257n22; Islamicate terminology and, 69–77

sunnat (habits/behaviors): embodied ideology of, 76–77; jihād and hijarat as, 71–73

Sunni Islam: Islamicate terminology and, 69–77; jihād and, 244n11; lesser and greater jihāds in, 183–85; Muslim community obligations under, 74–75

Surat-ul-Anfāl, 179–81

Tablighi Jamaat, 185–86

Taussig, Michael, xxi

tehsils (taxation units), 36, 129

temporary allotments and resettlements: family structure and, 130–36; Kashmiri refugees, 99–101, 123–27

territorial disputes: Kashmiri identity and, 59–66; LoC and, 46–48, 54–56; origins of, 248n2; protective migration and, 78–96

torture: accounts of, 88–91, 175–78, 213–19, 271n19; documentation of, 155–58, 175–76; refugees and, 53, 139–140, 161–62, 252–53; research on, 7, 272n22; human rights and, 173–75; jihād and, 4, 190,199–200, 205

Treaty of Amritsar (1846), 34–36; Princely State of Jammu and Kashmir and, 36–40

two-nation theory: Kashmir Dispute and, 56, 255n86; refugee identity and, 259n16

United Jihad Council (UJC), 194–98, 270n27, xiii

United Nations Ceasefire Line. *See* Line of Control

United Nations Appeal for Children (UNAC), Pakistan and, 110–11, 114–116

United Nations Commission on India and Pakistan (UNCIP), 43–46, 252n51; AJK refugee camps and, 137–40; Kashmiri refugees and, 116–17, 262n57

United Nations East Pakistan Relief Organization (UNEPRO), 267n26

United Nations High Commission for Refugees (UNHCR), 100–101, 267nn26–27; Afghan refugees and, 144–46; Kashmiri refugees and, 137–140, 175–176; India, in 143–144, 267n30 Pakistan earthquake relief and, 239–42; relief-development projects and, 141–46, World Food Program and, 144–46; World Health Organization and, 144–46

United Nations Human Rights Commission, 178

United Nations International Children's Emergency Fund (UNICEF), 102–3, 110; Afghan refugees in Pakistan and, 144–46

United Nations Security Council: refugee law and, 116, 142; resolutions on Jammu and Kashmir, and 43–44, 116, 252n51, 253n63

Universal Declaration of Human Rights, 57

Urdu language, categorical confusion about refugees and militants in, 160–67

Urūf (publication), 179–81

victim-refugees. *See also* refūjī: body sovereignty and, 171–75; documentation of, 155–56; gender distinctions concerning, 162; human rights and, 142–43; victimization of family members, 215–17

violence. *See also* rape *and* torture: contemporary jihadists and spectacle of, 5–11; documentation of, in refugee camps, 148–60; documentation of, language of human rights in, 175–81; jihād and hijarat and limits of, 73–75; social order and organization of, 229–35

Wadud, Abdul, 161–62

war: ethnographic research in context of, xv–xxi; Indo-Pakistan in Kashmir and, 31–33, 46–47, 52–54, 80–87; xiii–xv; jihād associated with, 5–11; hijarat and, 80–87, 150–51

War of Liberation: Bangladesh and, 56, 143–46; Jammu and Kashmir and, 45–46, 120–22

War on Terror: contemporary jihadist violence and, 5–11; Kashmir and, xiii–xv warriors. *See* mujāhids

Waseem, Nasir, 67, 85

Weiss, Thomas, 141

women: depoliticization of refugee categories for, 15–16, 232–35; in Islamic social hierarchy, 271n9; mujāhids as defenders of, 179–81, 271n9; protective migration experiences of, 82–87; refugee camp experiences of, 156–57; refugee crises and role of, 114–16; as refūjīs, 162–64; sexual violence against, 15–16, 205; temporary resettlements' impact on, 130–36

Women's Relief Committee (WRC), 115–16, 262n51

Yasmeen Begum, 218–19

Zollberg, Aristide, 14